MEDICAL LEADERSHIP

Today's healthcare systems need doctors and consultants to act as leaders, within the multi-disciplinary team, in addition to carrying out their clinical role. This book identifies the key elements of successful leadership through 'medically led' service development and system transformation and shows how this can benefit patient care, particularly when patients become partners in the process.

The authors provide a conceptual framework of medical leadership and a set of scientific methods and tools that make a significant contribution to advancing quality and transforming services in healthcare. On top of this, they present analytical tools which medical professionals can use to support their own improvement or system transformation strategy, including ways of measuring improvement and the returns on investment of medical leadership.

Weaved throughout the book are real-life case studies from medical leaders across the world, providing students with valuable practical insights. Chapter summaries and reflections are provided to support learning.

Medical Leadership will be essential reading for students on medical and clinical leadership courses internationally as well as for all practising doctors, consultants and General Practitioners.

Jill Aylott is Consultant in Autism and CEO at the International Academy of Medical Leadership (IAML) and Head of Programmes for Medical Leadership, Social Care and Quality Improvement.

Jeff Perring is Consultant Intensivist and Medical Director, Sheffield Children's NHS Foundation Trust.

Ann LN Chapman is Consultant in Infectious Diseases and General Medicine, and Clinical Director for Medicine, NHS Lanarkshire; Honorary Clinical Associate Professor, University of Glasgow.

Ahmed Nassef is Consultant Vascular Surgeon at Sheffield Teaching Hospitals Foundation NHS Trust, Council member & Deputy Convener of Exams for the Royal College of Surgeons Edinburgh, Lead of Communication Skills for the Intercollegiate Board of Surgical Exams, UK, and Medical Director, International Academy of Medical Leadership.

MEDICAL LEADERSHIP

A Toolkit for Service Development and System Transformation

*Edited by Jill Aylott, Jeff Perring,
Ann LN Chapman and Ahmed Nassef*

Routledge
Taylor & Francis Group

LONDON AND NEW YORK

First published 2019
by Routledge
2 Park Square, Milton Park, Abingdon, Oxon OX14 4RN

and by Routledge
711 Third Avenue, New York, NY 10017

Routledge is an imprint of the Taylor & Francis Group, an informa business

British Library Cataloguing-in-Publication Data
A catalogue record for this book is available from the British Library

Library of Congress Cataloging-in-Publication Data
Names: Aylott, Jill, editor. | Perring, Jeff, editor. | Chapman, Ann, Dr.,
    editor. | Nassef, Ahmed, editor.
Title: Medical leadership : a toolkit for service development and system
    transformation / edited by Jill Aylott, Jeff Perring, Ann Chapman and
    Ahmed Nassef.
Description: Abingdon, Oxon ; New York, NY : Routledge, 2019. |
    Includes bibliographical references and index.
Identifiers: LCCN 2018020299 | ISBN 9781138217348 (hbk.) |
    ISBN 9781138217355 (pbk.) | ISBN 9781315440880 (ebk.)
Subjects: MESH: Leadership | Health Services Administration |
    Delivery of Health Care | Physician's Role | Organizational
    Case Studies
Classification: LCC RA971 | NLM W 84.1 | DDC 362.1068—dc23
LC record available at https://lccn.loc.gov/2018020299

ISBN: 978-1-138-21734-8 (hbk)
ISBN: 978-1-138-21735-5 (pbk)
ISBN: 978-1-315-44088-0 (ebk)

Typeset in Bembo
by Apex CoVantage, LLC

Printed and bound in Great Britain by
TJ International Ltd, Padstow, Cornwall

CONTENTS

Foreword   *ix*
Contributor bios   *xi*

PART 1
A global emergent context for medical leadership   **1**

1 An introduction   3
   Ahmed Nassef, Mathew Fortnam and Jill Aylott

2 'Leadership' and 'medical leadership'   8
   Bolarinde Ola and Aishin Lok

3 Quality improvement as the goal of medical leadership   16
   Rachael Baines

4 Understanding patient experience as a clinical leader   22
   Suvira Madan

5 Primary care and general practice: medical leadership for all   33
   Mathew Fortnam

6 A theoretical model to engage doctors in medical leadership   38
   Ahmed Nassef

PART 2
Medical leadership   **57**

7 An introduction   59
Ann LN Chapman

8 Medical leadership and reducing health inequalities   61
Gilly Ennals

9 Medical leadership and reducing variation in healthcare   65
Ravishanka Sargur

10 Developing and analysing effective teams   79
Walaa Al-Safi

11 A strategy for engaging primary and secondary care
doctors in medical leadership   86
Simon Boyes

12 Medical engagement – strategies for engagement from the
'grass roots'   95
Paddy Dobbs and Alix Fonfe

13 Leadership diagnostics and reflections on personal
leadership development   106
Michael Robinson and Eleni Lekoudis

PART 3
**Improvement science, medical leadership and
measurement for improvement**   **127**

14 An introduction   129
Jill Aylott

15 Data analysts building capability in partnership with
medical leaders   132
Lisa Fox

16 Root cause analysis and simulation to improve quality   137
Adam Burns

17 Leadership diagnostics for self-awareness and bespoke
   course design   141
   Prosenjit Giri

18 Medical leadership and the use of data for a continuous
   quality improvement collaborative (CQIC) in an accident
   and emergency department   153
   Prakash Subedi, Jill Aylott, Prosenjit Giri,
   Martha Zaluaga Quintero, Sanjay Sinha, Sanjai Subramanian
   and Sathi Permaul

19 Developing a human transplantation health service in
   Nepal with ethical and moral medical leadership   163
   Pukar C. Shrestha

PART 4
Service development   **173**

20 An introduction   175
   Jeff Perring

21 'Patient reported outcome measures': we have barely
   started to walk let alone run   176
   Fiona Kew

22 Service improvement to reduce early deaths of children in
   hospital: the design of an electronic observation system   189
   Victoria Hemming

23 Innovations in person-centred service redesign for
   young carers   197
   Samantha Wong

24 Service improvement in paediatric dentistry   203
   Halla Zaitoun

25 Reflections on service improvement by medical leaders   210
   Jeff Perring, Fiona Kew, Victoria Hemming, Samantha Wong and
   Halla Zaitoun

PART 5
System transformation   **223**

26 Introduction to critical issues in health system transformation   225
    Jill Aylott and Ahmed Nassef

27 System transformation for health and social care   229
    Branko Perunovic

28 A strategy for engaging teams and motivating staff through
    system transformation   232
    Rachael Baines and Prasad Godbole

29 Transforming operating theatre services with medical leadership   238
    Ahmed Othman, Jayarama Mohan, Prabhakar Motkur, Salma
    Noor, Milind Rao, Adam Wolverson, Amit Shukla, Gurdip Singh
    Samra, Mohit Gupta, Chloe Scruton, Jill Aylott, Karen Kilner
    and Prasad Godbole

30 Transforming the emergency medicine medical workforce:
    a new 'hybrid' doctor with integrated speciality
    training and a competency-based Fellowship in Quality
    Improvement (FQim)   244
    Prakash Subedi, Jill Aylott, Naushad Khan, Prosenjit Giri
    and Lesley Hammond

31 Quality improvement and system transformation in
    emergency medicine   251
    Elizabeth Hutchinson

32 Transforming the quality of hospital care through advocacy
    for people with a learning disability and/or autism   257
    Jonathan Sahu

33 Transforming services for patients with spinal cord injury –
    a national review of standards and practice   263
    Pradeep Thumbikat

Index   *279*

FOREWORD

Medical leadership: a toolkit for service development and system transformation

In 2008, during my time as health minister, I produced the report *High Quality Care for All*, in which I addressed leadership as a fundamental component of the NHS. The report focused on the importance of encouraging clinicians to not only be practitioners but also to be partners and leaders with patients within the NHS.

With empowered leaders comes a motivated workforce who will drive forward the quality and safety agenda. I previously highlighted the need for a stronger role for clinical leadership and management throughout the healthcare system. Since 2008, we have seen some drive towards this with national leadership schemes, courses and frameworks. However, leadership is not just about individuals, but also about teams, and there is still a long way to go to empowering staff to fully take on these roles. We need to encourage staff to step up and make a case for change. As I once said – "It is relatively easy to set out a vision, much harder to make it a reality".

This insightful book offers a toolkit that can be applied for those wanting to develop their medical leadership skills in order to see service development and system transformation.

The book covers the key principles of leadership, developing a strong foundation of the role of medical leadership in various settings, and the fundamental principle of ensuring that care remains patient-centric. The second part of the book builds on the foundations laid out by the first part, discussing more specific aspects of leadership such as how it can reduce variation in quality of healthcare and help to reduce health inequalities. The latter parts of the book delve deeper into how we measure improvement to ensure we see service transformation and system development.

Medical Leadership: A Toolkit for Service Development and System Transformation offers not only a toolkit, but also well-chosen case examples offering a greater understanding of what healthcare professionals need to know when fostering leadership for safer care and how to take on the practical and theoretical challenges when doing so. This book will undoubtedly empower the leader in everyone who reads it.

Foreword by Lord Ara Darzi

CONTRIBUTOR BIOS

Walaa Al-Safi – Dr Al-Safi is Consultant Obstetrician and Gynaecologist and Fetomaternal Medicine Lead with a PG Cert Medical Leadership and Founder and Director of Mafraq Obstetric Emergency Training Program. Previously (2010–2014) she was Consultant Obstetrician and Gynaecologist and Lead for Fetomaternal Services at Rotherham General Hospital, South Yorkshire and Senior Lecturer at the University of Sheffield.

Jill Aylott – Dr Aylott is Consultant in Autism and CEO at the International Academy of Medical Leadership (IAML) and Head of Programmes for Medical Leadership, Social Care and Quality Improvement. Previously she was MBA and MSc Medical Leadership Programme Director (2010–2016) at Sheffield Hallam University and held Programme Director roles at Birmingham University, Anglia Ruskin University and Kings College, London.

Rachael Baines – Miss Baines is Registrar in Plastic Surgery in Yorkshire and the Humber and graduated with an MBA Medical Leadership in 2016. She specialises in paediatric plastic surgery reconstruction and was one of the first Yorkshire and the Humber Medical Leadership Quality Improvement Fellows in 2011. She is a Teaching Fellow and Associate at the International Academy of Medical Leadership, specialising in Quality Improvement methodologies for bespoke programme design and Clinical Microsystems Coaching.

Simon Boyes – Mr Boyes is Consultant in General Surgery and Clinical Director for General Surgical Services at Sheffield Teaching Hospitals. He specialises in workforce planning for surgical services and medical leadership engagement and development of doctors. He graduated with an MBA Medical Leadership in

2016. He is a Teaching Fellow and Associate Professor at the International Academy of Medical Leadership, specialising in competency framework development and workforce planning.

Adam Burns – Dr Burns is Consultant in Medicine and was Leadership and Simulation Fellow at Mid Yorkshire Hospitals NHS Trust 2014. He and his team were shortlisted for the Patient Safety Care Awards in 2014. He has innovated in the use of simulation techniques to advance the learning from Root Cause Analysis to improve patient safety.

Ann LN Chapman – Dr Chapman is Consultant in Infectious Diseases and Medicine and Clinical Director for Medicine and Associated Specialties in NHS Lanarkshire. She is also Honorary Clinical Associate Professor at the University of Glasgow and Teaching Fellow and Associate Professor at the International Academy of Medical Leadership, advising on research and development of Medical Leadership styles and 360-degree feedback for appraisals and revalidation. She is involved in medical leadership development locally and nationally at undergraduate and postgraduate level.

Paddy Dobbs – Dr Dobbs is Consultant in Anaesthesia and Neuro Critical Care, Clinical Lead for Anaesthetics and Associate Medical Director for Patient Safety, Sheffield Teaching Hospitals NHS Foundation Trust. He graduated with an MBA Medical Leadership in 2013. He is a Teaching Fellow and Associate Professor at the International Academy of Medical Leadership, leading Medical Engagement Strategies for Patient Safety and Quality Improvement.

Gilly Ennals – Dr Ennals is General Practitioner at Nexus Health in South West London. Her GP training was completed in Barnsley, Yorkshire. She completed a Medical Leadership Fellowship post with Health Education England, Yorkshire and the Humber and graduated with a PG Cert Medical Leadership award in 2016, specialising in Quality Improvement in General Practice. She is passionate about primary care and has an interest in tackling health inequalities.

Alix Fonfe – Dr Fonfe is a paediatric trainee who took part in the Future Leaders Programme in Yorkshire and the Humber in 2016–2017 where she worked for Better Start Bradford and designed services with families to improve children's life chances. She is currently planning a career which incorporates her interests in public health and neonatal medicine.

Mathew Fortnam – Dr Fortnam is a General Practitioner, having recently completed a year as a Leadership Fellow in Primary Care with Health Education England, graduating with a PG Cert. Medical Leadership. During the year, he developed a keen interest in developing the Primary Care workforce and advancing Medical Leadership amongst undergraduate and postgraduate doctors.

Lisa Fox – Mrs Fox MSc Health and Social Care Leadership is a Health Information Manager at Calderdale and Huddersfield Foundation Trust. She has a passion for raising the profile of the importance of measurement in relation to co-design of systems and processes which aim to make health systems safer. She is also Teaching Fellow and Associate for the International Academy of Medical Leadership.

Prosenjit Giri – Dr Giri is Consultant in Occupational Medicine, conferred to Fellowship in 2016. He is an examiner, journal reviewer, national appraiser and Secretary of the Society of Occupational Medicine Yorkshire Group. He is a Teaching Fellow and Associate Professor at the International Academy of Medical Leadership, leading on Medical Leadership Diagnostic research to improve the healthcare system and is a national and international speaker on the merits of Leadership diagnostics as a tool for reflection and self-awareness for medical leadership development.

Prasad Godbole – Mr Godbole is Consultant Paediatric Urologist and Deputy Medical Director at the Sheffield Children's Hospital NHS Foundation Trust. He is also an Honorary Professor at Sheffield Hallam University and Honorary Senior Lecturer at the University of Sheffield. He completed his MBA Medical Leadership from Sheffield Hallam University and is a member of the Faculty of Medical Leadership and Management.

Mohit Gupta – Mr Gupta is Consultant Ophthalmologist and has worked at United Lincolnshire Hospitals Trust since 2005. He has also been the Head of Service for Ophthalmology in the past and is now the Clinical Director for Head and Neck. He is a high-volume cataract surgeon and also has a special interest in Glaucoma, providing a service to the local population. He has been involved in quality improvement activity in the Trust and continues his interest in this area.

Lesley Hammond – Ms Hammond is NHS Manager for Barnsley Hospital with a passion for Emergency Medicine and workforce development. Lesley set up the first UK Quality Improvement Medical Education Training Centre, (QiMET) to advance the integrated Hybrid International Emergency Medicine Programme.

Victoria Hemming – Dr Hemming is Paediatric Consultant at Scarborough Hospital, York Teaching Hospitals NHS Foundation Trust. She is a Health Education England, Yorkshire and the Humber Future Leaders Programme Fellow alumnus, graduating with a PG Cert. Medical Leadership, completing projects that included implementing electronic observations in paediatric services at York Hospital. She is interested in Quality Improvement and service development to improve patient safety.

Elizabeth Hutchinson – Dr Hutchinson is an Emergency Medicine Registrar based in Yorkshire and the Humber. She recently graduated with a PG Cert. in Medical Leadership whilst completing a Leadership Fellowship as part of the Future Leaders Programme 2016–2017. Since going back into speciality training, she has continued her interest in Quality Improvement whilst currently chairing the Junior Doctors' Quality Improvement group at Hull Royal Infirmary as well as mentoring and supporting medical students at Hull York Medical School in their service improvement projects.

Fiona Kew – Miss Kew is Consultant Gynaecological Oncologist specialising in minimal access and robotic surgery. She graduated with an MBA Medical Leadership in 2016 and is a Generation Q fellow with the Health Foundation. She is lead clinician for 'Seamless Surgery' – a surgical pathways improvement programme and Clinical Director of Obstetrics, Gynaecology and Neonatology. She is a Teaching Fellow and Associate Professor at the International Academy of Medical Leadership specialising in the development of Quality Improvement metrics to measure improvement in surgical and healthcare practice.

Naushad Khan – Dr Khan is Consultant in Emergency Medicine at Doncaster & Bassetlaw Teaching Hospital NHS Foundation Trust, UK. He graduated in Sri Lanka in 1998 and completed an MSc in Diabetes. He is actively involved in developing and implementing the unique 'Hybrid' International Emergency Medicine training programme (HIEM) within the Quality Improvement Medical Education Training Centre (QiMET) in the UK, presenting this work in Nepal, Sri Lanka and the UK.

Karen Kilner – Dr Kilner is Senior Lecturer and Research Fellow at Sheffield Hallam University and has a PhD in Medical Informatics. She undertook the teaching of Statistical Process Control and measurement for improvement across the MBA Medical Leadership programme (2010–2016) and the MSc Health and Social Care Leadership award. She is also part of a teaching team delivering a Masters degree in Public Health. She has authored and co-authored several papers with medical colleagues to provide robust quantitative data analysis.

Eleni Lekoudis – Miss Lekoudis is Consultant in Obstetrics and Gyneacology, Labour Ward Lead, Fertility Lead and College Tutor. She undertook a Fellowship in Medical Leadership, graduating with a PG Cert. Medical Leadership in 2015–2016 and has undertaken evaluation research in the simulation of competence in ultrasound within the multidisciplinary team. She is a Teaching Fellow and Associate at the International Academy of Medical Leadership.

Aishin Lok – Dr Lok is a Neonatal Registrar Doctor, currently training with Yorkshire and the Humber School of Paediatrics. She has a keen interest in medical simulation and technology enhanced learning. She completed a Fellowship in Medical Leadership graduating with a PG Cert. Medical Leadership and has produced a publication on the identification of latent risks through in situ simulation training to prevent harm.

Suvira Madan – Dr Madan is Consultant Geriatrician at Sheffield Teaching Hospitals NHS Foundation Trust with special interests in perioperative medicine, orthogeriatrics and community geriatrics. She is privileged to work in Sheffield with caring colleagues, crossing traditional boundaries, to deliver high-quality integrated medical care for the frailest of the frail. She specialises in exploring ways to include the voice of the most vulnerable and frail patients.

Jayarama Mohan – Mr Mohan is Consultant in General/Vascular Surgeon and Clinical Director, General and Colorectal Surgery, Pilgrim Hospital, Vascular Surgery, Breast Surgery at United Lincolnshire Hospitals Trust. He is passionate about system improvement and transformation across medical and clinical specialties and provides collaborative leadership in this area. He was instrumental in the development of a business case in 2015 to inspire the NHS Trusts' Theatre Transformation programme 2016.

Prabhakar Motkur – Mr Motkur is Consultant Orthopaedic and Upper Limb/Shoulder Surgeon and Clinical Director at United Lincolnshire Hospitals NHS Trust. He has several years of Trauma and Orthopaedic surgery experience since 1990 and was instrumental in the development of a business case in 2015 to inspire the Theatre Transformation programme 2016.

Ahmed Nassef – Mr Nassef is a Consultant and Clinical Lead of Vascular Surgery at Sheffield Teaching Hospitals Foundation NHS Trust, Council Member & Deputy Convener of Exams for the Royal College of Surgeons in Edinburgh and lead of 'Communication Skills' for the Intercollegiate Board of Surgical Exams UK. He trained in Cairo, London and lately Sydney as an Endovascular Fellow (2016–2017). He graduated with an MBA Medical Leadership in 2016 and is Medical Director for the International Academy of Medical Leadership. Mr Nassef has presented his work on Self Determination and Medical Leadership programme design at UK and International conferences.

Salma Noor – Miss Noor is Consultant in Obstetrics and Gynaecology at United Lincolnshire Hospitals NHS Trust and trained with the London Deanery, UK. Her special interest areas are Minimal Access Surgery, Reproductive Medicine and theatre usage and improvement in its efficiencies in the NHS. In addition, she has a keen interest in working with medical colleagues to support health system transformation.

Bolarinde Ola – Mr Ola is Consultant, Advanced Reproductive Surgeon and IVF expert at Sheffield Teaching Hospitals NHS Trust, and he is also Training Programme Supervisor for Reproductive Medicine and Surgery. He has an MBA Medical Leadership (2016) and advanced accreditations in Reproductive Medicine, Assisted Reproduction, Reproductive Surgery, Laparoscopic Surgery, Hysteroscopic Surgery and Gynaecological Ultrasound Scanning. Furthermore, as Chairman of the RCOG-Nigeria Liaison Group, he worked tirelessly to make the Department of Health's Medical Training Initiative (MTI) more accessible to West African Doctors. He is a Research Fellow at the International Academy of Medical Leadership, specialising in critical appraisal, metasynthesis and social research methods for medical leadership.

Ahmed Othman – Mr Othman is Consultant in Orthopaedic Surgery and Clinical Lead for Grantham at United Lincolnshire Hospitals NHS Trust. His speciality is in primary and revision hip and knee aggravated arthroplasty. He has a Post Graduate Diploma in Medical Education and has experience in leading whole system change across a rural NHS Trust in Lincolnshire. He is Associate Professor at the International Academy of Medical Leadership, leading on Medical Leadership and whole system transformation relating to operating theatres.

Sathi Permaul – Dr Permaul is an Emergency Medicine Doctor with extensive experience in acute medicine, general and plastic surgery and medical oncology in Ireland, UK and South Africa. He currently works at Doncaster and Bassetlaw NHS Trust and has an interest and experience in Quality Improvement in the application of 'LEAN' methodology in Hospital Accident and Emergency Departments.

Jeff Perring – Dr Perring is Consultant Intensivist and Medical Director, Sheffield Children's NHS Foundation Trust. His interest is in the development of effective team working to improve patient safety and is the Joint Lead for Yorkshire and Humber Paediatric Critical Care Operational Delivery Network. He is a Teaching Fellow at the International Academy of Medical Leadership.

Branko Perunovic – Dr Perunovic is Consultant Histopathologist, Clinical Director of Laboratory Services at Sheffield Teaching Hospitals NHS Trust and Honorary Senior Lecturer at the University of Sheffield. Graduating with an MBA Medical Leadership in 2016, he applies entrepreneurialism to his role as Clinical Director for Laboratory Services. He developed an innovative pathology service to provide 'real time', innovative procedures to allow for cancerous tissue diagnostics to guide the surgeon while the patient is still in the operating theatre. He is a Teaching Fellow and Associate Professor at the International Academy of Medical Leadership, leading on the development of Strategic Management and Entrepreneurialism for medical and clinical leaders.

Milind Rao – Mr Rao is Consultant in Colorectal and General Surgery, specialising in the management of patients with colorectal disease including colorectal cancer, IBD and pelvic floor disorders. He is passionate about Medical Leadership and Engagement to transform the NHS to improve and maintain the quality of services to patients through Continuous Quality Improvement at the United Lincolnshire Hospitals NHS Trust.

Michael Robinson – Dr Robinson is a Consultant Anaesthetist and Improvement Fellow with an interest in Recovery. His leadership work has included mortality review, improving recovery from surgery and improving out-of-hours non-elective services which has been recognised nationally with an award for partnership working in delivering NHS services seven days a week.

Jonathan Sahu – Dr Sahu is Consultant in Cardiology and Cardiothoracic surgery, graduating with an MBA Medical Leadership in 2016. He specialises in general cardiology, electrophysiology, pacing and complex device implantation. He trained in Manchester and North America before specialising in Sheffield. He has a keen interest in developing inclusive services in the acute sector for people with Autism and multiple and complex needs and is Teaching Fellow and Associate Professor at the International Academy of Medical Leadership.

Gurdip Singh Samra – Dr Samra is Consultant in Anaesthesia and Intensive Care and Associate Medical Director at United Lincolnshire Hospitals NHS Trust. He is an experienced consultant with a demonstrated history of working in the hospital and healthcare industry. He is skilled in Clinical Research, Medical Education, Medical Devices, Clinical Anaesthesia, and Intensive Care Medicine. He graduated from St Bartholomew's Hospital Medical College.

Ravishanka Sargur – Dr Sargur is Consultant in Immunology and Clinical Lead for Sheffield Immunology Protein Reference unit. He is currently the chair of the JRCPTB Speciality Advisory Committee (Immunology) and was Training Programme Director, Immunology for HEEM and HEYH. He represents Immunology on the UKAS Professional Advisory committee. He has a keen interest in Quality Control and Quality Assurance and developed the Laboratory Atlas of Variation with Sheffield CCG to optimise laboratory test utilisation in primary care. He is a Teaching Fellow and Associate Professor at the International Academy of Medical Leadership, leading on the teaching of variation of healthcare for doctors and healthcare professionals.

Chloe Scruton – Miss Scruton is Business Manager for Orthopaedics at the United Lincolnshire Hospitals NHS Trust. She works closely with senior medical leaders and the wider multi-professional and non-clinical teams to support NHS Trust wide system transformation. She has successfully supported the implementation of small- and large-scale change, in partnership with medical leaders, based on the regular collection and analysis of data through PDSA cycles.

Pukar C. Shrestha – Dr Shrestha is a kidney and liver transplant surgeon and Executive Director of the Human Organ Transplant Centre (HOTC) Nepal. He initiated the first successful kidney transplant in Nepal at Bir hospital in 2008, subsequently undertaking ninety-nine kidney transplants with 99% success. He established the Aarogya Foundation in 2009, which is a 'not for profit' organisation set up to raise awareness and to provide logistic support for dialysis and kidney transplantation such as the HLA lab. He established HOTC in 2010 with facilities for kidney and liver transplantation for the people of Nepal. In Nepal, he has undertaken the first pair exchange kidney transplant, the first-ever deceased donor kidney transplant and the first liver transplant while also setting up six dialysis centres. He played a key role in influencing the organ transplant act 2072 and regulations 2073, which has widely expanded live donor pool, pair exchange and 'brain death donor transplant' facility. In recognition of his contribution to developing the Nepali healthcare system, he has been decorated with the first-ever 'Excellent Health Service Award' by the Ministry of Health in 2012 and given the 'Prabal Jan Sewa Shree', a national honour by the President of Nepal in 2013.

Amit Shukla – Mr Shukla is Consultant Colorectal surgeon and Head of Service for Colorectal and General Surgery at United Lincolnshire Hospitals NHS Trust. He has a keen interest in developing medical professionals in the multi-professional team to improve the quality of theatre services for patients.

Sanjay Sinha – Dr Sinha is Consultant in Emergency Medicine at Doncaster and Bassetlaw NHS Trust. He is also the Department Lead for Quality Improvement and Audit and provides leadership for trainees in the registering of audit and quality improvement projects. He is co-leading the advancement of the Continuous Quality Improvement Collaborative (CQIC) to improve the quality of care to patients and to improve job satisfaction for the team working in the emergency department.

Prakash Subedi – Dr Subedi is Consultant Emergency Physician at Doncaster and Bassetlaw Teaching Hospitals NHS Trust, with a special interest in developing a sustainable medical workforce through the development of a new 'hybrid' International Emergency Medicine (HIEM) speciality doctor. His PhD research is in Continuous Quality Improvement and medical leadership in Emergency Medicine with the development of an integrated clinical and leadership medical training programme. He is co-founder of REPSIN a Remote Emergency and Primary Services Improvement-Nepal, a programme that builds the Emergency Practitioner skills of Health Assistants in rural locations. He is a Teaching Fellow and Associate Professor at the International Academy of Medical Leadership, leading on the development of organisational resilience in the development of Continuous Quality Improvement.

Sanjai Subramanian – Dr Subramanian is a Consultant in Emergency Medicine at Doncaster and Bassetlaw Teaching Hospitals NHS Trust. He is co-leading on the advancement of the Continuous Quality Improvement Collaborative (CQIC) in the Emergency Medicine Department to create a culture of improvement as opposed to one of target setting.

Pradeep Thumbikat – Dr Thumbikat is Consultant in Spinal Injuries and Honorary Senior Lecturer, University of Sheffield. He is the Vice Chairman of the specialist advisory committee RCP in Rehabilitation Medicine and Chair of the education committee of British Association of Spinal Cord Injury Specialists. He graduated with an MBA Medical Leadership in 2016, undertaking a strategic evaluation of the national clinical pathway for spinal injuries patients in England, UK, and continues this national work in his role as executive member of the spinal cord injury clinical reference subgroup. He has published widely on spasticity and contracture management, complex pressure management, surgical rehabilitation and hand function following high spinal cord injury.

Adam Wolverson – Dr Wolverson is Consultant in Intensive Care Medicine at Lincoln County Hospital and at a major Trauma Consultant at Nottingham University Hospitals. He is a fellow of the Royal College of Anaesthetists and Fellow of the Faculty of Intensive Care Medicine and has been Clinical Director for Theatres, Anaesthesia and Intensive Care Medicine for 10 years. He has been a member of the East Midlands Clinical Senate and in the past served as a member of the National Clinical Reference Group for Adult Critical Care. He is also the Medical Quality and Service Improvement lead for Mid Trent Critical Care Network and leads on Quality Improvement in Critical Care for the Network and the joint Clinical Governance Lead for East Midlands Major Trauma Network. He is a member of the faculty of Medical leadership and management.

Samantha Wong – Dr Wong is a General Practitioner who has received recognition not only for her work with support for young carers but also from the Royal College of General Practitioners for creating work experience in General Practice for sixth formers and potential medical school applicants from deprived areas.

Halla Zaitoun – Miss Zaitoun graduated with honours from Newcastle Dental School in 2000. Following vocational training in the Northeast and Senior House Officer posts in Manchester, she completed MFDS (2002). In 2003, she started speciality training in paediatric dentistry in Liverpool, attaining Membership in Paediatric Dentistry and Masters in Clinical Dentistry. She completed the Intercollegiate Fellowship examination (ISFE) in 2008. She currently works full time as an NHS Consultant in Paediatric Dentistry at Charles Clifford Dental Hospital in Sheffield, the Clinical Lead for Paediatric Dentistry and Departmental Audit Lead. She teaches at the Dental Hospital and is also a Teaching Fellow at the International Academy of Medical Leadership, specialising in Measurement for Improvement

Martha Zaluaga Quintero – Dr Zaluaga Quintero is Doctor in Emergency Medicine and Primary Care, having trained and worked in Spain in Emergency and Primary Care and has several years of Emergency Medicine experience in the UK. She specialises in working with vulnerable adults to identify appropriate responses in emergency situations to treat pain. She is part of a team of UK-based doctors who have designed, developed and taught on an Emergency Medicine programme (REPSIN) for Health Assistants in rural Nepal.

PART 1

A global emergent context for medical leadership

1

AN INTRODUCTION

Ahmed Nassef, Mathew Fortnam and Jill Aylott

'Medical Leadership' describes an additional set of skills and knowledge in leadership and management for doctors, who are then expected to apply and integrate this new learning into their everyday practice. There have been various attempts to explain and outline what these leadership and management skills are, usually by the introduction of competency frameworks in healthcare leadership and management, for example in the UK, The Medical Leadership Competency Framework (NHS Institute for Innovation and Improvement, 2013), the Clinical Leadership Competency Framework (NHS Leadership Academy, 2011), the Leadership Framework (The NHS Leadership Academy, 2011) and the Leadership and Management Standards for Medical Professionals (Faculty of Medical Leadership and Management, 2014). While doctors and other health professions are encouraged to develop skills in leadership, there is also an equivalent Leadership Qualities Framework for adult social care (National Skills Academy for Social Care, 2014) and a leadership competency framework for Nursing, Allied Health Professions and Managers with the Healthcare Leadership Model (NHS Leadership Academy, 2013) and a Healthcare Leadership Alliance Model in the United States and in the international global context (Stefl, 2008; The International Hospital Federation, 2015). But in the UK the competency frameworks have been insufficient to impact upon and prevent the reported failures in healthcare (Francis, 2010, 2013; Kirkup, 2015) and increases in clinical errors (Bulman and Deardon, 2017). The problems within healthcare continue, regardless of the plethora of leadership competency frameworks, with poor and average healthcare the norm, with extensive variations in healthcare and a lack of an organisational culture of improvement.

Part 1 of this book argues for a new framework for the development of international models of medical leadership to support access to Universal Health Care (UHC) for all, as championed by the World Health Organization (WHO, 2013, 2014, 2016). Globally, many people are unable to access healthcare, and the skills of healthcare workers are variable (WHO, 2013, 2014, 2016). Even where health systems are well developed and resourced, there is clear evidence that quality remains a concern (WHO, 2006) while the challenges for future healthcare systems across the world strive for a more sustainable, affordable and equitable healthcare system (Deloitte, 2016).

However, with a global shortage of healthcare workers estimated to be 12.9 million by 2035 (WHO, 2013), the fastest growing part of the healthcare workforce is and will continue to be the health assistant workforce (Imison et al., 2016), with the professions required to take a lead in professionalising workforce planning and to lead the training of the assistant workforce (Aylott and Montesci, 2017). This growth in demand for healthcare combined with a shortage of health workers will stimulate a growth in the 'democratisation of professional knowledge' inspired by the model developed in Mexico and worldwide by Dr Sanjeev Arora (Bornstein, 2014) to develop the assistant workforce to become competent to deliver quality healthcare. This will require a more engaged, informed and 'conceptually different' medical and clinical workforce, with all doctors accepting their need to grow and develop their non-clinical skills in 'leadership', 'management', 'quality improvement' and 'health system transformation'. The future will require more collaboration between the professions, managers, assistants and patients, with less defensiveness about the 'scope of professional practice' and with less disputed professional boundaries (King et al., 2015; Aylott et al., 2017).

Chapter 2 outlined by Bolarinde Ola and Aishin Lok provides a chronology of the development of leadership theory and a critique of these theories and their relevance to doctors. The authors review key concepts such as 'leadership' and 'management' and critique how leadership theories have changed over time and evolved with a developed evidence base which has informed the development of new leadership theories. Perhaps the most striking evidence from leadership theory is the power of an awareness of 'Emotional intelligence'. Emotional intelligence is an important indicator of a leader's ability to succeed. Many studies link emotional intelligence with individual and group performances in the workplace. Evidence suggests that the best leaders and best 'medical leaders' will develop a heightened level of awareness of their 'emotional intelligence' and use the four styles – democratic, authoritative/visionary, affiliative and coaching – interchangeably according to the needs of individuals and team members. The styles of coerciveness and pace-setting are less likely to be effective and can create tension, a damaged culture and poor performance (Goleman et al., 2002). Goleman (2013) describes emotional intelligence as the foremost leadership skill, which harnesses four domains: self-awareness, self-management, social awareness and relationship management. Good leaders are aware of self and their physical and social environment, which facilitates how they influence people around them in a positive way. Demonstration of positive emotions like happiness, laughter and optimism can lift workers to achievements and progress; whereas negative emotions like anger, hostility, fear and anxiety can be demoralising to a workforce.

In Chapter 3, Rachael Baines explores the concept of 'quality improvement' and its origins, definition and application to healthcare. As 'medical leadership' develops within a contemporary global and emergent healthcare context, we argue that it is the goal of quality improvement and health system transformation in co-production with patients and the wider stakeholders, that requires the focus for current and future models of medical leadership.

Quality Improvement (QI), as a goal for healthcare, can unite clinicians and managers within 'shared', 'distributed' and 'collective' models of leadership to advance the quality of healthcare for patients and their families. It shares a common language and a common goal, however for QI to be effective it must embrace a new culture of working with patients and families as partners in all stages of the co-production of QI. Doctors are best placed to lead this process but are often unprepared, with a lack of integrated leadership and management skills developed throughout their medical training. However, all doctors are authoritative leaders because of their intensive training and experience in a clinical speciality, and without their engagement, healthcare will not transform. QI is required for all doctors regardless of their speciality alongside nurses, therapists, technicians and the assistant health workforce with support from managers in partnership with patients. Allowing patients to lead the Quality Improvement process is a challenging concept for all healthcare professionals, and future health systems depend on empowered patients managing their own healthcare conditions, with families which will lead to more 'experience-based redesign' of health and social care systems (Bate and Robert, 2006).

Much of the development of leadership programmes over time has developed with an absence of values (Moscrop, 2012). It is the ambition of this book to embed the core values of patient, service user and family engagement at the centre of reconceptualising 'medical leadership'. We strongly believe that medical leadership should embody the core values of medical and clinical practice, and to this end, all leadership development should be patient focused. The patient experience particularly for the vulnerable patient presenting with complex and multiple comorbidities is not always a positive one. Future models of medical leadership will require different ways of working with patients to engage and support them in quality improvement using new mixed methods and qualitative approaches. In Chapter 4, Suvira Madan outlines *hermeneutic inquiry,* which focuses on what humans experience rather that what they consciously know. Heidegger used the term *lifeworld* to express the idea that individuals' realities were invariably influenced by the world in which they were living. *Being-in-the-world* meant that humans could not abstract themselves from the world. Suvira Madan draws upon the life experience of elderly hip fracture patients to create new forms of knowledge and new forms of knowing to shape medical leadership learning about future healthcare scenarios. Where patients struggle to engage due to their vulnerability, we can learn from the patient experience to inform service improvement. All doctors as 'medical leaders' are unique in their proximity to the patients' care and are best situated to lead this process and understand the potential impact of any policy changes to national healthcare structures and their funding mechanisms on patients' care (Bohmer, 2012). Patient involvement is central to the most successful healthcare systems in the world, where integrated systems of service delivery focus on securing patient and carer involvement and embed 'patient personas' (please see the Institute for Health Improvement Esther project as an example (www.ihi.org/resources/Pages/ImprovementStories/ImprovingPatientFlowTheEstherProjectinSweden.aspx), which has been credited with being one of the main factors of success in Jonkoping, Sweden for sustainable Quality Improvement.

Medical Leadership within General Practice is a relatively recent emergence with guidance for doctors' revalidation (RCGP, 2014) and its 2022 vision (RCGP, 2013). It is emphasised that "trainees must engage with systems of quality management and quality improvement in their clinical work and training" (see Royal College of General Practitioners website: www.rcgp.org.uk). In Chapter 5, Mathew Fortnam reviews the role of the General Practitioner in relation to the scope and practice of quality improvement and explores the future role of General Practice and Medical Leadership.

Within global austerity, healthcare quality cannot be separated from costs, and new ways of capturing the cost of healthcare while demand for services increases is urgently required (Porter and Lee, 2013). The increasing complexity and rising costs of modern healthcare has presented healthcare providers with difficult trade-offs as they try to balance the allocation of scarce resources to individual patient care and that of the population at large. Here, too, doctors find themselves being able to contribute and lead a debate, grounded in the core training of their values and commitment to patients through their Hippocratic oath and to make these trade-offs through a unique combination of specialist medical knowledge and insight into their organisations' imperatives (Brook, 2010). Indeed, the creation of clinical commissioning groups with doctors positioned at the forefront of purchasing care has once again focused attention on the need for medical leadership (Bohmer, 2012).

Finally, Part 1 concludes with Chapter 6 by Ahmed Nassef, offering a conceptual model of Medical Leadership with underpinning theories of Adult Learning, Social Identity Theory, Self Determination Theory, co-production and communities of practice. This chapter concludes with the recommendation that medical leadership works better when it is 'self-determined' (Nassef and Aylott, 2016; Nassef et al., 2017; Giri et al., 2017) and when it is directly related to the interests and passions of the doctor at the individual level to pursue quality within the organisation. However, 'self-determined' medical leadership requires investment in the infrastructure of the organisation to support it, and in this book, we look for evidence of successful healthcare organisations that have embedded medical leadership and provide case studies to illustrate examples of this. The benefits of an engaged medical workforce reaps substantial organisational benefits including a more dynamic and engaged medical workforce who can deliver a better patient experience, with better outcomes, less clinical errors and lower absenteeism, and at the same time, results in engaged patients in the quality improvement process and in their own care (Clark et al., 2008; Rowling, 2011; Spurgeon et al., 2011a, 2014).

The advocacy of 'medical leadership' as a disaggregated and distinct entity, however, is neither to undermine the contribution of other healthcare professionals to the essential teamwork demanded by modern healthcare enterprises nor to imply that a doctor should necessarily be a better leader in all circumstances (Spurgeon et al., 2011b). It is merely a recognition that within any team, the professional identity, training and perspective of an individual is part of how the leadership role is enacted. Accordingly, Spurgeon et al. (2014) argue that doctors' individualistic expertise, autonomy in practice and their differential power bases within the NHS all make for a unique perspective that in turn influences their role and contribution to the leadership process.

2

'LEADERSHIP' AND 'MEDICAL LEADERSHIP'

Bolarinde Ola and Aishin Lok

'Leadership' vs 'management'

Kotter (1996) differentiates between leadership and management, describing management processes as those that are concerned with planning, budgeting, organising staffing, controlling and problem solving and leadership processes as those that involve establishing direction, aligning people, motivating and inspiring (Kotter, 1996). However, leadership still requires considerable management skills. But it is more than just management, which might be concisely summarised as 'getting the job done'. Leadership is differentiated from management in as much as managers seek to exert their control over an employee with the use of an employment contract, whereas leaders exert influence (Blom and Alvesson, 2015).

Leadership is about influence, influencing across the system at the micro level with patients and families, to influence with peers, team members, other teams and influencing upwards. The skills utilised for leadership will be variable and will require assessment of the situation, the context, the history of the organisation and knowledge about motivational strategies of those who are being influenced. There needs to be an assessment of followship. An effective leader is only as good as his or her communication skills to transmit a message. There is a level of conscious decision making and a level of risk taking, but overall there is a level of measured assessment as to which leadership strategy to use and when. The outcome of effective leadership should be quality improvement for patients and an improved and efficient healthcare system. Leadership is much more effective than management in achieving effective team participation, positive workplace well-being and personal levels of motivation. A study has shown that motivated employees are more happy and productive (Sgroi, 2015). Managed employees are more likely to feel resentment and negativity and are likely to go off sick. If individuals are unhappy at work, then this is associated with lower productivity, an affect that can last up to 2 years

(Sgroi, 2015). Even when managers manage, it will be more effective to use leadership skills to manage and support the person in their job role. Using punitive measures will merely thwart teamwork and productivity and generate a poor culture.

Other definitions of leadership that can be found in the literature include leadership as the art of motivating a group of people to achieve a common goal. This demands a mix of analytic and personal skills in order to set out a clear vision of the future and define a strategy to get there. It requires communicating that to others and ensuring that the skills are assembled to achieve it. It also involves handling and balancing the conflicts of interests that will inevitably arise.

Leaders can also transform their concepts, convictions and vision into organisational changes through their influence over other people (Gill, 2011; Hellriegel et al., 2004:286). Leaders such as Mother Teresa, Florence Nightingale, Mary Seacole and Nelson Mandela show outstanding examples of leadership. With each of the named individuals, we are offered a study in leadership theory, leadership styles and emotional intelligence as reflected by Goleman's six leadership styles (Goleman, 2000; Goleman et al., 2002) which he described as: democratic, authoritative/visionary, pace-setting, affiliative, coaching and coercive/commanding. The more aware a leader is of themselves the greater the level of Emotional Intelligence. There is a vast and confusing number of definitions for emotional intelligence, also called emotional literacy by others (Wolmarans and Martins, 2001). Martinez (1997:72) defines emotional intelligence as "a set of non-cognitive skills, capabilities and competencies that influence a person's ability to cope with environmental demands and pressures". Thorndike (1920) is widely credited with the first modern theory of emotional intelligence. He described three types of intelligence: abstract, concrete and social. Abstract intelligence, measured by intelligent quotient, measured how clever a person is. Concrete intelligence he felt was needed for manipulating objects and shapes, and social intelligence that was needed to interact and associate with people evolved into emotional intelligence as we know it today. Other researchers such as Howard Gardner (1983) extended the concepts of Thorndike to include other forms of intelligence that were not measurable by intelligent quotient.

The work of Salovey and Mayer led to the development of the ability model and subsequently the Multifactor Emotional Intelligence Scale (MEIS) (Mayer et al., 1998; Palmer et al., 2001). The MEIS also called the Mayer–Salovey–Caruso Emotional Intelligence Test (MSCEIT), describes twelve tasks designed to measure a person's ability to perceive, assimilate, understand and manage emotions (Mayer et al., 1998). Goleman (1998) built on existing work by proposing five components of emotional intelligence – self-awareness, self-regulation, self-motivation, social awareness and social skills – that can have a significant impact on an individual's perception and response to organisational environments. Self-awareness is all about understanding one's likes and dislikes and one's innate abilities and weaknesses. Self-regulation is the capacity to exercise proportionate control in the face of external influences. Self-motivation describes the ability to keep focused in the pursuit of goals by optimism, resoluteness and commitment. Social awareness is the emotion of empathy or feeling what others feel – an important attribute of a leader in the workplace. Social skills, according to Goleman (1998), include effective communication, conflict resolution, collaboration, cooperation, managing change and team building.

Emotional intelligence is an important indicator of a leader's ability to succeed. Many studies link emotional intelligence with individual and group performances in the workplace. Research by Schutte et al. (1998) demonstrated a positive link between emotional intelligence and effective outcomes like optimism, task mastery, mental well-being and job satisfaction but a negative link to symptoms of depression. The impact of emotional intelligence on group performance has also been investigated (Kelley and Caplan, 1993; Dulewicz and Higgs, 2000), with evidence suggesting that emotional intelligence can determine high and average performance in the workplace.

Evidence suggests that the best leaders and best 'medical leaders' will develop a heightened level of awareness of their 'emotional intelligence' and use the four styles – democratic, authoritative/visionary, affiliative and coaching – interchangeably according to the needs of individuals and team members. The styles of coerciveness and pace-setting are less likely to be effective and can create tension, a damaged culture and poor performance (Goleman et al., 2002). Goleman (2013) describes emotional intelligence as the foremost leadership skill, which harnesses four domains: self-awareness, self-management, social awareness and relationship management. Good leaders are aware of self and their physical and social environment, which facilitates how they influence people around them in a positive way. Demonstration of positive emotions like happiness, laughter and optimism can lift workers to achievement and progress, whereas negative emotions like anger, hostility, fear and anxiety can be demoralising to a workforce.

Understanding leadership styles and approaches and what motivates people is an essential aspect of developing as an effective 'medical leader'. This approach has evolved significantly since early leadership theories, when, for many years, it was a commonly held belief that some people were born to lead because they had inherited traits and qualities found in leaders (Swanepoel et al., 2000). The initial studies into trait theory concluded that many leaders had personality and psychological traits, which were inherited and were transferrable from one situation to another (Bernard, 1926; Kilbourne, 1935; Stogdill, 1974; Hersey and Blanchard, 1969; Maude, 1978). Such desirable traits included an extrovert personality, charisma, masculinity and dominance. Trait theories have been found to lack any scientific basis, as they focus too much on physical and personality characteristics like domineering masculinity, charisma, extrovertness and conservatism (Epstein, 1994; Derue, 2011). Trait theory works against concepts such as equality and diversity and the democratic approach of seeking a range of leadership strengths and attributes in a team, socio-cultural and geopolitical differences across regions or against confounding effects of job training and professional development (Epstein, 1994; Ayman and Korabik, 2010).

Contingency theories of leadership focus on particular variables related to the environment that might determine which particular style of leadership is best suited for the situation. According to this theory, no leadership style is best in all situations. Success depends upon a number of variables including the leadership style, qualities of the followers and aspects of the situation. In time, further research sought to improve understanding of leadership styles in the face of evolving challenges. For example, in a situation where the leader is the most knowledgeable and experienced member of a group, an authoritative style might be most appropriate. In other instances where group members are skilled experts, a democratic style would be more effective (Goleman et al., 2002).

Several theories were formed to explain how effective leaders change their styles according to situations and contingencies, as they arise. These theories, including Fielder's contingency theory of leadership, the path-goal theory of leader effectiveness, Hersey and Blanchard's life-cycle theory, the cognitive resource theory and the decision process theory (Hersey and Blanchard, 1969; Bass, 1998; Mullins, 2007) were based on studies of leaders under different situations. They concluded that good leaders can respond to situations around them and that leadership performance can also be enhanced or diminished by resources available. The emergence of leadership theories over time is summarised in Figure 2.1.

More recently and evidenced in the development of leadership and management competency frameworks is the theory of leadership from a behavioural perspective. This suggests that all people can learn the skills and knowledge of leadership, as great leaders, women, men, black and white, are made and not born. Rooted in behaviourism, this leadership theory focuses on the actions of leaders and not on psychological or emotional states and suggests leaders develop through teaching, learning and observation. As the validity of the trait theory became increasingly questioned, there was a move towards an investigation of how leadership behaviours, and not personal traits, influenced whether they succeeded or failed

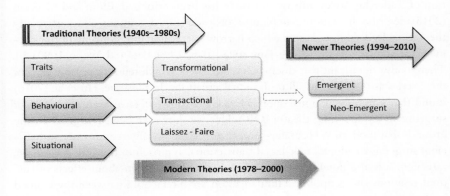

FIGURE 2.1   The development of leadership theories

Source: Adapted from Ola (2017).

(Shriberg et al., 1997; Draft, 1999). Such behavioural research led to several leadership models, including McGregor's Theory (1960), the Ohio State University of Michigan Models (Bass, 1990) and the Managerial Grid Model of Blake and Mouton (1964). Behavioural theorists can be criticised for focusing on laboratory and field data, which are not only detached from workplace reality, but also have an inability to explain how effective behaviours in one situation can be translated to unsuccessful outcomes in other circumstances. Behaviourism also fails to consider the impact of structural power imbalances in the workplace, where, despite some employees developing competence as leaders and managers, they face a glass ceiling. There is a general and more global phenomenon of gender inequalities, with women earning 77% of what men earn, and with women only marginally represented at CEO positions (4% in the US; 2.5% in India), and in the UK, 73% of female managers believe there are barriers to advancement (Snowdon, 2011). In the UK NHS, Trust Board membership is disproportionately male and white in comparison with the local population and the NHS workforce (Kline, 2014). With 35% of the consultant and registrar workforce from black and minority ethnic (BME) populations, only 15% are Medical Directors in London, where the local population is 45% BME. A diverse workforce where all staff contributions are valued is linked to good patient care (West et al., 2012; Dawson, 2009, Kline, 2014) yet, structurally, efforts to change this imbalance have been ineffective to date.

Medical leadership possibilities

Modern organisations have evolved and changed significantly over time, which has presented new challenges for the development of the skills and styles of leadership. More recently, research has focused more on two main modern theories of leadership: transformational and transactional (Bass, 1990; Robson, 1993; Bass and Avolio, 1990a; Crossman, 2013; Johnson et al., 2011). Recently, this compartmentalisation of leadership styles into two or three has been criticised. Blom and Alvesson (2015) describe 'hegemonic ambiguity' of leadership definitions and particularly the within-leadership concepts which narrow everything into convenient transformational, transactional or laissez-faire styles (Bass, 1990; Bass and Avolio, 1990a, b). There is also significant pan–disciplinary vagueness, which tends to portray each of these styles as one-size-fits-all professional situations. To illustrate, Hu et al. (2016) found that a transformational approach was the most effective leadership style of surgeons in an operating theatre (OR). This has, however, been critiqued on the grounds that modern WHO safer-surgery checklists actually requires safe and efficient surgeons to adopt a task-based transactional approach in the OR (Ola, 2016, 2017:59). It is also notable that not enough has been written about effects of cultural, religious and geopolitical influences on the interactions between these broad leadership styles and followership.

Leadership styles have a significant impact on team processes and followership in the workplace (Crossman, 2013, Johnson et al., 2011 and Robson, 1993). The Full Range Leadership Development Model by Bass and Avolio (1997) (Figure 2.2)

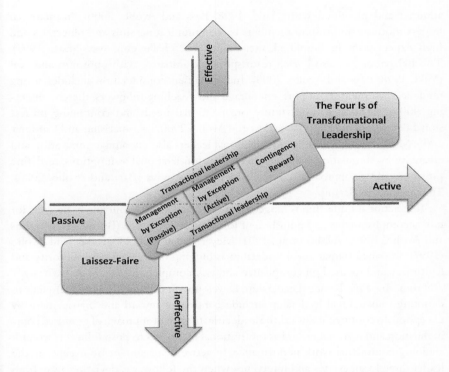

FIGURE 2.2   Schematic representation of Full Range Leadership Development Model

Source: Adapted from Bass and Avolio (1994); cited in Ola (2017).

Note: The four Is are: Idealised influence, inspirational motivation, individualised consideration, and intellectual stimulation.

grouped eight leadership criteria into active, passive, effective and ineffective leadership tendencies. These eight criteria are Idealised attributes (IA), Idealised behaviours (IB), inspirational motivation (IM), intellectual stimulation (IS) individual consideration (IC), contingency reward (LR), management by active expectation (MEA) and management by passive expectation (MEP). These four were then regrouped under transformational, transactional or laissez-faire leadership styles (Bass and Avolio, 1994).

Transformational leadership

The Full Range Leadership Development Model (Figure 2.2) identified four criteria characterising the active, effective tendencies of transformational leadership. These are Idealised influence, inspirational motivation, individualised consideration and intellectual stimulation (Bass and Avolio, 1994). Leaders with Charisma (Idealised influences) are role models for their followership. Such leaders are trusted, admired and identified with (Yukl, 1998; Bass and Avolio, 2000). Inspirational leaders motivate and inspire members by communicating aims and objectives and high expectations in simplified, meaningful, but challenging ways (Bass, 1997). This behaviour can also enrich team spirit and initiative with optimism and zeal (Yukl, 1998; Bass and Avolio, 2000). Individualised consideration includes strong tendencies to mentor, support, encourage and coaching followers, thereby directing skill acquisition towards future organisational needs and continuing professional development (Yukl, 1998; Bass and Avolio, 2000; Lagomarisino and Cardona, 2003; Mester et al., 2003). Transformational leaders also encourage innovation and creativity by stimulating followership to question irrational assumptions, re-define problems and re-approach old challenges in new ways (Bass and Avolio, 2000). Transactional leadership

Transactional leadership is hinged on a carrot-and-stick principle of benefits for task accomplishments and punishment for poor performance (Burns, 1978, in Bass and Avolio, 1990a; Avolio et al., 1991; Meyer and Botha, 2000). Bass and Avolio (1997) described transactional leadership as hinging on bureaucratic authority and legitimacy and focused on compliance and task completion.

From the Full Range Leadership Development Model (Figure 2.2), actions denoting transactional leadership include contingent reward and management by exception. In contingent reward, the leader uses the carrot approach of promises, commendation and material reward as motivational incentives to push followers towards attaining contractual work performance. In active management-by-exception, the leader directly supervises and intervenes when the follower is deviating away from agreed guidelines or target. By contrast, in passive management-by-exception, the leader monitors indirectly and can intervene only when standards are not met (Bass and Avolio, 1990b; Bass and Avolio, 1997; Mester et al., 2003).

Both styles of leadership are frequently complementary. Indeed, transactional leadership is entrenched in the curricula of postgraduate medical and surgical training, where trainees are expected to show learning curves in skill acquisition from direct to indirect supervision leading to independent practice. In such a system, transactional leadership offers corrective management either actively on the spot, or passively at quarterly formative assessment meetings. In modern-day NHS an understanding of leadership is complex, with leaders also having to be more emotionally intelligent, as they are expected to provide moral leadership, helping and listening skills that form the foundation stones for implementing trust strategic directions and commitment and dedication by followership (Bolden, 2003; Xirasagar et al., 2005).

Leadership and performance

There is a consensus that the most important factor in organisational performance is leadership. There is, however, no doubt that the skills, qualification, motivation, stimulation and dedication of members are also crucial to organisational performance, particularly in voluntary organisations; nevertheless, it is the leader who must be able to harness and optimise these attributes towards a collective goal. An effective leader can enhance the output of the entire workforce by bringing out the best in individuals and collectively (Bass, 1997, 1999; Mullins, 2007). Bass and Avolio (1994) demonstrated that transformational leadership has a greater influence on organisational performance when compared with transactional leadership. Other researchers (Pruijn and Boucher, 1994) have also concluded that transactional is an extension of transformational leadership; whereas the former brings out the expected performance from a group, the latter can motivate group and individual performance beyond expectations (Bass and Avolio, 1994; Bass, 1997). Furthermore, it is argued that transactional leadership is more suited to organisations engaged in stable markets without rivals or competitions, whereas transformational leaders are more adapted to the modern dynamic marketplace with fierce rivalry and competitions for scarce resources and more demanding clientele (Brand et al., 2000).

The Future model of Healthcare Leadership: Shared, collective and distributed leadership

Turnbull-James (2011) describes the 'post-heroic' model of leadership, which encompasses shared leadership involving multiple actors who take up leadership roles both formally and informally and by working collaboratively. Leadership is distributed away from the top of an organisation to many levels. The new leadership is a dynamic, interactive processes of influence and learning which will transform organisational structures, norms and work practices (Pearce and Conger, 2003). The NHS has moved beyond the outdated model of heroic leadership to recognise the value of leadership that is shared, distributed and adaptive. Leaders must focus on systems of care and not just institutions and on engaging staff and followers in delivering results. At a time of huge transition and challenge, leaders at all levels and from all backgrounds have a responsibility to ensure that the core purpose of the NHS – to deliver high-quality patient care and outcomes – is at the heart of what they do.

3

QUALITY IMPROVEMENT AS THE GOAL OF MEDICAL LEADERSHIP

Rachael Baines

'Quality Improvement' is now recognised across the globe as an effective vehicle to enable the application of leadership development in an experiential and applied way (Nelson et al., 2011; Benn et al., 2009; Bevan, 2004). In a paper titled 'Why the NHS Needs a Quality Improvement Strategy' (Kings Fund, 2016), the author argues that "even simple [healthcare] improvements, take intention and method", suggesting that a culture of improvement is required and that staff need the skills to use such methods. This section will focus on the method of 'clinical microsystems' to advance an organisational culture of quality improvement.

Quality Improvement is about engaging with patients in co-production to advance new ways of delivering healthcare services. The most successful healthcare systems embed values of patient involvement and patient engagement to achieve effective quality improvement: "Patients and their carers should be present, powerful and involved at all levels of healthcare organisations from wards to the boards of Trusts" (Berwick, 2013).

Clinical Microsystems (CMS)

In the last 20 years, there has been an explosion in healthcare QI methodologies (Nicolay et al., 2012; Balasubramanian et al., 2000). Despite this, little is known which is the most appropriate (Nicolay et al., 2012; Boaden et al., 2008; Øvretveit and Gustafson, 2002) or about how one should improve care across a variety of settings (Nicolay et al., 2012; Auerbach et al., 2007; Mittman, 2004).

CMS methodology originally developed in the US by TDI has been used globally to develop sustainable healthcare improvements in quality of care and efficiency (Downes, 2012; Bojestig, 2010; Godfrey et al., 2008). The approach thinks of health organisations as being made up of small building blocks that come together to provide care. The coaching programme supports each individual within each microsystem to enable healthcare improvement through learning and adapting improvement knowledge, developing skills and abilities, receiving encouragement and seeing improved group dynamics (Godfrey et al., 2008).

CMS coaching is internationally validated and is pivotal to the IHI White Paper outlining a framework for system level execution (Nolan, 2007; Sheffield Teaching Hospitals Foundation Trust (STHFT) Quality Strategy 2012; Godfrey et al., 2008). Such a programme has not previously been undertaken in the UK; however, significant investment by STHFT has been based on local pilot projects and success in other countries, such as Cincinnati Children's Hospital, Maine Medical Centre (US) and Haukeland University Hospital (Norway) and Qulturum in Jönköping County (Sweden) (Downes, 2012; Baker, 2011; Bojestig, 2010; Bodenheimer et al., 2007).

Clinical Microsystems as a method has evolved over time; however, it was a method originally developed from the statistician W. Edward Deming (Deming, 2000) and Professor Quinn (Quinn, 1992), who taught us that systems by their nature must have an aim, and their subcomponents must be working synergistically to achieve the overarching aim (Deming, 2000). The seminal idea for the CMS stems from the work of Quinn, whose work was based on analysing the world's best-of-best service organisations, such as FedEx, McDonalds's, Nordstrom and Scandinavian Airlines. He focused on determining what these extraordinary organisations were doing to achieve high-quality, explosive growth, high margins and wonderful reputation with customers (Best et al., 2012). He found that they organised around, and continually engineered, the frontline relationships that connected the needs of customers with the organisation's core competency (Foster, 2007). He called this frontline activity that embedded the service delivery process the 'smallest replicable unit' (Quinn, 1992), which we now call a 'microsystem'.

It was then that Paul Batalden and Eugene Nelson who pioneered Quinn's work and translated it into the healthcare sector (Nelson et al., 2002, 2011; Batalden et al., 2011; Batalden and Davidoff, 2007) noted that clinical units such as the operating room are also microsystems. A CMS in healthcare can, therefore, be defined as a small group of professionals who work together on a regular basis, or as needed, to provide care to discrete populations of patients (Best et al., 2012). The systems evolve over time and are (often) embedded in larger systems or organisation; these systems are called 'mesosystems' and 'macrosystems', respectively (Nelson et al., 2011).

Based on Deming's (2000) proposition that an organisation requires the 'square root of n' QI staff to achieve a critical mass for change (where 'n' is the number of employees in the organisation) (Deming, 2000), the STHFT MCA predicts the need to train approximately 125 coaches ($\sqrt{15,000}$ employees) (Reinertsen, 2004), achieving this within 2½ years, and by 3½ years, every patient experience in STHFT will have benefitted (Downes, 2012). This is in order to reach a tipping point (Gladwell, 2000) of mass cultural change creating a culture of sustained patient-centred continuous QI (Gladwell, 2000) within and beyond the STHFT (please see Case Study 1 at the end of this chapter).

The overall improvement in the quality of patient care will be defined and owned by the individual support and clinical microsystems. Rigorous measurement and records of clear and specific improvement against the dimensions of quality of patient care, as defined by the Institute of Medicine (IOM), will be made by the academy (IOM, 2001).

Although CMS are new to the NHS in some respects, many of the fundamental underpinning principles are fairly well established within the literature pertaining to organisational behaviour and change (Nelson et al., 2011; Williams et al., 2009). In a study of performance and productivity within the private sector, Quinn (1992) noted the importance of reducing large and complex organisations to key building blocks (named 'smallest replicable unit' or 'minimum replicable unit'), so that staff can respond to the needs of customers and changes within the external environment (Godfrey et al., 2008).

The conceptual framework derived from Deming (2000) and Quinn (1992) provides a clinical and business case supporting the need to focus and empower frontline teams with robust data and that performance measures should reflect how these teams interact rather than promulgate the outdated notion of solely measuring individual performance (Likosky, 2014).

Many QI initiatives rely on changing the clinical system, yet factors that influence the sustainability of QI are poorly understood (Hovlid et al., 2012). In a systematic review, the median follow-up time for interventions that sought to improve the quality of care was less than 1 year (Alexander and Hearld, 2009; Hovlid et al., 2012). Consequently, little is known about the factors that contribute to the sustainability of improvements over a longer period of time (Alexander and Hearld, 2009).

The UK NHS and world healthcare systems have to now move beyond just pockets of innovation and isolated examples of high-performing organisations to create a social movement for improvement (Bevan et al., 2011; Ham, 2009; Benn et al., 2009). Policymakers and healthcare professionals face the challenge of increasing the efficiency and quality of services provided (Best et al., 2012; Ham, 2004).

Microsystems that have coaching support are more likely to be successful in improvement through learning and adapting improvement knowledge, skills and abilities offering crucial encouragement and enhancing group dynamics (www.clinicalmicrosystem.org, 2012).

Strategic recommendations are made to the Hospital Trust Board based on challenges faced when scaling up large-scale change initiatives. Much of what is known about the effects of large-scale improvement efforts comes from a select organisation (such as the Institute for Healthcare Improvement) (Narine and Persaud, 2003). This is not to say pockets of established interventions, powerful ideas and examples of success and breakthrough results don't exist. A primary standard data or intervention registry for improvement efforts would be useful in order to analyse and develop context-specific assessment tools (Perla et al., 2011). The literature tends to suggest that large-scale change efforts tend to be fragmented from an implementation standpoint and weak from an evaluation standpoint (Perla et al., 2011). A more systematic approach is needed to assess and evaluate the effects of large-scale initiatives (Narine and Persaud, 2003). Many interventions are not well controlled or understood with a lack of rigorous data, which then makes it extremely difficult to know what did or did not work (Perla et al., 2011). More work needs to be done to understand the economic and infrastructure requirements of large-scale spread (Perla et al., 2011) in terms of startup costs and likely return on investments (Ovretveit, 2001). Other factors such as optimal collaboration (learning networks) need to be further understood (Narine and Persaud, 2003).

The CMS approach is essentially centred on empowering individuals in the clinical team to lead the improvement work themselves (Institute of Medicine, 2001; Nelson et al., 2002) by using a variety of tools. Much of the evaluation literature surrounding CMS has come from a US context, where the Dartmouth Hitchcock Medical Center has produced a series of nine papers based almost exclusively on two studies (Nelson et al., 2011; Williams et al., 2009). Nelson et al. (2002) reported a study of twenty high-performing clinical microsystems from across North America drawn from five categories: primary care, speciality care, inpatient care, nursing home care and home healthcare. The authors draw quite strong conclusions, particularly given that they studied just twenty sites out of the 'tens of thousands' (Nelson et al., 2002:486) of clinical microsystems, which operate across the US. Nevertheless, they identify nine characteristics of successful microsystems (Nelson et al., 2002:485–486):

1   Leadership
2   Culture
3   Organisational Support;
4   Information and Information Technology
5   Staff Focus
6   Patient Focus
7   Independence of Care Team
8   Process Improvement
9   Performance Patterns.

The study found substantial variation in the frequency with which each characteristic was mentioned by interviewees from the microsystems (Williams et al., 2009), which suggested that the balance of success characteristics differed across the five clinical settings. The most highly rated was that of process improvement (Nelson et al., 2011; Nelson et al., 2002). Brandrud et al. (2011) also describes three successful factors with regard to CMS and continual QI (refer to Table 3.1):

There is little evidence of the effectiveness of the CMS in the NHS available within the literature (Ham, 2014). In a review by Williams et al. (2009) examining its role in the NHS, there is agreement with the wider claims made by Godfrey et al. (2008) and Nelson et al. (2002) that by flattening hierarchy and motivating a range of staff groups, this can lead to demonstrable higher staff morale, empowerment, commitment and clarity of purpose (Williams et al., 2009). This in turn

TABLE 3.1 Factors for successful continual QI

No.	Success Factor	Description of Success Factor
1	Information	Provide continual and reliable information about best and current practice
2	Engagement	Anchor the improvement work to leadership; focus on and engage staff, patient and families in all stages of work
f	Infrastructure	Base the system in improvement knowledge; use multidisciplinary teams; develop systems to facilitate improvement work and a follow-up system to secure sustainability (Brandrud et al., 2011)

Source: Adapted from Brandrud et al. (2011).

leads to enhanced predisposition to improvement and innovation and a seemingly embedded sense of improvement as an ongoing process (Williams et al., 2009).

How the CMS approach is institutionally 'framed' is important; that is, how the approach is presented to staff members in a way that captures their interest and encourages them to engage, and then to sustain credibility to remain engaged, is an ongoing concern within a specific organisational context (Williams et al., 2009). People are much more likely to embrace change if it is framed as something that builds positively upon what they are familiar with, rather than as something that seems far away and unachievable (Bevan et al., 2011). There are many quality frameworks applied to healthcare that aim to reduce waste in the system, just like the CMS. It can be argued that the serial 'pumping and dumping' of a host of different QI methodologies in healthcare over the last 20 years has led not to sustained and continuing improvement but to some waste of effort and resources and a failure to achieve in all healthcare organisations the benefits that sustained and consistent investment in QI could have brought (Walshe, 2009). Parallels can be drawn from CMS when compared with Toyota Production System (TPS), which aims to achieve waste reduction and efficiency whilst simultaneously improving product quality, using fewer employees to produce more cars with fewer defects (Westwood and Sylvester, 2007). Also several of the impacts of Lean implementation reported noticeable reduction of processing or waiting time, an increase in quality through a reduction of errors, reduction in costs through less resource and better process design (Silvester et al., 2004) as well as increased employee motivation and satisfaction and increased customer satisfaction (Radnor and Boaden, 2008, Fillingham, 2007).

It is proposed that to effect change, implementers must first gain commitment to the change (Narine and Persaud, 2003). This is done by ensuring organisational readiness for change, surfacing dissatisfaction with the present state, communicating a clear vision of the proposed change, promoting participation in the change effort and developing a clear and consistent communication plan (Narine and Persaud, 2003). However, gaining commitment is not enough. Many change programmes have been initially perceived as being successful, but long-term success has been elusive (Narine and Persaud, 2003). Therefore, it is vitally important to maintain commitment from colleagues during the uncertainty associated with the transition period.

Bate et al. (2004) estimate that just 15% to 20% of NHS staff is currently actively engaged in quality improvement work, yet in order to achieve the goals set out in *The NHS Plan*, Bate and colleagues suggest that it will require 80% or 100% staff engagement. Thus, "*the next step of the NHS modernisation journey is about making improvement mainstream; transforming patient care by building improvement into everyday work at every level of the system*" (Bevan, 2004). Therefore, the next step in terms of NHS improvement is about having improvement embedded into the everyday activities of all staff.

When implementing change efforts on a large scale, Perla et al. (2011) has suggested four key elements that should inform the QI strategy of choice: a compelling vision and aim for the work, a carefully developed intervention, solid management of the overall effort and sufficient resources to run the initiative both centrally and within participating organisations (Perla et al., 2011).

In considering how individuals engage with innovation, the theme of person-centred values emerges strongly in the literature (Perla et al., 2011; Benn et al., 2009; Bleakley, 2005; Bate et al., 2004). Perla et al. (2011) identifies three elements of engagement an organisation should appreciate before embarking on large-scale change: a highly credible evidence base, a genuine belief that this new model provides better patient care and an organisational appetite for the innovation (Perla et al., 2011). Benn et al. (2009) suggests adopters of the innovation need the appropriate implementation capacity, decision-making authority, leadership and 'time is right' to succeed with large-scale change (Benn et al., 2009).

There is overwhelming evidence demonstrating that coaching behaviours improve ownership, engagement and performance and that an engaged workforce delivers better outcomes for patients. Coaching and not a military style of top-down leadership or performance management will produce the embeding of Quality Improvement in Healthcare settings. Enablement at all levels of the organisation has often proved to be a lever for successful CMS projects. Where CMS teams are given the time and space to meet regularly and feel able to discover and work on improvements important to them and their patients they often galvanise in terms of meeting and taking ownership of the work (Bojestig, 2010). Ham (2014) states the importance of in-house training is to develop a sustainable foundation for improvement and local ownership, by encouraging this approach rather than the provision of training through central bodies, such as the former Modernisation Agency. He also points to evidence from high-performing organisations which manage the pressures of external stimuli, whilst having a sustained commitment to a consistent quality improvement approach, enabling them to relentlessly focus on reducing waste and understanding variation.

4

UNDERSTANDING PATIENT EXPERIENCE AS A CLINICAL LEADER

Suvira Madan

The highest priority for the focus of leadership and quality improvement pro-grammes should be given to improving the quality of care patients receive and the services they use. This chapter will focus on learning from the experience of frail and vulnerable patients with one particular condition, a fractured hip, during their pathway of care from admission through to discharge into the community. The quality of care provided along this pathway has traditionally been considered from a clinical viewpoint, but this does not take into account the patient's own views on the care delivered to them and the outcomes they expect from it.

Within an organisation, strong leadership is required to drive forward the patient experience agenda. Fully engaged leaders can drive the patient experience agenda, empowering staff to make changes that improve the patient's experience, set up processes that capture feedback in real time, model good management from the top, capture patients' stories and ensure feedback from patients is turned into action plans (Hudson, 2013).

In order to take forward patient experience as an essential aspect of quality healthcare, new approaches to capture that experience are required. Hermeneutics is one such approach which helps clinicians to understand the uniqueness of indi-vidual patients, their meanings and their interactions with others, such as carers and family members, and their environment.

Heidegger Hermeneutic Interpretive Phenomenology Method

Hermeneutics brings out that which is normally hidden in human relations and experiences. It helps us to understand core concepts and meanings embedded in common life practices by gleaning them from narratives produced by participants.

Hermeneutic inquiry when applied to healthcare focuses on those narratives to understand the patient experience.

Heidegger used the term *lifeworld* to express the idea that individuals' realities were invariably influenced by the world in which they were living. *Being-in-the-world* meant that humans could not abstract themselves from the world. *Situated freedom* was where our subjective experiences were linked with the social, cultural and political contexts. Our freedom was not absolute and was circumscribed by the existing conditions of our daily lives. Heidegger also described *co-constitutionality*, which meant that the interpretive research was a blend of the meanings articulated by the participants and the researcher (Lopez and Willis, 2004).

A Hermeneutic circle interprets a whole in terms of its parts and parts in terms of the whole to which it belongs (Boell and Cecez-Kecmanovic, 2010). By using Heidegger's hermeneutic phenomenological approach to review the literature on patient experience of hip fractures, we can produce interpretations that go beyond individual studies and contribute to a conceptual and theoretical understanding of the deeper experience of these patients (Figure 4.1).

In order to take this approach forward, we need to consider the meaning of patient experience. Patient experience can be defined as "how well people understand healthcare, how they feel about it while they are using the health services,

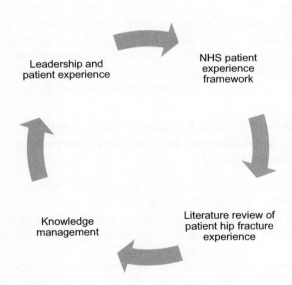

Leadership and patient experience

NHS patient experience framework

Knowledge management

Literature review of patient hip fracture experience

FIGURE 4.1 Heidegger Hermeneutic Interpretive Phenomenology approach to a literature review describing the meanings of hip fracture patients' being-in-the-world and how these meanings influenced the choices they make

Source: Adapted from Lopez and Willis (2004).

how well it serves its purpose and how well it fits into the context in which they are using it" (Bate and Robert, 2006).

In visualising desirable patient experience, three main attributes need to be considered (Liu et al., 2010):

- *Physiological*: high standards of clinical care along with an efficient system of admissions, discharge and dealing with emergencies
- *Psychological*: humanistic care, empathy, respect and communication
- *Environmental*: food, room layout and equipment.

An interpretation of a patients' lived experience can bring understanding and empathy that can be used to improve their care and ultimately their lives (Finch, 2004; Charalambous, 2010). When we begin to 'really know' patients and their world view, we can begin to co-produce services with them to improve their experience of them. Patients in different health groups report differences in their experience (Robert et al., 2011) and, therefore, we need to consider their experience within specific pathways to target improvement interventions such as greater clinical engagement, a healing environment and professional empowerment (Gorman and Watson, 2010).

By reviewing the literature from a Hermeneutic perspective, the experience of each patient with a hip fracture, from injury to recovery, can be subjected to analysis at different levels. The patient's narrative of their experience, the choice of treatment, rehabilitation and recovery pathways can be subjected to formal analysis. In doing this, both the content and nature of care should be considered of equal importance in determining patient experience. A good patient experience is, therefore, multi-dimensional; it is about both the *what* (functions or transactions) and the *how* (relational) of interactions between health services and patients.

National Institute Clinical Excellence (NICE) and A framework for Heidegger Hermeneutic Interpretive Phenomenology Method

NICE Quality Standards along with NHS National Quality Board have developed a patient experience framework to guide NHS staff in this cultural shift towards patient-centred care (Table 4.1). This guidance is the first attempt in standardising and defining healthcare from a patient's perspective (National Clinical Guideline Centre, 2012).

This needs to be considered in light of past healthcare failings such as that at the Mid-Staffordshire NHS Foundation Trust. In his final report of the inquiry, Francis (2013) looked at, amongst other areas, the experience of patients with hip fractures (Table 4.2). Themes that emerged from these patient experiences included the lack of clear nursing responsibilities, poor food and nutrition, lack of team working, poor communication with and about patients and a lack of involvement of patient families. Patient surveys taken during this period showed a decline in

TABLE 4.1 Summary of NHS Patient Experience Framework

	Themes	*Description*
1	Respect of patient-centred values, preferences and expressed needs	This includes cultural issues; the dignity, privacy and independence of patients and service users; an awareness of quality-of-life issues and shared decision making.
2	Coordination and integration of care	This is across the health and social care system.
3	Information, communication and education	This is on clinical status, progress, prognosis and process of care in order to facilitate autonomy, self-care and health promotion.
4	Physical support	This includes pain management, help with activities of daily living and clean and comfortable surroundings.
5	Emotional support	Alleviation of fear and anxiety about such issues as clinical status, prognosis and the impact of illness on patients, their families and their finances.
6	Welcoming the involvement of family and friends	On whom patients and service users rely, in decision making and demonstrating awareness and accommodation of their needs as caregivers.
7	Transition and continuity	As regards information that will help patients care for themselves away from a clinical setting and coordination, planning and support to ease transitions.
8	Access to care	With attention, for example, to time spent waiting for admission or time between admission and placement in a room in an inpatient setting, also waiting time for an appointment or visit in the primary care or outpatient or social setting.

Source: Department of Health Gateway Reference Number 17273 (2012).

patient feedback with the Trust being in the bottom 20% of hospitals for some of the standards of nursing care (Francis, 2013). The Report recommended that hearing and understanding patients must come first, at all levels of the system, from the individual interactions between staff, patients and families, to the hospital management and board, local and national regulatory and supervisory bodies and the Department of Health. Further, it recommended a statutory duty of candour in the NHS to support the development of a culture of patient-focused care at the frontline. In the setting of care standards, the care of frail, vulnerable older people, such as those with fractured hips, should come first (Nuffield Trust, 2013).

Heidegger was one of the first to write on the dehumanising implications of technological advances such as those associated with modern healthcare. By putting the emphasis on systems and processes, we face the consequences with an increasing lack of intimacy between our experiences and the world around us. Our human sense of identity can be affected; we can become like objects ourselves, trying to fit into impersonal systems and production lines (Todres et al., 2007).

TABLE 4.2 Hip fracture patients' and carers' written evidence from the Mid-Staffordshire NHS Foundation Trust inquiry – summary

Hip Fracture Patient and Carer Written Evidence	Year
Following a fall, an elderly patient was admitted to A and E at Stafford Hospital. She required a hip-bone replacement but had to wait for a week for the procedure. During her 7-week stay following the operation, her son observed a number of problems. His mother's bed was left soaking in urine, and she developed a number of bedsores. The emergency button was left out of reach, and her son had to leave work early to ensure someone was there to help feed her. She also received minimal physiotherapy and is now wheelchair bound.	2005
When the patient was dying, no staff came to see or check on her condition and she was left to die on a noisy ward with visitors coming in and out. Not one member of the staff noticed when the patient died. It was left to her daughter to check her mother's pulse, inform staff of the death and ask for her monitor to be turned off.	2006
Following a fall at home, the patient, an 86-year-old man, required hip replacement surgery. The patient was confused and frightened, and the nursing care provided to him was inadequate. He was left on a commode for long periods, he developed bedsores and no attention was given to his nutritional needs. Despite being vulnerable and distressed, the patient was asked directly by a doctor whether he wished to be resuscitated.	2006
Despite the pain it caused to the patient's hip, he was moved on six occasions at the hospital. When enquiries were made by his family as to why the patient was not eating, the nurse simply replied that he had not "ordered anything from the menu".	2007
The following day, her family noticed that she had bruises on her face and arms. They were informed that this was "normal" for old people, but the family were unhappy and asked for their mother-in-law to be transferred to another ward. In this new ward, little assistance was given with feeding. The patient was often found lying in her own faeces and her catheter was rarely emptied.	2007
Following a fall, a 75-year-old woman was taken to A and E and put into a side room for 5 hours, where she was left without pain relief. A doctor finally X-rayed her and told her that she would be operated on the following day. The patient was kept nil by mouth for 5 days as her operation kept being delayed. Her family was appalled by the uncompassionate nature of the staff and the lack of general hygiene.	2007
After being admitted for tests, the patient fell and broke her hip. She had been left to wander the ward, despite the requests by the doctors that she be kept seated.	2008
Following a fall and fracturing her hip at community hospital, the patient was admitted to the Clinical Decisions unit. She spent 5 days on the unit waiting for a bed to become available on the orthopaedic ward. When she was transferred, she was placed on a ward with five other male patients, which caused her upset. Staff refused to provide her with morphine that her doctor had already prescribed. On the ward, she was extremely distressed when the staff told her to urinate in her bed, as using a bedpan had become painful.	2009

Source: Francis (2010).

In reviewing the literature on patient experience of hip fractures, there was a striking similarity between these experiences and those described in the Francis report, creating concern that the failings Francis described were more widespread than a single hospital trust and that more widespread work needs to be undertaken to address them.

This literature has been reviewed in more detail using Heidegger hermeneutic interpretive phenomenology to gain a greater understanding of the patient experience. To provide a framework for the themes developed, the NHS Patient Experience Framework has been used.

Respect for patient-centred values, preferences and expressed needs

The overwhelming patient experience described in these studies was suffering. The meaning of suffering resulting from healthcare experiences can be described through its attributes (Berglund et al., 2012):

- To be mistreated
- To struggle for one's healthcare needs and autonomy
- To feel powerless
- To feel fragmented and objectified.

It is important for healthcare professionals to realise that hip fractures generally create a crisis by activating both fear and the reality of dependency in patients (Borkan et al., 1991).

The philosophy of 'no decision about me, without me' is an important mantra to provide a patient-centred healthcare service which meets the emotional and physical needs of the hip fracture population (Hudson, 2013). The value of being human needs to be evident in the patient-healthcare professional relationship, and the evidence suggests that this was not the case. Negative attitudes by healthcare staff can cause suffering to these patients and their caregivers. 'Suffering from care' emerged from a feeling of unworthiness and was not linked to the illness itself (Hedman et al., 2011).

All healthcare professionals interacting with these patients need to consider the experience and fear of these patients and not merely focus on their physical injury and disability. Hip fracture rehabilitation programmes supporting patients' self-reliance and hope of recuperation should, therefore, be given priority (Ziden et al., 2010).

An awareness of where hip fracture patients are in their process of recovery will help clinicians establish a plan of care and set realistic goals with them. Active listening by healthcare professionals can help unburden patients' fear of falling, thereby helping in the recovery process (Archibald, 2003). Meaningful activity is more likely to engage the patient in rehabilitation to achieve goals rather than meaningless or contrived activities. By asking questions and listening carefully, health professionals can discover patients' perceptions and develop a collaborative relationship between equals so that the patients' values and meanings are understood (Boutin-Lester and Gibson, 2002). An absence of skill, time or organisational priority can make health professionals interact with the patients less sympathetically.

Nurse–patient interactions and a nurse's understanding of the hip fracture patient's world or lived experience can be viewed as an interrelationship between rhetoric and hermeneutics that is necessary and integral to them carrying out the role of caregiving. Heidegger's views were "the know-how of rhetorical competence must be appreciated as having much to do with the (everydayness) of being with one another" (Finch, 2004). Older hip fracture patients are particularly vulnerable to poor practice such as having to use a commode behind a curtain or being disrespected because of their age. Frail, elderly patients have particular issues in relation to dignity and respect, and this may reflect the persistence of ageist attitudes (Robert et al., 2011). There is a need for the nurses and all healthcare professionals to maintain respect regardless of the patients' vulnerable status.

Clinicians need to act on, understand and reflect on the confused hip fracture patient's actions from an individual as well as a historic point of view (Andersson et al., 1993). The conditions for rehabilitation for hip fracture patients with dementia are their competence, absence of support, environmental factors and staff's judgement of the patient's ability to cope with the rehabilitation programme. It relies on healthcare professionals having the right knowledge, skill and kindness to treat these patients. Verbal and non-verbal communication and environmental stimuli are important factors that can help patients with dementia and hip fractures recover. Confused older patients must be taken seriously and treated with skill and kindness (Hedman and Grafstrom, 2001). The witness statements to the Mid-Staffordshire Foundation NHS Trust Inquiry revealed how those with dementia, often with no relatives to advocate on their behalf, were particularly vulnerable to poor standards of care and were least able to report it (Nuffield Trust, 2013).

Archibald (2003) used a phenomenological approach through hip fracture patients' sequential recovery process to generate a rich description of their experiences to inform nursing practices. The themes that emerged were classed into four stages of experience: injury, pain, recovery and disability. Hip fracture patients described their experience of being dependent in hospital and their motivation to recover enough to meet their functional needs independently. The study highlighted the need for caregivers to meet patient needs sensitively, with particular regard to personal cleaning, dressing and toilet needs (Archibald, 2003).

In 2016, the NHS Executive reported that nearly two thirds of NHS Trusts require improvement (NHS Executive, 2016), with reports available on the Care Quality Commission website in the United Kingdom showing which parts of the NHS are still failing to provide elderly and vulnerable patients with compassionate and dignified care as well as lacking basic standards in areas such as continence, nutrition and communication. The reasons for these failures are complex and deep-rooted and are associated with culture, behaviour, resourcing and prioritisation. In the words of the NHS constitution, the very purpose of healthcare is to support people "at times of basic human need when care and compassion are what matters most" (Department of Health, 2015). There is an urgent need to ensure that elderly and vulnerable patients receive dignified and compassionate care in every part of the NHS (Flory, 2011).

Organisational goals and management philosophy can influence how healthcare staffs deal with their patients in an organisation. Negative attitudes and biases towards older patients by healthcare staff can be a substantial barrier to rehabilitation. Optimism on the part of the rehabilitation staff, believing that restoration and recovery is possible, can be a powerful determinant of outcome in hip fracture patients.

Coordination and integration of care across the health and social care system

Frequent patient transfers that can be considered as 'passing them as parcels' and high patient turnover may decrease safety and quality by increasing the risk of medication errors, healthcare-acquired infections, patient falls and mortality (Riehle and Hyrkas, 2012).

For the elderly hip fracture patient, the very needs that necessitate the involvement of healthcare services also limit their autonomy to decide upon them. Instead, healthcare teams have a tendency to use their judgements of competency, mobility, function and access to resources to address these needs. For example, in the routine process of transferring a patient from an acute care to rehabilitation setting, designed to shorten their stay in an acute hospital bed, the overruling of patient choice can be smooth, undramatic and taken for granted because the power rests with the expertise of the healthcare team. Many of the relocation offerings are not timely or adequate solutions because of lengthy waiting lists and financial constraints and are inconsistent with the patient's preference to remain in his or her own home (Hicks et al., 2012).

Organisational effectiveness is required when patients are under the care of several specialists and when there are multiple providers who deliver the care. There is a risk that the overall care of a single hip fracture patient as she moves along the care pathway can easily become ineffective and un-integrated as the healthcare provided is cross-cut by multiple boundaries between hospital and community care. A hip fracture patient with limited medical knowledge, frailty, multiple comorbidities and cognitive impairment may not be able to master an overall pattern of chronic illness care in a sustainable way (Kerosuo, 2010). To counter this, a patient-centred approach is required when organising care pathways, within and across organisations, to ensure the integration required to provide the individualised care each patient requires.

Information and communication

A number of studies have found that the information provided to patients with hip fractures both improves their experience (Johansson et al., 2012) and reduces the likelihood that their families may perceive that care has been mismatched

(Slauenwhite and Simpson, 1998). However, it needs to be recognised that individual patients will differ in their perceptions regarding their need for information and views of their own responsibility in the rehabilitation process (Olsson et al., 2007).

Lack of information can, therefore, lead to misconceptions, anxiety and fear amongst these patients, but to do so, this information needs to address the patient's actual rather than assumed concerns. The information has to be personalised, specific and tailored to their individual circumstances, so that a patient with dementia can receive care from staff who understand that dementia is a condition which requires adjustments in the communication relationship with the care giver (Robert et al., 2011).

A lack of knowledge when dealing with elderly patients, alongside work overload, stress, ethical and spiritual distress, inappropriate facilities and the development of professional burnout, can all have an adverse effect on the quality of patient care. These areas need to be addressed at managerial and organisational levels to ensure that staff meet the needs of their frail, elderly patients (Merkouris et al., 2004). The planning of clinical time must be realistic, based not only on the technical tasks required but also on each patient and their caregiver's expectations and needs including the time required for therapeutic communication.

Finally, these patients with hip fractures are often not only concerned about losing control but also have a fear of falling again. They, therefore, need information and support to develop a healthy risk awareness that can overcome their fear of falling and mitigate their perceptions of future risk (McMillan et al., 2012).

Physical comfort

Physical comfort is an important aspect of patient experience. Pain needs to be addressed by accurate assessment, an appropriate use of comfort measures alongside prescribed analgesics and by ongoing evaluation of the effectiveness of implemented pain relief measures for each unique individual by the clinical team (British Pain Society and British Geriatrics Society, 2007). For example, good collaboration between nurses and physiotherapists is critical for achieving effective pain relief before mobilisation, thereby helping to achieve rehabilitation goals (Hommel et al., 2012).

It should also be considered that the unexpectedness and suddenness of the hip fracture with its functional impairments could alter how pain is perceived by patients and, therefore, the management required for it (Perry et al., 2012).

Emotional support

Maslow's hierarchy of needs makes it clear that not only primary needs such as food and drink have to be met by clinical staff but also secondary and meta needs, such as a sense of security and meaning of life, have to be more clearly addressed during the recovery pathway of a patient with a hip fracture (Hommel et al., 2012).

Perry et al. (2011) used an interpretative phenomenological analysis to explore the experiences of older patients discharged after lower limb orthopaedic surgery.

Patients wanted to please the various health professionals and were impressed with the 'clockwork' running of the orthopaedic wards. A paternalistic medical model was apparent wherein the patients fitted into the system, did as they were told and patiently waited for the surgeon's approval. This paternalistic model can run into problems where the patients may either not adhere to medical advice or worry needlessly and demand more attention from health professionals (Perry et al., 2011).

Carers and family

The complexity and the multidisciplinary needs of the frail hip fracture patients support the need for coordination, communication and collaboration among patients, their family and healthcare professionals. Although older people can demonstrate a remarkable ability to adjust, adapt to and even manage in an environment that seems to foster both physical and psychological dependency, the families' need for education and psychological and emotional support cannot be ignored (Congdon, 1994).

Transition and continuity

Transitions are conceptualised as complex multi-dimensional processes that both cause and affect changes in life, health, relationships and environment. For patients with hip fractures, worries about permanent dependency and impaired walking ability are prominent and can present as a hurdle to successful rehabilitation that needs to be considered by the clinicians caring for them. For example, undertaking a 'fear of falling' screening process at hospital discharge might be beneficial in tailoring rehabilitation efforts to the individuals' needs, thereby helping with their independence, reducing loneliness, frustration and isolation when recovering at home (Jellesmark, 2012). Rehabilitation programmes must have a major psychosocial component with a focus on existential well-being of patients (Wykes et al., 2009).

Perry et al. (2011), in their metasynthesis of older people's experiences of hospital discharge following orthopaedic intervention, identified four main themes: mental outlook, loss of independence, function and activity limitations and coping with pain. Disability can influence values and perceptions of quality of life, and it was found to be important to remain positive, be motivated and have faith. Pain, loss of independence, functional and activity limitations had negative influences on mental outlook. Older hip fracture patients strived to protect their independence for as long as possible. Dependency on others challenged a previously independent patient's sense of identity and self-esteem built up over time.

Access to care

Discharge planning and follow-up for patients after a hip fracture has been found to require greater attention with resources being identified soon after admission for it

(Robinson, 1999). Reducing waiting times for hip fracture surgery has a positive impact on functional status like reducing hospital-acquired infections and pressure sores but also on improving physical comfort, nutrition and dependency levels as well as alleviating fear and anxiety amongst these patients.

Conclusion

Hip fractures are a common and life-changing injury for the frail, elderly members of our society. By reviewing the literature from a Hermeneutic perspective, the importance of the patient experience can be highlighted in such a way as to provide clear areas for intervention and improvement, such as in the provision of training and time to meet not only physical but also psychosocial needs. The patient with a hip fracture embarks on a therapeutic journey through acute services and rehabilitation, and for many they have a prospect of returning home. The whole journey needs to be considered from the patient's perspective alongside the transitions between each part of that journey. Only by doing this will we provide the quality of care these patients deserve. Clinical leaders need to recognise both the importance of the patient experience and the methodologies used to understand this experience. Only by doing so can a culture of 'patient centred' service improvement be promoted within the wider multi-professional team in coproduction with patients and their families.

5

PRIMARY CARE AND GENERAL PRACTICE

Medical leadership for all

Mathew Fortnam

In the UK, *The Five-Year Forward View* (NHS, 2014) outlined new models of care, with greater emphasis on the importance of integration of health and social care and the collaboration of existing providers to develop more community-oriented services and to improve patient pathways. This follows the implementation of the Health and Social Care Act (HM Government, 2012) (England, UK), in conjunction with developments in Primary Care services (*General Practice Forward View*, NHS England, 2016a), the introduction of Sustainability and Transformation Programmes (NHS England, 2016b) and the outcomes of Vanguard projects (NHS England, 2016c) which collectively are all shaping the landscape for health and social care reform. It is possibly more important than ever before that all clinicians will need to engage in a process to develop new skills and knowledge to meet these challenges in organisational change, which are high on the political agenda (Rose, 2015:3–10) and of extreme national and international importance (Barker, 1996:5–47). As Smith (2015:1) articulates, "we need to ensure strong leadership and improvement capability across healthcare", whilst "responsibility for this is everybody's business at both national and local level".

The concept that leadership is for everybody and for all doctors and it is not just 'another competency', defined by a competency framework is further supported by Rughani and Lees (2013), indicating that development of such skills later in postgraduate training may well be too late to allow the talented leaders in waiting to flourish. Development in both leadership and management is needed for all doctors, and it is now recognised that it is not 'an optional extra' (Clark, 2012). Leadership development must not focus purely on technical competencies, but also on the ability to create climates in which individuals can themselves act to improve services and care. Staff at all levels need to be given the skills to have the courage to challenge poor practice and to lead effectively, becoming adaptive and flexible in the way services evolve. A new and emergent type of leadership is 'shared leadership', which seeks to build upon the work of transformational leadership, suggesting that "transformational leadership could be shared amongst team members . . . inspiration would come from a sharing of mutually articulated goals" (Bass, 1998:157). A definition of shared leadership is "a dynamic interactive influence process among individuals in groups for which the objective is to lead one another to the achievement of a group or organisational goals or both" (Pearce and Conger, 2003:1). It is argued that once shared leadership is combined with participative leadership behaviours, this provides the platform to recognise all team members' contributions, which then provides a level of integration and communication amongst the team that allows it to begin to engage in a reciprocal influence process where no single team member is presumed to be more powerful (Hernandez et al., 2011).

Previously, much of the literature on leadership development focused on the leader and his or her followers (Hernandez et al., 2011; Howieson and Thiagarajah, 2011) with previous taxonomies of leadership omitting the inclusion of 'context' in which leaders and their followers are embedded (Hernandez et al., 2011). An exploration of the type of organisations and culture in which leaders function has also previously not been sufficiently explored in the leadership literature when organisational context can both exert influence on and receive influence from organisational members (Howieson and Thiagarajah, 2011).

The changing external context of healthcare requires primary and secondary care doctors to operate in a vastly different environment which will require a different form of organisational leadership. As shared leadership is developed within different and specific contexts, it is

> a group level phenomenon that moves away from the traditional notion of top down influence and argues that the leadership role can be shared by team members either simultaneously or in a rotating fashion resulting in lateral and upward influence.
>
> *(Pearce and Conger, 2003)*

Leadership can be assumed by any team member who feels able to do so based on a competency framework. The future models of 'shared leadership' results in a 'leadership network' (Carson et al., 2007).

Not all hospitals will survive in the future (Leech and Cox, 2008), and there will be a demise of hospital care as technology makes it possible for more healthcare to be provided in community settings. Medical leaders need to be at the forefront of these changes and involved in organisational decision-making processes, as this is most likely to enhance organisational performance. Organisations that invest in leadership and management development and succession planning tend to do appreciatively better than those that do not (Rowling, 2011:28; Castro et al., 2008). The evidence suggests that more effective organisational change occurs when leadership is a collective process across clinical, administrators and political

leaders (Toutati et al., 2006) and as a team effort of different clinical professionals and people with a management background (Chantler, 2010). A further study
supports this and argues that it is not the effectiveness of a leader in isolation that
affects organisational performance, but the alignment of leaders across hierarchical
levels that is associated with the successful implementation of a strategic change
(O'Reilly et al., 2010). The authors undertook a study with forty-one medical
departments in an American healthcare system and found that professional service organisations present leaders with a different set of challenges and constraints
than conventional firms (O'Reilly et al., 2010). Some of the external and internal
challenges include the unique regulatory environment of hospitals, the presence
of unions and the presence of strong professional groups. These findings suggest a
continued need to develop shared leadership strategies as well as shared leadership
skills in strategic ways.

The changing of the doctor's role from clinician to 'clinician/manager' in the
United States in the 1990s led to commentators suggesting there is a need for doctors to influence rather than to control, to develop a more external than internal
focus, with the physician leading by listening, influencing and supporting others. The type of leadership development required now and for future UK healthcare organisations includes understanding leadership in its broader context of the
organisation. No longer can leadership be considered at a purely psychological level
in terms of just 'leaders and followers'. It has been argued that the way the NHS
is changing requires a focus on developing the organisation and its team . . . and
to understand leadership that is shared, disturbed and adaptive (Rowling, 2011).
Rowling (2011) argues that the new model and direction for leadership development will need leaders to focus on systems of care and on engaging staff and followers in delivering results. This changing focus of leadership development towards
a more organisational perspective is supported by Hardacre et al. (2011) who argue
that the more complex the environment and improvement initiative, the more
the leader needs to draw on his or her managerial skills as well as relational skills.
The increased complexity of the healthcare environment is a result of the need to
develop more integrated services, more specialisation and more cost-effectiveness
in service provision while maintaining quality.

What clinicians say and what they do has a significant impact on those they lead,
as they will be tasked with communicating the organisation's priorities and values
(King's Fund, 2013). Therefore, all clinicians need to be competent managers and
leaders in their practitioner roles. This is due to their direct and far-reaching impact
on patient experience and outcomes and their broad legal duty, which means they
have an intrinsic leadership role within healthcare services. It is also about the recognition that without doctors actively involved in the management, leadership and
transformation of health services, initiatives to improve the patient experience are
unlikely to succeed (Clark and Armit, 2010).

Medical leadership is inextricably linked to medical engagement, providing
the rationale and steer for the aspiration that medical leadership development

programmes will result in greater medical engagement from doctors. Medical engagement has been defined as "*the active and positive contribution of doctors within their normal working roles to maintaining and enhancing the performance of the organisation which itself recognises this commitment in supporting and encouraging high quality care*" (Spurgeon et al., 2008:214). A study of medical engagement suggests that "medical engagement plays a crucial role in supporting organisational achievement and that leadership is essential to creating the appropriate culture for medical engagement to flourish" (Atkinson et al., 2011). This is supported by Goldstein and Ward (2004) who explain 'medical engagement' in an American context as "the involvement of physicians in strategic decision making" and argue that this is "one of the critical links between strategic planning and the clinical function". The authors argue for more physician involvement in strategic decision making, as their own research findings suggest a direct correlation between physician involvement and hospital performance. Their research concludes by suggesting that relegating the clinical leadership of hospitals to a purely technical role by leaving physicians out of important strategic decisions appear to be associated with lower organisational performance.

In the UK, there has been a global drive to engage doctors in non-clinical matters in healthcare, and this has been acknowledged for several decades; in the Griffiths report of 1983, for example, it was argued that hospital doctors "*must accept the management responsibility which goes with clinical freedom*" (Griffiths report, 1983:18). It is only, however, more recently that medical engagement has been more directly associated with quality improvement and not just concerned with leadership and management. Leadership though quality improvement has resonated with clinicians, as this is at the heart of the work that we are passionate about. As the pressures on our healthcare systems intensify, the need to develop leaders capable of delivering change becomes even more apparent. However, the change must not be change for change sake, but be led by what patients value in terms of change.

In summary, there is good evidence that organisations that are clinically led outperform those where clinical leadership is lacking (Goodall, 2011; West and Dawson, 2012; West et al., 2015:6, Roebuck, 2011:5–9), and that good medical engagement is key to the delivery of organisational performance, as outlined by the *Medical Engagement Scale* (Spurgeon et al., 2011b:81–98). When doctors are more engaged with service development and quality improvement, hospitals perform better financially and clinically (Spurgeon et al., 2011a, b). This is particularly so where doctors are in senior leadership roles (Clark, 2012). Indeed, "*the future well-being of the NHS is closely associated with a commitment by clinicians and doctors in particular, to be at the heart of local management*" (Paton et al., 2005), with doctors leading at a range of levels in the organisation (Howieson and Thiagarajah, 2011). Medical engagement appears to be crucial to healthcare transformation (Best et al., 2012); a major challenge facing the NHS is how to overcome the cynicism of clinicians after a decade in which change has been driven top down, with many initiatives taken to improve performance, most of them lacking strong evidence (Ham, 2009). Historically, in many health systems, physicians have been the principal players in either opposing change efforts or supporting successful transformative efforts, and in such cases, physicians' champions have taken a lead role. This has led many experts to point to physician engagement as critical for change efforts to be successful (McDonald et al., 2008). The future challenge is for the development of more shared forms of medical leadership across the primary and secondary care sector.

6

A THEORETICAL MODEL TO ENGAGE DOCTORS IN MEDICAL LEADERSHIP

Ahmed Nassef

There is no doubt from the literature that medical leadership is one of the 'means to the end' of a high-performing healthcare system (Ham, 2009). Medical leaders must actively engage with improving services, especially in hard financial times, and clinicians need to lead the process of innovation and improvement and the elimination of waste (Ham, 2009, 2014). However, this will need to be supported by the development of key skills in leadership, management and quality improvement. At the same time, the organisation needs to create a culture where medical leadership is supported, sustained over time and becomes part of the embedded culture of the organisation.

Medical leadership programmes should be developed and designed as bespoke programmes and tailored to meet the needs of patients and service users from within a given local population, encouraging shared learning across primary and secondary care and collaborating with patient groups. The evidence suggests that a 'one-size' approach does not fit all (Rose, 2015; Smith, 2015) and programmes should be co-designed and co-developed with doctors (Nassef and Aylott, 2016; Nassef et al., 2017:30–33) and underpinned by Adult Learning Theory (including behaviourism, cognitivism and social learning theory) (Allen, 2007); Work-Based Learning (Boud and Solomon, 2011; Raelin, 2008); transformative learning and reflective practice (Allen, 2007; Mezirow, 2000); Social Identity Theory (Tafjel and Turner, 1982) and Self Determination Theory (Deci and Ryan, 1985, 2000).

Medical leaders are themselves adult learners who bring their lifelong experiences to any learning environment. They are practical and goal oriented and prefer learning that will be immediately relevant to their life and work-related problems. They are autonomous and self-directed and like to partake in co-designing their own learning endeavours. They value experiential learning techniques over traditional pedagogical instruction methods. And although they might suffer with physical disabilities or emotional barriers to one area of learning or another, they are purposeful and aspire to competence in whatever they do or engage with (Merriam et al., 2006). Finally, we advocate for the development of 'communities of practice' for medical leadership programmes to support the informal and formal networks and relationships that need to be facilitated in the development of new and innovative transformation of services (Weick, 2001; Nassef et al., 2017:32).

Behaviourism: Under this paradigm, Leadership Development Programmes (LDPs) should incorporate a number of 'real time' opportunities for learners to perform newly acquired behaviours with adequate feedback in a supportive environment. Leadership needs to be practiced to develop proficiency, and 'work-based learning' (WBL) must be a core component. WBL is a process of making work-related learning both conscious and deliberate. Theory and practice are not separate when undertaking WBL. Theory makes sense through practice and practice only makes sense through reflection enhanced by theory (Raelin, 2008). When practitioners begin to understand the insights they gain during practice then this becomes legitimate as a source of knowledge, and the process and outcomes of learning become more meaningful (Higgs and Titchen, 2001). During WBL, some 'invisible' aspects of practice, for example, beliefs, values and attitudes are clarified.

Boud and Solomon (2011) identify common ingredients of WBL and these include:

- Specifically established partnerships to foster learning which benefit the learner, and the organisation.
- Formal arrangements that benefit all parties and enable understanding of the CPD needs of the individual and the quality improvement and system transformation requirements of the organisation(s).
- WBL can be targeted towards individuals or groups of employees.
- Partnerships and infrastructure are to be established which identify key roles and responsibilities.
- Work is the curriculum, standard modules may not always be a good match and the organisation and the learner should lead the content.
- Needs of the workplace and the learner are represented in forms which can be utilised by the organisation.
- Different learners/groups may follow different pathways depending on opportunities, experiences and aspirations.
- The starting point is the competency and aspiration of the individual or group.
- The negotiated programmes are assessed by standard and across all levels in Higher Education and need to be transdisciplinary.
- The outcome of WBL should ultimately benefit the users/patients of the service.

WBL can provide a carefully thought out course of study or guided learning and can also be a vehicle for the Recognition of Prior Learning. Creation of a learning environment in the workplace in which the learner constructs and directs their studies and in turn can increase motivation to learn.

Cognitivism: unlike behaviourism, the focus here is on the internal aspects of learning. Cognitivists view people as part of their environment. They hold that individuals experience life through external and internal stimuli and that it is how they interpret these events that define how they make meanings and acquire knowledge of their worlds (Ertmer and Newby, 2013). Accordingly, cognitivists rely on experience-centred instruction methodologies and focus on developing learners' understanding of their individual micro-, meso- and macro-spheres rather than simply by changing their behaviour. They promote the use of case studies and real life problems of immediate relevance to guarantee maximum learners' engagement, encourage them to think in new ways and optimise their problem-solving skills. They emphasise the need for a non-threatening learning environment that will allow and provide participants with opportunities to test new assumptions through activities (Merriam et al., 2006). And as it relates to LDPs, cognitivism would advocate active learning and the crucial role of participants in developing their own objectives and co-designing their learning experiences, for example, through self-determined service improvement projects (Allen, 2007; Nassef and Aylott, 2016).

Social Learning Theory (SLT): SLT complements cognitivism and suggests that individuals learn behaviour (e.g. leadership) based on modelling in their environment (McLeod, 2011). Behaviour, therefore, is a function of the person's interaction with their environment, and as such is a reciprocal concept: People influence their environment which in turn influences the way they behave (Merriam et al., 2006). SLT supports the use of interactional instruction techniques: group learning, action learning sets and, once again, work-based service improvement projects (Prideaux and Ford, 1982).

Transformative Learning: this theory closely examines the learner's meaning-making system (similar to cognitivism) and explores the notion of learning through perspective transformation. Mezirow and Associates (2000) argue that learning is the process of using a prior interpretation to construe a new or revised interpretation of the meaning of one's experience in order to guide future action. Thus, central to Mezirow's transformative learning is critical reflection of one's own environment and existing frames of reference to develop new perspectives and understanding of the world. Indeed, critical reflection assists learners to confront their assumptions and validate their meaning structures – frames of reference, points of view, habits of mind, and so on – through a process of deliberate reasoning and critical appraisal of logic. Transformative learning is facilitated through Action Learning in the workplace to enable a closer connection to the context of practice.

Social Identity Theory

Social Identity Theory (SIT) (Tafjel and Turner, 1982) helps to explain intergroup conflict and has particular relevance in healthcare where there are many different types of professional groups and subgroups. Although groups can give us an important sense of pride and a sense of belonging, they can also contribute to others feeling excluded and forming part of an 'outgroup'. The central hypothesis of SIT is that group members of an 'ingroup' will seek to find negative aspects of an outgroup, to enhance their own self-image and self-esteem. This can create feelings of 'them' and 'us' in the organisation, and this will act as a barrier to achieving shared and collective leadership to improve and transform services. Tafjel and Turner (1982) proposed that there are three mental processes involved in evaluating others as 'us' or 'them':

Catgorisation: we categorise objects in order to understand them. We use categories like black, white, male, female, working class and middle class and assign them into a group. We position ourselves into groups that we value and dissociate from those that we don't value. We can belong to many different groups.

Social Identification: in the second stage, we adopt the identity of the group we have categorised ourselves as belonging to. There will be an emotional significance to our identification to the group and self-esteem will be affected.

Social Comparison: in the final stage, once we have decided which group we belong to then we will compare ourselves to others in that group. If our self-esteem is to be maintained our group needs to compare favourably with other groups.

While SIT explains the alignment of an individual with a group, Identity Theory (IT) is concerned with self-categorisation as the occupant of a role and the incorporation, into self of the meanings and expectations associated with that role (Stets and Burke, 2000). The two theories of SIT and IT co-exist: one always and simultaneously belongs to a group and at the same time occupies a role. Furthermore, both identities are relevant to and influential on perception, attitudes and behaviour (Burke and Stets, 1999).

In SIT, relationships are within a given social identity and all group members will pull in the same direction. In IT, they are reciprocal, with each role being related to, but set apart from counter roles within the group. Burke and Stets (1999) highlight the importance of successful negotiation between individual holders of these roles to iron out competing interests over finite resources, differential performances and relational standpoints – if group harmony is to be maintained and development of both the self and the collective are to be achieved.

The third identity and what Brewer (1991) describes as the most insular level of self-categorisation is Personal Identity. This is the unique self as a separate identity and distinct from any group affiliation or societal role it occupies. Personal Identity penetrates all others and is sometimes powerful enough, Brewer (1991) maintains, to override them both for the sake of the individual's own goals and desires.

Motivation and Self-Determination Theory (SDT): Deci and Ryan (1985) define motivation as a cognitive and psychological construct that constitutes the mobilisation of action. The nature of motivation, they add, concerns energy, direction and commitment. They distinguish between intrinsic motivation – where actions are taken because of genuine interest and satisfaction in the activity itself – and extrinsic motivation driven by an external source such as tangible rewards or punishments.

Through their SDT, Deci and Ryan (2000) argue that people are psychologically active, growth oriented and inherently proactive in mastering their inner drives and emotions to achieve their potential. However, optimal development requires nurturing from the surrounding social environment through the satisfaction of three innate psychological 'nutrients': autonomy, competence and relatedness.

They acknowledge the supremacy of intrinsically motivated behaviours and the thwarting impact of external regulation on physical and psychological health and well-being. However, they describe 'internalisation' as an active and natural process in which individuals attempt to transform socially sanctioned processes into personally endorsed values for self-regulation. When this functions optimally, people identify with the importance of social regulations, assimilate them into their integrated sense of self and accept them as their own.

Communities of practice

At all stages of a Leadership Development programme, learners should be encouraged to draw upon their own 'concrete experience' of leadership for improvement or transformation. A 'community of practice' is defined as a group of people who share a concern or passion for something they do and learn how to do it better as they interact regularly (Lave and Wagner, 1991). This is most usefully done in Action Learning Sets where participants will be asked to 'reflectively observe' the specific challenges and barriers to steering their improvement/transformation project (Nassef et al., 2017:32). The facilitator encourages participants to draw upon a wide range of theory with which to critically make sense of and critique what they observe. Learners are encouraged to develop their own capacity for sense-making (Langley, 1999; Weick, 2001). In light of new, theoretically informed understandings, learners will be required to develop and extend their managerial and leadership practice, to observe the consequences of their own actions and so pragmatically test out and develop theory in the complex and challenging context of medical leadership practice.

Participants should be encouraged to check the extent to which their projects demonstrate 'shared' leadership by exploring the following criteria:

- To what extent are others in the team 'buying in' to the improvement project?
- Which leadership strategies could be useful to encourage 'buy-in' from those more fearful of change?
- Is a decision maker or executive sponsor involved in the improvement project who can action small monthly PDSA changes based on the team's data collection and analysis?
- Are patients involved in the improvement project? If not, then how is the patient voice being captured?
- Is there clarity in terms of aims, objectives and projected outcomes?
- Has trust been established amongst the team members?
- Is there a sharing of power and influence amongst the team members, and is this clarified in 'roles and responsibilities'?
- Is it clear who the leader of the improvement project is? This should be a clinician with the most advanced knowledge of the patient speciality area to ensure quality standards are maintained in the improvement process.

- Are there 'Terms of Reference' for the QI group?
- How are individual members supported to develop their skills?
- What mechanisms are being using for reflection? (Action Learning? Self-reflection?)
- Is a 'collaborative' social leadership identity being formed, or is there still 'Them' and 'Us' in the group?
- Are all written reports showing the names of all the team members? Are all names on any papers for publication or poster presentation to show a commitment to sharing and building knowledge?

Co-production

In summary and to conclude, there are multiple factors that can create barriers to medical engagement, but the key to enabling and sustaining medical engagement is to explore what are the motivating drivers for engagement and also how might this be challenged by personal factors in Identity Theory, Social Identity and Personal Identity Theory.

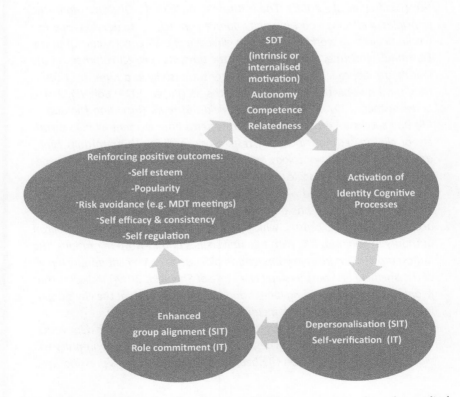

FIGURE 6.1   A cyclical relationship between theories to support a bespoke medical leadership development programme

Case Study 1: developing an organisation-wide Clinical Microsystems Academy at Sheffield Teaching Hospitals Foundation Trust, UK

In June 2012, a shared purpose programme commenced funded by a grant from the Health Foundation. Shared purpose formed the third round of the Health Foundation's closing the gap improvement programme which has sought to identify improvements, build knowledge and skills and create new approaches to transform the quality of healthcare in the UK (Downes, 2012). The specific aim of the programme was to develop and implement an innovative way for corporate and support services and clinical teams to work together to improve quality of care delivered to patients. To this end, the MCA academy project set out to develop capability amongst clinical and corporate support staff to coach QI initiatives using the CMS methodology developed in the US by TDI.

TDI in the US is a leading institution for academia focusing on examining the causes and consequences of unwarranted variations in healthcare practice (Godfrey et al., 2008). The institute's coaching in QI draws upon the principles of effective coaching and improvement science to develop expertise within healthcare workforce to coach clinical microsystems to lead QI at the Dartmouth Institute, United States. At the time, this project commenced the Dartmouth approach had been used very successfully in a number of countries, most notably the US, Sweden and the UK (Baker, 2011; Bojestig, 2010; Bodenheimer, 2007). Staff within Sheffield's SI team (including the author RB) had successful experiences of microsystems improvement work in a variety of clinical settings, including respiratory medicine, hospital falls clinic, ambulatory haemato-oncology and the cystic fibrosis service. This past experience had been small-scale use of CMS in a defined closely bound service as opposed to the proposed wide-scale implementation of the MCA.

The city of Sheffield has a growing population of just over half a million according the 2012 census, which makes it the third largest metropolitan authority in England, UK. With two universities and in-ward migrations, the largest growth has been in younger and older people. A recent annual report of the Sheffield first partnership (The State of Sheffield, 2014) indicates that people in Sheffield are living longer and the overall health of the city's population is improving; however, inequalities persist (CQC, 2009).

Despite Sheffield being a diverse and growing city, it still has deprivation higher than UK average (Downes, 2012). The changing demographics will place significant demand on the health services, and there is pressing need to deliver value (STH Quality Strategy, 2012; Downes, 2012). The recent merger with Community Services has changed the nature of STHFT, providing an opportunity to explore ways of redesigning care (Downes, 2012).

STHFT is the major provider of adult hospital and community healthcare for the city. The trust manages five NHS adult hospitals in Sheffield: Royal Hallamshire, Northern General, Jessop Wing, Western Park and Charles Clifford Dental Hospital in addition to community health services (STH Quality Strategy, 2012). Apart from the Charles Clifford Dental Hospital, all other services provided by the trust have been involved in the MCA initiative (Downes, 2012).

STHFT has made a significant investment in using CMS as their QI methodology to roll out over the next 3–5 years. In total, the full award from the Health Foundation to include set-up and implementation of the MCA amounted to £420,000 over 3 years. The MCA has demonstrated the capacity to generate income (e.g. through the training of coaches external to Sheffield) and is now funded centrally for the roles of MCA manager and CA Program Support Officer (HFSP, 2016). This is the UK's first MCA aiming to train coaches across clinical and corporate support areas at STHFT and will be led by the trust SI team, in collaboration with the human resources (HR) department (HFSP, 2016). Overall, the project will train around 150 coaches in six cohorts over 5 years, reaching 15,000 employees, and within 5 years, every patient experience in the trust is set the benefit from the initiative (Downes, 2012).

References for Part 1

Alexander, J. A., and Hearld, L. R. (2009). What can we learn from quality improvement research? A critical review of research methods. *Medical Care Research and Review*, 66(3), 235–271.

Allen, S. (2007). Adult learning theory and leadership development. *Leadership Review*, 7, 26–37.

Andersson, E., Knutsson, I., Hallberg, I., and Norberg, A. (1993). The experience of being confused: A case study. *Geriatric Nursing*, 14(5), 242–247.

Archibald, G. (2003). Patients' experience of hip fracture. *Issues and Innovations in Nursing Practice*, 44(4), 385–392.

Atkinson, S., Spurgeon, P., Clark, J., and Armit, K. (2011). Engaging doctors: What we can learn from trusts with high levels of medical engagement? *NHS Institute for Innovation and Improvement*, 1–16.

Auerbach, A. D., et al. (2007). The tension between needing to improve care and knowing how to do it. *New England Journal of Medicine*, 357, 608–613.

Avolio, B. J., Waldman, D. A., and Yammarino, F. J. (1991). Leading in the 1990's: The four I's of transformational leadership. *Journal of European Industrial Training*, 15, 1–8.

Aylott, J., Godbole, P., and Burke, D. (2017). Clinicians versus clinicians versus managers or a new patient centred culture that eradicates them and us? In: Godbole, P., Burke, D., and Aylott, J. (eds). *Why hospitals fail: Between theory and practice*. Basel, Switzerland: Springer International Publishing AG 2017.

Aylott, J., and Montesci, L. (2017, July). Nurses need to professionalise workforce planning as one of the urgent goals for the NHS MBA. *Learning Disability Practice*.

Ayman, R., and Korabik, K. (2010). Leadership: Why gender and culture matter. *American Psychologist*, 65(3), 157.

Baker, G. R. (2011). *The role of leaders in high-performing health care systems*. London: The Kings fund.

Balasubramanian, B. A., and Cohen, D., et al. (2000). Learning evaluation: Blending quality improvement and implementation research methods to study healthcare innovations. *Implementation Science*, 10, 31.

Barker, C. E. (1996). *The health care policy process*. London: Sage Publications.

Bass, B. M. (1990). *Bass and Stogdill's handbook of leadership: Theory, research and managerial applications*. New York: Free Press.

Bass, B. M. (1997). Concepts of leadership. In: Vecchio, R. P. (ed). *Leadership: Understanding the dynamics of power and influence in organizations*. Notre Dame: University of Notre Dame Press.

Bass, B. M. (1998). *Transformational leadership: Industrial, military, and educational impact*. Mahwah, NJ: Lawrence Erlbaum and Associates.

Bass, B. M. (1999). Two decades of research and development in transformational leadership. *European Journal of Work and Organizational Psychology*, 8(1), 9–32.

Bass, B. M., and Avolio, B. J. (1990a). Developing transformational leadership: 1992 and beyond. *Journal of European Industrial Training*, 14(5), 21–27.

Bass, B. M., and Avolio, B. J. (1990b). *Transformational leadership development: Manual for MLQ*. Palo Alto: Consulting Psychologist Press.

Bass, B. M., and Avolio, B. J. (1994). *Improving organisational effectiveness through transformational leadership*. Thousand Oaks, CA: Sage Publications.

Bass, B. M., and Avolio, B. J. (1997). *Full Range Leadership Development – Manual for the multifactor leadership questionnaire*. Redwood City, CA: Mind Garden.

Bass, B. M., and Avolio Bruce, J. (2000). *Multifactor leadership questionnaire*. Redwood City, CA: Mind Garden.

Batalden, P. B., and Davidoff, F. (2007, February). What is "quality improvement" and how can it transform healthcare? *Quality and Safety in Health Care*, 16(1), 2–3.

Batalden, P. B., Davidoff, F., Marshall, M., Bibby, J., and Pink, C. (2011). So what? Now what? Exploring understanding and using the epistemologies that inform the improvement of healthcare. *Quality and Safety in Health Care*, 20(1), 95.

Bate, P., Bevan, H., and Robert, G. (2004). *Towards a million change agents: A review of the social movements literature: Implications for large-scale change in the NHS*. London: NHS Modernisation Agency.

Bate, P., and Robert, G. (2006). Experience-based design: From redesigning the system around the patient to co-designing services with the patient. *Quality and Safety in Health Care*, 15, 307–310.

Benn, J., Burnett, S., Parand, A., et al. (2009). Studying large-scale programmes to improve patient safety in whole care systems: Challenges for research. *Social Science & Medicine*, 69(12), 1767–1776.

Berglund, M., Westin, L., Svanstrom, R., and Sundler, A. (2012). Suffering caused by care-patients' experiences from hospital settings. *International Journal of Qualitative Studies on Health and Well-Being*, 7(8), 1–9.

Bernard, Luther Lee. (1926). *An introduction to social psychology*. New York: Henry Holt and Company.

Berwick, D. (2013). *A promise to learn – a commitment to act: Improving the safety of patients in England*. National Advisory Group on the Safety of Patients in England. London: DoH.

Best, Greenhalgh T., Lewis, S., et al. (2012). Large-system transformation in health care: A realist review. *The Milbank Quarterly*, 90(3), 421–456.

Bevan, H. (2004, 8 April). On the power of theory. *Health Service Journal*.

Bevan, H., Winstanley, L., and Plsek, P. (2011). *Leading large-scale change*. Warwick: NHS Institute for Innovation and Improvement.

Blake, R. R., and Mouton, J. S. (1964). Management by grid® principles or situationalism: Which? *Group & Organization Management*, 6(4), 439–455.

Bleakley, A. (2005). Stories as data, data as stories: Making sense of narrative inquiry in clinical education. *Medical Education*, 39, 534–540.

Blom, M., and Alvesson, M. (2015). All-inclusive and all good: The hegemonic ambiguity of leadership. *Scandinavian Journal of Management*, 31(4), 480–492.

Boaden, R., et al. (2008). *Quality improvement: Theory and practice in healthcare*. NHS Institute for Innovation and Improvement. www.institute.nhs.uk/service_transformation/quality_improvement/quality_improvement%3A_theory_and_practice_in_healthcare.html. (Accessed on 2 January 2013).

Bodenheimer, T., Bojestig, M., and Henriks, G. (2007). Making system wide improvements in healthcare: Lessons from Jonkoping County, Sweden. *Quality Management in Health Care*, 16(1), 10–15.

Boell, S., and Cecez-Kecmanovic, D. (2010). Literature reviews and the hermeneutic circle. *Australian Academic and Research Libraries*, 41(2), 129–144.

Bohmer, R. (2012). *The instrumental value of medical leadership: Engaging doctors in improving services*. London: The Kings Fund.

Bojestig, M. (2010). *Healthcare in Jonkoping County*. Presentation in Singapore. www.lj.se/info_files/infosida35432/singapore_2010.pdf. (Accessed on 12 November 2015).

Bolden, R., et al. (2003). *A review of leadership theory and competency frameworks*. Centre for Leadership Studies. Exeter: University of Exeter.

Borkan, J. M., Quirk, M., and Sullivan, M. (1991). Finding meaning after the fall: Injury narratives from elderly hip fracture patients. *Social Science and Medicine*, 33(8), 947–957.

Bornstein, D. (2014). The power to cure, multiplied. *New York Times*.

Boud, D., and Solomon, N. (2011). *Work based learning: A new higher education?* Buckingham: Open University Press.

Boutin-Lester, P., and Gibson, R. W. (2002). Patients' perceptions of home health occupational therapy. *Australian Occupational Therapy Journal*, 49, 146–154.

Brand, C., Heyl, G., and Maritz, D. (2000). Leadership. In: Meyer, Marius and Botha, Eben (eds). *Organisational development and transformation in South Africa*. Durban: Butterworths.

Brandrud, A. S., Schreiner, A., et al. (2011). Three success factors for continual improvement in healthcare: An analysis of the reports of improvement team members. *BMJ Quality & Safety*, 20(3), 251–259.

Brewer, M. (1991). The social self: On being the same and different at the same time. *Personality and Social Psychology Bulletin*, 17, 475–482.

British Pain Society and British Geriatrics Society. (2007). *Evidence on the assessment of pain of older people*. National Guidelines.

Brook, R. H. (2010, 28 July). Medical leadership in an increasingly complex world. *JAMA*, 304(4), 465–466.

Bulman, M., and Deardon, L. (2017). Mistakes by hospital staff see sharp rise: Official NHS Figures reveal. *Independent*. (Accessed on 31 December 2016).

Burke, P., and Stets, J. (1999). Trust and commitment through self verification. *Social Psychology Quarterly*, 62, 347–366.

Burns, James M. (1978). *Leadership*. New York: Harper and Row Publishers.

Carson, J. B., Tesluk, P. E., and Marrone, J. A. (2007). Shared leadership in teams: An investigation of antecedent conditions and performance. *Academy of Management Journal*, 50, 1217–1234.

Castro, C. B., Perin, M.V., and Bueono, J. C. (2008). Transformational leadership and followers attitudes: The mediating role of psychological empowerment. *The International Journal of Human Resources Management*, 19(10), 1842–1863.

Chantler, C. (2010). Paper prepared for the Mid Staffordshire inquiry seminar on the role of leaders in setting a positive organisational culture.

Charalambous, A. (2010). Interpreting patients as a means of clinical practice: Introducing nursing hermeneutics. *International Journal of Nursing Studies*, 47, 1283–1291.

Clark, J. (2012). Medical leadership and engagement: No longer an optional extra. *Journal of Health Organisation and Management*, 26(4), 437–443.

Clark, J., and Armit, K. (2010). Leadership competencies for doctors: A framework. *Leadership in Health Services*, 23(2), 115–129.

Clark, J., Spurgeon, P., and Hamilton, P. (2008). Medical professionalism: Leadership competency – an essential ingredient. *International Journal of Clinical Leadership*, 16(1), 3–9.

Congdon, J. (1984). Managing the incongruities: The hospital discharge experience for elderly patients, their families, and nurses. *Applied Nursing Research*, 7(3), 125–131.

Crossman, A. (2013). *Deductive reasoning versus inductive reasoning*. http://sociology.about.com/od/Research/a/Deductive-Reasoning-Versus-Inductive-Reasoning.htm.

Dawson, J. F. (2009). *Does the experience of staff working in the NHS link to the patient experience of care?* www.gov.uk/government/uploads/system/uploads/attachment_data/file/215457/dh_129662.pdf.

Deci, E. L., and Ryan, R. M. (1985). The general causality orientations scale: Self-determination in personality. *Journal of Research in Personality*, 19, 109–134.

Deci, E. L., and Ryan, R. M. (2000). Self-determination theory and the facilitation of intrinsic motivation, social development and well-being. *American Psychologist*, 55(1), 68–78.

Deloitte. (2016). *Global health care outlook – Battling costs while improving care*. Blogs.deloitte.co.uk.

Deming, W. E. (2000). *Out of the crisis*. Cambridge, MA: MIT Press.

Department of Health. (2008). *High quality care for all*. (online). www.gov.uk/government/uploads/system/uploads/attachment_data/file/228836/7432.pdf.

Department of Health. (2015). *The NHS constitution for England* (updated 14 October 2015). London: Department of Health.

Derue, D. S., et al. (2011). Trait and behavioural theories of leadership: An integration and meta-analytic test of their relative validity. *Personnel Psychology*, 64(1), 7–52.

Downes, T. (2013, 30 October). 'Discharge to assess' at Sheffield Frailty Unit': The Health Foundation. *Newsletter*.

Daft Richard, L. (1999). *Leadership: Theory and practice*. Fort Worth, TX: Dryden Press Series in Management.

Dulewicz, V., and Higgs, M. (2000). Emotional intelligence – A review and evaluation study. *Journal of Managerial Psychology*, 15(4), 341–372.

Epstein, S. (1994). Trait theory as personality theory: Can a part be as great as the whole? *Psychological Inquiry*, 5(2), 120–122.

Ertmer, P. A., and Newby, T. J. (2013). Behaviourism, cognitivism, constructivism: Company critical features from an instructional design perspective. *Performance Improvement Quarterly*, 26(2), 43–71.

Faculty of Medical Leadership and Management. (2014). *Leadership and management standards for medical professionals*. www.fmlm.ac.uk/resources/leadership-and-management-standards-for-medical-professionals.

Fillingham, D. (2007). Can lean save lives? *Leadership in Health Services*, 20(4), 231–241.

Finch, L. (2004). Understanding patients lived experiences: The interrelationship of rhetoric and hermeneutics. *Nursing Philosophy*, 5, 251–257.

Flory, D. (2011). *The operating framework for the NHS in England 2012/13*. London: DH/NHS Finance, Performance and Operations, pp. 1–52.

Francis, R. (2010). *Independent inquiry into care provided by mid Staffordshire NHS foundation trust January 2005-March 2009*. London: The Stationery Office, pp. 1–367.

Francis, R. (2013). *Inquiry report of the mid Staffordshire NHS foundation trust*. www.gov.uk/government/uploads/system/uploads/attachment_data/file/279124/0947.pdf. (Accessed on 23 May 2016).

Gardner, H. (1983). *Frames of mind*. New York: Bantam.

Gill, R. (2011). *Theory and practice of leadership*. Thousand Oaks, CA: Sage Publications.

Giri, P., Aylott, J., and Kilner, K. (2017). Self-determining medical leadership needs of occupational health physicians. *Leadership in Health Services*, 30(4), 394–410.

Gladwell, M. (2000). *The tipping point: How little things can make a big difference*. Boston: Little Brown Ltd.

Godfrey, M., Melin, C., Muething, S., Batalden, P., and Nelson, E. (2008). Clinical microsystems, part 3. transformation of two hospitals using microsystem, mesosystem, and macrosystem strategies. *The Joint Commission Journal on Quality and Patient Safety*, 34(10), 591–603.

Goldstein, S. M., and Ward, P. T. (2004). Performance effects of physicians' involvement in hospital strategic decisions *Journal of Service Research*, 6(4), 361–372.

Goleman, D. (2000, March–April). Leadership that gets results. *Harvard Business Review*, 76–91. http://elibrary.kiu.ac.ug:8080/jspui/bitstream/1/480/1/Leadership%20That%20Gets%20Results.pdf.

Goleman, D. (2013). Leadership that gets results. *Harvard Business Review Onpoint*, 26–38. Hbr.org.

Goleman, D., Boyatzis, R., and McKee, A. (2002). *The new leaders – transforming the art of leadership into the science of results*. London: Time-Warner.

Goleman, Daniel. (1998). *Working with emotional intelligence*. New York: Bantam.

Goodall, A. H. (2011). Physician leaders and hospital performance: Is there an association? *Social Science and Medicine*, 73(4), 535–539.

Gorman, C., and Watson, J. (2010). *Feeling better? Improving patient experience in hospital*. London: The NHS Confederation, pp. 1–20.

Griffiths, R. (1983). *Community care: An agenda for action*. London: HMSO.

Ham, C. (2004). *Health policy in Britain*. Basingstoke: Palgrave Macmillan.

Ham, C. (2009a). *Health policy in Britain*, 6th edition. London, UK: Blackwell Books.

Ham, C. (2009b). *Learning from the best: What the NHS needs to do to implement high quality care for all*. NHS Institute for Innovation and Improvement. England, UK: Health Services Management Centre, University of Birmingham.

Ham, C. (2014). *Reforming the NHS from within: Beyond hierarchy, inspection and markets*. London: The Kings Fund.

Hardacre, J., Cragg, R., Shapiro, J., Spurgeon, P., and Flanagan, H. (2011). *What's leadership got to do with it?* London: The Health Foundation.

Hedman, A., and Grafstrom, M. (2001). Conditions for rehabilitation of older patients with dementia and hip fracture-the perspective of their next of kin. *Scandinavian Journal of Caring Sciences*, 15, 151–158.

Hedman, A. M., Stromberg, L., Grafstrom, M., and Heikkila, K. (2011). Hip fracture patients' cognitive state affects family members' experiences – a diary study of the hip fracture recovery. *Scandinavian Journal of Caring Sciences*, 25, 451–458.

Hellriegel, Don., et al. (2004). *Management: Second South African edition*. Cape Town: Oxford University Press Southern Africa.

Her Majestys Government. (2012). *The health and social care act*. www.local.gove.uk.

Hernandez, M., Eberly, M. B., Avolio, B. J., and Johnson, M. D. (2011). The loci and mechanisms of leadership: Exploring a more comprehensive view of leadership theory. *The Leadership Quarterly*, 22, 1165–1185.

Hersey, P., and Blanchard, K. H. (1969). Life cycle theory of leadership. *Training and Development Journal*, 23(5), 26–34.

Hicks, E., Sims-Gould, J., Byrne, K., Khan, K. M., and Stolee, P. (2012). "She was a little bit unrealistic": Choice in healthcare decision making for older people. *Journal of Aging Studies*, 26, 140–148.

Higgs, J., and Titchen, A. (2001). Framing professional practice: Knowing and doing in context. In: Higgs, J. and Titchen, A. (eds). *Professional practice in health education and the creative arts*. Oxford: Blackwell Science.

Hommel, A., Kock, M., Persson, J., and Werntoft, E. (2012). The patient's view of nursing care after hip fracture. *International Scholarly Research Network Nursing*, 6(1), 1–6.

Hovlid, E., Bukve, O., et al. (2012). Sustainability of healthcare improvement: What can we learn from learning theory? *BMC Health Services Research*, 12, 234.

Howieson, B., and Thiagarajah, T. (2011). What is clinical leadership? A journal based meta-review. *The International Journal of Clinical Leadership*, 17, 7–18.

Hu, Y. Y., et al. (2016). Surgeons' leadership styles and team behavior in the operating room. *Journal of the American College of Surgeons*, 222(1), 41–51.

Hudson, S. (2013). *The patient experience book*. Coventry: NHS Institute for Innovation and Improvement, pp. 1–96.

Imison, C., Castle-Clarke, S., and Watson, R. (2016). *Reshaping the workforce to deliver the care patients need*. Research report, Nuffield Trust, in association with NHS Employers, pp. 1–92.

Institute of Medicine. (2001). *Crossing the quality chasm: A new health system for the 21st century*. Washington, DC: IOM.

International Hospital Federation. (2015). *Leadership competencies for healthcare services managers*. American College of Healthcare Executives, ache.org, pp. 1–12.

Jellesmark, A., Herling, S., Egerod, I., and Beyer, N. (2012). Fear of falling and changed functional ability following hip fracture among community-dwelling elderly people: An explanatory sequential mixed method study. *Disability and Rehabilitation*, 34(25), 2124–2131.

Johansson, I., Baath, C., Wilde-Larsson, B., and Hall-Lord, M. (2012). Acute confusion states, pain, health, functional status and quality of care among patients with hip fracture during hospital stay. *International Journal of Orthopaedic and Trauma Nursing*, 1–11.

Johnson, Gerry, Whittington, Richard, and Scholes, Kevan. (2011). *Exploring corporate strategy*, 9th edition. Essex: FT Prentice Hall,.

Kelley, R., and Caplan, J. (1993). How Bell labs creates star performers. *Harvard Business Review*, 3(2), 100–103.

Kerosuo, H. (2010). Lost in translation: A patient-centred experience of unintegrated care. *International Journal of Public Sector Management*, 23(4), 372–380.

Kilbourne, C. E. (1935). The elements of leadership. *Journal of Coast Artillery*, 78, 437–439.

King, O., Nancarrow, S. A., Borthwick, A. M., and Grace, E. (2015). Contested professional role boundaries in healthcare: A systematic Review. *Journal of Foot and Ankle Research*, 8(1), 2.

Kings Fund. (2013). *Patient centred leadership: Rediscovering our purpose*. London: The Kings Fund.

Kings Fund. (2016). Why the NHS needs a quality improvement strategy: Chris Ham in conversation with Don Berwick. *The Kings Fund Insight Magazine*, summer.

Kirkup, B. (2015). *Morcambe Bay report publication*. London: Department of Health.

Kline, R. (2014). *The "Snowy White Peaks" of the NHS: A survey of discrimination in governance and leadership and the potential impact on patient care in London and England*. Middlesex University Research Repository. http://eprints.mdx.ac.uk

Kotter, J. P. (1996). *Leading change*. Boston: Harvard Business School.

Kramer, M. W., and Crespy, D. A. (2011). Communicating collaborative leadership. *The Leadership Quarterly*, 22, 1024–1037.

Lagomarisino, R. M., and Cardona, P. (2003). *Relationships among leadership, organisational commitment and OCB in Uruguayan health institutes*. IESE Working Paper No.D/494.

Langley, A. (1999). Strategies for theorizing from process data. *Academy of Management Review*, 24, 691–710.

Lave, J., and Wagner, E. (1991). *Situated learning: Legitimate peripheral participation*. Cambridge: Cambridge University Press.

Leech, D., and Cox, D. (2008). Working in and learning from a troubled system. *British Journal of Healthcare Management*, 14(10), 452–454.

Likosky, D. S. (2014). Developing and executing quality improvement projects. *The Journal of Extra Corporeal Technology*, 46(1), 38–44.

Liu, S., Kim, H., Chen, J., and An, L. (2010). Visualizing desirable patient healthcare experiences. *Health Marketing Quarterly*, 27, 116–130.

Lopez, K., and Willis, D. (2004). Descriptive versus interpretive phenomenology: Their contributions to nursing knowledge. *Qualitative Health Research*, 14(5), 726–735.

Martinez, M. N. (1997). The smarts that count. *HR Magazine*, 42(11), 72–78.

Maude, B. (1978). *Leadership in management*. London: Business Books.

Mayer, J. D., Caruso, D., and Salovey, P. (1998). Competing models of emotional intelligence. In: Steinberg, Robert J. (ed.) *Handbook of human intelligence*, 2nd edition. New York: Cambridge University Press.

McDonald, R., Harrison, S., and Checkland, K. (2008). Incentives and control in primary health care: Findings from English pay-for-performance case studies. *Journal of Health Organisation and Management*, 22(1), 48–62.

McGregor, D. (1960). *The human side of enterprise*. New York: McGraw-Hill 21(166.1960).

McLeod, S. (2011). *BoboDoll experiment, simply psychology*. Simplypsychology.org

McMillan, L., Booth, J., Currie, K., and Howe, T. (2012). A grounded theory of taking control after fall-induced hip fracture. *Disability and Rehabilitation*, 34(26), 2234–2241.

Merkouris, A., Papathanassoglou, E., and Lemonidou, C. (2004). Evaluation of patient satisfaction with nursing care: Quantitative or qualitative approach. *International Journal of Nursing Studies*, 41, 355–367.

Merriam, S. B., Caffarella, R. S., and Baumgartner, L. M. (2006). *Learning in adulthood: A comprehensive guide*, 3rd revised edition. Jossey Bass Higher & Adult Education. www.wiley.com

Mester, C., Visser, D., and Roodt, G. (2003). Leadership style and its relation to employee attitudes and behaviour. *SA Journal of Industrial Psychology*, 29(2), 72–80.

Meyer, Marius, and Botha, Eben. (2000). *Organisation development and transformation in South Africa*. Durban: Butterworths.

Mezirow, J. and Associates (2010). *Learning as transformation: Critical perspectives on a theory in progress (Higher Education)*. The Jossey Bass Higher and Adult Education Series. New York: John Wiley and Sons

Mittman, B. S. (2004). Creating the evidence base for quality improvement collaboratives. *Annals of Internal Medicine*, 140, 897–901.

Moscrop, A. (2012). Clinical leadership: Individual advancement, political authority and a lack of direction. *British Journal of General Practitioners*, 62(598), e384–e386.

Mullins, L. J. (2007). *Management and organisational behaviour*. Harlow: Financial Times Prentice Hall, 837p.

Narine, L., and Persaud, D. (2003). Gaining and maintaining commitment to large-scale change in healthcare organisations. *Health Services Management Research*, 16, 179–187.

Nassef, A., and Aylott, J. (2016). *Doctors in co-design of a medical leadership programme: Self-determination at Sheffield teaching hospitals NHS trust, UK*. In: Paper presented at the 6th International Conference on Self Determination Theory, Victoria, BC.

Nassef, A., Ramsden, L., Newnham, A., Archer, G., Jackson, R., Davies, J., and Stewart, K. (2017). Factors affecting failure. In: Godbole, P., Burke, D., and Aylott, J. (eds) *Why hospitals fail: Between theory and practice*. Basel, Switzerland: Springer International Publishing AG 2017.

National Clinical Guideline Centre. (2012). *Patient experience in adult NHS services: Improving the experience of care for people using adult NHS services*. London: National Clinical Guideline Centre, Royal College of Physicians, pp. 1–335.

National Skills Academy for Social Care. (2014). *The leadership qualities framework for adult social care*. Leeds: Skills for Care Ltd. Skillsforcare.org.uk

Nelson, E., Batalden, P. B., and Godfrey, M. M. (2011). *Quality by design: A clinical microsystems approach*. Jossey-Bass Publication, 508p.

Nelson, E. C., Batalden, P. B., Huber, T. P., Mohr, J. J., Godfrey, M. M., Headrick, L. A., and Wasson, J. H. (2002). Microsystems in health care: Part 1. Learning from high-performing front-line clinical units. *Journal on Quality Improvement*, 28, 472–493.

NHS. (2014). *Five year forward view*. www.england.nhs.uk/wp-content/uploads/2014/10/5yfv-web.pdf. (Accessed on 21 May 2016).

NHS England. (2016a). *General Practice Forward View*. www.england.nhs.uk/wp-content/uploads/2016/04/gpfv.pdf. (Accessed on 23 May 2016).

NHS England. (2016b). *New care models – vanguard sites*. www.england.nhs.uk/ourwork/futurenhs/new-care-models/ (Accessed on 23 May 2016).

NHS England. (2016c). *Sustainability and transformation plans*. www.england.nhs.uk/our work/futurenhs/deliver-forward-view/stp/ (Accessed on 23 May 2016).

NHS Executive. (2016, 18 April). *Nearly two thirds of NHS trusts require improvement*. NHS Executive. www.Nationalhealthexecutive.com

NHS Institute for Innovation and Improvement. (2013). *Medical leadership competency framework*, 3rd edition. Faculty of Medical Leadership and Management, NHS Institute for innovation and improvement and Academy of Medical Royal Colleges. www.fmlm.ac.uk.

NHS Leadership Academy. (2011). *Clinical leadership competency framework*. www.leadership academy.nhs.uk

NHS Leadership Academy. (2013). *Healthcare leadership model the nine dimensions of leadership behaviour*. www.leadershipacademy.nhs.uk/wp-content/uploads/dlm_uploads/2014/10/NHSLeadership-LeadershipModel-colour.pdf. (Accessed on 20 May 2016).

Nicolay, C. R., Purkayastha, S., et al. (2012). Systematic review of the application of quality improvement methodologies from the manufacturing industry to surgical healthcare. *British Journal of Surgery*, 99(3), 324–335.

Nolan, T. M. (2007). *Execution of strategic improvement initiatives to produce system-level results.* IHI innovation series white paper. Cambridge MA: Institute for Healthcare Improvement. www.IHI.org

Nuffield Trust. (2013). *The Francis public inquiry report: A response.* London: Nuffield Trust, pp. 1–16.

Ola, B. (2016). Leadership styles: Team behaviour or safer surgery? *Journal of the American College of Surgeons*, 222(5), 967.

Ola, B. (2017). *Leadership styles in why hospitals fail*, (eds) Burke, Godbole and Aylott, J. Basel, Switzerland: Springer International Publishing AG 2017, p. 59.

Olsson, L-E., Nystrom, A. E. M., Karlsson, J., and Ekman, I. (2007). Admitted with a hip fracture: Patient perceptions of rehabilitation. *Journal of Clinical Nursing*, 16, 853–859.

O'Reilly, C., Caldwell, D. F., Chatman, J. A., Lapiz, M., and Self, W. (2010). How leadership matters: The effects of leaders' alignment on strategy implementation. *The Leadership Quarterly*, 104–113.

Øvretveit, J. (2001). The Norwegian approach to integrated quality development. *Journal of Management in Medicine*, 15(2), 125–141. doi:10.1108/02689230110394543.

Øvretveit, J., and Gustafson, D. (2002). Quality improvement research – evaluation of quality improvement programmes. *Quality and Safety in Health Care*, 11, 270–275.

Palmer, B., et al. (2001). Emotional intelligence and effective leadership. *Leadership & Organization Development Journal*, 22(20), 1–7.

Paton, C., Whitney, D., and Coupe, J. (2005). Medical leadership: Doctors, the state and prospects for improvement. In: Edmonstone, J. (ed). *Medical leadership: Doctors, the state and prospects for improvement.* Chichester: Kingsham, pp. 21–30.

Pearce, C. L., and Conger, J. A. (2003). Shared leadership: Reframing the hows and whys of leadership. *Leadership and Organisation Development Journal*, 25(1), 111–113.

Perla, R. J., Bradbury, E., and Gunther-Murphy, C. (2011). Large-scale improvement initiatives in healthcare: A scan of the literature. *Journal for Healthcare Quality*, 1, 1–11.

Perry, M. A., Hudson, S., Meys, S., Norrie, O., Ralph, T., and Warner, S. (2012). Older adults' experiences regarding discharge from hospital following orthopaedic intervention: A Metasynthesis. *Disability and Rehabilitation*, 34(4), 267–278.

Perry, M., Hudson, S., and Ardis, K. (2011). "If I didn't have anybody, what would I have done?" Experiences of older adults and their discharge home after lower limb orthopaedic surgery. *Journal of Rehabilitation Medicine*, 43, 916–922.

Porter, M. E., and Lee, T. H. (2013, October). The strategy that will fix health care. *Harvard Business Review*, 91(10), 50–70.

Prideaux, S., and Ford, J. E. (1982). Management development: Competencies teams, learning contracts and work experience based learning. *Journal of Management Development*, 7(3), 13–21.

Pruijn, G. H. J., and Boucher, R. L. (1994). The relationship of transactional and transformational leadership to the organisational effectiveness of the Dutch national sports organisations. *European Journal of Sports Management*, 1, 72–87.

Quinn, J. (1992). *Intelligent enterprise: A knowledge and service based paradigm for industry.* New York: The Free Press.

Radnor, Z., and Boaden, R. (2008). Editorial: Lean in public services-panacea or paradox? *Public Money and Management*, 28(1), 3–7.

Raelin, J. A. (2008). *Work based learning: Bridging knowledge and action in the workplace*, 2nd edition. New York: Wiley.

Reinertsen, J. L. (2004). *A theory of leadership for the transformation for health care organizations.* www.uft-a.com/PDF/Transformation.PDF. (Accessed on 26 November 2012).

Riehle, M., and Hyrkas, K. (2012). Improving quality in healthcare – current trends. *Journal of Nursing Management*, 20, 299–301.

Robert, G., Cornwell, J., Brearley, S., Foot, C., Goodrich, J., Joule, N., Levenson, R., Maben, J., Murrells, T., Tsianakas, V., and Waite, D. (2011). *What matters to patients?* Coventry: NHS Institute for Innovation and Improvement, pp. 1–200.

Robinson, S. B. (1999). Transitions in the lives of elderly women who have sustained hip fractures. *Journal of Advanced Nursing*, 30(6), 1341–1348.

Robson, Colin. (1993). *Real world research: A resource for social scientists and practitioners-researchers.* Oxford: Blackwell Publishers Ltd.

Roebuck, C. (2011). *Commission on leadership and management in the NHS developing effective leadership in the NHS to maximise the quality of patient care: The need for urgent action.* www.kingsfund.org.uk/sites/files/kf/developing-effective-leadership-in-nhs-maximise-the-quality-patient-care-chris-roebuck-kings-fund-may-2011.pdf. (Accessed on 23 May 2016).

Rose, L. (2015). *Better leadership for tomorrow: NHS leadership review.* www.gov.uk/government/uploads/system/uploads/attachment_data/file/445738/Lord_Rose_NHS_Report_acc.pdf. (Accessed on 21 May 2016).

Rowling, E. (2011). *The future of leadership and management in the NHS: No more heroes, Report from the Kings Fund Commission on Leadership and Management in the NHS.* www.Kingsfund.org.uk

Royal College of General Practitioners. (2013). *Quality improvement project (QIP) guidance for GP trainees.* RCGP.org.uk.

Royal College of General Practitioners. (2014). *The 2022 GP: A vision for general practice in the future.* www.rcgp.org.

Rughani, A., and Lees, P. (2013). Leadership training: Fitness for purpose or fitness for the future? *Education for Primary Care*, 24(1), 15–18. doi:10.1080/14739879.2013.11493449.

Schutte, N. S., et al. (1998). Development and validation of a measure of emotional intelligence. *Personality and Individual Differences*, 25, 167–177.

Senior, B., and Fleming, J. (2006). *Organizational change.* London: Pearson Education.

Sgroi, D. (2015). *Happiness and productivity: Understanding the happy-productive worker.* Global perspectives series: Paper 4 CAGE: Competitive Advantage in the Global Economy. www.warwick.ac.uk/cage

Sheffield Teaching Hospital Quality Strategy. (2012–2017). *Safe, efficient, personal: Quality strategy.* www.Sth.nhs.uk

Shriberg, A., Shriberg, D., and Lloyd, C. A. (2002). *Practicing leadership: Principles and applications.* New York: J. Wiley & Sons.

Silvester, K., Lendon, R., Bevan, H., et al. (2004). Reducing waiting times in the NHS: Is lack of capacity the problem? *Clinician in Management*, 12, 1–8.

Slauenwhite, C. A., and Simpson, P. (1998). Patient and family perspectives on early discharge and care of the older adult undergoing fractured hip rehabilitation. *Orthopaedic Nursing*, 17(1), 30–36.

Smith, E. (2015). *Introduction by Ed Smith, lead for the review of leadership development and improvement, and deputy chair of NHS England.* www.england.nhs.uk/wp-content/uploads/2012/10/Introduction-by-Ed-Smith.pdf. (Accessed on 21 May 2016).

Snowdon, G. (2011 20 February). Women still face a glass ceiling. *The Guardian*.

Spurgeon, P., Barwell, F., and Mazelan, P. (2008). Developing a Medical Engagement Scale (MES). *The International Journal of Clinical Leadership*, 16, 213–223.

Spurgeon, P., Clark, J., and Ham, C. (2011a). *Medical leadership: From the dark side to centre stage.* London: Radcliffe Publishing.

Spurgeon, P., Clark, J., and Ham, C. (2011b). The development of the medical leadership competency framework. In: Spurgeon, P., Clark, J., and Ham, C. (eds). *Medical leadership: From the dark side to centre stage.* London: Radcliffe Publishing, pp. 99–118.

Spurgeon, P., Long, P., Clark, J., and Daly, F. (2014). Do we need medical leadership or medical engagement? *Leadership in Health Services*, 28(3), 173–184.

Stefl, M. E. (2008). Common competencies for all health managers: The leadership alliance model. *Journal of Healthcare Management*, 53(6), 360–373.

Stets, J., and Burke, P. (2000). Identity theory and social identity theory. *Social Psychology Quarterly*, 63(3), 224–237.

Stogdill, Ralph M. (1974). *Handbook of leadership: A survey of theory and research.* New York: The Free Press.

Swanepoel, Ben, Erasmus, Barney, and Schenk, Heinz. (2008). *South African human resource management: Theory and practice.* Cape Town: Juta and Co. Ltd.

Tafjel, H., and Turner, J. (1982). The social psychology of intergroup relations: An integrative theory of intergroup conflict. *Social Psychology of Intergroup Relations: Annual Review of Psychology*, 33, 1–39.

Thorndike, E. L. (1920). A constant error in psychological ratings. *Journal of Applied Psychology*, 4, 25–29.

Todres, L., Galvin, K., and Dahlberg, K. (2007). Lifeworld-led healthcare: Revisiting a humanising philosophy that integrates emerging trends. *Medicine, Healthcare and Philosophy*, 10, 53–63.

Toutati, N., Roberge, D., Denis, J. L., Cazale, L., Pineault, R., and Tremblay, D. (2006). Clinical leaders at the forefront of change in health care systems: Advantages and issues. Lessons learned from the evaluation of the implementation of an integrated oncological services network. *Health Services Management Research*, 19, 105–122.

Turnbull-James, K. (2011). *Leadership in context: Lessons from new leadership theory and current leadership development practice.* London: The Kings Fund.

Walshe, K. (2009). Pseudoinnovation: The development and spread of healthcare quality improvement methodologies. *International Journal for Quality in Health Care*, 21(3), 153–159.

Weick, K. E. (2001). *Making sense of the organisation.* Malden MA: Blackwell Publishers.

West, M., Armit, K., Loewenthal, L., Eckert, R., West, T., and Lee, A. (2015). *Leadership and leadership development in health care: The evidence base.* www.kingsfund.org.uk/sites/files/kf/field/field_publication_file/leadership-leadership-development-health-care-feb-2015.pdf. (Accessed on 23 May 2016).

West, M. A., and Dawson, J. F. (2012). *Employee engagement and NHS performance.* www.kingsfund.org.uk/sites/files/kf/employee-engagement-nhs-performance-west-dawson-leadership-review2012-paper.pdf. (Accessed on 13 May 2016).

West, M., Dawson, J., and Kaur, M. (2012). *Making the difference: Diversity and inclusion in the NHS.* London: The Kings Fund.

West, M., Echert, R., Steward, K., and Pasmore, B. (2014). *Developing collective leadership for healthcare.* London: The Kings Fund.

Westwood, N., and Sylvester, K. (2007). Eliminate NHS Losses by adding lean and some six sigma. *Operations Management*, 5, 216–230.

Williams, J., et al. (2009). Clinical microsystems and the NHS: A sustainable method for improvement? *Journal of Health and Organisation Management*, 23(1), 119–132.

Wolmarans, S., and Martins, N. (2001). *The 360 degree emotional competency profiler.* Unpublished manual. Johannesburg: Organisational Diagnostics and Learning Link International.

World Health Organization. (2006). *Working together for health: The world health report.* http://www.who.int/whr/2006/en/

World Health Organization. (2013). *Research for universal health coverage: World health report.* http://apps.who.int/iris/bitstream/handle/10665/85761/9789240690837_eng.pdf;jsessionid=0BB5871A938FB6BEE28BE1A0700E44CC?sequence=2

World Health Organization. (2014). *A universal truth: No health without a workforce.* http://www.who.int/workforcealliance/knowledge/resources/GHWA-a_universal_truth_report.pdf

World Health Organization. (2016). *Universal health coverage, fact sheet.* http://www.who.int/news-room/fact-sheets/detail/universal-health-coverage-(uhc)

Wykes, C., Pryor, J., and Jeawody, B. (2009). The concerns of older women during inpatient rehabilitation after fractured neck of femur. *International Journal of Therapy and Rehabilitation,* 16(5), 261–270.

Xirasagar, S., Samuels, M. E., and Stoskopf, C. H. (2005). Physician leadership styles and effectiveness: An empirical study. *Medical Care Research and Review,* 62(6), 720–740.

Yukl, G. (1998). *Leadership in organisations.* Englewood Cliffs: Prentice-Hall.

Ziden, L., Scherman, M. H., and Wenestam, C-G. (2010). The break remains-elderly people's experiences of a hip fracture 1 year after discharge. *Disability and Rehabilitation,* 32(2), 103–113.

PART 2
Medical leadership

7

AN INTRODUCTION

Ann LN Chapman

I am delighted to introduce this second section of the book. In this section, we will explore broader aspects of medical leadership. A key theme in this section is 'standardisation' or reducing variability, and how medical leadership can contribute to achieving this goal.

In Chapter 8, Gilly Ennals explores health inequalities across geographical regions and some of the reasons for these, drawing on the example of an innovative project established by General Practitioners (GPs) to reduce variability in standards of public health and to improve the quality of primary care services. One key aspect of this is supporting and encouraging junior doctors undertaking GP training, with the eventual aim of improving GP recruitment in the most deprived areas. In Chapter 9, Ravishanka Sargur explores variability but this time the focus is on variation of healthcare delivery and he draws a distinction between 'warranted' and 'unwarranted' variation. The latter of these refers to variation that cannot be explained through differences in population or clinical need – the chapter draws on the example of requesting blood tests, where requests for a particular test can vary substantially between regions without an obvious clinical explanation. Ravishanka Sargur explores how the NHS could potentially save billions of pounds annually if this unwarranted variation could be reduced, however such attempts to explore improvements in this area require clinical engagement in medical leadership and quality improvement.

A third type of 'standardisation' relates to the delivery of clinical care in emergency situations. There is evidence from within and outside of Medicine that performance in emergency situations is optimal if there is a standardised approach with a well-designated team, with team members aware of their roles and with knowledge and skills to carry out that role. In Chapter 10, Walaa Al-Safi describes a project to develop a training programme which teaches a standardised approach to the management of obstetric emergencies. Although the overall aim of the project was to improve maternal and neonatal morbidity and mortality, it was recognised that a major factor in achieving this aim was the effectiveness of the multidisciplinary team which responded to obstetric emergencies, in particular dynamics and communication between team members. The application of a theoretical framework for analysing team effectiveness to the obstetric emergency team illustrates the power of understanding and developing these non-clinical professional attributes as a means of improving both clinical outcomes for patients and also staff confidence and commitment to the team.

One critical factor in all of these pieces of work is the engagement and contribution of doctors. In Chapters 11 and 12, two different perspectives of engagement are presented. Both chapters demonstrate the benefits of medical engagement across a range of measures and argue that engagement is best achieved through a 'bottom-up' rather than a 'top-down' approach. Paddy Dobbs and Alix Fonfe (Chapter 12) argue that engaging doctors may be achieved best through the actions of other doctors and illustrate this with an example of how recruitment and retention of paediatric trainees was improved through a focus on engagement and communication. This work demonstrates how engagement strategies with doctors are critical to supporting them to become 'prepared' or 'quality improvement ready' to work with the multiprofessional team and with patients, to lead on service development. Simon Boyes (Chapter 11) discusses role theory and the potential conflict between an individual doctor's clinical and managerial roles. These concepts may apply to a greater or lesser extent across different scenarios and situations, but one further overarching requirement is that doctors have an understanding of their own behaviour and responses in different contexts, that is, that they are reflective practitioners not just in a clinical context but also when considering their non-clinical roles and behaviours. In the final chapter of this section, Chapter 13, Michael Robinson and Eleni Lekoudis review leadership styles in the context of medical leadership and highlight the importance of an individual medical leader having awareness and insight into his or her own personal leadership style preferences. They discuss the role of self-assessment of leadership styles using a range of diagnostic tools, illustrate the chapter with personal reflections on the use of these tools in their own personal leadership development and conclude with some strategies to facilitate personal leadership development, including coaching, mentoring and networking.

8

MEDICAL LEADERSHIP AND REDUCING HEALTH INEQUALITIES

Gilly Ennals

Medical leaders globally strive not only to increase population health across primary and secondary care but also to reduce health inequalities: "Health inequalities between individuals and groups of individuals are understood and measured as marked differences in life expectancy and levels of morbidity" (RCGP, 2015a). Understanding and tackling health inequalities has long been part of the WHO agenda (Crombie et al., 2005), and with successive UK governments and authorities trying, but failing, to improve health outcomes, health inequalities need to be championed by both primary and secondary care clinicians.

The causes of health inequalities are numerous and overlapping so they can be difficult to quantify. Deprivation is the biggest indicator of relative ill health: those living in areas of high deprivation are more likely to be affected by multi-morbidity, public health issues and poor living conditions. In the UK, The Marmot Review (2010) identified that individuals from the poorest neighbourhoods in England on average die 7 years earlier than those living in the richest areas. Individuals living in deprived areas suffer from multiple chronic health problems, most commonly long-term mental health problems (RCGP, 2015a), spending a substantial proportion of their lives with a disability as well as dying younger. It is predicted that the number of people with three or more long-term conditions will rise from 1.9 million in 2008 to 2.9 million in 2018 (Kings Fund, 2012a). Furthermore, individuals in deprived areas are more likely to be affected by public health issues including smoking, obesity and alcohol-related diseases. Between 1995–1997 and 2006–2008, the difference in life expectancy between the most and least deprived increased by 7% for men and 14% for women (National Audit Office, 2010). The same argument of concern for health inequalities has been outlined by Bambra (2016), suggesting that there is clear evidence for a north-south divide in the UK, and that the countries that have better Universal Health Coverage have less of a differential in income between the rich and poor.

Difficulties accessing healthcare and the wider social care system exacerbate health inequalities. Socially excluded groups such as the homeless, traveller communities, sex workers, refugees and asylum seekers struggle to engage with healthcare, having worse health outcomes. Homeless individuals are more vulnerable to mental health and drug abuse problems, affecting their own health and ability to engage with healthcare services. Life expectancy of a homeless individual is 30 years less than that of the general population (RCGP, 2013a). Asylum seekers face the additional barrier of not understanding healthcare services and of speaking limited English (RCGP, 2015b). Dr Tudor Hart coined the term *inverse care law* (Tudor Hart, 1971): "The availability of good medical care tends to vary inversely with the need for it in the population served".

GPs at the 'Deep End'

Primary care sits at the heart of the UK NHS, yet it is facing significant challenges due to chronic underfunding, increasing demand, workforce problems and low staff morale (RCGP, 2016b). As well as providing good quality, continuous care to patients general practitioners (GPs) need to act as leaders within large multidisciplinary teams across community and secondary care health and social care providers, working at different organisational levels: this "opens up opportunities in pathway design, service leadership, education, training or research, or developing areas of clinical interest" (RCGP, 2016b). Effective medical leadership and engagement is critical and central to all strategies to reduce health inequalities and improve quality of care for all (Darzi, 2008).

In the UK, the GP workforce is flatly distributed, leading to areas of most need not being serviced by enough doctors. This suggests that if primary care teams were better supported they could be more effective (Watt, 2013).

As GPs are expert generalists, knowing their patients and able to provide continuity of care, they can have an impact on efforts to understand and tackle health inequalities. By providing whole patient care in the context of their wider social environment, GPs can signpost patients towards relevant health or social services (RCGP, 2016b).

It is recognised by the General Medical Council (GMC, 2009) that an understanding of health inequalities must form part of all doctor's training. The Royal College of General Practitioners (RCGP) (RCGP, 2016a) also recognises the importance of trainee GPs gaining an understanding about health inequalities and strategies to tackle them, as part of their 3-year general practice training. A report conducted by the RCGP's Health Inequalities Standing Group (RCGP, 2013b) reviewed and developed a consensus on teaching this at undergraduate level. No such evaluation has been produced for postgraduate general practice training.

The Scotland 'Deep End' GP group formed in September 2009, following a meeting of GPs from sixty-three of the most deprived practices in Scotland, as identified by the proportion of their patients living in the most deprived 15% of Scottish postcode data zones (Scottish Government, 2012). The meeting revolved around sharing experience and views of working in deprived communities and discussed topics such as workforce, communication with secondary care and how to empower patients to manage their own health. The Deep End Group continues to meet regularly and now publishes reports on deprivation, informs Scottish Government policy and acts as an advocate for patients. It is a nationally and internationally recognised group which highlights the struggles and benefits of working in deprived areas and seeks to reduce health inequalities (Scotland Deep End, 2016).

The Yorkshire and Humber region sought to replicate this model. The 100 most deprived practices in the region were identified, and at their first meeting, in October 2015, the Yorkshire and Humber Deep End Group was established with the following objectives (Yorkshire and Humber GPs at the Deep End, 2016):

- Help practices tackle workforce and recruitment issues.
- Support and provide educational sessions relevant to deep end work.
- Provide a forum to share ideas on planning services and strategy.
- Act as an advocate for communities and develop networks for deep end practitioners.
- Establish links with the academic community and evaluate the effect of interventions on health inequalities.
- Provide academic support for the group to gain funding, facilitate organisation and write-up of sessions.

During the symposium, there was discussion of medical undergraduates' and GP trainees' understanding of the wider concepts of health inequalities and of how training programmes could encompass both theoretical aspects of health inequalities and also issues around personal resilience to prepare trainees for working in deprived areas.

It is difficult to attribute a firm financial value to improving trainee understanding of health inequalities. Recent evidence from Scotland (McLean et al., 2015) illustrates that practices in deprived areas have more cases of multi-morbidity and patients attend more consultations, but that current funding does not match clinical need. If GPs were more aware of health inequalities, and how policy and advocacy can help reduce them, they could more effectively lead communities in persuading governments to increase funding to general practice in deprived areas. Furthermore, investment in practices in deprived areas could improve access to a GP or a nurse. Patients from deprived areas are more likely to attend Accident and Emergency departments than those from affluent backgrounds (Scantlebury et al., 2015). This results in cost and flow pressures within acute hospitals. If patients are able to access treatment from their general practice, they are less likely to attend Accident and Emergency.

GP recruitment and retention is increasingly of concern: Blane and colleagues (2015) conclude that this is due to increasing pressure on GPs within practices, their perceived age and gender profile and the increased uptake of early retirement. A Scotland Deep End report (2010), suggested that trainees want to work in deprived areas if they have had a good experience as a trainee and feel supported in their development. However, McLean et al. (2015) argue that practices in deprived areas are less likely to be training practices compared with more affluent areas. Therefore, if trainees can be motivated to work in deprived areas, by improvements in education and supported opportunities during training, this may begin a positive cycle which increases training capacity, all of which benefits GPs and the communities they serve.

The Scottish Deep End project holds an annual health inequalities training day, which is compulsory for all trainees in their first or second year. Evaluation from trainees demonstrated that they found it thought-provoking, interesting and beneficial as well as being an enjoyable day. The day's syllabus included setting the scene about health inequalities, an introduction to the Deep End project's work, the challenges of dealing with addiction and homeless patients, the health needs of asylum seekers and refugees and case-based discussions of routine GP workloads in deprived areas.

These training days could be replicated across other areas. Another way of delivering teaching would be through weekly protected teaching time; however, this would rely on cooperation from training programme directors. Alternatively, an online model on health inequalities could be developed for trainees to complete – this would be easily accessible but may not allow for engaged discussion on topics and for trainees' beliefs to challenged or their questions answered.

Tackling health inequalities remains a challenging aspect of general practice work, and GPs of the future must be armed with the knowledge, skills and confidence needed to tackle inequality. However, tackling health inequalities is not just the responsibility of clinicians in primary care; but also it is the responsibility of every doctor to take opportunities to promote healthy living. A formal teaching programme will support and enhance these important attributes across all trainees and contribute to reducing heath inequality locally and nationally.

9

MEDICAL LEADERSHIP AND REDUCING VARIATION IN HEALTHCARE

Ravishanka Sargur

Variation in healthcare has become a major topic of inquiry influencing UK policy at national and local levels (Love and Ehrenberg, 2014a). Many studies have reported the existence of 'significant' variation in healthcare and its detrimental effect on quality of care and the contribution to healthcare inequalities (Santos, 2013). Such variation often cannot be explained by demographic factors or other determinants of health need (Love and Ehrenberg, 2014b). Jack Wennberg defined variation as "variation in the utilization of health care services that cannot be explained by variation in patient illness or patient preferences" (2010). The increasing complexity of decision-making processes in healthcare provision and the uniqueness of patients make the understanding and management of variation very challenging.

In this chapter, we argue that the term 'variation' is used as a homogenous concept, creating confusion between what is good and acceptable variation in healthcare and that which is unacceptable and unwarranted variation. We critically explore the research and evidence base behind variation in healthcare, its causes, effects and management strategies. This chapter reflects on the learning from the application of theories and models to a case study examining patterns in the request for laboratory blood tests by primary care practitioners situated in a small locality in a clinical commissioning group (CCG) in England, UK. In a time of austerity, there is much debate to explore how much money can be saved by reducing variation in healthcare; however, this chapter illustrates the complexity involved when seeking to improve outcomes and deliver better value through the understanding of variation and its various forms.

Variation in healthcare

Variation in healthcare was first noted by William A. Guy, in 1856, as he looked at per capita utilisation of resources between small geographical areas. He noted that annual per capita rates for hospitalisation in King's Hospital varied from 325 per 1,000 population in the parish of St. Mary-le-Strand to 1 per 1,000 in the district of Marylebone (Paul-Shaheen et al., 1987).

Several studies looking at population-based healthcare utilisation rates amongst geographic areas have demonstrated substantial variations in use amongst seemingly similar communities (Paul-Shaheen et al., 1987). The Dartmouth Atlas Project reported glaring variations in how medical resources have been distributed and used in the United States over the past 20 years (The Dartmouth Institute for Health Policy and Clinical Practice, 2015).

Laboratory testing costs the National Health Service £2.5 billion annually. In his review of pathology services in England, Lord Carter (2008) estimated that effective and efficient use of laboratory tests could save £500 million, despite an average annual increase of 8–10% in workload. One area of increasing importance is managing the demands for pathology tests and reducing inappropriate requesting. By understanding the reasons behind variability in requesting between areas and implementing appropriate measures to reduce this variability, it may be possible to improve both quality of care and efficiency of utilisation of healthcare resources.

The NHS Atlas of Variation in Diagnostic Services (NHS Right Care, 2015) highlights the wide variation in the use of laboratory tests between primary care trusts (Box 1). There is paucity of research exploring in depth the reasons behind why service users request tests 'inappropriately' (Fryer and Smellie, 2013). Given increasing financial constraints, there is a constant pressure to reduce costs and improve efficiency while maintaining quality.

The identification and examination of unexplained variations may help clinicians to understand what is going on in their area and where to focus attention to improve the care they provide. The NHS diagnostic Atlas (2013) highlighted the wide variation in diagnostic test utilisation. Such variations are unexplained and frequently occur despite clear national guidelines on diagnostic testing, for example, requests for testing rheumatoid factor in rheumatoid arthritis, where there is a 170-fold variation in testing across England. Unwarranted variation (both overuse and

---

BOX 1: *PRINCIPLES OF RIGHT CARE APPROACH (NHS RIGHT CARE, 2015)*

Reducing unexplained variation is an opportunity to increase effective healthcare and reduce healthcare inequalities for populations.

Develop understanding with clinicians (GPs) to help the local healthcare system use the resources effectively.

Help commissioners and providers understand the importance of a 'population perspective' whether based on geography or patient cohort (e.g. frail elderly), to maximise value and benefit to their populations.

underuse) in the rates of diagnostic testing has a significant impact on patient care and the local healthcare economy. It has an impact on effective capacity planning, and in addition can cause harm to patients, for example, through unnecessary blood sampling or exposure to ionising radiation.

Although the data presented in the Diagnostic Services Atlas may be open to more than one interpretation, it is widely recognised that the power of the Atlas series lies not in the answers they provide but in the questions they raise. There is an urgent need for work to improve our understanding of variation in the utilisation of many diagnostic services and to understand whether the variation observed is random (inherent in the system), warranted (i.e. true clinical variation) or caused by other factors such as poor access to services or a need for education or CPD update. Unexplained variation provokes questions about the effectiveness, efficiency and quality of healthcare services. Observations of variation have consequently been used to justify a variety of policies aimed at reducing variability, such as greater emphasis upon outcomes research, feedback to practitioners and closely monitored performance measures.

Causes of variation

It is recognised that variation is inevitable in healthcare. Healthcare systems are complex, with multiple system-level variables and variations at the level of professionals and patients. Deming (1993) reasoned that "variation is present everywhere" and he argued that it is fundamental to understand variation overtime in order to recognize and use observed differences for the purpose of improvement.

Variation in many instances represents appropriate care. The complex question, however, is which variations – or what proportions of variation – are 'good', or warranted, and which are 'bad', or unwarranted (Appleby et al., 2011). As Evans has noted:

> If variations represent evidence of inappropriate care, which care is inappropriate? Are the regions, or institutions, or practitioners with high rates over-providing, or are the low ones under-providing, or does the 'best' rate lie somewhere in the middle (or beyond either end)?
>
> *(Evans, 1990)*

Wennberg and Cooper (1998) observe in the Dartmouth Atlas that the patterns of variation in the discharge rates for medical conditions have recognisable 'medical signatures' and 'surgical signatures'. The 'surgical signature' predominantly reflects variability in practice as regards types and numbers of procedures with different associated lengths of stay. By contrast, discharge rates for a specific high variation medical condition tend to be more closely associated with the total discharge rate for all medical conditions in that hospital referral region. Medical admissions and discharge rates vary widely across different hospital regions; this variation appears to be independent of the level of morbidity in the community. It is important to increase our understanding of the causes of variability in admissions and discharges, as a major target of today's NHS is to reduce bed numbers and/or improve the efficiency of bed use. This has led to significant challenges both at the front door (Accident & Emergency and Acute admissions) and at the back door (discharging to social care), highlighting the need for a system-wide solution.

Unwarranted variation may be due to differences in supply of resources or access to facilities between populations. It may also be due to different definitions of appropriateness for intervention and referral, either by individual clinicians, sometimes even within the one institution, or between different groups of clinicians working in the different populations. Varying attitudes, both individual and population based, may result in differences in use of services by different ethnic groups or different age groups. Understanding the complex reasons behind variation is challenging. As Mulley (2011) suggests, that if all variation were bad, solutions would be easy. He goes on to argue that the difficulty is in reducing the bad variation, which reflects the limits of professional knowledge and failures in its application, yet the good variation is a marker for good patient centred care.

Appleby and colleagues, in their King's Fund Report Variations in healthcare (2011), concluded that unwarranted variation in healthcare had a negative impact on equity of access to services, the health outcomes of populations and efficient use of resources. They recommended that NHS data need to be mapped in a systematic way to identify variations and then analysed at a local level to determine whether these are warranted or unwarranted (Love and Ehrenberg, 2014a). The focus is to tackle clinical decisions through greater emphasis on shared decision making with patients as a way of driving out unwarranted, and promoting warranted, variation.

This can be done by mapping the many possible causes of variation, from possible spurious variations caused by demographics of the population, data quality problems, the geographic pattern of illness through to substitution effects arising from differences in the use of private healthcare and differences in clinician behaviour arising from the interaction of payment systems and the characteristics of clinicians. There is complex interplay between these causes which will vary between and within geographical locations (Appleby et al., 2011).

Clinical practice variation, utilisation of healthcare resources and productivity

Several studies have reported existence of variation in clinical practice (Wennberg, 1999, 2014; Winchester et al., 2014; O'Connor et al., 1999; Bojke et al., 2013; Nuti and Seghieri, 2014). In the UK, The King's Fund review of variations in healthcare published nearly 30 years ago (Ham, 1988) raised issues about efficiency, equity and patient safety and cause of variations – the influence of demand, supply and professional decision making; these issues remain the same today.

Wennberg (2006) reports a curious finding: "There is no relationship between quality in one measure and quality in another. Health care systems that perform well on one effective care measure – are no more or less likely to perform well on others".

The NHS is under significant financial stress coupled with the challenge of achieving productivity savings of around £ 22 billion by 2020–2021. Better Value in the NHS: the role of changes in clinical practice (Alderwick et al., 2015) looks at past trends in NHS productivity and identifies the following opportunities.

- Tackling inappropriate care – overuse, underuse and misuse;
- Identifying and removing unwarranted variation in clinical practice;
- Using evidence of better ways of delivering care and support for specific patient groups.

Bojke and colleagues (2013) reported that productivity between strategic health authorities (SHAs) varied from 5% above to 6% below the national average. Productivity was highest in South West SHA and lowest in East Midlands, South Central and Yorkshire and The Humber SHAs. They estimated that if all regions were as productive as the most productive region in England, the NHS could treat the same number of patients with £3.2bn fewer resources each year.

Studies from the US have suggested that the principal driver of variation in per capita spending is not from variations in costs per admission but in rates of admission (Gottlieb et al., 2010). Wennberg and colleagues proposed that there was scope by tackling admission rate variations to reduce spend on Medicare (for the elderly) by nearly 30% ($40 billion) (Wennberg et al., 2002). However, although admission rates vary widely, it does not necessarily mean that doctors in areas with low or with high admission rates make more appropriate clinical decisions. To the contrary, studies of discretionary admissions in the US in the 1980s (Chassin et al., 1987; Leape et al., 1990) found no relationship between rates of appropriateness and overall admission rates: high proportions of admissions were classed as inappropriate or equivocal for areas with both high and low admission rates. In England, a similar study into admissions for coronary angiography and coronary artery bypass operations (when compared with the US and England as a whole) found that only about half of these to have been appropriate irrespective of high or low rates of admission (Gray et al., 1990).

Lord Carter's report on "Operational Productivity and Performance in English NHS Acute Hospitals: Unwanted Variations" highlights the challenges faced by the NHS: the NHS is expected to deliver efficiencies of 2–3% per year, effectively setting a 10–15% real terms cost reduction target by 2021 (Lord Carter of Coles, 2016). This report looked at the wide 'variation' in clinical staff, pharmacy and medicines, diagnostics and imaging, procurement, back office functions and estates and facilities. For Pathology (diagnostic tests which included primary, secondary and specialist care), the costs as a proportion of trust operating expenditure ranged from less than 1.5% to over 3.0%.

Looking specifically at blood test requests, it is recognised that healthcare professionals request unnecessary tests for a wide range of reasons, including fear of litigation (risk avoidance), lack of experience, uncertainty, lack of awareness of guidelines or the cost of investigations, as a consequence of protocol-based requesting (QOF) or as a result of patient anxiety or patient pressure (Figure 9.1). Time available for consultation is a significant factor influencing the decision about doing diagnostic tests. Diagnostic tests are also used a 'placebo' to allay patient anxiety. Internet searching by patients increases anxiety (cyberchondria), and GPs are put under pressure to do tests.

GPs use tests in a variety of ways, and patient reassurance by getting a negative test result is considered a legitimate use of a test. There may also be a lack of understanding by GPs about the limitations of the diagnostic tests. Moreover, given that patient factors influence decision making, some of the variation can be attributed to shared decision making.

Measuring variation

There is a significant amount of confusing terminology in the literature about the different types variation in healthcare which generates a lack of clarity amongst clinicians. The term is often used as a homogenous term, including all forms and types of variation. There is a need for agreement about the meaning of the terminology used and consistency in the terms used. Wennberg's definition of variation in healthcare services utilisation (2010) focused on variation which cannot be explained by variation in patient illness or patient preferences. This 'unexplained' variation presupposes knowledge of 'explainable variation'. This would include components of acceptable variation.

The variation of concern to clinicians and for those focused on quality improvement or service development projects is 'Unwarranted'/'Unjustifiable'/'Unacceptable'/'Bad' variation (Uv) – which is best defined as the 'difference' between 'total Variation in the system' (TV), 'Explainable Variation' (Ev) and 'Acceptable Variation' (Av) (Table 9.1).

The key challenge is to define 'acceptable variability' in a complex system in which human factors are involved. Before deciding whether variation is a problem, clinicians need to step back and assess how much variation one should actually expect to see, given the variability in patient, physician and system factors. Ultimately the question of how much variation is too much is a judgement, and pragmatically should depend upon what is believed about the impact of variation, and whether there are ways of addressing it. If there is substantial variation in some measure, but it does not provoke concerns about quality, equity or efficiency, then it may not be worth devoting precious quality improvement resources to addressing the issue. By contrast, if even a relatively small level of variation raises serious issues about quality of care, then it is worthy of attention and follow-up (Love and Ehrenberg, 2014b).

Reducing 'unwarranted variation': strategic perspectives

Having identified unwarranted variation, the challenge is how to reduce this variation to realise the benefits to patient care and to secure financial savings. Health

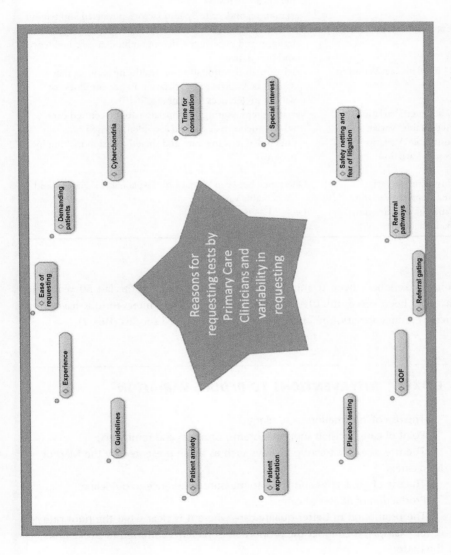

FIGURE 9.1 Reasons for requesting and factors influencing variability in requesting tests in primary care

TABLE 9.1 Terminology of 'variation'

Terminology	Definition
Total Variation (TV)	Differences in utilisation of healthcare resources and healthcare delivery
'Explainable' Variation (Ev)	Variation secondary to system factors, physician and patient factors: resource allocation, healthcare policy, physician training and experience, demographics, disease incidence and prevalence
'Unexplainable' Variation	'Variation' in the utilisation of healthcare services that cannot be explained by variation in patient illness or patient preferences (Wennberg, 2010)
'Warranted' Variation 'Acceptable' Variation (Av) 'Justifiable' Variation 'Good' Variation	Variation representing appropriate patient-centred care which encompasses effective evidence-based care, preference sensitive care and shared decision making by patients
Unwarranted Variation Unacceptable Variation (Uv) Unjustifiable Variation 'Bad' Variation	Difference between 'Variation', 'Explainable Variation' and 'Acceptable Variation' $Uv = TV - (Ev + Av)$

policymakers have been trying to address this challenge for the last 50 years and have not been successful. Over the last 5 decades, many interventions have been tried to reduce variation in clinical practice with limited success (Box 2).

BOX 2: *INTERVENTIONS TO REDUCE VARIATION*

The use of information technology;

Point of care decision support systems, prompts and reminders;

The use of explicit care pathways such as those presented by the Map of Medicine;

The use of guidelines and audit to measure adherence to guideline;

Production of atlases of care;

The promotion of better quality care where it is clear what the right rate is, for example, the higher the proportion of patients admitted to stroke units the better;

Analysis of both high and low rates of activity when it is not clear what rate offers the best value.

Shared Decision Making (Appleby et al., 2011)

The UK NHS is a complex system with a history of constant change. Scholes and colleagues (2011) comment that a useful way of thinking about the role and influence of history is through the concept of 'Path dependency' (Figure 9.2). Path dependency is where early events and decisions establish 'policy paths' that have lasting effects on subsequent events and decisions (Arthur, 1989).

Organisational decisions are, therefore, historically conditioned. Path dependency's origins, its impact and how it can be understood are, therefore, important. It is important to understand the path dependencies created by healthcare policy which influence variation. These include the purchaser/provider split, Quality Outcomes Framework, business models for providing laboratory services to primary care, technology, a drive to reduce new-to-follow-up patient ratio, drive to reduce secondary care referrals and a drive to reduce interventions. All of these decisions have an unintended influence on how other parts of the system function. There is constant pressure to reduce costs, and in this context, improvement initiatives in the area of diagnostic tests are used to realise efficiency and cost savings.

However the situation is more complex and there is a need to understand variation at an individual organisational level, to map the reasons behind that variation and then address those variations identified using a system-level approach. The variation at an individual organisational level needs to be looked at from the perspective of 'cultural frames of reference'. One way of understanding a 'cultural frame of reference' is to explore the policies, systems and norms within a 'community of organisations'. Scholes et al. (2011) explain that a community of organisations are those that interact more frequently with one another and the authors term this a 'field of organisations'. A field of organisations will have developed a shared meaning system together. They will share a common technology, a set of regulations or similar education and training. GP surgeries can be looked at as a community of organisations as they are independent healthcare providers being contracted by the Clinical Commissioning Group to provide primary healthcare to the population.

Developing a strategy to address small area variation is challenging, as it needs multiple strategy development processes as the nature of environment and human factors is complex (Figure 9.3). The complexity of the NHS combined with the complexity of the environment it operates within is one of the reasons why efforts to reduce variation have so far been far from successful. A useful model to further understand variation within complex healthcare organisations is to consider how quality of care is understood against a framework of Structure, Process and Outcome (Figure 9.4).

According to Donabedian (1988), good structure increases the likelihood of good process and a good process increases the likelihood of a good outcome. Quality of care can be measured by evaluating 'structures', 'processes' and 'outcomes'. Figure 9.4 captures the structures and processes which result in variation as one of the outcomes.

One reason why approaches to reducing 'unwarranted variation' in the last few decades have had limited success is because the solutions tried lead to unintended consequences because of systems archetypes (Senge, 1990). The phenomenon of

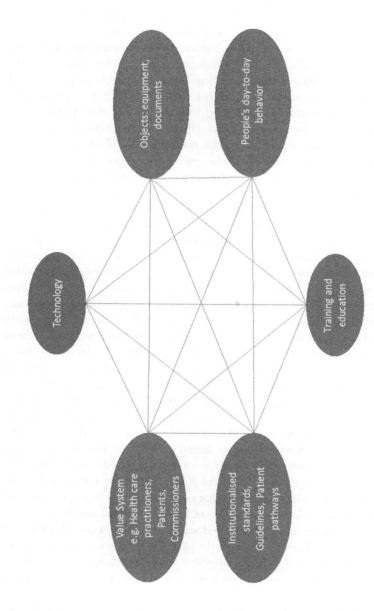

FIGURE 9.2 Path dependency

Source: Adapted from Scholes et al. (2011).

Nature of Environment   **Nature of Organisation**

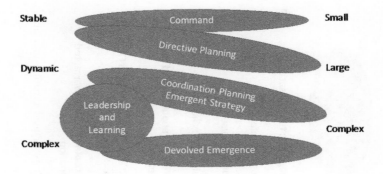

FIGURE 9.3   Strategy development contexts

Source: Adapted from Scholes et al. (2011).

Shifting the Burden was described by Senge (1990): a short-term solution is used to correct a problem, with seemingly positive immediate effects. As this correction is used more and more, more fundamental long-term corrective measures are used less and less (Figure 9.5). The principal strategic perspective is to focus on the fundamental solution, and if the symptomatic solution (referral gating) is imperative (because of delays to fundamental solution), use it to gain time while working on the fundamental solution (Senge, 1990).

Another system archetype relevant to 'Unwarranted Variation' is that of 'Fixes That Fail': a fix, effective in the short term, has unforeseen long-term consequences which require even more of the same fix. The utilisation of Quality Outcomes Framework (QOF)to drive quality and reduce variation is an example of this archetype. This failed to achieve its intended objectives, as a long-term focus on improving capacity in social care and investing in primary care was not realised and QOF became an outcome objective in itself (Figure 9.6).

Given the complexity of the NHS, limited funding and the need to improve productivity (Alderwick et al., 2015), the approach to reducing variation needs to be multifaceted and should take into account structures, systems and strategy. However, although understanding where the opportunities lie is important, the real challenge facing the NHS is being able to turn these opportunities into tangible improvements in care (Appleby et al., 2011). Making change happen requires a fundamental shift in approach by government and NHS leaders – away from using external pressures to improve performance, towards a sustained commitment to supporting reform from within. These changes will require action and alignment at all levels of the system, aimed at supporting clinical teams to make improvements to the way they deliver services in collaboration with their patients (Alderwick et al., 2015).

Structure

Physician experience

Organi ational structure

Guidelines

QOF

Reimbursement structures

Laboratory

Technology

Process

Physician – Patient interaction

Patient expectations, anxiety

Professional decision making

Human factors

Time for consultation

Ease of requesting

OUTCOME

Diagnostic test utilisation

Hospital referral

Antibiotic use

Patient satisfaction

PREMs – Patient-Related Experience Measures

PROMs – Patient-Related Outcome Measures

Acceptable and Unwarranted Variation

FIGURE 9.4   Quality of Care framework (Donabedian, 1966), adapted to capture 'unwarranted variation in a small locality'

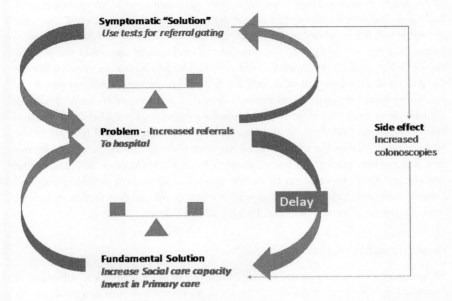

FIGURE 9.5   'Shifting the Burden Archetype' to represent how overuse of Faecal Cal-
protectin by GPs led to unexpected consequences

Source: Archetype adapted from Senge (1990).

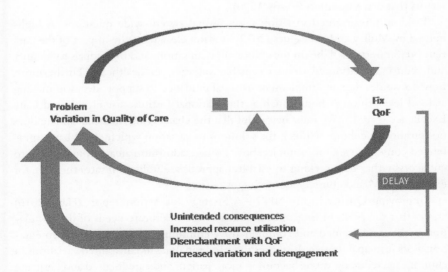

FIGURE 9.6   'Fixes That Fail Archetype' to represent unintended consequences from
QOF

Source: Adapted from Senge (1990).

An alternative, or perhaps complementary, approach is to focus on the process leading to individual clinical decisions – decisions to 'test' or 'not to test', 'to refer' or 'not refer', 'to treat' or 'not to treat', 'to treat in one way' and 'not another' – rather than attempt to specify the outcome of decisions in aggregate for populations (Mulley et al., 2012; Appleby et al., 2011). The key here is to create space for the patient–doctor interaction, which has become increasingly difficult given the decreasing time for consultation. Patients should be encouraged to think about the available screening, treatment or management options and the likely benefits and harms of each so that they can communicate their preferences and help select the best course of action for them. Shared decision making (SDM) is, of course, not new, but implementation has been difficult. Elwyn and colleagues (2010) note that ready access to evidence about treatment options, guidance on weighing pros and cons of different options and a supportive clinical culture that facilitates patient engagement are critical to successful adoption of SDM.

Final thoughts

To summarise, there is evidence of wide variation in clinical practice, utilisation of diagnostic tests, healthcare resource utilisation, hospital admissions and productivity locally, nationally and internationally. Although variation is inherent in the healthcare systems, the key issue is to distinguish 'acceptable' and 'warranted' variation from that which is 'unwarranted' or 'unacceptable', a task that is not always easy across varying contexts even with statistical modelling of disease prevalence and factors that drive variation (Evans, 1990).

Tackling unwarranted variation raises several system-wide questions, as highlighted by Mulley and colleagues (2012). It is not clear what the impact of the current NHS reforms will be on the ability of organisations and individuals to identify and reduce unwarranted or unacceptable variation in healthcare. Furthermore, how do we develop and implement national guidance to support decision making at local level, through bodies such as the National Institute for Health and Care Excellence (NICE)? We must be careful that the challenging financial climate does not promote a culture of 'quick fix' solutions to variation which could have unintended consequences, for example, above average admission areas aiming simply to cut access rather than seeking to establish appropriate utilisation rates through, for example, SDM and consideration of equity issues.

'Improving Quality in the NHS – A Strategy for Action' report (Ham, 2016) argues that the NHS in England cannot meet the healthcare needs of the population without a sustained and comprehensive commitment to quality implementation as its principal strategy. It stresses the need for attacking unwanted variations in clinical care, reducing waste, becoming more patient and care focused and ensuring that quality and safety are at the top of health policy agenda. As highlighted in the 'Better Value in NHS' Kings Fund Report (Alderwick et al., 2015), the challenge facing the NHS over the coming years is fundamentally about improving value rather than reducing costs. Reducing 'unwarranted variation' will be a key part of this strategy.

10

DEVELOPING AND ANALYSING EFFECTIVE TEAMS

Walaa Al-Safi

Effective team working can promote better patient health outcomes. One area where this is particularly important is in Obstetrics where the effectiveness of the team can literally make a difference between life and death. Obstetric emergency training has significantly increased the knowledge of obstetric emergencies (Crofts, 2007). In a centre in Bristol, introducing obstetric emergency training was associated with a significant improvement in perinatal outcome (Draycott et al., 2006), and this improvement has been sustained as the training continued. Practical shoulder dystocia training can result in improved neonatal outcome (Draycott et al., 2008).

Here, we report an innovative obstetric emergency multi-professional training programme, developed at Mafraq Hospital in the United Arab Emirates, to improve the effectiveness of the clinical Obstetric team. Mafraq is a general hospital regulated by the Health Authority of Abu Dhabi (HAAD). Mafraq Obstetric Emergency Program (MOEP) has been developed as a localised version of the United Kingdom's Practical Obstetric Multi-professional Training (PROMPT) (www.promptmaternity.org).

Over the past few years, Mafraq Hospital has sought to improve its maternity services through its reports to the Patient Safety Network (PSN). An analysis of data identified a need to improve team working and communication.

Established in October 2014, MOEP aims to train clinicians providing maternity care leveraging PROMPT's philosophy of introducing obstetric simulation training programmes to improve care and improve communication and team working. Educational material was prepared by trainees using local resources, and MOEP went live in May 2015.

Establishing the MOEP team

Based on his study of twenty-seven different types of teams, Hackman (1990) identified three hurdles that every team had to surmount to achieve effectiveness. The
team members had to:

- Expend sufficient effort to achieve their task (motivation);
- Bring sufficient knowledge and skill to their group task (composition);
- Use group processes appropriate for the task (processes).

Authors have sought to explain the continuing popularity of team working.
Buchanan (2000) and Marchington and Wilkinson (2005) have pointed to the fact
that in Western societies, the term *team working* conveys the notion of collaboration and commitment and carries with it connotations of shared skills, problem
solving and making decisions together. Good team-working skills have become a
required competency sought by employers in selecting new employees (Buchanan
and Huczynski, 2010) and a key aim of MOEP was to develop an effective leadership team.

Team effectiveness has been defined as the capacity a team has to accomplish
the goals or objectives administered by an authorised personnel or the organisation
(Aubé, 2011). A team is a collection of individuals who are interdependent in their
tasks, share responsibility for outcomes and view themselves as a unit embedded
in an institutional or organisational system which operates within the established
boundaries of that system (Halvorsen, 2013).

Team effectiveness can be defined in terms of three criteria (Hackman, 1987):

- *Output*: this should meet or exceed the performance standard of the people
  who review the output. MOEP members discussed potential output measures
  for the team and agreed that the output would be 'Improvement in trainees'
  knowledge of obstetric emergencies'. The plan was for this to be assessed using
  pre- and post-course testing, and a large pool of multiple choice questions was
  developed by senior clinicians of the team. MOEP trainers also undertook a
  pre-test and a post-test assessing their knowledge and skills prior to training
  others.
- *Social Processes*: the internal social processes operating as the team interacts
  should enhance, or at least maintain, the group's ability to work together in the
  future.
- *Learning*: the experience of working in the team environment should act to
  satisfy rather than aggravate the personal needs of team members.

In a local survey about trainers' own experience in the first 6 months of developing MOEP, all reported a positive experience, high satisfaction rate about improved
knowledge, confidence in managing obstetric emergencies as well as improved
communications skills and attitude towards teamwork (Figure 10.1).

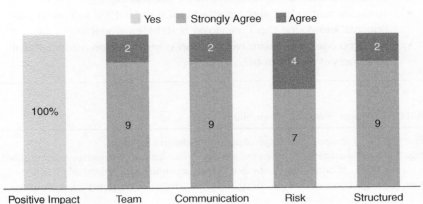

FIGURE 10.1   Impact of MOEP training on MOEP on trainers' performance during Obstetric Emergency Management (OEM)

From the early days, MOEP founders set clear aims, one of which was to measure team effectiveness (Box 1). This was planned to be achieved in three successive stages with an ultimate aim of improving maternal and neonatal morbidity and mortality. Targets were set in such a way as to ensure sustainable effectiveness and ongoing improvements (Table 10.1). Increase in participants' knowledge was successfully implemented as the first target in May 2015. Four months later and owing to the encouraging improvement in trainees' knowledge, funding was approved to allow the core team to enhance their expertise through attending the UK's official Train the Trainers PROMPT course.

BOX 1:   AIMS OF THE MULTIDISCIPLINARY OBSTETRIC EMERGENCY TRAINING TEAM

- Executive group to steer the project;
- To develop MOEP training packages/resources/data and so forth;
- To train representatives in the principles of managing obstetric emergencies to educate trainees;
- To facilitate discussion of the content of training material and methods of objective assessment of the effectiveness of the programme;
- To determine staff members mandated to attend training courses, frequency of training courses, number of trainees per course and to set standards for frequency of training updates;

- To look into methods of recording MOEP compliance;
- To discuss methods of auditing effectiveness of MOEP in increasing participants' knowledge about managing obstetric emergencies;
- To encourage better team working and communication across cultural differences of team members.

TABLE 10.1 Stages of MOEP effectiveness

Stage 1	Increased knowledge of managing obstetric emergencies
Stage 2	Managing obstetric emergencies in line with departmental guidelines, level of compliance to be determined according each individual guideline
Stage 3	Improving team working and communication when managing obstetric emergencies

Ecological framework for analysing work team effectiveness

Sundstrom et al. (1990) presented an ecological framework for analysing performance or effectiveness of work teams. This framework provides a perspective which looks at teams as embedded within their organisation (Buchanan and Huczynski, 2010).

They have provided perhaps the most creative model of work team performance. The framework suggests that, at any time, a team's effectiveness is the outcome of team development and the organisational context, mediated by the team's boundaries. It depicts team effectiveness as interdependent with organisational context, boundaries and team development (Sundstrom et al., 1990). Key context factors include:

- organisational culture
- technology and task design
- mission clarity
- autonomy
- rewards
- performance feedback
- training/consultation
- physical environment.

In this framework, team effectiveness is the dependent variable and is measured using two criteria – performance and viability. Team performance is focused on meeting the needs of the customers and assessed using measures such as quantity, quality and time. The customer's assessment of the team's output is important in assessing performance, in a similar way to Hackman's model (2001), where work team performance can be measured as the acceptability of output to customers who receive team services. Team viability is the social dimension, which is internally focused and concerns the enhancement of the group's capability to perform effectively in the future. Team viability indicators include group cohesion, shared purpose and the level of member commitment. They indicate team members' satisfaction and willingness to stay together over the long term. The two are closely related because the team may get a job done but self-destruct in the process.

Sundstrom and colleagues chose not to use the input-process-output format for displaying the factors believed to be most crucial to work team performance because they felt such a format implies that performance is an end state rather than a continual process. Instead, they presented their model in such a way as to avoid temporal dynamics and highlight the interrelationships between the major sets of work team factors, including the organisational context, team boundaries and team development (Dale and Cloyd, 1998).

Analysing effectiveness of the MOEP team

Following their first meeting in October 2014, MOEP core members established regular weekly meetings where they recruited seven additional members to complement the team, prepared teaching material and obtained educational and administrative approvals. MOEP went live in May 2015, delivering monthly courses and 4 months later, forty-two candidates were trained.

Sundstrom's ecological framework was used as a template to analyse the team effectiveness of the MOEP team (Sundstrom et al., 1990). This model highlights that performance is affected by three major components, focused on external conditions and internal processes of the team:

- *The Organisational Context*: this includes organisational cultures, characteristics of the task, mission clarity, autonomy, rewards, training and the physical environment. These factors can augment team performance by providing resources. This is viewed as ties to the team via team boundaries.
- *Team Boundaries*: the boundary for the team is like fence around a piece of property. Described by Sundstrom et al. (1990), these boundaries mediate between the organisational context and the team's development, having direct ties to the team's performance. If the boundary becomes too open, the team might lose its identity. If too closed, this might lead to isolation of the team and loss of touch with suppliers, managers and customers (Buchanan and Huczynski, 2010).
- *Team Development*: over time, teams change and develop new ways of operating as they adapt to their contexts. Factors included here are interpersonal processes, norms, cohesion and roles.

The MOEP team agreed to observe and measure team performance in three successive stages, ultimately aiming to improve maternal and neonatal morbidity and mortality.

The first stage was comparison of trainees' knowledge before and after training. Change in trainees' knowledge were measured using a Multiple-Choice Questionnaire (MCQ) of twenty-five questions completed at the start of the day and immediately after training before trainees received their attendance certificates. Test scores were analysed every month, and results were compiled in a cumulative manner.

MCQs are recognised as an efficient method to objectively assess knowledge; a short assessment allows a breadth of sampling of many subject areas. However, they have been criticised as being unfair and promoting factual regurgitation over higher order thinking (McCoubrie, 2004). The true/false format used in this study has drawbacks, namely guessing and the cueing effect. Trainees are aware of this drawback, and in order to discourage guessing, they have been looking to introduce a suitable alternative such as the use of negative marking (Schuwirth et al., 1996).

A criticism of the validity of MCQs, and therefore of this small study, is that testing cognitive knowledge does not guarantee competence. Nonetheless, it has been demonstrated that knowledge of the cognitive domain is the single best determinant of expertise and best assessed using written test forms thinking.

Training has been defined as the systemic acquisition of knowledge (what we think), skills (what we do) and attitudes (what we feel) that leads to improved performance in a particular environment (Benjamin et al., 1964).

Kirkpatrick (1998) describes four levels for evaluation of the effect of training programmes:

- Level 1 Reaction (satisfaction following training)
- Level 2 Learning (MCQ test, skill acquisition)
- Level 3 Behaviour (patient care)
- Level 4 Results (patient outcomes).

To date, the performance of this MOEP programme has reached Level 2 only. Previous studies assessing other obstetric emergency training programmes have also reported an increase in knowledge (Level 2); however, in these studies, knowledge assessments were not multi-professional and were completed by very small numbers of trainees (Johanson R et al., 2002 and Johanson RB et al., 2002).

The gold standard evaluation of any obstetric training programme would be to demonstrate an improvement in maternal or neonatal outcome following the instigation of training (Crofts, 2007). Our study does not reach this goal; however, since the official start of the course, trained staff have reported that training has had a positive impact on their management of obstetric emergencies in terms of knowledge, communication and teamwork skills. They are confident that future data will provide evidence of attainment of Level 4, that is, improved patient outcomes.

BOX 2:   PERSONAL REFLECTION ON TEAM WORKING WITHIN THE MOEP PROJECT

The team enjoyed sufficient autonomy and invested much time and effort in the development phase. Members are aware that organisational factors can significantly affect performance. Members encountered several incidents that clashed with their performance, such as staff shortages and unexpected changes of course venue.

In hindsight, it would have been useful to invite a representative from the senior management team to be involved in the project group in order to communicate the vision and support project implementation.

I have learnt about team viability and the social dimension that can affect performance. In a particular incident, the course's venue had to be changed at the last minute. The team responded promptly, identified an alternative venue and worked hard over a weekend to set it up. The alternative venue was a success, and the team leader organised a social event to enhance the team's coherence and reward the group.

The weekly meetings held by the team have helped maintain member's coherence and interaction, exchange of best practices, maximising effectiveness and evaluating accomplishments. With recent staff shortages, the MOEP group has found it difficult to maintain their weekly meetings. The group is now considering other ways of maintaining group coherence, for example, incorporating some work time within social activities or meeting outside working hours.

I have learnt that the composition of a multidisciplinary team is crucial to its success. Having a diverse range of interdependent skills, experiences and personal attributes, MOEP members have set a true example of a multidisciplinary team. The wide skill mix has ensured sufficient cross-cover and role rotation helped sustainable performance.

11

A STRATEGY FOR ENGAGING PRIMARY AND SECONDARY CARE DOCTORS IN MEDICAL LEADERSHIP

Simon Boyes

Within the literature there is increasing evidence that engagement by doctors in leading and managing healthcare is important when seeking to improve the quality of healthcare to patients and to reduce health inequalities. The challenge is to define what is meant by engagement so that it gives context in which to understand how, why and for whom engagement leads to improvement.

Defining engagement

The concept or term *engagement* has been used to refer to a psychological state (involvement, mood attachment), performance construct (effort or observable behaviour including organisational citizenship behaviour) or disposition (positive affect) (Macey and Schneider, 2008). Kahn (1990) proposed that engagement is "the harnessing of an organisation's members selves to their work role . . . people employ and express themselves physically, cognitively and emotionally during role performance". Kahn (1990:694) determined through an inductive analysis that the level of engagement an individual would have within the organisation was determined by three psychological states:

- *Meaningfulness*: the individual's sense of return on investing themselves in their organisational role. This may be by feeling valued, having influence and a job that provides variety and challenge.
- *Safety*: where the individual is able to show their self without worrying about a negative impact on their standing, career or self-image.
- *Availability*: how able an individual is to invest in their role at any particular moment dependent on their physical, emotional or psychological well-being, which may be influenced by factors within or out of the work environment.

Kahn (1992) expanded his original model further and theorised that the extent an individual experienced the three conditions of meaningfulness, safety and availability influenced how psychologically present they are in their role and thus how behaviourally engaged they were. This in turn has an impact on outcomes, whether this is personal experience, performance or productivity. The feedback received around those outcomes can in turn have a positive or negative effect on their experiential state and thus how psychologically present an individual remains. Macleod and Clarke (2009a, 2009b), in their report *Engaging for Success*, proposed that there are three components to engagement which can trigger and reinforce one another: attitude, behaviour and outcome.

Maslach (2003) defines engagement as the positive antithesis of burnout. Burnout had been conceptualised as having three psychological components: emotional exhaustion, depersonalisation and reduced personal accomplishment (Maslach, 1997). At the opposite end of the scale, engagement is defined as comprising energy, involvement and sense of efficacy (Maslach, 2003). Schaufeli et al. (2002) conceptualised engagement as the persistent positive affective emotional state of employee fulfilment. They defined three components that were characteristic of employee engagement. Vigour is categorised by high levels of energy, resilience in the face of complications and the desire to invest effort in one's job role. Dedication represents the individual's deep-seated involvement in their job giving rewards of pride, enthusiasm and being inspired. The final characteristic is absorption and refers to being immersed in your work with the feeling time passes quickly and being unable to detach from the task in hand.

It is more difficult to define what is meant by engagement as a directly observable behaviour and how it is different to other performance-related behaviours. Macey and Schneider (2008) conceptualised behavioural engagement as proactivity, personal initiative, role expansion or extra, discretionary and atypical effort beyond that would be typical or expected within a role. However, they conceded that these terms in themselves are difficult to define and thus measure. Newman and Harrison (2008), in their commentary on Macey and Schneider (2008), disagreed with their construct around behavioural engagement that normal task behaviour (doing your job well) excluded an individual from being defined as engaged in their role. They proposed that employee engagement could be understood by the presence of three behaviours: job performance, involvement and citizenship behaviour. Outcomes are dependent on the individual's behavioural engagement; contrary to Newman and Harrison's thesis, it is the psychological state of the individual that is instrumental in defining the level of behavioural engagement.

The NHS National Workforce Project defined engagement, which, on many levels, reflects the theoretical concepts defined by the literature:

A measure of how people connect in their work and feel committed to their organisation and its goals. People who are highly engaged in an activity feel excited and enthusiastic about their role, say time passes quickly at work, devote extra effort to the activity, identify with the task and describe themselves to others in the context of their task (doctor, nurse, NHS manager), think about the questions or challenges posed by the activity during their spare moments (for example when travelling to and from work), resist distractions, find it easy to stay focused and invite others into the activity or organisation (their enthusiasm is contagious).

(NHS National Workforce Projects, 2007)

It is clear that there is no unifying definition of engagement though all seem to agree that it involves positive attributes coming from slightly different perspectives. Without a single definition, it means that it is not feasible to develop a standard research tool to measure engagement, and thus comparing studies across the literature becomes much more difficult.

Measuring engagement

The Enhancing Engagement in Medical Leadership Project commissioned the development of a tool to measure and differentiate two aspects of medical engagement on a personal level and from an organisational context. The authors utilised data collected over a 10-year period on the stress and attitudinal ratings of 23,782 NHS staff from twenty organisations. They identified three key areas related to engagement:

* relationships with other professionals, managers and the organisation;
* involvement in planning delivery and transforming services;
* motivation defined by job satisfaction, commitment and dedication.

Following testing for reliability and validity, the resultant commercially available Medical Engagement Scale can be administered as an 18-item instrument composed of three meta scales, or as a 30-item instrument composed of the three meta scales comprising each of two subscales, allowing for an organisational or individual context, depending on the depth of analysis of engagement that is required (Clark et al., 2008) (Table 11.1).

The impact of medical engagement

Though there is some understanding of what medical engagement is, it is unclear how to assess its impact. Organisational performance is usually used as a surrogate marker to measure the impact of medical leadership and engagement. The World Health Organisation in a report published in 2003 identified five principal areas of measurement of organisational (hospital) performance:

* Regulatory inspection, for example, by the Care Quality Commission (CQC);
* Patient experience questionnaires including patient-reported outcome/experience measures (PROM or PREM);

TABLE 11.1 Medical Engagement Scale

Medical Engagement Scale (O) organisation, (i) Individual	Scale definition:-The scale is concerned with the extent to which . . . .
Index: Professional engagement	. . . doctors adopt a broad organisational perspective with regard to their clinical responsibilities and accountability
Meta scale 1:Working in an open culture	. . . doctors have opportunities to authentically discuss issues and problems at work with all staff groups in an open and honest way
Subscale 1: (O) Climate for positive learning	. . . the working climate for doctors is supportive, and problems are solved by sharing ideas and joint learning
Subscale 2: (I) Good interpersonal relationships	. . . all staff are friendly towards doctors and are sympathetic to their workload and work priorities
Meta scale 2: Having purpose and direction	. . . medical staff share a sense of common purpose and agreed direction with others at work, particularly with regard to planning, design and delivery of services
Subscale 3: (O) Appraisal and rewards effectively aligned	. . . doctors consider that their work is aligned to the wider organisational goals
Subscale 4: (I) Participation in decision making and change	. . . doctors consider that they are able to make a positive impact through decision making about future developments
Meta scale 3: Feeling valued and empowered	. . . doctors feel that their contribution is properly appreciated and valued by the organisation and not taken for granted
Subscale 5: (O) Development and orientation	. . . doctors feel that they are encouraged to develop their skills and progress their career
Subscale 6: (I) Commitment and work satisfaction	. . . doctors feel satisfied with their working conditions and feel a real sense of attachment and commitment to the organisation

Source: Adapted from Spurgeon et al. (2008).

- Third-party assessment by peer review, ISO 9000 standards and other accreditation schemes;
- Statistical indicators such as mortality rates, length of stay and readmission rates;
- Internal assessment.

Within the literature, there is no consistent measure of organisational performance, but they all use a combination of the aforementioned areas. The lack of standardised, reliable and validated measurement tools for organisational performance doesn't allow for comparison of the results within the literature or comparisons across organisations (Shaw, 2003).

Parand et al. (2010) highlighted that an organisation's previous record on its approach to quality and service improvement had a significant impact on doctors' motivation to become engaged. Multiple initiatives with little provision of support were unlikely to achieve buy-in. Macleod and Clarke (2009a, 2009b) argued that medical engagement is important due to the increasing evidence that it correlates with improving organisational improvement. Hospital Chief Executives identified engagement of physicians in service improvement initiatives as a significant healthcare challenge; better performing hospitals that engaged with physicians saw improvements in safety, operational performance and quality of patient care (Guthrie, 2005). In a longitudinal study looking at the impact of leadership qualities on performance, the only statistically significant domain was that of engaging others, which in turn led to achievement of goals (Alimo-Metcalfe et al., 2008). However, this study used only one measure of organisational performance: reduction in bed occupancy. Although the authors argued that this outcome measure strongly associated with organisational performance as a whole, the use of only one measure of organisational performance limits the validity of their study. A further study ranked seventy-nine Academic Medical Centres by scoring them for quality and safety on their discharge date. Three top and three average performers were selected for qualitative site visits. It was evident, though on a small sample size and not the including of poor performers, that the top performing institutions achieved their outcomes by a mixture of excellent organisational leadership and clinical engagement (both medical and nursing) (Keroack et al., 2007). A qualitative study looking at quality and safety improvements in ten high-performing US hospitals found that medical engagement was essential to the delivery of organisational objectives around quality and safety (Taitz et al., 2012).

The Medical Engagement Scale (MES) is a validated measure for predicting the level of engagement of medical staff within an organisation (Spurgeon et al., 2008). Independently collected performance indicators within the same time scale as the collected MES were analysed to see whether there were observable links between medical engagement and organisational performance. Across all three of the performance areas analysed, engagement was associated with improvements in mortality, patient safety and the organisational CQC rating (Spurgeon et al., 2011). A study of 8,597 hospital-based nursing staff in Canada showed a positive correlation for employee engagement and patient safety outcomes (Laschinger and Leiter, 2006). As part of the innovation series for the Institute for Healthcare Improvement, Reinertsen and colleagues (2007) cite several key organisations that have seen improvements in quality and safety which would not have been achieved without physician engagement.

Therefore, although research is limited, there is increasing evidence that increased medical engagement is associated (although not necessarily causal) with improved organisational performance, quality improvement and safety. At the same time as the importance of medical engagement has been recognised, it has also been acknowledged that medical leadership may also play an important role in improving performance and quality.

Medical leadership

Ham (2003), in his viewpoint on clinical leadership, stated that for improvement to occur within an organisation, both managerial and medical leadership is required.

Mountford and Webb (2009) agreed that clinical leadership is required to bring about the transformation of healthcare services necessary to combat the huge challenges now faced by the healthcare industry. Their premise was that clinicians not only make decisions around quality of care but also have the specialised knowledge to make long-term strategic decisions around service delivery. Medical leadership in several studies has been linked to organisational performance and delivery both in the UK and internationally. During the evaluation of 'national booking admissions scheme' pilots in several UK hospitals, it was found that those achieving highest success had medical leadership involvement in the pilot (Ham et al., 2003). Goodall (2011) examined the professional background of Chief Executive Officers of the top 100 hospitals ranked by an Index of Hospital Quality in the US and found that hospitals were more successful if they were led by a medical leader. There was a positive association ($p < 0.001$) between high ranking and a CEO who was a medical leader rather than a professional manager. A study that assessed management practice in 126 hospitals across the UK showed that strong operational effectiveness, performance management and talent management were linked to improved indicators of safety, quality, productivity and finance. It was also evident that medical leadership involvement in the way the hospital was managed had a significant positive impact on delivery of those indicators (Castro et al., 2008). A qualitative study that looked at eleven cases of clinical service improvement within the NHS found that those led by medical leaders were less likely to run into difficulty and more likely to be delivered successfully (Fitzgerald et al., 2006). Data from 1,987 hospitals across nine countries including the UK and US were collected using an interview-based tool to assess management practices across three broad categories of operations, targets and human resources. Those hospitals that scored highest for management practices also had a positive link to hospital performance, having lower mortality for acute myocardial infarction and general surgery operations, lower staff turnover and decreased length of stay. Predictors of having good management practices were size, private ownership, competition and medical leadership (Bloom et al., 2009, 2013). A survey of fourteen UK hospitals between 2006 and 2009 showed an increase in management practice scores which correlated with an increase in medical leaders. The UK had the lowest proportion of medical leaders out of seven countries surveyed: the obvious question is what could be achieved if this proportion were increased (Dorgan et al., 2010)?

There does seem to be an increasing evidence base that medical leadership is necessary to deliver improved organisational performance and outcomes. The development and training of medical leaders is still in its infancy, so the ability of medical leaders to deliver must be partially down to other factors. To have undergone medical training, doctors need to be hardworking, intelligent, able to make decisions (sometimes under intense pressure) and lead a team in delivering clinical care. This gives them a unique position as a medical leader in that they will have credibility with their peers and non-medical staff, be able to communicate in a language clinical staff will understand and understand the clinical challenges faced by the organisation. It would be naïve to believe that this is all that is required to be good medical leader, but leadership development can be used to enhance further the knowledge and skills required for continued success. Greener et al. (2011) proposed that training in leadership could be effective only if it included both managerial and clinical perspectives within the NHS context. Armit and Roberts (2009), in their review on engaging doctors, proposed that enhanced medical engagement could be achieved with a model of shared leadership where influence is exercised across relationships, system and culture. The authors argue that it should apply to all, not the few. This view could be attained only if the organisation has a culture that encourages doctors to participate in medical leadership.

Medical leadership does, however, throw out its own challenges. Those individuals who are involved in medical leadership can find it difficult to reconcile their role as a clinician with that of being a medical leader having conflicting commitments across both of these roles (Spehar et al., 2014; Kippist and Fitzgerald, 2010). Limited evidence suggests that medical leaders maintain their legitimacy and credibility with their peers and their organisation by continuing in a clinical role (Hoff, 1999; Mo, 2008; Bruce and Hill, 1994). Davies et al. (2003), in a survey of acute medical trusts, demonstrated that Clinical Directors had a negative perspective on non-clinical managers' capabilities and the balance of power between clinicians and managers. Joffe and McKenzie-Davey (2012), in their study looking at medical directors in hybrid medical management roles, highlighted that even in these roles there is a negative construct of NHS management, suggesting little has changed in the intervening years. Hallier and Forbes (2005) conducted semi-structured interviews with present and past clinical directors over a 5-year period. They found that the pre-role expectation was that they would receive support in their relationship with hospital managers. The reality was reluctance by hospital managers to involve the clinical directors in the operation of the hospital and a lack of enthusiasm over their input. Forbes et al. (2004), in a qualitative study interviewing medical leaders, found that lack of understanding by hospital managers of the dual responsibilities that medical leaders had resulted in conflict. A small study of fourteen medical leaders who were involved in a clinical leadership development programme also demonstrated professional conflict between the medical leaders' values and beliefs and the organisation's management objectives (Kippist and Fitzgerald, 2009). As part of a reflective analysis of two longitudinal completed studies in the UK healthcare system, Fitzgerald and Ferlie (2000) found that many doctors did not consider non-medical professionals qualified to manage a medical service. This mainly came down to their lack of credibility due to a shortage of specialist knowledge that would allow an understanding of the issues related to service delivery. To achieve improvements in engagement of doctors in medical leadership roles, it is evident that the cultural divide between clinicians and managers will need to be addressed.

These issues are not unique to individuals or healthcare organisations: a brief discussion of role theory may give some insight into how those challenges may be addressed. It is evident that without resolution to such issues, they will have a confounding effect on organisational performance. Role theory is defined as the way humans behave in ways that are different and predictable depending on their respective social identities and situation (Biddle, 1986). There are three components to role theory: role behaviour, role relationships and role expectations. The consensus is that expectations are the major influence on role, learnt through experience and that persons are aware of the expectations they hold (Biddle, 1986). There are five approaches to role theory, but only one is relevant here: organisational role theory.

Roles in an organisation follow the assumption that they are associated with an identified social position and will be generated by normative expectations. Norms may vary amongst individuals and may reflect the expectations of peers and managers and the demands of the organisation and other employees. This variability in norms inevitably leads to role conflict, as there is inadequate or inappropriate role expectations for the individual (Willcocks, 1994; Biddle, 1986). Related to role conflict are three conditions that have relevance to medical leadership.

Role ambiguity is where there is a lack of clarity around the expectations of a role. This may be seen as a challenge for some and be empowering (Willcocks, 1994), but the converse can be true and it has an impact on job satisfaction and performance (Singh, 1998). When there is an excess of roles or differences in expectation leading to extremely demanding workload in the context of the medical leader this would be being a clinician, manager and trainer. This is defined as role overload and was associated with decreased job satisfaction amongst clinical directors (Willcocks, 1994). The last is role incompatibility where there are conflicting expectations due to two or more contradictory roles; from the medical leader perspective this would be the managerial vs clinical roles. Willcocks (1994), in the case study of clinical directors, considered this to be a potential role conflict and may lead to role stress. Role theory allows a better understanding of how behaviour changes within social interactions and expectations. Improved understanding may lead to strategies that deal with the key challenges associated with medical leadership, particularly the hybrid role and managerial relationships.

Conclusions

It is difficult not to argue from the evidence cited that medical engagement and medical leadership are instrumental in enhancing organisational performance and outcomes. What is less clear is whether it requires medical leadership to be present within an organisation as a prerequisite to increasing the level of medical engagement within that organisation. In theory, if all the factors that relate to medical engagement are in play, then medical leadership should not be a dependent variable. This probably ignores that healthcare organisations are 'Professional Bureaucracies': this is where professionals within an organisation exert power due to their expertise, not their position in the organisation. Managers are not in a position to enact normal top-down control mechanisms like budgeting, operating procedure or supervision (Mintzberg, 1979; Abernethy and Stoelwinder, 1990; Currie and Procter, 2005). Professionals are less likely to see supervision or operating procedures as bureaucratic control mechanisms if they come from expertise delivered by the profession and not from non-professional hierarchy (Abernethy and Stoelwinder, 1990). This would suggest that the maximal impact of engagement in medical leadership occurs when doctors lead doctors, avoiding the negative construct of hierarchical bureaucratic control.

12

MEDICAL ENGAGEMENT – STRATEGIES FOR ENGAGEMENT FROM THE 'GRASS ROOTS'

Paddy Dobbs and Alix Fonfe

Broader tools to engage staff in healthcare may not necessarily work for doctors. This is evident in the low response rate of doctors in staff engagement surveys. There needs to be practical and innovative ways to engage and listen to doctors, and such initiatives are often led by doctors, as there is a level of trust and connection with medical peers. Investment in bespoke initiatives to engage doctors in particular specialties is worth considering. Our own experience is that we have been able to increase medical engagement through a 'bottom-up' approach focusing on direct communication and involvement with doctors in our own respective specialties in anaesthesia and paediatrics.

Engagement is defined as the action of engaging or being engaged (OED, 2012), that is, being participatory or involved. However, in recent medical politics, the meaning has become rather more difficult to understand, a nebulous concept possibly meaning that the person is actively trying to improve quality within the financial framework that exists today. Chris Ham, in the Kings Fund leadership review (2012), argues that "stronger engagement between staff, clinicians and patients is crucial to improving patient outcomes, delivering integrated care, and tackling the unprecedented financial and organisational challenges facing the NHS", but does not actually define engagement. Macleod and Clarke (2009a, 2009b) define engagement as "the business values the employee and the employee values the business", suggesting that engagement is a two-directional process with accountability both on the business and the employee. Within the NHS, engagement is also reported to mean that clinicians are involved with decision making or more generally the openness of communication with management (Kings Fund, 2012a). West and Dawson (2012) describe engagement as a psychological state, a performance construct, a disposition or a combination of these. However, engagement can mean different things to different people. Erlandson and Ludeman (2003) found that administrators, when speaking of physician engagement, mean what they would like doctors to do but can't get them to do, and doctors, when speaking about engagement, mean what they already do that is not supported, appreciated or valued by the administrators. Such reference in the literature suggests that doctors are a homogenous group, but our own experience is that this is not the case.

The NHS constitution pledges to

> engage staff in decisions that affect them and the services they provide, individually, through representative organisations and through local partnership working arrangements. All staff will be empowered to put forward ways to deliver better and safer services for patients and their families.
>
> *(Department of Health, 2012:11)*

The Government confirms its commitment to staff engagement in Equity and Excellence (2010).

At an organisational level, the Standard Contract (NHS England, 2013) requires providers to complete the NHS staff survey, part of which involves engagement; the Quality Accounts guidance recommends including the staff survey results in returns (Monitor, 2013).

The benefits of staff engagement are a better patient experience, fewer errors, lower infection and mortality rates, improved financial management, higher staff motivation and morale with less absenteeism (Kings Fund, 2012b; NHS Employers, 2013). In investigating variations in quality of care, Clarke et al. (2010) found that clinician engagement was critical in leading change to improve quality.

Clinicians have not, however, universally embraced engagement (Gollop, 2004; Ovretveit, 1996). Wilkinson et al., (2011:16) says, "overall, healthcare professionals are reluctant to engage. In part this is because they perceive that the initiatives will be ineffective and a waste of scarce personal and organisational resources" and "increasing clinician engagement is likely to be difficult: non-engagement of clinicians is a long-standing, multi-factorial and international problem". Gollop (2004: 108–113) further states "the opinions and behaviour of doctors are particularly important, and their support is vital".

The roots of this lack of engagement lie in the origin of the health service when clinical autonomy was the price the government paid to entice doctors into the fledgling NHS (Dickinson and Ham, 2008). The autonomy has led to a state of 'professional bureaucracies' (Mintzberg, 1979) where frontline staff have a high level of control over content of work by virtue of their training and specialist knowledge. Professional bureaucracies are oriented towards stability rather than change and also silo mentality. Since the Griffiths (1983) report, attempts have been made to challenge the level of autonomy that doctors have enjoyed, with variable success.

A further issue is the consequence of poor engagement: burnout. Burnout is perceived as the opposite end of a continuum from engagement and is described as a negative psychological syndrome strongly linked to stress (Maslach and Leiter, 2008).

Dickinson and Ham (2008), in reviewing the literature related to medical engagement, point out that it is how engagement in leadership is defined which will have implications for the way it is measured. Previous studies examined physician presence in particular roles as a marker of engagement (Weiner et al., 1996); in contrast, another study used qualitative interviews to determine the degree of influence an individual doctor has, to determine the level of engagement (Buchanan et al., 1997). Mohapel and Dickson (2007) describe the use of a Likert scale to rate physicians' feelings and behaviours relating to leadership. All these methods of assessing engagement focus on leadership or management, especially of clinicians in positions of authority. None of the metrics described attempt to assess the level of engagement of a group of clinicians with the organisation they work for or to investigate individuals without the traditional hierarchical roles such as clinical director. Indeed, Dickinson and Ham (2008) conclude that any metric that is used must reflect the definition of medical leadership that is utilised. The NHS staff survey is a universal tool which, in part, assesses the level of engagement of the individual with their organisation and as such would appear to be suitable for the research question posed in this evaluation.

Impact of staff engagement

From the work by West and Dawson (2012) for the King's Fund, and work published on the NHS Employers website – Staff engagement toolkit (2013, online), there is a significant body of evidence that staff engagement can affect organisational performance.

The main areas in which links can be shown between staff engagement and outcomes are:

- Staff Absenteeism
- Patient Satisfaction
- Staff Health and Well-being
- Hospital Standardised Mortality
- CQC Financial Performance
- CQC Quality of Services.

Staff absenteeism

Staff absenteeism is a significant problem for the NHS. The Boorman review, NHS Staff Health and Well-being (2009) found that staff are absent from work for an average of 10.3 days a year, costing £1.75 billion. When organisations with high staff engagement are compared with others, there is a significant difference in absenteeism, especially going from medium to high engagement (Figure 12.1). It follows that a reduction in absenteeism could make significant financial benefit for

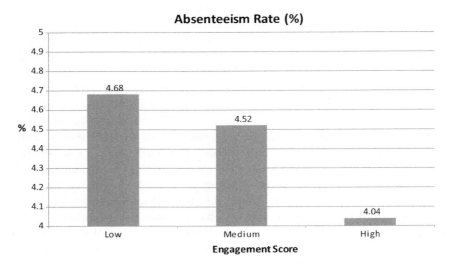

FIGURE 12.1 Absenteeism rate compared with engagement level

Source: Adapted from NHS Employers Staff Engagement Tool online (2013).

organisations in a time of austerity. This saving has been calculated as £235,000 in 2013 for the average acute trust (NHS Employers, online, 2013). Across the whole NHS, Boorman predicted that if staff sickness absence were reduced by one third, 3.4 million additional available working days a year for NHS staff would be available, equivalent to an extra 14,900 whole-time equivalent staff with an estimated annual direct cost saving of £555 million.

Patient satisfaction

Patient satisfaction also correlates with engagement (Figure 12.2). West and Dawson (2012) suggest that the patient satisfaction scores are closely linked with the advocacy dimension of engagement. This reflects the symbiotic relationship between staff and patient experience: if staff perceive that the patients are satisfied with the care provided, they will view the quality of care more positively themselves.

Staff health and well-being

Improved staff health and well-being are associated with higher levels of staff engagement (Figure 12.3) and are themselves positively associated with a number of clinical outcomes. Boorman (2009) argues that organisations that prioritised staff health and well-being performed better, with improved patient satisfaction, stronger quality scores, better outcomes, higher levels of staff retention and lower rates of absence.

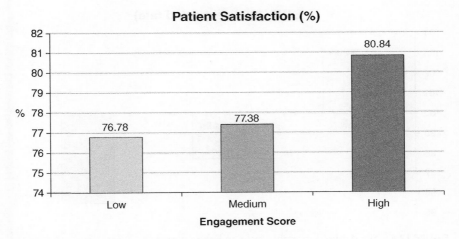

FIGURE 12.2   Engagement and patient satisfaction

Source: Adapted from NHS Employers Staff Engagement Tool online (2013).

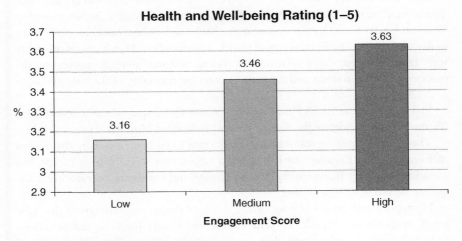

FIGURE 12.3   Engagement and staff health and well-being

Source: Adapted from NHS Employers Staff Engagement Tool online (2013).

Hospital standardised mortality

Perhaps one of the strongest motivators for clinicians is quality related to patient outcomes. The hospital standardised mortality ratio (SMR) shows the overall rate of deaths within the NHS trust each hospital belongs to. Rates are given as better, worse, or as expected compared with the national average (NHS Choices, 2013, online). It can be seen that there is a clear relationship between SMR and staff engagement.

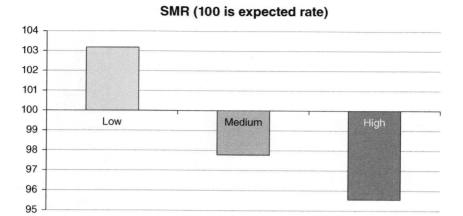

FIGURE 12.4   Standardised mortality ratio and engagement

Source: Adapted from NHS Employers Staff Engagement Tool online (2013).

The SMR is lower than average in hospitals with high levels of staff engagement. The reverse correlation is that poor staff engagement can lead to higher mortality. This can be illustrated by the events at the Mid-Staffordshire hospitals NHS Trust in the mid-2000s. The Francis report (2013) describes how high levels of mortality were ignored or put down to incorrect coding, and staff were disengaged by the push for foundation status and the 'targets or terror' mentality of the time (Propper et al., 2007).

In a lecture at the Kings Fund, Robert Francis QC displayed the following text (Figure 12.5) to evidence the disengagement at Stafford Hospital (Francis, 2013).

There are compelling reasons for organisations to embrace a culture that fosters staff engagement. Engagement is not just a target, or a score to be achieved, but a marker of quality that requires cultural change and consistent monitoring if the quality agenda is to be achieved.

Hertzberg and others as part of the content theory of motivation describe levels or needs that should be achieved before higher levels of self actualisation or becoming everything that one is capable of becoming (Maslow cited in Mullins, 2010:261). In Hertzberg's theory, hygiene or maintenance factors include:

- Salary
- Job Security
- Working Conditions
- Level and Quality of Supervision
- Company Policy and Administration
- Interpersonal Relationships.

A lack of meetings and other opportunities for communication would fit into the working conditions and interpersonal relationships domains. The theory suggests these hygiene factors are related to job context and concerned with job environment and extrinsic to the job itself, and they act to prevent dissatisfaction. In Maslow's theory, increasing the percentage satisfaction at lower levels of the hierarchy leads to increased satisfaction at higher levels; cohesive work group and professional associations are mid-levels in the social domain, and poor satisfaction at this level will inhibit growth and satisfaction in the higher esteem and self-actualisation levels.

Team working and appraisal

West (2002, 2006) and West and Dawson (2012) suggest that appraisal and team working are important antecedents of engagement. In reviewing the NHS staff survey and relating engagement to appraisal type (well-structured, poor appraisal or no appraisal), West and Dawson found a correlation between well-structured appraisal and high levels of engagement. Similarly, West and Dawson (2012) found that the quality of team working correlated with engagement levels. The employees working in well-structured teams were most engaged, with those who worked in pseudo-teams (defined as those who thought they worked in a team but didn't answer the three questions in the staff survey as a positive response) being less engaged than those who didn't consider that they worked in teams. Team working has been shown to be beneficial to organisations and directorates:

> The best and most cost-effective outcomes for patients and clients are achieved when professionals work together, learn together, engage in clinical audit of outcomes together, and generate innovation to ensure progress in practice and service.

Perhaps I should have been more forceful in my statements, but I was getting to the stage where I was less involved and I was heading to retirement . . . I did not have a managerial role and therefore I did not see myself as someone who needed to get involved. Perhaps my conscience may have made me raise concerns if I had been in a management role, but I took the path of least resistance. In addition, most of my patients were day cases and there was less impact on those patients. There were also veiled threats at that time, that I should not rock the boat at my stage in life because, for example, I needed discretionary points or to be put forward for clinical excellence awards.

Evidence given to the Public Enquiry

© 2013 Robert Francis

FIGURE 12.5 Disengagement as described by Robert Francis

There is a significant and negative relationship between the percentage of staff working in teams and the mortality in these hospitals, taking account of both local health needs and hospital size. Where more employees work in teams the death rate is significantly lower.

(Borrill et al., 2001)

Implications for leadership

A new approach to leadership and management in healthcare is required to promote better medical engagement. The previous heroic/pacesetter styles are not sufficient or appropriate alone. There needs to be recognition of alternative models, both formal and informal, which both encourage and nurture the talent of doctors working at all levels of the organisation.

A more meaningful and sustained solution would be to develop an organisational strategy that works at directorate level and to embed this within the organisation. It should be down to medical specialties to develop the detail for an implementation plan, to respond to the specific requirements of the speciality.

NHS Employers have developed a staff engagement toolkit (NHS Employers, 2013. online) which highlights areas where organisations can develop to improve staff engagement.

The Institute for Healthcare Improvement has published a framework by Reinertsen et al. (2007) to help organisations engage clinicians with quality and

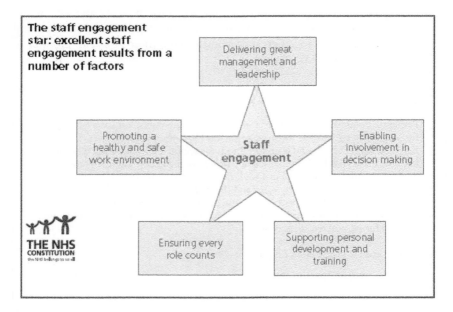

FIGURE 12.6   NHS Employers staff engagement toolkit

safety. The framework articulates a plan for improving engagement with six key phases:

*   Discovering a common purpose (reduce hassles and wasted time);
*   Reframe values and beliefs (make physicians partners, not customers);
*   Segmenting the engagement plan (identify and activate champions);
*   Use engaging improvement methods (make the right thing easy to do);
*   Show courage (providing back-up all the way to the board);
*   Adopting an engaging style (involve physicians very visibly and valuing their time).

This framework has been used to much success by McLeod hospital in Florida, US, to improve staff engagement, which has been vital to transforming the hospital's quality agenda (Gosfield and Reinertsen, 2010). It provides a useful 'toolkit' which can be applied to specific situations or challenges, increasing engagement of clinicians involved and empowering them to find solutions (Box 1).

In conclusion, clinician engagement is associated with a number of positive healthcare outcomes, including clinical effectiveness, patient experience and staff well-being, as shown earlier. However, engagement is not an automatic process – it needs to be encouraged within an organisation through creating an atmosphere of trust, mutual support and encouragement. This is not something that can be imposed in a 'top-down' manner but needs to be 'grown' from the grass roots. Organisations can encourage this process through some of the strategies outlined earlier, as illustrated in Box 1.

BOX 1: APPLICATION OF THE ENGAGEMENT FRAMEWORK TO RECRUITMENT/RETENTION OF PAEDIATRIC TRAINEES

There has been an increase nationally in vacancies in paediatric training posts: the Royal College of Paediatric and Child Health (RCPCH) reported an increase in vacancies from 10.4% in March 2012 to 14.9% in March 2016 (RCPCH, 2012 and RCPC, 2016) and noted that rota gaps and vacancies raise concern about the sustainability of paediatric services, patient safety and quality of care and trainees' well-being (RCPCH, 2016). These gaps arise because of doctors leaving training, and anecdotally this occurs because of low morale and concerns about work-life balance. Morale in doctors who continue training is reduced because of work pressure in covering increasingly arduous rotas.

Discovering common purpose

The engagement framework was applied in order to determine why morale was so low amongst paediatric trainees. A trainee highlighted to the Paediatric School Board that a key reason for low morale was a lack of notice for the allocation of rotation locations, resulting in poor work-life balance. At that time, notification of location and speciality for paediatric rotations at this time was 6–8 weeks.

Reframing values and beliefs

A survey of paediatric trainees was conducted. This showed that only 5% of trainees thought they were given sufficient notice of each new paediatric rotation. Seventy-four percent said that knowing their rotations in advance would significantly improve work-life balance. Free text responses reflected low morale, for example: "I handed in my notice for paediatric training this morning and one of the main reasons was how difficult it is to have a life when you don't know where you'll be in a few months' time".

Segmenting the engagement plan

A 'champion' was agreed. Her first action was to find out how other deaneries allocated trainees to rotations and what notice period they were given. It was determined that the majority of deaneries allocated rotations 1–3 years in advance.

Using engaging improvement methods

Presenting evidence of trainee morale and providing information how the timings of allocations is done elsewhere to the board, provided the leverage required to make changes which the trainees wanted.

Showing courage

The trainee survey results were presented to the School of Paediatrics Board meeting for the deanery. Consequently, the board committed to allocating trainees to their rotations 1 year in advance rather than 6–8 weeks.

Adopting an engaging style

A follow-up survey was conducted which showed that 75% of trainees felt they were given sufficient notice of their paediatric rotations and that 82%

of trainees agreed that being allocated their rotations 1 year in advance has improved their work-life balance.

This was a small but significant step to improving morale for doctors in training in one area. Further work is required locally and nationally. Junior doctor forums are developing in many hospitals: these have the potential to unite trainees in identifying areas for change to improve morale and consequently to retain trainees in the speciality.

13

LEADERSHIP DIAGNOSTICS AND REFLECTIONS ON PERSONAL LEADERSHIP DEVELOPMENT

Michael Robinson and Eleni Lekoudis

Leadership is a complex concept without a universal definition (Grint, 2000), although it might be best defined as a process whereby an individual influences and motivates people to achieve a common goal (Northouse, 2007; King's Fund, 2011). Leadership differs from management by using influence rather than hierarchical authority (Edmonstone, 2009) and promoting change rather than stability (Kent, 2005).

With global austerity, and rising costs of healthcare worldwide, there is a continued interest in leadership research (Mumford, 2011) to identify the most effective leadership approach to produce an engaged medical workforce. At the same time there is an ever-growing demand for high-quality leadership development, especially for clinicians, to deliver the changes required to transform healthcare into a more integrated system and to improve and create a sustainable NHS (NHS Confederation, 2009; King's Fund, 2011; Edmonstone, 2009). Arguably, the lack of medical involvement in NHS leadership and management has been one of its defining weaknesses (King's Fund, 2011). This chapter will explore how a particular type of 'medical leadership', grounded in practice and supported by reflection is the way forward. The use of facilitated reflection in different forms can be a useful process for doctors to become more effective medical leaders, particularly in the area of driving forward quality improvement and service development initiatives.

Empirical research demonstrates that service improvements are likely to succeed when they are clinically led (Mountford and Webb, 2009) by leaders who are authentic, relying upon their credibility and integrity to develop trust (Edmonstone, 2009). In a UK context, Sir Ian Carruthers (2007) outlined the importance of the engagement of clinical leaders in the service improvement process as they play a vital role in building public and patient confidence. He also concluded that those areas that do not have such strong clinical and frontline leadership face criticism that proposals are primarily motivated for financial or managerial reasons, rather than by patient safety or quality of care.

Xiragasar and colleagues (2005) go on to identify which leadership styles more successfully influence doctors to achieve measurable clinical goals. Doctors are less likely to be influenced by someone who simply occupies a particular hierarchical position and more likely to respond to individuals who influence others through their personality and power of persuasion. To a large degree, getting doctors interested in re-engineering service delivery involves persuasion that is often informal, one doctor at a time, and interactive over time.

Alimo-Metcalfe (2005) described the six factors of leadership as valuing individuals, networking and achieving, enabling, acting with integrity, being accessible and being decisive.

Leadership styles

Transformational or transactional leadership

The most commonly explored leadership style paradigm is that of transformational versus transactional leadership. There is a general acceptance that the transformational leadership style is associated with better outcomes and performances across a wide range of business, educational and public sector contexts, borne out by several large meta-analyses such as that by Judge and Piccolo (2004). Transformational leadership for healthcare has been promoted by some who argue it is most effective at influencing others to accept change (Dickinson and Ham, 2008; Department of Health, 2009). Leaders and followers engage in a mutual process of raising one another to higher levels of morality and motivation according to Burns (1978). Bass and Avolio (1994) described the four essential components of transformational leadership as charisma or idealised influence, inspirational motivation, intellectual stimulation and individualised consideration.

The contingent rewards offered by leaders to others in return for compliance may have a positive effect on followers' satisfaction and performance (Burke et al., 2006). However, the main limitation of transactional leadership is the prevailing assumption that a person will be largely motivated by money and simple reward, and hence that their behaviour is predictable (Johnson, 2014).

Situational leadership

Situational leadership occurs when leaders adapt their leadership style to manage particular situations (Crevani et al., 2010). The core competencies of situational leaders are the ability to identify the performance, competence and commitment of others and to be flexible (Lynch et al., 2011).

Goleman (2000) analysed a leader's emotional intelligence and identified six different leadership styles, and it seems likely that most leaders would adapt their style according to the situation. Commanding leaders are driven, self-controlled individuals who demand immediate compliance. Authoritative leaders mobilise people towards a vision. Their style works best when a clear direction is needed and often acts like a 'change catalyst'. On the contrary, affiliative leaders create emotional bonds and harmony within the team. They tend to be empathetic, calm individuals with excellent communication skills and time to listen to the team's suggestions. Similarly, democratic leaders build consensus through encouraging the participation of all team members. They focus on achieving results through collaboration, good communication and input from valued employees. Pace-setting leaders expect excellence and self-direction, setting high standards of performance. They provide initiative and have a drive to achieve by leading a highly motivated team. Finally, coaching leaders develop people for the future by increasing self-awareness and asking the right questions at the right time in order to assist the followers to improve performance or develop long-term strengths.

Distributed leadership

Distributed leadership should improve organisational performance by enabling collaboration, which challenges the stability associated with the traditional role culture and promotes innovative change (Kean and Haycock-Stuart, 2011). However, caution is needed in assuming that distributing leadership automatically leads to organisational improvement, as much of its potential benefits depend upon the reasons for, and the method of, distributing it (Harris et al., 2007) and asking the right questions at the right time in order to assist the followers to improve performance or develop longer-term strengths. Chapman and colleagues (2014) reported self-assessment of use of Goleman's leadership styles in a cohort of clinical and medical directors and found that democratic and affiliative styles predominated.

Change agents who use hierarchical authority often resist ideas and counter offers from followers, and so may be as responsible for failed change initiatives as others' so-called resistance. Distributing leadership generates dialogue which helps to create 'multi-authored' change: this is more sustainable than the unquestioning acceptance of top-down directives (Thomas, 2011).

Ideal leadership style for doctors

Transformational leadership for healthcare has been promoted by some who argue it is most effective at influencing others to accept change (Dickinson and Ham, 2008; Department of Health, 2009), but this emphasis on transformational leadership should be questioned. First, it seems that the criticisms of the heroic model of leadership could also apply to the idea that only charismatic transformational leaders (Bass, 1985) are capable of medical leadership.

Second, it is not clear if distributed and transformational leadership are separate entities and can co-exist or if one is a sub-set of the other (Timperley, 2005). In either case, distributed leadership seems to have a better conceptual basis in healthcare. O'Brien et al. (2008) argue that transactional and directive doctors fail to motivate other healthcare professionals and so doctors who distribute leadership are 'transformational'. In this sense, 'transformational' relates to the collaboration associated with distributed leadership rather than charisma, and this emphasis on shared leadership seems more suited to healthcare organisations given the interdependence of healthcare professionals (Johns, 2010).

Finally, transformational leaders lacking moral values are exploitative, self-consumed and destructive (Sun and Anderson, 2011), and this pseudo-transformational leadership may promote harmful change. As such, moral values clearly have a role in medical leadership, and this is not necessarily apparent in traditional transformational theory.

If we conclude that the emphasis should be on distributed, rather than transformational leadership, we need to consider how leadership is distributed. Tyler and De Cremer (2005) argue that ensuring procedural justice by making accurate evaluations and acting consistently at all times will enable followers to accept change. However, this rational decision making ignores the importance of values and beliefs (Hernandez et al., 2010; Sun and Anderson, 2011). Indeed, the best clinical leaders behave authentically by endlessly examining their beliefs and relying upon their credibility and integrity to develop trust (Edmonstone, 2009). Acting on beliefs and values motivates, positively influences and increases the optimism of others (Kean and Haycock-Stuart, 2011).

Although authentic and distributed leadership styles address leadership of self and others, leadership is also needed at organisational levels and ideally should be strategic, where the performance and strategic choices of an organisation reflect the values, behaviours and thoughts of senior leaders (Hernandez et al., 2011; NHS Confederation, 2009).

Despite the benefit of strongly held values in leading others, values will improve organisational performance only if they are externally oriented on communities and patients (Ogbonna and Harris, 2000). Evidence shows that externally focused leaders increase physician engagement (Dickinson and Ham, 2008), create externally oriented organisational cultures (Ogbonna and Harris, 2000) and are more likely to deliver change than bureaucratic and internally focused leaders (Department of Health, 2009; NHS Confederation, 2009). Indeed, if leaders are capable of a high level of leadership of self, others and the organisation, they become transcendent and are more likely to deliver the best organisational performance (Crossen, 2008).

Leading across organisational boundaries in the external environment requires the additional consideration of how to foster multi-organisation collaboration, which is increasingly important due to the variety of healthcare provider organisations in the UK (Allen et al., 2011). For this, transformational leadership is also inadequate because there is no formal authority between diverse organisations (Sun and Anderson, 2011). Only by developing civic capacity, the means and motivation to bring together groups and organisations may leaders work to solve complex social problems across organisational boundaries (Sun and Anderson, 2011).

Leaders with civic capacity are motivated to be involved in social issues, are able to translate social opportunities into practical reality and, crucially, have widespread social connections (Sun and Anderson, 2011). Connectedness enables successful collaboration across organisational boundaries (King's Fund, 2011) and so is an increasing focus of leadership development especially by those seeking to influence policy and create systems change (Hoppe and Reinelt, 2010).

Thus, having considered medical leadership with a focus on leadership styles, we conclude that medical leaders should distribute leadership to ensure others are motivated, involved in decision making and inspired to change. They should be continually aware of their beliefs and values, acting on them authentically to develop trust. Medical leaders working to improve their organisations need to have an external focus and think strategically, but only by developing strong networks across organisational boundaries will medical leaders be capable of the multi-organisational collaboration required to engender positive system-wide change.

In order to develop as leaders it is important to have self-knowledge of one's own preferences and predilections across a range of behaviours (NHS Confederation, 2009). Although there are criticisms of self-assessment diagnostic tools, they can be valuable in aiding reflection, personal development and enabling personal adaptation of leadership style and approach. In Boxes 1 and 2, we provide two case studies exploring personal reflections on their use and value. Most of the diagnostic tools used here (Appendix 1) are based on traditional leadership theories, and not the more contemporary theories, which have had less time to become established and accepted as validated diagnostic tools. The tools require leaders, and occasionally their associates, to answer questions about the leader and their preferred ways of dealing with people, groups or situations.

BOX 1:   CASE STUDY 1 – PERSONAL REFLECTION ON LEADERSHIP STYLES

The 'what sort of leader are you' situational leadership and path-goal questionnaires help assess a leader's participatory style. They reveal that I have a strongly participatory style, which is reassuring considering the arguments for distributed leadership. Hernandez et al. (2011) emphasised the need to involve all team members equally in distributed leadership, and the outgroup questionnaire allows leaders to assess the extent they do this. I obtained an average score in the outgroup questionnaire, suggesting that, like many others, I may undervalue the inclusion of outgroup members. This has helped me realise that I should make greater efforts to include others with different opinions, but it is also interesting to consider why this might be the case.

Fielder's Least Preferred Co-worker (LPC) and the path-goal questionnaires may provide an answer, as both suggest I have a strong task- or achievement-oriented style. Although in isolation Fiedler's LPC is potentially questionable, because it may be skewed if the LPC is genuinely nasty, the path-goal questionnaire confirms my achievement-orientated style and on balance this is a characteristic I recognise. An achievement orientation would suggest that I might be frustrated by outgroup members, especially if I perceive them as obstructing progress and preventing the group from meeting its goals. This raises an interesting question about my empathy with outgroup members. Both the transformational leadership and leadership traits questionnaires ask about empathy and whilst both I and my associates believe I am empathetic, this is an area where I can probably improve. Arora et al. (2010) found that empathy in doctors was associated with improved interpersonal communication and improved patient satisfaction and so making greater attempts to empathise with others is likely to improve my own leadership of others.

Beyond managing outgroup members, an achievement orientation has other interesting connotations. Highly skilled professional jobs are often designed to stimulate a professional's intrinsic motivation (Johns, 2010), which includes achievement (Herzberg, 1959) and perhaps explains why autonomy is strongly valued by doctors (Dickinson and Ham, 2008). However, too great a level of autonomy may threaten effective team working, especially in highly interdependent healthcare organisations (Johns, 2010). Job design supporting high in-role performance might encourage individualism at the expense of the citizenship and ethical behaviour. Thus, high levels of autonomy may be at odds with distributed leadership, and perhaps doctors' historical autonomy has been detrimental to patients and the organisations that they work in. As teamwork is vital to securing patient safety in the theatre environment, my recent anaesthetic training has emphasised its importance, and I feel positive that completing this training has allowed me to strongly value effective team working. Understanding the theory underpinning distributed leadership and the challenge that high levels of autonomy may place on interdependent working is helpful in further developing my leadership style.

The managing conflict questionnaire provides additional learning about working with others and managing conflict. I have a consistent style with regards to compromise, collaboration and accommodation, and my high collaboration style is reassuring given the leadership theory. However, I appear to vary my levels of avoidance and competition depending on the situation. In a situation with conflict with my line manager, I have tended to use avoidance rather than competition; however, in a scenario without hierarchical authority, I tend to be more competitive, which is something I need to be aware of. Although appropriate at the time, an overuse of a competing conflict style may be at odds with the need to collaborate and share leadership.

Having considered my leadership style regarding distributed leadership and working with others, I will move on to discuss my core values. I answered the core values questionnaire before evaluating the leadership theories, which is interesting because my two core values are integrity and authenticity. These values are clearly linked with contemporary leadership theory, and it is reassuring that I rate these values highly.

Evidence from the leadership traits questionnaire shows that others and I perceive myself similarly most of the time. However, I feel less outgoing and confident than perhaps I should. My learning from contemporary leadership theory highlighted the importance of social ties and networks, and in order to develop this side of my leadership, I need to ensure that I am not inhibited in developing social networks.

Finally, the setting the tone questionnaire shows that I score above high-moderate for all of the setting the tone styles – building structure, clarifying norms, promoting excellence and building cohesiveness. I score especially high for promoting standards of excellence, which correlates with my achievement orientation and is also reassuring given the need for leaders to make quality their priority.

In summary, the tools have added some useful information regarding my leadership style. I am keen to distribute leadership and involve others but need to ensure I empathise with outgroup members to ensure I can involve them fully. I have a high achievement orientation, which is similar to many doctors, but I need to consider the potential conflict between team working and autonomy. I have values that are consistent with the medical leadership theory, but to develop my leadership, I need to ensure a lack of confidence does not inhibit broadening my social networks.

BOX 2: CASE STUDY 2 – PERSONAL REFLECTION ON LEADERSHIP STYLES

The completion of a range of leadership diagnostic questionnaires has helped me reflect on my leadership style and see myself through the eyes of others. It has highlighted certain areas that I need to work on in the future.

My conclusion, having completed the questionnaires and considering the leadership styles above, is that I am a situational leader. I can relate using all the above leadership styles depending on the situation; however, the style that I predominantly use is the democratic style.

My two most important core values deriving from the questionnaire are integrity and family.

I believe leadership styles are shaped within time and can change depending on the leader's personal and professional experiences. For example, had

I answered the same questionnaires when I first graduated from medical school, my results would be very different from now. Having been an Obstetrics and Gynaecology registrar and then becoming a Consultant in Obstetrics and Gynaecology, my personality and behaviour as a leader has changed due to the amount of responsibility that the role of a labour ward Consultant necessitates. When I am on call for the labour ward, I feel I am responsible for the well-being of staff and patients and can be authoritarian if things are not done my way. My team would expect me to lead in an emergency situation, and my patients would expect me to look after them in labour, delivering their baby safely. I, therefore, need to get the job done using the right tools within the right time frame to achieve a successful result.

When I am not on call, however, and I am taking part in a meeting, for example, my style is a lot more democratic, as I feel my role is to be part of the team, encouraging all members to speak and be part of a team decision. I would frequently use a coaching approach with junior doctors, as I feel that asking the right questions is more helpful than telling someone what to do. I recently had a situation where one of the junior doctors decided that Obstetrics and Gynaecology was not for her and was considering applying to another speciality. We had a lengthy chat about the pros and cons of each speciality and the kind of life she would like to have in the future. By asking the right questions and allowing her to answer, she discovered what was important for her and the kind of job she wanted to do. I felt she knew the answer all along but needed someone to coach her to facilitate her to come to her own understanding.

I would rarely use the laissez-faire leadership style unless I feel that a situation is under control and my input is not necessary. This is a situation I come across when I am asked to review patients in the midwifery-led part of the labour ward where normality is the golden standard and the labouring women are low risk from a medical point of view. I would, however, tend to try and 'medicalise' labour and increase observations to the mother or the baby despite the fact that the labour is progressing well 'just in case' I miss a disaster waiting to happen. I find it extremely difficult to do nothing. As doctors, we are asked to review patients who have complications, and as time goes by, experiences of new cases add to the medical 'paranoia'. Many a time I have found myself caring for an unwell patient in the high dependency unit, for example, and calling as soon as I get up in the morning to see what the blood results and observations have been overnight.

Leader or Leadership development?

Having undertaken leadership diagnostic questionnaires and reflected on our own personal development needs, the question arises: how can we as medical leaders develop our own leadership capability? It is important for every doctor to become aware of themselves, their default style of leadership and specific areas for personal development, while at the same time facilitating and supporting the development of others in the multi-professional team. There is, however, an important distinction between 'leader' development, with a concentration on developing a leader's inter-personal skills and abilities, and 'leadership' development, which is the development of social capital by building networked relationships and enhancing cooperation to create organisational value (Day, 2001; Bolden, 2007). Traditionally healthcare organisations have concentrated on leader, rather than leadership, development or others have supported multiprofessional 'leadership development' without 'leader' development. However, reflecting on our experience it is that both leader and leadership development are essential for doctors who must develop themselves to become the most effective medical leaders when working with others.

There are a variety of tools that may enable 'leader' development. First, mul-tisource feedback is a method of systematically collecting perceptions of an indi-vidual's performance from a variety of sources (Day, 2011), which encourages self-analysis and an exploration of leadership styles (Bolden, 2007).

Second, coaching, which involves practical, goal-focused, one-to-one learn-ing and behavioural change, attempts to enhance organisational performance by improving individual performance and personal satisfaction. Indeed, the effective-ness of multisource feedback may be improved by linking it to follow-up coach-ing, and coaching itself should increase a person's weak and strong network ties, so developing social capital (Day, 2011).

Third, mentorship is an ongoing personal developmental relationship compris-ing learning, dialogue and challenge between a mentor and a mentee (Day, 2011). This may be formal or informal and may involve colleagues who are direct line managers or in an unrelated role. A mentor in a similar work role may have greater understanding of the immediate context and help the mentee to consider specific leadership issues and other work aspects within that context. However, an unrelated mentor may be able to provide more generic support as an independent observer.

Fourth, networking, the development and strengthening of relationships amongst leaders (Day, 2001), is important for working across organisational boundaries and one of the principles of a learning organisation (Watson, 2007). It is important to make the most of opportunities for building relationships, for example, through regional peer Leadership Fellow networks (Hoppe and Reinelt, 2010). This can be challenging in the face of significant work commitments. At a national level, the Faculty of Medical Leaders and Managers (FMLM) is a field-policy leadership network (Hoppe and Reinelt, 2010) and has the capacity to influence and propose medical leadership policy and issues.

Finally, developing leaders should consider the possibility of postgraduate medi-cal leadership courses. Evidence shows that additional degree courses develop deeper and more strategic learning in medical students (McManus, 1999). Many courses combine theoretical learning with work-based and experiential learn-ing, allow networking with other leadership fellows and provide opportunities for

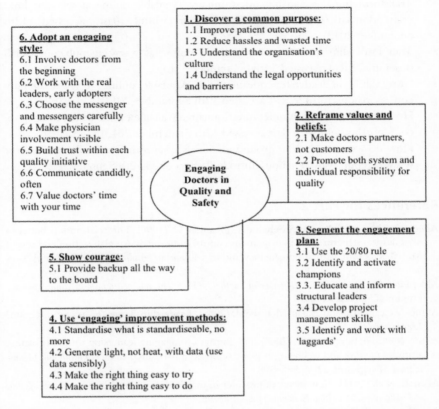

FIGURE 13.1   Reinertsen et al.'s (2007:4) framework for engaging doctors in quality and safety

reflection with action learning (Day, 2001), all of which stimulate learning and help to develop deep thinking (Gleeson, 2010).

Appendix 1 – Leadership diagnostic tools

- Leadership styles questionnaire 'What sort of leader are you?' Available online at www.sagepub.com/northouseintro2e (last accessed 12th September 2013).
- Fiedler's least preferred co-worker questionnaire. Available online at www. mindtools.com/pages/article/fiedler.htm (last accessed 12th September 2013).
- Situational leadership questionnaire. Available online at www.FlexibleTrain ingPartners.com (last accessed 12th September 2013).
- Path–goal questionnaire. Available online at www.sagepub.com/northou se6e/study/materials/Questionnaires/03409_07lq.pdf (last accessed 12th September 2013)

- Transformational leadership questionnaire. Available online at www.nwlink. com/~donclark/leader/transformational_survey.html (last accessed 12th September 2013).
- Trait leadership questionnaire Available online at www.sagepub.com/north ouseintro2e (last accessed 12th September 2013).
- Core values in leadership questionnaire. Available online at www.sagepub. com/northouseintro2e (last accessed 12th September 2013).
- How do you manage conflict questionnaire. Available online at www.sagepub. com/northouseintro2e (last accessed 12th September 2013).
- How do you manage 'out group individuals' questionnaire. Available online at www.sagepub.com/northouseintro2e (last accessed 12th September 2013).

References for Part 2

Abernethy, Margaret A., and Stoelwinder, Johannes U. (1990). The relationship between organisation structure and management control in hospitals: An elaboration and test of Mintzberg's professional bureaucracy model. *Accounting, Auditing & Accountability Journal*, 3(3).

Alderwick, H., et al. (2015). *Better value in the NHS – The role of changes in clinical practice.* London: The King's Fund.

Alimo-Metcalfe, B., and Alban-Metcalfe, J. (2005). Leadership: Time for a new direction? *Leadership*, 1(1), 51–71.

Alimo-Metcalfe, Beverly, et al. (2008). The impact of engaging leadership on performance, attitudes to work and wellbeing at work: A longitudinal study. *Journal of Health and Organization Management*, 22(6), 586–598.

Allen, P., et al. (2011). New forms of provider in the English national health service. *Annals of Public and Cooperative Economics*, 82(1), 77–95.

Appleby, J., et al. (2011). *Variations in health care: The good, the bad and the inexplicable.* London: The King's Fund.

Armit, K., and Roberts, H. (2009). Engaging doctors: The NHS needs the very best leaders. *Asia Pacific Journal of Health Management*, 4(2), 25.

Arora, S., et al. (2010). Emotional intelligence in medicine: A systematic review through the context of the ACGME competencies. *Medical Education*, 44, 749–764.

Arthur, W. B. (1989). Competing technologies: Increasing returns and lock in by historical events. *Economic Journal*, 99, 116–131. www.nhsemployers.org/EmploymentPolicyAnd Practice/staff-engagement/Staff-engagement-toolkit/Pages/Staff-engagement-toolkit. aspx.

Aube, Caroline, and Rousseau, Vincent. (2011, September). Interpersonal aggression and team effectiveness: The mediating role of team goal commitment. *Journal of Occupational and Organizational Psychology*, 84(3), 567.

Bambra, C. (2016). *Health divides: where you live can kill you.* University of Bristol, UK: Policy Press.

Bass, B. M. (1985). *Leadership and performance.* New York: Free Press.

Benjamin, S., Bloom, B. B. M., and Krathwohl, D. R. (1964). *Taxonomy of educational objectives.* New York, NY: David McKay.

Biddle, Bruce J. (1986). Recent development in role theory. *Annual Review of Sociology*, 67–92.

Blane, D. N., McLean, G., and Watt, G. (2015). Distribution of GPs in Scotland by age, gender and deprivation. (online). *Scottish Medical Journal*, 60(4), 214–219.

Bloom, Nicholas, et al. (2009). *Management practices in hospitals.* Manuscript. London: School of Economics.

Bloom, Nicholas, Sadun, Raffaella, and Van Reenen, John. (2013). *Does management matter in healthcare.* Centre for Economic Performance. www.semanticscholar.org

Bojke, C., et al. (2013). Regional variation in the productivity of the English national health service. (online). *Health Economics*, 22(2), 194–211.

Bolden, R. (2007). Trends and perspectives in management and leadership development. *Business Leadership Review*, IV(II), 1–13.

Boorman, S. (2009). *NHS staff and well-being – final report.* London: Department of Health.

Borrill, C., et al. (2001). *The effectiveness of health care teams in the national health service.* Birmingham: Aston Centre for Health Service Organization Research, Aston University.

Bruce, Allan, and Hill, Sandra. (1994). Relationships between doctors and managers: The Scottish experience. *Journal of Management in Medicine*, 8(5), 49–57.

Buchanan, D. A. (2000). An eager and enduring embrace: The ongoing rediscovery of teamworking as a management idea. In: Procter, Stephen, and Mueller, Frank (eds). *Teamworking.* Houndmills and London: Macmillan Business, pp. 25–42.

Buchanan, D., et al. (1997). Doctor in the process: The engagement of clinical directors in hospital management. *Journal of Management in Medicine*, 11, 132–156.

Buchanan, D. A., and Huczynski, A. A. (2010). Ecological framework for analyzing work team effectiveness. In: *Organizational behaviour*, 7th edition. London: Pearson, pp. 405–416.

Burke, S. C., Stagl, K. C., Klein, C., Goodwin, G. F., Salas, E., and Halpin, S. M. (2006). What type of leadership beahviours are functional in teams? A meta-analysis. *The Leadership Quarterly*, 17: 288–307.

Burns, J. M. (1978). *Leadership.* New York: Harper and Row.

Carruthers, Sir Ian. (2007). Presentation at the 'Clinical Leadership Health Summit' 28 February 2007. http://webarchive.nationalarchives.gov.uk/+/http://www.dh.gov.uk/en/Managingyourorganisation/Healthreform/DH_073231

Castro, Pedro J., Dorgan, Stephen J., and Richardson, Ben. (2008). A healthier health care system for the United Kingdom. *McKinsey Quarterly*. McKinsey & company. www.washburn.edu/faculty

Chapman, Ann LN, et al. (2014). Leadership styles used by senior medical leaders: patterns, influences and implications for leadership development. *Leadership in Health Services*, 27(4), 283–298.

Chassin, M. R., et al. (1987). Does inappropriate use explain geographic variations in the use of health care services? A study of three procedures. (online). *Journal of American Medical Association*, 258(18), 2533–2537.

Clark, J., Spurgeon, P., and Hamilton, P. (2008). Medical professionalism: Leadership competency – an essential ingredient. *International Journal of Clinical Leadership*, 16(1), 3–9.

Crevani, L., Lindgren, M., and Packendorff, J. (2010). Leadership, not leaders: on the study of leadership as practices and interactions. *Scandinavian Journal of Management*, 26, 77–86.

Crofts, J. F., et al. (2007). Change in knowledge of midwives and obstetricians following obstetric emergency training: A randomised controlled trial of local hospital, simulation centre and teamwork training. *BJOG*, 114(12), 1534–1541.

Crombie, Iain K., Irvine, Linda, Elliott, Lawrie, and Wallace, Hilary. (2005). *Closing the health inequalities gap: An international perspective. Other.* Denmark: World Health Organization Regional Office for Europe.

Crossen, M., Vera, D., and Nanjad, L. (2008). Transcendent leadership: Strategic leadership in dynamic environments. *The Leadership Quarterly*, 19, 569–581.

Currie, Graeme, and Procter, Stephen J. (2005). The antecedents of middle managers' strategic contribution: The case of a professional bureaucracy. *Journal of Management Studies*, 42(7), 1325–1356.

Dale, E.Y., and Cloyd, H. (1998). Contemporary theories. In: *High-performing self-managed work teams: A comparison of theory to practice by.* Thousand Oaks, CA: Sage Publications, p. 35.

The Dartmouth Institute for Health Policy and Clinical Practice. (2015). *Dartmouth atlas of health care.* (online). www.dartmouthatlas.org.

Davies, H.T., Hodges, C. L., and Rundall, T. G. (2003). Views of doctors and managers on the doctor–manager relationship in the NHS. *BMJ* (clinical research ed.), 326(7390), 626–628.

Day, David. (2001). Leadership development: A review in context. *The Leadership Quarterly*, 11(4), 581–613.

Day. (2011). *Leadership Development.* The Sage Handbook of Leadership. Sage Publications.

Deming, W. E. (ed.) (1993). *The new economics for industry, government, education,* 2nd edition. Cambridge, MA: MIT Press.

Department of Health. (2009). *Inspiring leaders: Leadership for quality.* https://eoeleadership. hee.nhs.uk/sites/default/files/1234220929_NbJb_inspiring_leaders_-_leadership_for_quality.pdf

Department of Health. (2010). *Equity and excellence: Liberating the NHS.* London: The Crown. (ISBN: 9780101788120).

Department of Health. (2012). *The NHS constitution.* London: The Crown. (2900013).

Dickinson, H., and Ham, C. (2008). *Engaging doctors in leadership: Review of the literature.* Birmingham: NHS Institute for Innovation and Improvement.

Donabedian, A. (1966). Evaluating quality of medical care. *Milbank Memorial Fund Quarterly*, 44(3), 166–206.

Donabedian, A. (1988). The quality of care: How can it be assessed? *Jama*, 260(12), 1743–1748.

Dorgan, Stephen, et al. (2010). *Management in healthcare: Why good practice really matters.* London: McKinsey and Company/London school of economics.

Draycott, T. J., Sibanda, T., Owen, L., Akande, V., Winter, C., Reading, S., and Whitelaw, A. Bjog. (2006 February). Dose training in obstetric emergencies improve neonatal outcome? *British Journal of Obstetrics and Gynecology*, 113(2), 177–182.

Draycott, T. J., Crofts, J. F., Ash, J. P., Wilson, L. V., Yard, E., Sibanda, T., Whitelaw, A. (2008 July). Improving neonatal outcome through practical shoulder dystocia training. *Obstetrics Gynecology*, 112(1), 14–20.

Edmonstone, J. (2009). Clinical leadership: The elephant in the room. *International Journal of Health Planning and Management*, 24, 290–305.

Elwyn, G., et al. (2010). Implementing shared decision making in the NHS. (online). *BMJ* (clinical research ed.), 341, c5146.

Erlandson, E., and Ludeman, K. (2003). Physician engagement and shared accountability: Buzzwords, dilemma or choice. *Michigan Health and Hospitals*, 39(6), 28–29.

Evans, R. G. (1990). The Dog in the night-time: Medical practice variations and health policy. In: Anderson, T. F., and Mooney, G. (eds). *The challenges of medical practice variations.* London: Palgrave Macmillan, pp. 117–152.

Fitzgerald, Louise, et al. (2006). *Managing change and role enactment in the professionalised organisation.* London: NCCSDO.

Fitzgerald, Louise, and Ferlie, Ewan. (2000). Professionals: Back to the future? *Human Relations*, 53(5), 713–739.

Forbes, T., Hallier, J., and Kelly, L. (2004). Doctors as managers: Investors and reluctants in a dual role. *Health Services Management Research*, 17(3), 167–176.

Francis, R. (2013 27 February). *Lessons from Stafford. The Francis inquiry: Assuring patient safety and quality across the system of care.* London: The Kings Fund.

Fryer, A. A., and Smellie, W. S. (2013). Managing demand for laboratory tests: A laboratory toolkit. (online). *Journal of Clinical Pathology*, 66(1), 62–72.

Gleeson, C. (2010). Education beyond competencies: A participative approach to professional development. *Medical Education*, 44, 404–411.

GMC. (2009). *Tomorrow's doctors*. (online). www.gmcuk.org/Tomorrow_s_Doctors_1214.pdf_48905759.pdf.

Goleman, D. (2000, March–April). Leadership that gets results. *Harvard Business Review*, 76–91. http://elibrary.kiu.ac.ug:8080/jspui/bitstream/1/480/1/Leadership%20That%20Gets%20Results.pdf.

Gollop, R., et al. (2004). Influencing sceptical staff to become supporters of service improvement: A qualitative study of doctors' and managers' views. *Quality and Safety in Health Care*, 13, 108–114.

Goodall, Amanda H. (2011). Physician-leaders and hospital performance: Is there an association? *Social Science & Medicine*, 73(4), 535–539.

Gosfield, A. G., and Reinertsen, J. L. (2010). *Achieving clinical integration with highly engaged clinicians*. Reinertsengroup.com

Gottlieb, D. J., et al. (2010). Prices don't drive regional Medicare spending variations. (online). *Health Affairs*, 29(3). http:\\content.healthaffairs.org.gate2.library.lse.ac.uk/cgi/reprint/2 9/3/537?maxtoshow=&hits=10&RESULTFORMAT=&fulltext=Gottlieb&andorexac tfulltext=and&searchid=1&FIRSTINDEX=0&resourcetype=HWCIT.

Gray, D., et al. (1990). Audit of coronary angiography and bypass surgery. (online). *The Lancet* (London, England), 335(8701), 1317–1320.

Greener, Ian, et al. (2011). *A realistic review of clinico-managerial relationships in the NHS: 1991–2010.* National institute for health research, service delivery & organisation programme. Netscc.ac.uk

Griffiths report. (1983). London: Department of Health and Social Security.

Grint, K. (2000). *The arts of leadership*. Oxford: Oxford University Press.

Guthrie, Michael. (2005). Engaging physicians in performance improvement. *American Journal of Medical Quality*, 20(5), 235–239.

Hackman, J. R. (1990). *Groups that work (and those that don't)*. San Francisco, CA: Jossey-Bass.

Hackman, J. Richard. (1987). The design of work teams. *Handbook of Organizational Behavior*, 315–342.

Hackman, J. R. (2001). Leading Teams: Setting the stage for great performances. *Harvard Business Review*.

Hallier, Jerry, and Forbes, Tom. (2005). The role of social identity in doctors' experiences of clinical managing. *Employee Relations*, 27(1), 47–70.

Halvorsen, Kristin. (2013). Team decision making in the workplace: A systematic review of discourse analytic studies. *Journal of Applied Linguistics & Professional Practice*, 7(3), 273–296.

Ham, C. (1988). *Healthcare variations: Assessing the evidence*. London: The King's Fund.

Ham, C. (2012). Why engagement matters. (online). www.kingsfund.org.uk/blog/2012/05/why-engagement-matters. (Posted 24 May 2012. (Accessed on 29 October 2012).

Ham, C., Berwick, D. M., and Dixon, J. (2016). *Improving quality in the English NHS – A strategy for action*. London: The King's Fund.

Ham, Chris. (2003). Improving the performance of health services: The role of clinical leadership. *The Lancet*, 361(9373), 1978–1980.

Ham, Chris, Kipping, Ruth, and McLeod, Hugh. (2003). Redesigning work processes in health care: Lessons from the national health service. *Milbank Quarterly*, 81(3), 415–439.

Harris, A., Leithwood, K., Day, C., Sammons, P., and Hopkins, D. (2007). Distributed leadership and organizational change: Reviewing the evidence. *Journal of Educational Change*, 8, 337–347.

Hart, J.T. (1971). The inverse care law. (online). *The Lancet*, 1(7696), 405–412.

Hernandez-Mogollon, R., Cepeda-Carrion, G., Cegarra-Navarro, J. G., and Leal-Millan, A. (2010). The role of cultural barriers in the relationship between open-mindedness and organisational innovation. *Journal of Organisational Change Management*, 23(4), 360–376.

Hernandez, M., et al. (2011). The loci and mechanisms of leadership: Exploring a more comprehensive view of leadership theory. *The Leadership Quarterly*, 22(6), 1165–1185.

Herzberg, F. (1959). *The motivation to work*. New York: John Wiley and Sons.

Hoff, Timothy J. (1999). The social organization of physician-managers in a changing HMO. *Work and Occupations*, 26(3), 324–351.

Hoppe, B., and Reinelt, C. (2010). Social network analysis and the evaluation of leadership networks. *The Leadership Quarterly*, 21, 600–619.

Joffe, Megan, and Mackenzie-Davey, Kate. (2012). The problem of identity in hybrid managers: Who are medical directors? *International Journal of Leadership in Public Services*, 8(3), 161–174.

Johanson, R., Akhtar, S., Edwards, C., Dewan, F., Haque, Y., Jones, P. Moet. (2002). Bangladesh – an initial experience. *Journal of Obstetrics Gynaecology Research*, 28, 217–223.

Johanson, R. B., Menon, V., Burns, E., Kargraymanya, E., Osipov, V., Israelyan, M., et al. (2002). Managing Obstetric Emergencies and Trauma (MOET) structured skills training in Armenia, utilising models and reality based scenarios. *BMC Medical Education*, 2(5).

Johns, G. (2010). Some unintended consequences of job design. *Journal Organizational Behaviour*, 31, 361–369.

Judge, T. A., and Piccolo, R. F. (2004). Transformational and transactional leadership: A meta-analytic test of their relative validity. *Journal of Applied Psychology*, 89(5), 755–768.

Kahn, William A. (1990). Psychological conditions of personal engagement and disengagement at work. *Academy of Management Journal*, 33(4), 692–724.

Kahn, William A. (1992). To be fully there: Psychological presence at work. *Human Relations*, 45(4), 321–349.

Kean, S., and Haycock-Stuart, E. (2011). Understanding the relationship between followers and leaders. *Nursing Management*, 18(8), 31–35.

Kent, T. W. (2005). Leading and managing: It takes two to Tango. *Management Decision*, 3(7/8), 1010–1017.

Keroack, M. A., et al. (2007). Organizational factors associated with high performance in quality and safety in academic medical centers: Academic medicine. *Journal of the Association of American Medical Colleges*, 82(12), 1178–1186.

King's Fund. (2011). *The future of leadership and management in the NHS: No more heroes*. London: The King's Fund.

King's Fund. (2012a). *Long-term conditions and multi-morbidity*. (online). www.kingsfund.org.uk/time-to-think-differently/trends/disease-and-disability/long-term-conditions-multi-morbidity.

Kings Fund. (2012b). *Leadership and engagement for improvement in the NHS*. London: The Kings Fund.

Kippist, L., and Fitzgerald, A. (2009). Organisational professional conflict and hybrid clinician managers: the effects of dual roles in Australian health care organisations. *Journal of Health Organisation and Management* 23(6), 642–655.

Kippist, L., and Fitzgerald, A. (2010). The paradoxical role of the hybrid clinician manager. In: *Mind the gap: Policy and practice in the reform of healthcare 7th biennial conference in organisational behaviour in health care*. Birmingham: University of Birmingham.

Kirkpatrick, D. (1998). *Evaluating training programs: The four levels*, 2nd edition. San Francisco, CA: Berrett-Kochler Publishers.

Laschinger, Heather K. Spence, and Leiter, Michael P. (2006). The impact of nursing work environments on patient safety outcomes: The mediating role of burnout engagement. *Journal of Nursing Administration*, 36(5), 259–267.

Leape, L. L., et al. (1990). Does inappropriate use explain small-area variations in the use of health care services? (online). *Jama*, 263(5), 669–672.

Lord Carter of Coles. (2008). *Report of the second phase of the review of NHS pathology services in England.* London: Department of Health.

Lord Carter of Coles. (2016). *Operational productivity and performance in English NHS acute hospitals: Unwarranted variations.* An independent report for the Department of Health by Lord Carter of Coles. London: Information Policy Team, The National Archives, Department of Health.

Love, T., and Ehrenberg, N. (2014a). *Addressing Unwarranted Variation: Literature Review on Methods for Influencing Practice.* Published April 2014 by the Health Quality & Safety Commission, PO Box 25496, Wellington 6146, New Zealand ISBN: 978-0-478-38568-7 (print) ISBN: 978-0-478-38569-4. (online). www.hqsc.govt.nz. (online). New Zealand, Health Quality & Safety Commission, Wellington, New Zealand. www.hqsc.govt.nz/ assets/Health-Quality-Evaluation/PR/Variation-literature-review-on-methods-for-influencing-practice-May-2014.pdf.

Love, T., and Ehrenberg, N. (2014b). *Variation and improving services: Analysing and interpreting variation.* New Zealand: Health Quality and Safety Commission, Sapere Research Group. hqsc.govt.nz.

Lynch, B. M., McCormack, B., and McCance, T. (2011). Development of a model of situational leadership in residential care for older people. *Journal of Nursing Management*, Nov: 19(8) 1058–1069.

Macey, William H., and Schneider, Benjamin. (2008). The meaning of employee engagement. *Industrial and Organizational Psychology*, 1(1), 3–30.

Macleod, D., and Clarke, N. (2009a). *Engaging for success: Enhancing performance through employee engagement.* London: Department for Business Innovation and Skills.

Macleod, David, and Clarke, Nita. (2009b). *Engaging for success: Enhancing performance through employee engagement: A report to government.* London: Department for Business, Innovation and Skills.

Marchington, M., and Wilkinson, A. (2005). *Human resource management at work*, 3rd edition. London: Chartered Institute of Personnel and Development.

The Marmot Review. (2010). *Fair society, healthy lives.* (online). www.instituteofhealthequity. org/projects/fair-society-healthy-lives-the-marmot-review.

Maslach, C., and Leiter, M. (2008). Early predictors of job burnout and engagement. *Journal of Applied Psychology*, 93, 498–512.

Maslach, Christina. (2003). Job burnout new directions in research and intervention. *Current Directions in Psychological Science*, 12(5), 189–192.

Maslach, Christina, Jackson, Susan E., and Leiter, Michael P. (1997). Maslach burnout inventory. *Evaluating Stress: A Book of Resources*, 3, 191–218.

McCoubrie, P. (2004). Improving the fairness of multiple-choice questions: A literature review. *Medical Teacher*, 26, 709–712.

McLean, G., et al. (2015). General Practice funding underpins the persistence of the inverse care law: Cross-sectional study in Scotland. (online). *British Journal of General Practice*, 65(641), 799–805.

McManus, I. C., Richards, P., and Winder, B. C. (1999). Intercalated degrees, learning styles, and career preferences: Prospective longitudinal study of UK medical students. *British Medical Journal*, 319, 542–546.

Mgbere, O. (2009). Exploring the relationship between organizational culture, leadership styles and corporate performance: An overview. *Journal of Strategic Management Education*, 5(3/4), 187–202.

Mintzberg, Henry. (1979). Structuring of organizations: A synthesis of the research. In: Mintzberg, Henry (ed). *Theory of management policy series.* Prentice-Hall. https://www.nrc.gov/ docs/ML0907/ML090710600.pdf

Mo, Tone Opdahl. (2008). Doctors as managers: Moving towards general management? The case of unitary management reform in Norwegian hospitals. *Journal of Health, Organisation and Management*, 22(4), 400–415.

Mohapel, P., and Dickson, G. (2007). *Physician engagement: Principles to maximise physician partici-pation in the health care system.* Victoria, BC: The Centre of Health Leadership and Research.

Monitor. (2013). *NHS foundation trust annual reporting manual.* (online). www.monitor-nhsft. gov.uk/home/news-events-publications/our-publications/browse-category/guidance-health-care-providers-and-co-25. (Accessed on 3 June 2013).

Mountford, James, and Webb, Caroline. (2009). When clinicians lead. *McKinsey Quarterly.* McKinsey United states.

Mulley, A. L. (2011). *Learning from variations to increase value for money in the NHS.* (online). www.kingsfund.org.uk/blog/2011/07/learning-variations-increase-value-money-nhs.

Mulley, A. L., Trimble, C., and Elwyn, G. (2012). *Patients' preferences matter – Stop the silent misdiagnosis.* London: The King's Fund.

Mullins, L. (2010). *Management and organisational behaviour,* 9th edition. Harlow: Prentice Hall.

Mumford, M. D. (2011). A hale farewell: The state of leadership research. *The Leadership Quarterly,* 22, 1–7.

National Audit Office. (2010). *Tackling inequalities in life expectancy in areas with the worst health and deprivation.* (online). www.nao.org.uk/wp-content/uploads/2010/07/1011186.pdf.

Newman, Daniel A., and Harrison, David A. (2008). Been there, bottled that: Are state and behavioral work engagement new and useful construct "wines"? *Industrial and Organiza-tional Psychology,* 1(1), 31–35.

NHS Atlas of Variation in Healthcare for people with liver disease. (2013). Reducing unwar-ranted variation to increase value and improve quality.

NHS Choices. (2013). *Mortality ratios; deaths in hospitals.* (online). www.nhs.uk/scorecard/Pages/IndicatorFacts.aspx?MetricId=95 HYPERLINK "www.nhs.uk/scorecard/Pages/IndicatorFacts.aspx?MetricId=95&OrgType=5" & HYPERLINK "www.nhs.uk/scorecard/Pages/IndicatorFacts.aspx?MetricId=95&OrgType=5"OrgType=5. (Accessed 19 May 2013).

NHS Confederation. (2009). *Future of leadership: Reforming leadership development . . . again.* London: NHS Confederation Publications.

NHS Employers. (2013). *Staff engagement toolkit.* (online). (Accessed on 19 May 2013).

NHS England. (2013). *2013/2014 standard contract.* (online). www.england.nhs.uk/nhs-standard-contract/. (Accessed on 3 June 2013).

NHS Right Care. (2015). *Diagnostics: The NHS atlas of variation in diagnostic services.* (online). www.rightcare.nhs.uk/index.php/atlas/diagnostics-the-nhs-atlas-of-variation-in-diagnostics-services/.

NHS Workforce Project. (2007 July). *Maximising Staff Engagement.* http://www.em-online. com/download/medical_article/36269_nwp%20max%20staff%20engag%20brief-ing%20v5%20in%20-%20final.pdf

Northouse, P. (2007). *Leadership: Theory and practice,* 4th edition. London: Sage Publications.

Nuti, S., and Seghieri, C. (2014). Is variation management included in regional healthcare governance systems? Some proposals from Italy. (online). *Health Policy* (Amsterdam, Netherlands), 114(1), 71–78.

O'Brien, J., Martin, D., Heyworth, J., and Meyer, N. (2008). Negotiating transformational leadership: A key to effective collaboration. *Nursing and Health Sciences,* 10, 137–143.

O'Connor, G. T., et al. (1999). Geographic variation in the treatment of acute myocardial infarction: The cooperative cardiovascular project. (online). *Jama,* 281(7), 627–633.

Ogbonna, E., and Harris, L. C. (2000). Leadership style, organizational culture and perfor-mance: Empirical evidence from UK companies. *International Journal of Human Resource Management,* 11(4), 766–788.

Ovretveit, J. (1996). Medical participation in and leadership of quality programmes. *Journal of Management in Medicine*, 10(5), 21–28.

Oxford English Dictionary. (2012). (online). http://oxforddictionaries.com/definition/eng lish/engagement?q=engagement. (Accessed on 11 December 2012).

Parand, A., et al. (2010). Medical engagement in organisation-wide safety and quality-improvement programmes: Experience in the UK safer patients initiative. *Quality & Safety in Health Care*, 19(5), e44.

Paul-Shaheen, P., Clark, J. D., and Williams, D. (1987). Small area analysis: A review and analysis of North American literature. *Journal of Health Politics, Policy and Law*, 12(4), 741.

Practical Obstetric Multiprofessional Training. www.promptmaternity.org. (Accessed on 12 June 2016).

Propper, C., Sutton, M., Whitnall, C. and Windmeijer, F. (2007). Did 'targets and terror' reduce waiting times in England for hospital care? Working paper No. 07/179 published in the *B.E. Journal of Economic Analysis and Policy* 8(1), Article 5 (2008) published as Public Service Programme Discussion paper number 0706 (2007).

RCGP. (2013b). *A core curriculum for learning about health inequalities in UK undergraduate medicine.* (online). www.rcgp.org.uk/policy/rcgp-policy-areas/~/media/Files/Policy/A-Z-policy/RCGP-A-Core-Curriculum-for-Learning-About-Health-Inequalites-in-UK-Undergraduate-Medicine.ashx.

RCGP. (2015a). *Health inequalities.* (online). www.rcgp.org.uk/policy/rcgp-policy-areas/~/media/Files/Policy/A-Z-policy/2015/Health%20Inequalities.ashx.

RCGP. (2015b). *Patient access to general practice.* (online). www.rcgp.org.uk/policy/rcgp-policy-areas/access-to-general-practice.aspx.

RCGP. (2016a). *The RCGP curriculum: Professional & clinical modules.* (online). www.rcgp.org.uk/training-exams/gp-curriculum-overview/~/media/Files/GP-training-and-exams/Curriculum-2012/RCGP-Curriculum-modules.ashx.

RCGP. (2016b). *General practice forward view.* (online). www.england.nhs.uk/wp-content/uploads/2016/04/gpfv.pdf.

RCGP and University of Birmingham. (2013a). *Improving access to health care for gypsies and travellers, homeless people and sex workers.* (online). www.rcgp.org.uk/news/2013/december/~/media/Files/Policy/A-Z-policy/RCGP-Social-Inclusion-Commissioning-Guide.ashx.

RCPCH. (2011 December–2012 March). *Rota vacancies and compliance survey findings.* Royal College of Paediatrics and Child Health. www.rcpch.ac.uk/sites/default/files/user31401/Rota%20vacancies%20and%20compliance%20Winter%202011.pdf. (Accessed on 17 August 2016).

RCPCH. (2015/2016 Winter). *Paediatric Rota vacancies and compliance survey.* 2016. Royal College of Paediatrics and Child Health. www.rcpch.ac.uk/sites/default/files/user31401/Rota%20vacancies%20and%20compliance%20survey%20-%20FINAL.pdf. (Accessed on 17 August 2016).

Reinertsen, J. L., Gosfield, A. G., Rupp, W., and Whittington, J. W. (2007). *Engaging physicians in a shared quality agenda.* IHI innovation series white paper. Cambridge, MA: Institute for Healthcare Improvement.

Santos, M. (2013). *Variation in healthcare processes: Implications for quality of care.* PhD, Chalmers University of Technology, Göteborg, Sweden.

Scantlebury, R., et al. (2015). Socioeconomic deprivation and accident and emergency attendances: Cross sectional analysis of general practices in England. (online). *British Journal of General Practice*, 65(639), 649–654.

Schaufeli, Wilmar B., et al. (2002). Burnout and engagement in university students a cross-national study. *Journal of Cross-Cultural Psychology*, 33(5), 464–481.

Scholes, K., Johnson, G., and Whittington, R. (2011). *Exploring strategy: Text & cases.* 9th edition. Harlow: Pearson Education.

Schuwirth, L. W., Van der Vleuten, C. P., Stoffers, H. E., and Peperkamp, A. G. (1996). Computerized long-menu questions as an alternative to open ended questions in computerized assessment. *Medical Education*, 30, 50–55.

Scotland Deep End Group. (2010). *Deep end report 7 general practitioner training in very deprived areas.* (online). www.gla.ac.uk/media/media_153245_en.pdf.

Scotland Deep End Group. (2016). (online). www.gla.ac.uk/researchinstitutes/healthwell being/research/generalpractice/deepend/.

Scottish Government. (2012). *Scottish index of multiple deprivation.* (online). http://simd.scot land.gov.uk/publication-2012/.

Senge, P. M. (1990). *The fifth discipline.* New York, NY: Doubleday.

Shaw, C. (2003). *How can hospital performance be measured and monitored?* Copenhagen: WHO Regional Office for Europe (Health Evidence Network Report).

Singh, Jagdip. (1998). Striking a balance in boundary-spanning positions: An investigation of some unconventional influences of role stressors and job characteristics on job outcomes of salespeople. *The Journal of Marketing*, 69–86.

Spehar, Ivan, Frich, Jan C., and Kjekshus, Lars Erik. (2014). Clinicians in management: A qualitative study of managers' use of influence strategies in hospitals. *BMC Health Services Research*, 14(1), 1.

Spurgeon, Peter, Barwell, Fred, and Mazelan, Patti. (2008). Developing a medical engagement scale (MES). *The International Journal of Clinical Leadership*, 16(4), 213–223.

Spurgeon, P., Mazelan, P. M., and Barwell, F. (2011). Medical engagement: A crucial underpinning to organizational performance. *Health Services Management Research*, 24(3), 114–120.

Sun, Pyt, and Anderson, M. H. (2011). Civic capacity: Building on transformational leadership to explain successful integrative public leadership. *The Leadership Quarterly 2011*. doi10.1016/j.leaqua.2011.05.018.

Sundstrom, E., de Meuse, K. P., and Furtell, D. (1990). Work teams: Applications and effectiveness. *American Psychologist*, 120–133.

Taitz, Jonathan M., Lee, Thomas H., and Sequist, Thomas D. (2012). A framework for engaging physicians in quality and safety. *BMJ Quality & Safety*, 21(9), 722–728.

Thomas, R., Sargent, L. D., and Hardy, C. (2011). Managing organizational change: Negotiating meaning and power-resistance relations. *Organization Science*, 22(1), 22–41.

Timperley, H. S. (2005). Distributed leadership: Developing theory from practice. *Journal of Curriculum Studies*, 37(4), 395–420.

Tudor Hart, Julian. (1971). *The inverse care law.* (online). www.sochealth.co.uk/ national-health-service/public-health-and-wellbeing/poverty-and-inequality/ the-inverse-care-law/.

Tyler, T. R., and De Cremer, D. (2005). Process-based leadership: Fair procedures and reactions to organizational change. *The Leadership Quarterly*, 16, 529–545.

Watson, M. (2007). Knowledge management in health and social care. *Journal of Integrated Care*, 15(1), 27–33.

Watt, G. (2013). What can the NHS do to prevent and reduce health inequalities? (online). *British Journal of General Practice*, 63(614), 494–495.

Weiner, B., Alexander, J., and Shortell, S. (1996). Leadership for quality improvement in healthcare: Empirical research on hospital boards, managers and physicians. *Medical Care Research and Review*, 53, 397–416.

Wennberg, D. (2006, May). Pay-for-performance through the lens of unwarranted variation in the delivery of health care. *Health Watch*, 52.

Wennberg, J. E. (1999). Understanding geographic variations in health care delivery. (online). *The New England Journal of Medicine*, 340(1), 52–53.

Wennberg, J. E. (2010). *Tracking medicine: A researcher's quest to understand health care*, 1st edition. New York: Oxford University Press.

Wennberg, J. E. and Cooper, M. (1998). *The Dartmouth atlas of health care*. Chicago: AHA Publishing Inc.

Wennberg, J. E., Fisher, E. S., and Skinner, J. S. (2002). Geography and the debate over Medicare reform. *Health Affairs*.

Wennberg, John E. (2014). Forty years of unwarranted variation – And still counting. (online). *Health Policy*, 114(1), 1–2.

West, M., and Dawson, J. (2012). *Employee engagement and NHS performance*. London: The Kings Fund.

West, M., et al. (2002). The link between the management of employees and patient mortality in acute hospitals. *International Journal of Human Resource Management*, 13, 1299–1310.

West, M., et al. (2006). Reducing patient mortality in hospitals: The role of human resource management. *Journal of Organizational Behavior*, 27, 983–1002.

Wilkinson, J., Powell, A., and Davies, H. (2011). *Are clinicians engaged in quality improvement?* London: The Health Foundation.

Willcocks, Stephen. (1994). The clinical director in the NHS: Utilizing a role-theory perspective. *Journal of Management in Medicine*, 8(5), 68–76.

Winchester, D. E., et al. (2014). Clinician-dependent variations in inappropriate use of myocardial perfusion imaging: Training, specialty, and location. (online). *Journal of Nuclear Cardiology: Official Publication of the American Society of Nuclear Cardiology*, 21(3), 598–604.

Xiragasar, Sudha, Samuels, Michael E., Stoskopf, Carleen H. (2005). Physician leadership styles and effectiveness: An empirical study. *Medical Care Research and Review*, 62, 720–740.

Yorkshire & Humber GPs at the Deep End. (2016). (online). https://yorkshiredeependgp.org/.

PART 3

Improvement science, medical leadership and measurement for improvement

14

AN INTRODUCTION

Jill Aylott

Management Science is defined as a multidisciplinary and interdisciplinary approach to problem solving and decision making in industry, manufacturing and all human services organisations. However, the term *Improvement Science* is much more likely to be used in healthcare and is defined as "*finding out how to improve and make changes in the most cost-effective way. It is about systematically examining the methods and factors that best work to facilitate quality improvement*" (Health Foundation, 2011:3). Improvement science suggests the use of evidence-based models and approaches and underpinning theories. The emphasis is on data collection and statistical analysis, drawing upon various scientific methods (Deming, 2000). Applying the skills of Improvement Science is critical to effectively utilising Quality Improvement methods and is often used in association with The Model for Improvement (Table 14.1; IHI, 2003) to develop 'profound knowledge' about how systems can be improved in relation to four component parts: appreciation of the system; knowledge of variation in the system; the theory of knowledge and the limits of what can be known and the knowledge of psychology (Peden and Rooney, 2009)

The use of descriptive statistics (with a minimum sample of 30) used in conjunction with run charts and/or statistical process control are the data collection and analysis methods of choice that can support the PDSA process (Table 14.1). Such data can also be an effective tool to use with individuals and teams for quality performance evaluation (Deming, 2000; Wrazen and Soliman, 2017:85) to enable effective benchmarking in pursuit of continuous quality improvement and steering a service towards a culture of quality (Deming, 1986). PDSA cycles are a flexible and dynamic tool to support a process that enables team learning from process changes in the quality improvement process. As healthcare is delivered from within complex systems, small adaptive monthly changes can be undertaken and evaluated with the use of data, collected within specific, measurable and evidence-based methods (Reed and Card, 2015).

TABLE 14.1 The Model for Improvement

Plan –	What are we trying to accomplish?
	How will we know that a change is an improvement?
Do –	What change can we make that will result in an improvement?
Study –	Measure to find out if the change has made an improvement
Act –	Implement the change in practice

Source: Adapted from Deming (2000) and Langley et al. (2009).

The aim of Part 3 of this book is to explore key issues relating to measurement for improvement within Improvement Science and to support the development of an awareness of the broader principles of the management of data within improvement science. It has been reported that the skills and expertise required for the collection of high-quality data and analysis for improvement are sufficiently underdeveloped in some areas of healthcare with information and data specialists having a critical role to play in supporting organisation-wide change programmes (Crisp, 2017).

This section explores a model of joint and multidisciplinary working, proposed by Lisa Fox which seeks to explore the complimentary roles between data analysts, managers and medical leaders, drawing upon Self Determination Theory (SDT) (Deci and Ryan, 1985, 2000; Ryan and Deci, 2000) to help explain this joint approach. Adam Burns outlines the use of Root Cause Analysis (RCA) and proposes how this method can be better utilised to create a greater generation of 'profound knowledge' (Peden and Rooney, 2009) and organisational learning (Senge, 2006) with the use of simulation training.

We then examine improvement science in an applied way in relation to three concepts from systems theory: the Microsystem (The system closest to the individual); Mesosystem (Relationships amongst the systems in an environment) and, finally, the Macrosystem (a larger system that influences the infrastructure such as policies, administration of entitlement programmes and culture).

First we examine the use of data for improvement at the individual level (the micro level), where Prosenjit Giri examines how personalised leadership diagnostic self-assessment tools can create effective data for planning for personal development goals. Such personal development for personal improvement is required to enable medical leaders to build capability to engage with quality improvement projects within the organisation. This section draws upon work undertaken by Prosenjit, who has researched a wide range of leadership development tools freely available from the internet and tested them on himself, reflecting upon their usefulness for doctors to develop self-awareness of their own medical leadership skills. We explore how such tools can be used to reflect upon one's own development for professional revalidation purposes. Although it is not the scope of this chapter, such broader use of leadership diagnostic tools can be used with a collective group of clinicians to help them self-determine and design their own bespoke medical leadership programme to meet the individual, group and organisation's needs (Nassef et al., 2017:31; Giri et al., 2017).

Second, Prakash Subedi and colleagues look at the meso environment and how data can be collected within a process of continuous quality improvement at an Emergency Medicine Department within a hospital. We examine how the multiple stakeholders of doctors, nurses, managers and patients within a meso system can be supported to engage in a process of quality improvement through a Continuous Quality Improvement Collaborative (CQIC) by using the regular collection and analysis of data and feedback as a vehicle to foster collaboration for change. We then examine how this process of data collection and analysis can create a system of continuous quality improvement collaborative (CQIC) to address some of the difficult and challenging everyday problems in an Emergency Medicine department in a UK hospital. Prakash Subedi set up the CQIC to facilitate the monthly collection of data from the A&E shop floor based on specific problems that were presented to him and encountered by patients and frontline staff. This medical leadership initiative provides an example of collaborative and shared leadership, where all stakeholders including patients, staff, porters, receptionists, nurses and doctors participate in the collection of data to explore specific everyday problems occurring in a busy A&E department.

Finally, Pukar C. Shrestha shares the learning and insight into his role as a renal surgeon who engaged with the macro-system perspective across the wider political, economic, social, technical and legal macro environment in his home country of Nepal. He set up a successful human transplantation health system in Nepal, which required a broader understanding of data from social and political systems to challenge cultural, social and economic healthcare inequalities.

Acquiring skills in data collection and data analysis for quality and system improvement across the micro, meso and macro environments largely involves the acquiring of technical skills and will mostly involve the development of individual clinician skills in statistical analysis with the competent use of Excel spreadsheets. Using data to motivate and engage other clinicians and teams will require getting 'buy-in' from team colleagues to support specific strategies for improvement. This requires effective Medical Leadership strategies, which will involve drawing upon a range of leadership theories, models and perspectives outlined in Part 1 of this book. Determining which leadership strategies to use and 'how' to use them first requires the development of an awareness of one's own leadership and management skills, style and behaviour (Goleman, 2000) and a reflection on self as explored in Chapter 13.

15

DATA ANALYSTS BUILDING CAPABILITY IN PARTNERSHIP WITH MEDICAL LEADERS

Lisa Fox

All clinicians are now expected to engage in quality improvement projects, and the UK specialty training programmes for doctors require skills in undertaking clinical audits as well as quality improvement projects. Although doctors are reasonably familiar with the collection of data for audit purposes (as this is set out in their speciality training curriculum), collecting data for the measurement of service and quality improvement requires an additional skill set. Understanding measurement, how to define it, what to count and why it should be seen as extending beyond an individual's expertise is a requirement of effective medical leaders of the future.

> *At a service level, quality improvement relies on a level of analytical support to drive change – yet often this is absent and as a result there are weaknesses in the systems for monitoring and evaluating changes.*
>
> *(Bardsley, 2016)*

Bardsley (2016) points out that health systems cannot function without data and information and that there should always be intelligence to inform clinical and non-clinical decision making on how things are run and where money is spent. This is required not only for large macro system health planning but also for helping better understand the impact of small tests of change through the use of PDSA cycles to inform the development of new service models.

The NHS needs people who are skilled in the analysis and interpretation of data; these healthcare analysts can be from a number of different disciplines. These skills need to be seen as essential components of a modern healthcare system (Bardsley, 2016). Data analysis and a thorough understanding of measurement helps to shape the care provided for individual patients across the health economy.

> *The NHS was awash with innovations in how to deliver care – changes triggered by either a desire to improve quality of care, the need for financial solvency, or both.*

> *Yet despite the hunger for new models of care, there is often no way of knowing what really works. Often, there is not the capability to know whether the changes people are working so hard to implement are having the desired effects, e.g. reducing emergency admissions.*
>
> *(Bardsley et al., 2013:4)*

When describing healthcare analysts, they were referring to a team of people with a range of skills and expertise, which might include statistics, manipulating and linking large data sets, social research methods such as survey design, mathematical skills (e.g. operational research and modelling), economics, epidemiology, methods and measurement, public health, improvement science, health policy and evaluation.

Why measurement is key?

Improvement science advocates that in order to improve something you must be able to measure it (Langley et al., 2009). There is a general belief that you cannot improve what you don't measure, but not all measurement is created equally. Measurement without improvement is just harassment (Deming, 1986).

You can weigh yourself every day, but if you don't make an intervention then simply generating data will not release improvement. You can have measurement without improvement, but it is rare you can have sustained improvement without measurement.

Tracking how your chosen project is doing, figuring out when to stop doing something and when to start, and determining what the most cost-effective intervention is critical.

How do we measure?

One of the important elements in health service analytics is that often good analytics may be catalysed by the involvement of interested and engaged clinicians. These are most commonly doctors, though examples from nursing and allied health professionals (AHPs) also exist (Bardsley, 2016).

Parand et al. (2010) state that *"medical engagement is a complex technical, socio-political and motivational issue that is underpinned by a series of inter related factors associated with organisational context, the design of improvement programs and how they are promoted"* (p. 1).

Using the lens of Self Determination Theory (SDT) (Deci and Ryan, 1985, 2000; Ryan and Deci, 2000), insight is offered into the motivational element of Parand et al.'s (2010) findings, creating a theoretical framework to consider what motivational factors might support individuals to more meaningfully engage in quality improvement initiatives and how the measured components could support ongoing interest in these initiatives. According to SDT, the internalisation process is fostered by three innate psychological needs:

- *Autonomy*: feeling that you are determining your own behaviour;
- *Competence*: knowing what you are doing and having the skills to do it;

- *Relatedness*: having a sense of belonging with at least five other individuals or work groups in the work environment.

Connecting these psychological needs to the improvement programme via the use of measurement may prove to be a positive force helping to create changes in a medical leaders' engagement that ultimately could result in a wider organisational culture shift.

SDT highlights that not only do people have different amounts of motivation but that there are also different types of motivation (Ryan and Deci, 2000). An appreciation of this enables leaders to consider why it is that measurement is so important to sustain improvement and engagement.

Ryan and Deci's (2000) research is based in educational settings, and although there is very little literature specifically looking at SDT in relation to individual involvement quality improvement programmes, there are clear parallels between the need to understand how best to motivate clinicians and patients in a quality improvement process and the needs of leaders to develop medical engagement strategies that maximises engagement of all staff in quality improvement.

There are improvement programmes that are sometimes referred to as 'nice to do's' and the lack of any perceived rewards, internal or external, mean that they never really get off the ground. At the opposite end of the spectrum, there is intrinsic motivation, occurring when the individual has complete internal freedom regarding the choice to engage (Ryan and Deci, 2000). This takes place in the total absence of any extrinsic motivational factors: the behaviour is being carried out solely for personal enjoyment or interest.

Between these two points SDT places a continuum of internalisation, running from motivation, which has some external regulation (e.g. some consequence of not performing well) to motivation, which has become internalised and integrated (e.g. is part of own self-development). Sufficiently internalised extrinsically motivated actions will become self-determined so the difference between each type of extrinsic motivation is the degree of 'internalisation'. Encouraging more doctors to become involved in quality improvement projects will require supporting their own ideas for improvement as opposed to 'top-down' driven improvement objectives. This requires a change in organisational culture, with new models of devolved clinician leadership improvement initiatives which can be achieved only with new levels of trust formed between frontline clinicians and managers.

Measurement supporting the psychological need for autonomy

Doctors play an essential role in quality improvement (Berwick, 1992, 2013) and clinical expertise appears critical for success in many health improvement projects, not just for the obvious reason of needing to understand the terminology but also to bring credibility to any findings which may then require further participation in improvement projects (Wright and Butterworth, 2014).

The BMA stipulate that the role of the consultant, aside from delivering clinical care is to be *"involved in running departments, managerial decisions, teaching, training, researching, developing local services – generally being involved in the wider management and leadership of the organisations they work in, and the NHS generally" (BMA, 2008).* This broad and complex role does not always allow for time to get involved in new initiatives; the structuring of consultant job plans is a done in such a way that it should assist in carving out time for personal development through the designated Specialist Programed Activities (SPA) slots. In 2010, the Consultant Contract said there was a recommendation of 2.5 SPAs in a 10 Programed Activity (PA) contract; however, in recent times, the SPA time has come under debate, with NHS Hospital Trusts looking to cut costs by asking consultants to voluntary forgo 0.5 of SPA time (Broad, 2010).

The BMA cites a number of activities which could count as SPA and quality improvement features within the Audit section. Consultants will have many competing demands, and there may well be resistance to using SPA time to support corporate initiatives if they do not have the belief that such initiatives will contribute to organisational wide improvement or at the very least directly impact their own service.

As Ryan and Deci (2000) note, people must experience their behaviour as self-determined if intrinsic motivation is to be maintained or enhanced, and therefore leaders need to choose to actively use their time.

Measurement feedback relates to reinforcing a sense of competency

The importance of clear training to collect and analyse data is twofold. First, it provides the opportunity to address the case for change (Kotter, 1996), and second, it instils confidence in those participating in a Quality Improvement project that they are making informed and useful judgements to steer the improvement process.

Training in data collection and analysis is seen as paramount in order to ensure reliability and validity of the data. The training enables a sense of competence and confidence in completing quality improvement projects (Hogan et al., 2012). Berwick (2013) believes that if you give the clinical workforce *"the tools, and the information and the psychological safety to pursue improvement, we'll see it"*.

According to SDT, a sense of competence will result in increased intrinsic motivation, however this competence comes from more than just knowing how to do the job, it comes from being aware that they are doing a good job and receiving positive feedback is a key component of this psychological need (Deci and Ryan, 2000).

Measurement supporting relatedness

Measurement feedback relates to reinforcing a sense of relatedness, Ryan and Deci (2000) point out that people are more likely to be willing to act if they are valued by significant others to whom they feel (or would like to feel) connected to. They suggest that the internalisation process can be further facilitated by providing a sense of belonging and being connected to the persons, or group which is setting the goals. For Deci and Ryan (1985, 2000), this is the primary reason why people are willing to engage.

To conclude, Self Determination Theory provides a theoretical rationale for the teaching of competence in data collection and data analysis for quality improvement. Measurement is critical for the engagement of medical leaders and to provide critical feedback on continuous improvement activity that is the focus of much coveted SPA time of doctors. Without measurement, such time could be at risk with a continued drive for efficiency savings in healthcare.

16

ROOT CAUSE ANALYSIS AND SIMULATION TO IMPROVE QUALITY

Adam Burns

A Root Cause Analysis (RCA) is "a systematic investigation technique that looks beyond the individuals concerned and seeks to understand the underlying causes and environmental context in which an incident happened" (NPSA, 2004). As an investigation technique for patient safety incidents, it looks beyond the individuals concerned and seeks to understand the underlying causes and environmental context in which an incident happened. It is used as a tool to learn from systems errors and to improve the quality of a service provided to patients. The tool can be effective only if it is used as a learning tool, and poor dissemination of RCA outcomes is often an indicator of poor communication with clinical staff. For an RCA to have best effect, it needs to be used in a culture that seeks continuous system improvement and team building and not used as a tool that seeks to blame individuals. In order to maintain communication, it is important that everyone involved in submitting information to it, is briefed on its outcome after the investigation is concluded. The outcome should be clear and accessible and should incentivise changes in behaviour and compliance with a revised system. For example, when working as a junior member of staff, with limited knowledge of the RCA process, I was provided with a long RCA report that did not enhance my learning or support me to understand how things would now be different.

Reflecting on my conversations with colleagues, it became apparent that current local policy did not promote organisational learning from RCAs with findings ineffectively conveyed to key individuals. Subsequently, I chose to use the 'plan, do, study, act' or PDSA cycle (Langley et al., 2009) as a method of quality improvement to promote organisational learning from critical clinical incidents and their subsequent RCAs. Ultimately, I wanted to improve the number of junior staff attending RCA meetings, improve staff knowledge and perceptions of the RCA process and to build a way to rapidly test and implement findings. With these objectives,

I planned to improve organisational learning for both clinicians and management staff (Senge, 2006).

Following the events at Mid-Staffordshire, the Francis report brought patient safety issues back to the national stage (Francis, 2012). The twelfth recommendation of the Francis report stated:

> Reporting of incidents of concern relevant to patient safety, compliance with fundamental standards or some higher requirement of the employer needs to be not only encouraged but insisted upon. Staff are entitled to receive feedback in relation to any report they make, including information about any action taken or reasons for not acting.

Increasing learning from clinical incidents and reducing harm to patients is a high priority for National Health Service in the United Kingdom. These priorities directly reflect the priority of its regulatory body, Care Quality Commission (CQC), which stated that there must be an appropriate system in place to monitor quality of care for patients. RCAs are a crucial part of this system but may have limited benefit for quality improvement if not paired with simulation.

An incident reporting system can create a reactor or opportunistic approach to quality improvement (Shortell et al., 1995). In a reactor system, staff perform their normal role and react to local issues. Little learning is generated that could be applied to other situations or systems. Introducing a structured simulation, the intervention changes the approach to an analyser approach. In this approach, a single or limited number of issues are assessed with data collected in a structured format before changes are introduced (Shortell et al., 1995). It can be argued that a standard RCA model that does not involve simulation only offers similar benefits to the analyser model.

Simulation can be defined as an instructional process that substitutes real patients with artificial models, live actors, or virtual reality patients (Gaba, 2004). A variety of simulation methods exist including patient actors, online virtual simulation, mannequins and high fidelity electronic patient simulators. Therefore, simulation can encompass a wide range of scenarios and environments encountered by the healthcare professional. Simulation gives the opportunity to repeatedly rehearse clinical scenarios and receive prompt feedback without the fear of adverse patient outcome. In such a manner, technical skills can be assessed alongside interpersonal and professional skills (Ottestad et al., 2007).

Staff involvement is crucial to the success of any intervention. Wallace et al. (2007) found that overall risk management was improved through a multidisciplinary approach. When working with multiple professions, the greater the number of persons involved in incident reporting the more likely the chance the results of RCAs will be driven forward in order to effect organisational change. This effect was enhanced by teaching delegates about basic processes in risk management such as RCAs.

Simulation and RCA

Simulation has mostly been used as an education tool. However, with accurate recreation of real world environments now possible, a new use for simulation within RCA has become apparent. First, by recreating a real incident within the simulation lab, the RCA team can have multiple opportunities to apply a contributory factors framework without the risk of further patient harm, thereby offering additional insight when searching for the root cause. Additional factors such as staff experience, clinical complexity and distractions can be factored into the scenario. Simms et al. (2012) found that a simulated re-enactment of a clinical incident involving a failure to recognise post-operative bleeding recreated the root cause on two out of six occasions when candidates were not aware of the incident prior to commencing the simulation. This dramatically highlighted system as well as personal factors in the incident. This study found additional 'special cause variation' in reduced monitoring by nursing staff and 'common cause variation' in reduced physician presence post-operatively when the simulation was used, items that were not identified using standard RCA models. In this, RCAs are using simulation in a similar way to that which has been used in air accident investigation over many years, perhaps most famously in the forced landing of an American Airlines A320 on the Hudson River in 2009 (NTSB, 2010).

Simulation can be also used to assess the impact of any potential intervention post-RCA. Using video analysis of simulated incidents, the potential impact of a variety of interventions can be assessed. They could also be used as a preliminary assessment prior to implementing an intervention to look for negative consequences that may not be immediately apparent (Tenner, 1997).

Finally, if an RCA establishes training needs or key information to be disseminated, simulation can be used in its more traditional role as an educational tool to meet these requirements. One study looked at attitudes to quality improvement after a simulation-based RCA programme. Following the programme, positive attitudes to patient safety and to RCA principles were significantly increased in the simulation group when compared with a standard RCA model (Qurashi et al., 2011). This creates a powerful argument for involving staff in simulated RCA analysis, as they can take skills and attributes learnt back to the clinical environment to improve patient safety in their workplace.

It has been argued that unless RCA is joined up with systems thinking, the recommended action for change will result in little change especially when senior managers are not involved (Peerally et al., 2017). The aim of this service improvement plan was to improve patient safety within the hospital by using the RCA within the completion of three PDSA cycles. Simulation was implemented within three separate RCAs, using the outcome from each to adjust the programme for the next. However, the primary aim was found to be too broad a term to measure accurately, making it impossible to complete the PDSA cycle because it was not possible to assess for potential improvements. Subsequently, more specific aims were included in design, such as improving staff attitude and engagement with the RCA process alongside more measurable improvements in quality. The core design of the service improvement project was also set before starting the PDSA cycle, that of introducing simulation-based RCAs. This limited the system improvement value of the PDSA cycle but was not found to reduce the effectiveness of the project in that simulation was universally well received by those working on the project.

To conclude, it has been argued that the investigation of incidents needs professionalising and requires advanced skills and expertise in investigation, including underlying theories of ergonomics, human factors and hands-on experience of using analytical methods from within Improvement Science (Peerally et al., 2017). In addition, patients and relatives need to be involved in the process in a planned and systematised way, ensuring that the learning from RCA are drawn together in an aggregated analysis across the micro, meso and macro health systems (Peerally et al., 2017).

17

LEADERSHIP DIAGNOSTICS FOR SELF-AWARENESS AND BESPOKE COURSE DESIGN

Prosenjit Giri

Measuring personal performance through self-assessment leadership diagnostics is a useful way to support doctors to consider their strengths and development needs as a medical leader driving quality improvement. This chapter examines a range of leadership diagnostic tools while reflecting on the learning acquired from them. The leadership diagnostics questionnaires aim to assess an individual's (1) leadership behaviours and (2) leadership style. For leadership behaviours, the NHS Leadership Academy the 'Healthcare Leadership Model' has been adapted, and for leadership style, a number of questionnaires have been included and reflected upon as to their relevance and usefulness to doctors.

1 Leadership behaviour: the healthcare leadership model

The Healthcare Leadership Model was produced by the NHS Leadership Academy in 2013 after extensive research and evidence review in order to support leadership development in health and social care. It is a practical way to approach leadership by incorporating the everyday practice of clinicians with a view to reflecting on how an individual might develop in specific leadership domains. The Healthcare Leadership Model has been developed to apply to staff working in a clinical or service setting to aid in becoming a better leader irrespective of a formal leadership responsibility or role or size of team. It applies to the whole variety of roles and care settings irrespective of a doctor's clinical and non-clinical commitment. The Healthcare Leadership Model aims to support individuals to understand how their leadership behaviours can impact on the culture and climate of their own team and organisation, the experience of patients and service users, the quality of care provided and the reputation of their organisation.

Each and every clinician in the healthcare setting should see themselves as a leader irrespective of their job title and hierarchy. The Healthcare Leadership

Model is made up of nine 'leadership dimensions', quantified on a four-part scale: 'essential', 'proficient', 'strong' and 'exemplary'. The Healthcare Leadership Model assesses leadership behaviours through a series of questions which explores an individual's self-perception under individual domains. Its purpose is to guide thought processes and to help doctors to understand their own strengths and weaknesses with a view to achieving the ultimate goal, which is to improve effectiveness as a leader. More importantly, the process of engaging with the Healthcare Leadership Model may raise a more critical understanding of leadership and help to develop emotional intelligence as a leader (as explored in Chapter 2 of this book). Whilst all nine domains are important, their relevance depends on the context of an individual's job role. It is for each person to decide which areas need development. A 360-degree tool has also been developed by the NHS Leadership Academy to complement the self-assessment process.

How a leader manages themselves, behaves and leads very much depends on the Personal Qualities that they possess. 'Personal Qualities' encompass emotional expressiveness, such as self-awareness, self-confidence, self-determination, self-control, self-knowledge, personal reflection, resilience and determination. It has a direct impact on the leader's colleagues and the team and influences the overall culture and climate within the team as well as within the organisation. It also has a strong impact on the quality of care and services provided to the patients, service users or their families irrespective of any role the doctor may have in providing direct patient care or as a support service. Awareness of an individual leader's strengths is vitally important as it helps a leader to build confidence to manage themselves and improve their effectiveness and efficiency by nurturing their strengths and addressing their areas for development.

The NHS Leadership Academy sets out the areas identified for development within the model relating to both self-management and leading others. The Healthcare Leadership Model targets every individual with a view to help them to think about their leadership practice, carry out appraisals and prepare personal and professional development plans. Within a team or organisational setting, personal leadership strategies should guide the recruitment criteria and processes, educational standards and curricula and training programme materials and assessment criteria. The self-assessment 360-degree feedback tool has been developed by the NHS Leadership Academy to enable every individual to use a developmental process to help fulfil their leadership aspirations.

Self-reflective case study using the healthcare leadership model

The NHS Healthcare Leadership Model self-assessment tool has eight questions under each domain with responses on a 5-point Likert scale, prompting the respondent to report the frequency that each statement applies to their work role (rarely; sometimes, frequently, usually and nearly always and scored from 1 to 5). Maximum score under each domain is 40. The tool is freely available to access and was used as a self-rating tool to help prepare and reflect on my own needs in preparation for an annual appraisal. The results of the tool are presented in Figure 17.1, and the code for each abbreviated domain is as follows

1   Inspiring Shared Purpose – ISP
2   Leading with Care – LC
3   Evaluating Information – EI
4   Connecting Our Service – CS
5   Sharing the Vision – SV
6   Engaging the Team – ET
7   Holding to Account – HA
8   Developing Capability – DC
9   Influencing for Results – IR.

An analysis of my own data showed that I have strengths in certain domains such as Inspiring Shared Purpose and Holding to Account, whereas I need to develop in the domains such as Developing Capability, Connecting Our Service and Sharing the Vision.

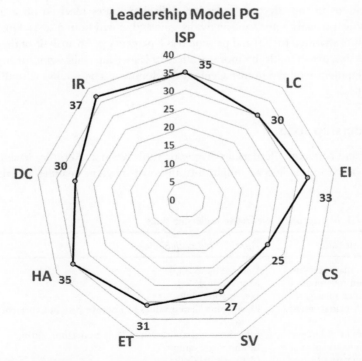

FIGURE 17.1   The Healthcare Leadership Model applied to PG to enable reflection on leadership development needs

Continuing in my journey of self-discovery of my own leadership development needs and a reflection on my strengths, I have accessed a range of tools to help me prepare for my annual appraisal. These are presented below.

2 Leadership and management skills

Another approach taken to assess leadership behaviour was by assessing my confidence in managerial and affective leadership skills. The questionnaire originated from the NHS Institute for Innovation and Improvement's Medical Leadership Competency Framework and used by a study on Medical and Clinical Directors (Giordano, 2010). Although it is important that leaders have effective leadership skills, it can be argued that managerial skills are equally relevant to look at problems analytically and make reasoned and informed decisions. It may not be possible for a leader to master both sets of skills, and a leader should have the ability to understand how managers think and how they make decisions. Clinicians do not need to have the same set of skills as, say, finance directors. Instead, they need the ability and confidence to move from clinical work and engage with a colleague in the Finance department to make decisions collaboratively.

A leadership diagnostic survey was constructed using the Giordano (2010) model. Ten questions were asked to assess the confidence in managerial skills and six questions in the affective leadership skills. Responses received on a 5-point Likert scale (strongly agree to strongly disagree and scored from 5 to 1). Finally, the scores were stratified to 100 and presented as a percentage. An analysis of these data revealed that my strengths lie more in affective leadership skills, with further areas of development required in management development. The results are outlined in Figure 17.2.

3 Leadership style

The second part of the leadership diagnostic tools was framed on leadership style, with a view to providing an insight into my own inherent qualities and the way

TABLE 17.1 Management vs affective leadership skills

Management Skills	Affective Leadership Skills
Resource management	Leading by example
System improvement	Motivational skills
Performance management	Negotiation skills
Safety risk management	Developing shared values to improve patient experience and safety
Management of budget	Effective communication skills in non-clinic setting
Making business plan	Leading by example
Improving patient care	Motivational skills

Source: Giordano (2010).

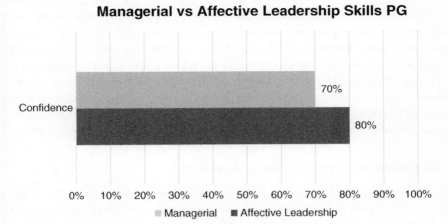

FIGURE 17.2 Managerial vs affective leadership skills (Giordano, 2010)

I am likely to lead others in the workplace. The theory behind the development of the Leadership Style survey is presented in Chapter 2 of this book and reported elsewhere (Chapman and Giri, 2017).

3a Authoritative, democratic and laissez-faire leadership style

The successes and failures of a leader can determine the fate of an organisation – make it a successful and profitable or a failed one. Leaders vary in their decision-making styles. All these styles could be relevant depending on organisational culture, type of industry employee's skill mix and business goal. Kurt Lewin et al. (1939) categorised three main leadership styles: autocratic, democratic, laissez-faire.

This leadership style was assessed through an 18-item questionnaire (six questions specific to each style) on a 5-point Likert scale (strongly disagree to strongly agree; scored 1 to 5). Out of maximum score of 30, a score of 26–30 indicates very high range, 21–25 high range, 16–20 moderate range, 11–15 low range and 6–10 very low range. Individual scores were analysed under each style and a graph showing their score after stratification to 100 (Figures 17.3 and 17.4).

There are limitations with the use of this tool as Lewin et al. (1939) were researching leadership before the emergence of research on motivation theory and particularly Self Determination Theory (Deci and Ryan, 2000; Giri et al., 2017). The use of the term *Autocratic Leader* is now separately defined from the term *Authoritative Leader*, although it sometimes appears in the literature that both terms are mistakenly interchanged. According to Lewin et al. (1939), the autocratic leader has total control over the decision-making process, with little input from group members, which can result in a negative and demotivating effect on group/team members. However, authoritative leaders as defined by Daniel Goleman (2000) (discussed in Chapter 2) are seen as experts in their field of work, able to clearly articulate a vision and the path to success and to mobilise people towards that vision. The difference between autocratic and authoritative leaders is that the former remove autonomy from the team members, whereas the latter supports, facilitates and encourages autonomy, which is one of the three core pillars of Self Determination Theory (Ryan and Deci, 2000; Giri et al., 2017). My own results reflect a more democratic and participative process of leadership, but I am mindful that such an approach takes time and can sometime risk deferment of a decision being made at the expense of continuous engagement and consensus forming amongst the group.

3b Collaborative and shared leadership skills

In a complex setting like healthcare, it is physically impossible for a leader to influence every aspect of patient care and decision making, and effective, quality and safe care needs to be deployed by the healthcare team. It is, therefore, important that leaders develop skills in collaborative leadership with other team members or ideally with everyone providing healthcare or supporting care to collectively reach the goal to provide a high-quality service to the patient. For shared leadership, leaders need to have a vision for the future, a strategy for appropriate delegation and an ability to facilitate collaboration and team-work. Table 17.2 outlines the core skills for collaboration and for shared leadership:

Collaborative skills have been assessed through a 21-item questionnaire on a 5-point Likert scale from low to high (scored 1 to 5), and the total score was stratified to 100. Shared Leadership skills were assessed through a 20-item Shared Leadership Survey questionnaire on a 5-point Likert scale from strongly agree to strongly disagree (scored 5 to 1). The score is presented under individual qualities (collaboration, vision, delegation and culture), and this can also be provided in a graphical representation of scores after stratification to 100. This gives the indication the specific skills leaders may wish to develop.

A summary of the analysis is presented in Figure 17.3 and presented in a bar chart in Figure 17.4

TABLE 17.2 Collaborative and shared leadership skills

Collaborative Skills	Shared Leadership Skills
Facilitation of collaborative interrelationship	• Facilitating **collaboration**
Innovation through exchange of knowledge	• Building a shared **vision**
Ability to create team dynamics	• Facilitating distributive leadership by promoting and facilitating **delegation**
Ability to support complex interaction	• Developing a **culture** of effective and efficient team working
Ability to motivate	

- 2a. Leadership style: Authoritarian (16/30; moderate), Democratic (27/30; very high), Laissez-Faire (14/30; moderate)
- 2b. Collaborative skill score – 100/105

Shared Leadership: Collaboration 21/25, Vision 15/20, Delegation 21/30, Culture 20/25

- 2c. Task/Relationship: Task (35/50; moderate), Relationship (45/50; very high)
- 2d. Leadership skill: Administrative (24/30; high) Interpersonal (27/30; very high) Conceptual (21/30; high)
- 2e. LMX – 7 score: 30/35 (high)

FIGURE 17.3   International Academy of Medical Leadership (IAML) leadership style scores and interpretation (PG)

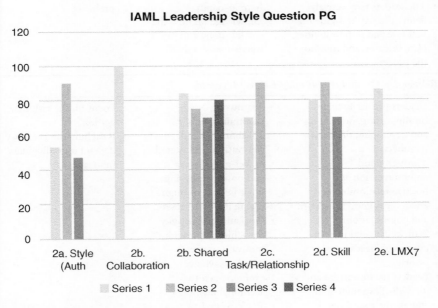

FIGURE 17.4   Analysis of leadership diagnostics

3c Leadership orientation: task-oriented vs relationship-oriented

Forsyth (2010) developed the task–relationship model which is a descriptive model of leadership which categorises most leadership behaviours as performance maintenance or relationship maintenance (this is set out in Table 17.3). In other words, if something needs to be done in an organisation and it has to be done right, a task-oriented leader is the best for the job. This person will focus on completing the task and worry much less about the roles and people who need to do them.

TABLE 17.3 The task-relationship model of leadership

Task-Oriented (Task-Focused) Leadership

Characteristics	Advantage	Disadvantage
• Here, leaders focus on the task that has to be done in order to achieve their goal. • Task, timeliness and achieving the desired standard remain the priority here. • Leaders are not concerned about the human impact of achieving their objectives. • The leaders may actively define the work; decide on staff role and responsibilities; plan, organise and monitor the process.	• It ensures that the deadlines are met and jobs are completed. • Helpful if the team members lack in self-management and organisational skills. • It achieves the desired standard. • These leaders usually have in-depth knowledge on how the work is done and can micro-manage them.	• Leaders may often behave like autocratic leaders. • Employee's well-being may be neglected. • This may lead to de-motivation amongst employees. • Retention of employees may be a problem.

Relationship-Oriented (Relationship-Focused) Leadership

• Leaders primarily focus on supporting, motivating and developing their team members. • Through good communication and positive relationship, it encourages good teamwork and collaboration. • Staff welfare and meeting everyone's needs are a priority. • Leaders try to nurture an individual's strength and address their weaknesses. • Transparency and openness are facilitated.	• Teamwork, communication, collaboration and innovation are fostered • A feel-good factor and positive working environment through caring leader is present. • Goal and productivity are achieved through motivation of staff members where everyone takes accountability. • Work-related dissatisfaction is reduced.	• Focus on the task may get lost. • Reaching the goal may depend on individual's motivation.

Source: Adapted from Forsyth (2010).

This is similar to the completer-finisher role found within Belbin's Self-perception Inventory (BPSI). Belbin (1981) argued that successful teams need a mix of nine types of individual team roles, with some people being effective at several roles at different times.

Although each style can be effective, studies have identified the scenarios when one or the other style is likely to be successful (Table 17.4).

A 20-item questionnaire was used to measure these leadership orientations; 10 for the task orientation and 10 for the relationship orientation. A 5-point Likert

TABLE 17.4 When leadership styles are most successful

Leader-Member Relations	Task Structure	Leader's Position Power	Most Effective Leader
Good	Structured	Strong	Task-oriented
Good	Structured	Weak	Task-oriented
Good	Unstructured	Strong	Task-oriented
Good	Unstructured	Weak	Relationship-oriented
Poor	Structured	Strong	Relationship-oriented
Poor	Structured	Weak	Relationship-oriented
Poor	Unstructured	Strong	Relationship-oriented
Poor	Unstructured	Weak	Task-oriented

scale (Never, seldom, occasional, often and always) was used and scored from 1 to 5. A score of 45–50 indicates very high range, 40–44 high range, 35–39 moderate high range, 30–34 moderately low range, 25–29 low range and 10–24 very low range. Scores were received under both these orientations and also a graphical representation of scores after stratification to 100. My own analysis revealed greater strengths in relationship-oriented leadership and lower results in task-oriented (Figures 17.3 and 17.4). My more effective collaborations with team colleagues is when I collaborate with more task-oriented colleagues, which contributes to my own strengths.

3d Leadership skills: administrative, interpersonal and conceptual

These sets of diagnostic questionnaires assess learnt competency of a leader. Every leader should possess these skills in order to perform to the highest level. This is deemed as an essential quality for successful leadership. They are broadly divided into three groups: Administrative; Interpersonal and Conceptual skills.

Administrative skills: these are the skills that every leader needs to possess to achieve the purpose and goals of any organisation. It has three pillars: planning, organisation and coordination. These skills also cover three distinct areas: managing people, managing resources and showing technical competence.

- *Managing People*: a successful leader needs to have the skill to manage its team members effectively and efficiently. It involves connecting staff with their task, protecting the environment and helping staff to perform to the best of their ability. To do it, leaders need to understand their staff as well as the task which is needed to be done. Successful people management helps team working, improves staff morale, reduces interrelationship conflicts and provides staff with job satisfaction.
- *Managing Resources*: leaders need to be competent in understanding what resources are required to finish the task in hand and have the competency in procuring and allocating them. Resources are vital in running any organisation and can vary widely from finance, equipment, space, time and supplies.

- *Showing Technical Competence*: leaders are required to understand the culture of an organisation and how the organisation works. Leaders may also need to understand the competency and effectiveness of their staff, but it does not call for micro-management. Having this functional competency helps a leader to run the team successfully and also help the organisation to achieve its goal.

Interpersonal skills: Leaders need to possess good interpersonal skills in order deal effectively with their subordinates, peers and higher authorities. This is important for an organisation to be successful. It involves three skill sets: being socially perceptive, showing emotional intelligence and managing interpersonal conflicts.

- *Being Socially Perceptive*: this involves understanding others' needs, and problems as well as how they react to change and how they can be motivated.
- *Showing Emotional Intelligence*: the ability to understand his or her own emotion and emotion of others is a vital skill for a leader. This helps the leader to understand the intellectual demand of individual team member, think appropriately before communicating, manage emotions effectively and regulate his or her own emotion for the ultimate goal of the team.
- *Managing Interpersonal Conflicts*: although conflict can be good for an organisation to progress and develop, conflict can be highly uncomfortable as well. Literature shows that conflict can lead to a dysfunctional team through inter-relationship problems, affect creativity and problem solving and produce work-related stress. However, as change is an integral part of an organisation to move forward, conflict may be inevitable. Managing interpersonal conflict is, therefore, an integral part of a leader's job.

Conceptual skills: this deals with the cognitive aspects of a leader involving problem solving, strategic planning and creating vision.

- *Problem Solving*: the ability to solve any problem and to complete the task is of vital importance for the success of an organisation. An efficient problem-solving approach involves identifying the problem, thinking of solutions, deciding on the most appropriate solution and implementing it.
- *Strategic Planning*: this involves careful thinking and setting up an action plan with a view to achieve a goal by utilising the available resources and to staff effectively and efficiently. A deep understanding of the people and their environment is essential to achieve the success here. It also calls for an ability to learn and a capacity to adapt.
- *Creating Vision*: this involves future planning. A leader has to have a vision and a future plan and to mobilise his or her staff to achieve this goal. It may involve influencing or shaping the ideals and values of an organisation.

These leadership skills were assessed through an 18-item questionnaire (six questions specific to each style) on a 5-point Likert scale (not true to very true; scored 1–5). Out of maximum score of 30, a score of 26–30 indicates very high range, 21–25 high range, 16–20 moderate range, 11–15 low range and 6–10 very low range. Individual scores are allocated under each style and a graph showing their score after stratification to 100. The results are summarised in Figure 17.3 and presented in a graph in Figure 17.4. It helps to identify areas of strength and weakness. My own results again show my strength in interpersonal leadership, second within administration and third in conceptual leadership (Figures 17.3 and 17.4).

3e Leadership-Member Exchange (LMX) Theory

This theory investigates the relationship between leaders and their subordinates, which may vary according to each group of individuals being led. The quality of the relationship is affected by the degree of mutual trust, loyalty, support, respect and obligation that exists between the leaders and their followers (Northouse, 1997).

According to the theory, leaders favour the group of staff whom they feel are an 'ingroup', by providing them with more attention and access to organisational resources. Leaders classify members as an 'ingroup' if they possess similar personalities as the leader or they are perceived to be more competent at performing their jobs. Usually this staff group are more involved, communicative and more dependable and have confidence in their leaders. Other members are classified as the outgroup and are less favoured. Although they are at work and do their own job they are not highly involved in the team.

A strong Leader-Member relationship with all team members has multiple benefits for the organisation in the form of:

* Increased motivation of staff
* Better performance
* Less turnover of staff
* More job satisfaction
* More attention and support from leader
* Better performance evaluation
* Promotion and career progression.

The LMX 7 questionnaires analyse the leadership styles that an individual has and whether he or she believes his or her team members are ingroup or outgroup members. Seven questions are asked on a 5-point Likert scale, with the score range from 1 to 5 (30–35: very high; 25–29: high; 20–24: moderate; 15–19: low and 7–14: very low). The scores acquired for my own personal self-assessment in the leadership style questionnaire (Figures 17.3 and 17.4) shows that I am good in collaboration, have good skills but will need to improve focus on task orientation and need to have my authority established in order to complete the task and reach the organisational goal.

In conclusion, the use of data for self-assessment has helped me to reflect upon my default leadership style and enable me to plan to develop areas of my leadership style that will be usefully applied in some situations and not in others. These self-assessment questionnaires have supported me to prepare for my appraisal and to argue for specific 'self-determined' areas of development.

18

MEDICAL LEADERSHIP AND THE USE OF DATA FOR A CONTINUOUS QUALITY IMPROVEMENT COLLABORATIVE (CQIC) IN AN ACCIDENT AND EMERGENCY DEPARTMENT

Prakash Subedi, Jill Aylott, Prosenjit Giri, Martha Zaluaga Quintero, Sanjay Sinha, Sanjai Subramanian and Sathi Permaul

Previous chapters (Chapter 13 and Chapter 17) explored the value of undertaking self diagnostic tools for reflection and personal development planning for appraisal. While preparing individuals to develop the skills for quality improvement, more distributed, collaborative and shared leadership models are required to engage all stakeholders on the front line of health and social care services. This is a very different approach to the view that 'leadership' as a concept can be taught, theoretically in classrooms, to a select few individual leaders who will be taught 'how' to direct others in the organisation to follow a certain direction. Often, people in senior positions or roles do not have the highest level of knowledge within the system that requires improvement or system change. However, they do have the power in their role to choose to reflect on their leadership style and to consider the impact of their behaviour on others, to either keep control or to devolve power to others. There is a dominant perspective from writers in the field of leadership suggesting that 'knowledge' will trickle down from the notional 'top' of the organisation and that leaders will set the tone and make the decisions (Thorpe et al., 2011). *A Systematic Review of the Literature: A Report for the NHS Leadership Centre* defined leadership development as "*the building of the capacity of individuals to help staff learn new ways of doing things that could not have been predicted*" (Hartley and Hinksman, 2003:10).

Successful organisations know that the speed of external change is now rapid (Thorpe et al., 2011). Change in a healthcare organisation has to be responsive, ever more fast and adaptive, in terms of workforce development, job design, systems change, motivation and employee assurances (Thorpe et al., 2011). There will be flatter structures, matrix structures, devolved leadership and networks, all of which show the limitations of many of the existing top-down models and the historical and prevailing view of leadership as 'the empty vessel' residing in the individual.

Where organisations are increasingly project based, knowledge based, professional and clinical based and where innovation occurs through knowledge of intensive exchange processes within networks – leadership is now moving to a form that is able to cope with a collective endeavour, where individuals can contribute to the establishment and the development of a common purpose. The more that is devolved, the greater the motivation amongst clinicians and the more likely that change will be successful and sustained over time.

New ways of leadership are required through 'collaborative interrelationships' (Careau et al., 2014). Such collaborative interrelationships are suggested to be a more effective method for creating new dynamics that share and support complex processes. This is the way to achieve more integrated services in the future.

A collaborative leadership model is defined as one that is:

> *focused on developing leaders that are able to **build a shared vision** within a group/ organisation, and who **facilitate the distribution of leadership processes** according to the groups expertise, **as well as act as a catalyst for shared decision making and collective actions**.*
>
> *(Careau et al., 2014)*

We have a global evidence base of what works in healthcare improvement (Bevan and Layton, 2000; Ferlie and Shortell, 2001; Ovretveit, 2002; Ovretveit and Gustafson, 2003; Nembhard, 2009; Nadeem et al., 2013) and how co-production with patients is key to delivering fitness for purpose service redesign (VonKorff et al., 1997; Bate and Robert, 2006; Skard Brandrud et al., 2011). A truly collaborative multidisciplinary approach to improvement in the NHS (Horak et al., 2014) is needed.

The collaborative leadership model is focused on developing leaders who are able to build a shared vision within a group, department or organisation and who facilitate the distribution of leadership processes to the group according to the group members' expertise. At the same time, the clinical leader acts as a catalyst for shared decision-making processes and collective actions (Careau et al., 2014). Most current day leadership programmes do not seek to achieve patient-centred outcomes or create system change (Careau et al., 2014; Frich et al., 2015).

Without effective clinical leadership (Ovretveit et al., 2002), engagement with managers and patients will not happen and healthcare improvement will not be sustained over time (Ovretveit et al., 2002; Skard Brandrud et al., 2011). Improvement science requires the facilitation of 'learning' from practice, as opposed to the dominant paradigm of 'teaching', and providing support to carry out the use of Plan Do Study Act (PDSA) learning cycles to test out small process changes, and the use of interpreting reliable and valid data to evaluate improvement options (Ovretveit et al., 2002; Nembhard, 2009; Skard Brandrud et al., 2011; Nadeem et al., 2013). Suh an approach requires clinicians to have 'time' scheduled in their workplan to improve their skills and apply them specifically to a problem in clinical practice. In addition they also need ongoing support on the 'front line' in the application of quality improvement methods and data analysis.

A case study: the Doncaster Emergency Medicine Continuous Quality Improvement Collaborative (EM-CQIC)

The hospital quality improvement collaborative was inspired by the American Institute for Healthcare Improvement (IHI) collaborative model for achieving Breakthrough Improvement (IHI, Langley et al., 2009). Its aims are to "improve healthcare by supporting change, though collaborative learning" (IHI, Langley et al., 2009). It is recognised that the Doncaster EM–CQIC developed on a much smaller scale to the American breakthrough series programmes and in addition the Doncaster programme set out to integrate quality improvement, clinical practice and medical leadership. The differences are set out in Table 18.1:

TABLE 18.1 Differences between IHI Breakthrough series and Doncaster EM–CQIC

IHI Breakthrough Collaborative (US)	Doncaster EM-CQIC (UK)
Short-term 6–15 months	Longer-term sustainable continuous QIC in ED
Brings together a large number of teams from hospitals or clinics to seek improvement in a focused topic area	Staff from different professional groups within ED were co-opted onto smaller subgroups for improvement projects to explore and test out process improvements
Size from 12 to 160 teams	Small scale with a focus on capacity development for improvement
Learning sessions consisting of quality improvement methods with the collaborative	Learning sessions that integrate clinical development, improvement science and leadership

Quality Improvement Collaboratives (QIC) aim to close the gap between what is the best and current practice and support a process whereby everyone contributes to a process of continuous quality improvement (Skard Brandrud et al., 2011). However, QIC require 'Collaborative learning' amongst a wide range of professional, technical and non–clinical team members, in a healthcare context where there is a continued risk of professionalised boundary disputes and defensiveness in professionalised 'scope of practice' (Aylott et al., 2017). New types of leadership will be required which support a change-oriented organisational culture, working in co-production with patients, who can recognise "complex multifaceted processes that focus on the development of individuals as well as the organisational contexts in which they are called to operate" (Marshall, 2006), working towards the development of generative and life-affirming learning communities by design (Marshall, 2006; Jones et al., 2014).

It is argued that this requires a shift away from a broad ontological perspective where leadership is seen as individual and hierarchical to model of shared and distributed leadership. But how prepared are senior leaders and managers for a fundamental shift in the way they relate to people in the organisation? The values of distributed leadership are based on respect rather than regulation with more support for individual autonomy (Woods, 2004). Distributed leadership is a form of shared leadership, which opens up spaces for the kind of personal development that is integral to active or developmental democracy (Woods and Gronn, 2009). Thorpe et al. (2011) are more optimistic in their view that leadership is now moving to a form that is able to cope with collective endeavour and development of common purpose with ideas such as participation, empowerment, engagement and delegation. But with a focus on conjoint actions rather than reliance on formal positions, this will require some individuals to give up power and move from a position of comfort and privilege to discomfort.

The Doncaster EM-CQIC was set up within an approach of 'collective endeavor' and with reference to the evidence base of what works in CQIC (Ovretveit et al., 2002). The CQIC aimed to develop wide-scale engagement and participation across all staff groups, managers and patients in a large emergency department in a busy teaching hospital. A timeline showing seven months of meetings for improvement with CQIC is presented in Table 18.2 and senior Managers and Clinical Leads were co-opted on to the collaborative with the agreement that the collaborative would make decisions following the PDSA approach (IHI, Langley et al., 2009; Reed and Card, 2015). Data are collected following a 4-week cycle (Table 18.3), and an analysis of the data is presented at a monthly meeting (Table 18.4).

TABLE 18.2 Timeline of Doncaster EM-CQIC

Meeting 1 – Launch of EM-CQIC	Agreed Terms of Reference decisions must be made based on the data presented at the meeting; working on a PDSA model; also three process changes are to be agreed at the end of each meeting to be tested out to see if the change has resulted in an improvement. Aims and Objectives based on QIC Breakthrough series. Project registered with the Research and Audit department; In the first meeting, we focused on the building of a coalition with representation across the organisation, head of service from A&E, director of care group, head of nursing, general manager, head of clinical governance. By the end of this meeting, we agreed what we were trying to accomplish and the aim was agreed and sent out to the team to encourage as much participation as possible. The aim is for collective leadership and learning and to engage all members of the team.
Meeting 2	Multidisciplinary discussion of the process on feedback and resources required to run and manage the EM-CQIC, we requested a EM-CQIC suggestion box, discussed how we want to use it in the department, levels of data analysis and how we will respond to the data, following the PDSA cycle of testing small process changes.

Meeting 3	Data were presented on consultant working pattern, number of hours required to be covered in the department and the number of consultant hour shortfall. At this meeting, a decision was made to increase the consultant numbers from 10 to 14. Agreed to collect data on nursing continuing professional development for the next cycle.
Meeting 4	Discussed nurses continuing professional development and core competencies of nurses in ED. One of the core outcomes of this meeting was the need for a strategy for Continuing Professional Development and medical education for nurses as emergency nurse practitioners (ENP) – There didn't exist any strategy for professional updating for nurses prior to this meeting. By the end of the meeting, it was agreed that the care group for nursing allocates 1 hour every week for professional updating. We planned two 2-hour teaching sessions a month, but need to identify a nurse coordinator. Agreed a plan to collect data on 'what can be done differently in the clinical decision unit (CDU)'.
Meeting 5	Fifty-seven feedback responses. The question for this month was: is there anything that can be done differently in relation to patient care in the CDU?, the team, the patient group? What feedback can be helpful to the patient – only one doctors round in a day and the doctor is not available when needed and nurses not sure who the responsible doctor is. All of this delays patient care. At this meeting, the managers agreed that there will be two rounds and not one each day, there will also bleep for the doctor – so they can be contacted with ease. Agreed to test out and evaluate the impact, bringing data to the next meeting.
Meeting 6	CDU – band 7 is responsible for gatekeeping as to who is in CDU. At this meeting, we agreed to collect data on patient care in the resuscitation room.
Meeting 7	Staff satisfaction and patient satisfaction data needed for the next meeting – and the seventh meeting is to focus on how to improve relationships between doctors and nurses and everyone else to achieve collective leadership.

TABLE 18.3 Four-week cycle of the EM–CQIC

Week 1	First day of week 1, send out the feedback form on the monthly selected topic, everyday all stakeholders are encouraged to write their ideas in response to the agreed improvement objective on a slip of paper and post the slip in the suggestion box; Make available printed forms and encourage people to give feedback, offer guidance to give it physically or ask the healthcare assistants to give it. Post it in the suggestion box. Move the box from behind the secretary's office to the common area by the receptionist. Give everyone three weeks to complete this. We want to encourage everyone to contribute to it, so everyday staff to be encouraged to engage with the improvement programme – with an aim to make it sustainable – not dependent on one person, create a system to make it happen.
Week 2	Encouragement and reminders every day for 14 days

(Continued)

TABLE 18.3 (Continued)

Week 3	By the third week (one week before the meeting), all data are analysed using descriptive statistics and summarised in a paper (the collective results are presented in Table 18.4) and free text subjected to thematic and content analysis.
Week 4	QIC meeting. Fourth week: open the box and the secretary will type up the comments verbatim – had to negotiate for 3 hours every week secretarial time. When she types up this then it goes to the audit department, who produces graphical presentations of the graphs which are then presented at 4pm every second Thursday every month at the Quality Improvement Team (CQIC).

TABLE 18.4 Results of data analysis for the Doncaster EM-CQIC

Audit A: Quality of Care in Resus (Total Response: 135)

Staffing level		40 (30%)
	Nursing	16/40 (40%)
	Doctor	7
	HCA	7
	Unspecified	6
	Specialist (ODP 2; Paeds Nurse 1; Cleaner 1)	4
Appropriate allocation of staff/efficient use		18 (13%)
Training to use equipment and proper stock		13 (10%)
Clinical Management issues		19 (14%)
	Inappropriate patients	9
	Transferring out	4
	Process issues	3
	Protocol issues	3
Equipment issues		58 (43%)
	Clinical equipment	44/58
	Non-clinical equipment (desk/IT/Phone)	14 (24%)

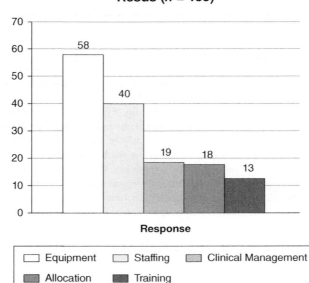

Resus (*n* = 135)

Inference
- An interesting audit with large number of participants
- Lack of equipment has been identified as the primary barrier (43%)
- Most of the equipment is simple equipment such as trolley/rack and is not cost intensive.
- 10% highlighted non–clinical logistics issues such as desk and phone, which is as high as identifiable training need.
- Whilst it is not surprising that 30% of responders highlighted staffing level, 13% indicated towards appropriate/efficient usage of staff.
- Clinical Management issues were identified by 14% of employees.

Staffing

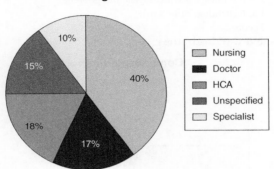

Service improvement opportunities
- Lack of simple equipment and training to use equipment has been the primary barrier by 53% of responders for an effective service. This should be an easy fix and should yield high with low investment.
- Whilst increasing staffing level may be unrealistic and cost intensive, affective use of available human resource should be a priority.
- Clinical management issues can be solved but may need time, effort and horizontal scanning before attempting.

Service Improvement Opportunities

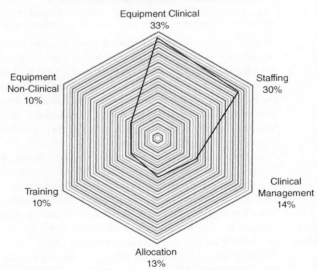

(Continued)

TABLE 18.4 (Continued)

Audit B: Communication on Shop Floor (Total Response: 38)

Preferred communication method	20 (53%)
Verbal (direct)	13 (34%)
By documenting in system	3
Involving patient	1
Unspecified	1
Board room communication	2
Attitude (respect/politeness/understanding/feedback)	17 (45%)
Communication with respect and politeness	9
Understanding other's role	7
Feedback	1
Handover issues and workload/stress	9 (24%)

Communication (*n* = 38)

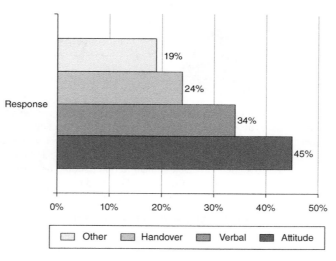

Inference:
- An interesting audit with a few participants but a powerful message
- As high as 45% of the responders asked for respect and politeness during communication. They believe that a lot can be achieved if their role and responsibility, limitation and pressure are understood by their colleagues before delegating them tasks. During the modern era of team working, interpersonal skills is a fundamental skill that each healthcare worker should possess. Every member of staff should be treated with respect and dignity.
- As high as one in three responders preferred verbal communication. A simple human touch can achieve a lot. A direct communication may be a fundamental prerequisite in delivering safe and effective patient care.
- One in four responses highlighted issues related to handover system.

Service improvement opportunities
- Team building may be a fundamental area the management can consider in order to achieve a quick success in the form of opening up channels for easy and effective communication.
- Whilst it may be difficult to implement, steps may be taken to promote direct face-to-face communication, although for the reasons of safety and to prevent near misses, it will need to be documented in system as well.
- Smooth handover systems may need to be established.

Access and Care		29 (52%)
	Regular round (ideally twice or more)	11
	Availability/ease to contact	7
	Attitude/joint working with nurses/team/junior doctor	6
	Taking ownership of patients/proactive	2
	Timeliness/Earlier ward round	2
	Earlier ward round over weekend	1
Documentation/Planning		18 (32%)
	Documenting outcome of ward round, discharge plan, discharge summary, care plan, completing drug card, referral to other doctor	12
	Availability of results before ward round	2
	Patients should have fully worked up management plan	1
	Named doctor	1
	Support from other consultant colleagues	1
	Support from colleagues	1
Inappropriate investigation, admission		2
Poor staffing level		2

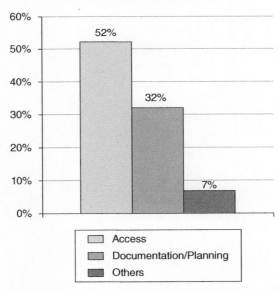

Consultant Cover CDU (*N* = 56)

Inference	• Access to a doctor/consultant has been the standout issue
	• Documentation, robust clinical management plan
Service improvement opportunities	• Access to a doctor can be easily managed by production of a robust rota which is visible to everybody
	• Doctors may carry bleep. Timelines is of vital important and so is documentation. Doctors should take ownership of their job.
	• A culture change may be necessary to address the fragmented documentation issue, which may take time and significant management involvement.

At the time of writing, the EM–CQIC is still in operation following a monthly cycle set out in Table 18.2. Data are presented to the group, and some of the projects are now collecting data from their second cycle. This CQIC seeks to change a shift in culture of the Emergency Medicine department from a reactive, crisis-driven culture to one that thrives on exploring the collection of data to understand and take collective action to improve systems in the department.

19

DEVELOPING A HUMAN TRANSPLANTATION HEALTH SERVICE IN NEPAL WITH ETHICAL AND MORAL MEDICAL LEADERSHIP

Pukar C. Shrestha

More 'leadership and less management' has been the trend in health systems in developed countries over recent years. The development of clinical/medical leadership roles in the UK served to engage clinicians to advance and improve the quality of care *within* clinical specialties in the NHS Healthcare system (Edmonstone, 2014; Giri et al., 2017). This promoted more leadership and less management, with much of this work undertaken at the micro levels of organisations and with some English NHS organisations adopting the Microsystems Coaching Academy (MCA) approach (please see Chapter 3). This approach was founded in the United States (Nelson et al., 2002; Narine and Persaud, 2003, 2014) along with other methods of improvement, for example, 'The Model for Improvement' (Chapter 14). Both the MCA and The Model for Improvement have been advanced in the developed world and may not necessarily apply in the same way or have the same priority in a developing country.

Developing countries face a raft of major macro level issues at a political, economic, geographical and of a social nature. Developing a healthcare system in a poor remote country will require a much broader set of medical leadership and management skills, as doctors will need to influence multiple systems across the country at the same time as they seek to develop and advance its healthcare services. Not only is this a different type of medical leadership to the model currently developed in the Western world but also the model requires embedding an ethical and moral framework, to ensure compliance with broader global standards of equality, financial risk protection and Sustainable Development Goals (Verguet, 2016). More traditional medical leadership programmes have largely overlooked the ethical and moral underpinning of leadership development programmes (Moscrop, 2012). The case study that follows outlines the application of a broader macro level approach to medical leadership and demonstrates how this approach provides an accountable ethical and moral framework in the development of a healthcare system. This case study is an account of the journey of the set-up of a human organ transplantation service in Nepal which started in 2008.

The development of human organ transplantation in Nepal

Nepal has a population of approximately 30 million people, with an estimated 3,000 people a year experiencing kidney failure and 1,000 people with liver failure. Prior to 2008, those who could afford it would fly to India for a kidney transplant, as Nepal lacked the physical infrastructure and the human resources to deliver this service. There were also insufficient policies and a lack of awareness of the cause of organ failure amongst the population at large. The trafficking in human organ transplantation had been a significant problem in Nepal, with reports of Nepalese villages being preyed upon by 'organ brokers' encouraging the sale of body parts to buy houses (Fleckner, 2015). Such practice led to restrictive organ donation policies to protect vulnerable people from human organ trafficking (Rasmussen et al., 2016). Although this policy aimed to protect vulnerable people, it later served to disable people, as the restrictive pairing arrangement meant that close friends, cousins and non-family members couldn't offer themselves as a donor.

One of the major problems that compounds the development of an equitable human organ transplantation service is that Nepali society is characterised by huge social diversity encompassing caste, ethnic and regional differences within a deeply patriarchal society, with 125 ethnic/caste groups and 123 languages (Richardson et al., 2016). Although Nepal signed up to the Convention on the Elimination of All Forms of Discrimination Against Women (CEDAW) in 1991, women donate kidneys out of self-protection and a sense of duty, whereas men rarely donate them to women (Rasmussen et al., 2016; Richardson et al., 2016).

Returning to Nepal from the UK in 2008 after six years as a surgeon in the English NHS, the social, economic and political situation in Nepal created significant challenges to the setting up of a human organ transplantation service. The first successful kidney transplantation in Bir hospital, the oldest Government hospital in the country was carried out in December 2008. This opened the door for the development of a human organ transplant service in Nepal, with the completion of 99 operations 4 years later, the first complicated multi-vessel kidney transplant, the first pair kidney transplant exchange and the first liver transplant surgery in 2016. Setting up this service against a challenging context meant that the clinical quality of the service needed to be high. There was a 99% graft survival rate, which created confidence in the new service.

A systems leadership approach is described by Fillingham and Goodson (2013), and the authors argue that at the macro level, there needs to be 'system enablers' Figure 19.1:

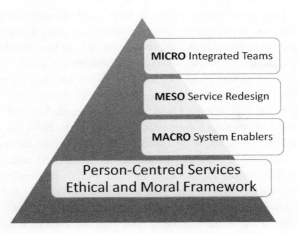

FIGURE 19.1   Person-centred macro health system development
Source: Adapted Fillingham and Goodson (2013).

TABLE 19.1   Skills and knowledge required for macro medical leadership

Skills and knowledge required for macro medical leadership		
Technical Know-How	Patient-centred/Ethical and moral framework Accessibility, fairness, equality	Service Design and co-production with communities; Governance arrangements; innovative contracting and financial mechanisms; Equality of opportunity; skills in technology
Improvement Know-How	Patient-centred/Ethical and moral framework Methods of engagement with multiple patient groups and communities	Systems thinking, partnership working with patients and community groups; engagement strategies, Improvement science, large-scale change
Personal Effectiveness	Patient-centred/Ethical and moral framework Core values demonstrated in medical leadership, such as integrity, trust, honesty, selflessness and a focus on the greater good rather and reducing poverty	Interpersonal skills and behaviour; A visionary participative style, embracing the core values of equality and a fair society

Source: Adapted from Fillingham and Goodson (2013).

Fillingham and Goodson (2013) suggest that there needs to be a balance of skills between technical and improvement know-how combined with personal effectiveness. However, this case study highlights the importance of two other domains: Person Centeredness and an Ethical and Moral Framework. The skills, knowledge and Ethical/Person Centredness is presented in Table 19.1

A series of large-scale change processes were implemented driven by systems thinking, but the core driver was the commitment that kidney transplants would be offered to all people in Nepal including those who did not have the financial means to pay. This generated a consensus amongst medical leaders, politicians and others that patients should not suffer financial hardship to pay for a kidney transplant, and the AAROGYA Foundation (www.aarogyafoundation.org.np) was set up in 2010 to raise money to fund the service. The AAROGYA Foundation paid for laboratory equipment so that samples no longer needed to be sent to India but instead could be undertaken with a next day service and at half the cost. The modern laboratory system includes tests such as human leukocyte antigen (HLA) which is critical to match patients and donors for blood or marrow and Tacrolimus levels testing to assess drug levels with transplantation patients. This is the only service in the country to provide results available within 12 hours at an affordable cost.

A major political and social marketing campaign ensued which aimed to spread the message about the human organ transplant service as well as to create positive messages about healthy lifestyle and kidney failure prevention. A public awareness campaign with health ministers led to 2,500 people registering as brain death kidney donors. The high-level support for this initiative led to the Prime Minister to becoming involved in World Kidney Day and political countrywide support was given to the first Transplant Games in Nepal.

It was 5 years later and after the first human transplant operation in Nepal that a dedicated Human Organ Transplant Centre was opened under the Ministry of Health in Bhaktapur, Nepal, 2012. This provided high-tech facilities for kidney and liver and pancreas transplantation. More patients were being diagnosed and treated, and between 2012 and 2016, the Haemo Dialysis service substantially increased the number of patients who were able to receive this service for free. Despite the successful growth in the service, two major problems were encountered while seeking to develop the service: (1) The current Transplant Act and Policy was limiting the amount of donors that were available, and (2) The patriarchal society in Nepal was creating substantial gender inequalities in the Human Organ Transplantation service. Both problems required further research and inquiry.

The transplant act and policy

The development of the service found that there were current restrictions with the Transplant Act, when a wider expansion of the live donor pool is required. To provide a wider accessible service, the live donor pool had to be expanded so that any relative could be a potential organ donor, and provision was made for organ donation of the deceased. After significant lobbying and influence of the AAROGYA Foundation, amendment of the Transplant Act 2072 and regulations 2073, with Transplant Regulation was passed in 2016, paving the way for the first liver transplant that occurred just 3 days after legislation had been passed. The law needed to change to facilitate and support any relative who wanted to be a donor including cousins and distant cousins. There also needed to be provision for deceased donor transplantation and brain death donors. One brain death can offer eight major organs for transplantation including two kidneys, two lungs, one liver, one heart, pancreas and one small intestine. The first deceased donor transplant (brain dead donor transplant) of two kidneys was undertaken in May 2017. With government support, kidney dialysis continues to be free alongside renal transplant. Surgery and post-transplant medications are delivered at a fraction of the cost of neighbouring countries and the Western world, and the quality of health outcomes are of a comparable standard.

Gender inequalities in human organ transplantation

There is a gender bias in the donation of human organs for transplantation, as 71% of donors are female and 29% are male, whereas 78% of recipients are male and 22% are female. Gender inequalities in organ transplantation are a global problem with no current framework for good practice guidelines for the appropriate handling of sex and gender issues in human transplantation research (Laprise et al., 2017). Research in Italy found that women seem to have more self-sacrifice and sense of responsibility than men (Puoti et al., 2016), and in Nepal, women more than men are obliged to suffer for the benefit of the greater family (Rasmussen et al., 2016).

A strategy to incentivise men to become donors in Nepal led the AAROGYA Foundation to pay the family if the man donates a kidney. This strategy has now started to show changes in reducing gender inequalities in human organ donation, but more needs to be done to challenge the entrenched gender inequalities in Nepal. The longer-term solution is suggested to be for women to secure dignified work as a way to lift themselves out of poverty and discrimination (Pfeffer, 2011). Gender inequalities in human organ transplantation are indicative of deeper levels of social and economic inequalities in Nepal where women's choices are limited. Fairer economic opportunities is a way that can challenge societal gender inequalities, and this is evidenced in the United States, where it was found that when individuals had the means to access human organ transplant services, there was no gender or ethnic differences found (OPTN/UNOS, 2010). In Nepal, the root causes of the gender bias are deeply rooted in Nepal's systemic, inequitable treatment of women, where women are seen as socially responsible for the health of their male kin (Rasmussen et al., 2016). Lack of access to education and employment opportunities particularly in remote and rural locations in Nepal is a challenge. But fair pay for fair work should be a vision for women's labour in Nepal, where the successful female volunteer service has made significant progress in achieving the countries immunisation targets, yet they continue to work as unpaid volunteers (Government of Nepal, 2067 programme strategy).

References for Part 3

Aylott, J., Godbole, P., and Burke, D. (2017). "Clinicians versus Clinicians versus Managers" or New Patient Centred Culture that eradicates 'Them and Us'? in *Why Hospitals Fail* (Eds) Prasad Godbole, Derek Burke and Jill Aylott, Springer.

Bardsley, M. (2016). *Understanding analytical capability in health care: Do we have more data than insight?* London: Health Foundation. www.health.org.uk/publication/understanding-analytical-capability-health-care.

Bardsley, M., Steventon, A., Smith, J., and Dixon, J. (2013). Evaluating integrated and community based-care: How do we know what works? www.nuffieldtrust.org.uk/evaluation.

Bate, P., and Robert, G. (2006). Experience-based design: From redesigning the system around the patient to co-designing services with the patient. *Quality & Safety Health Care*, 15, 307–310.

Belbin, R. M. (1981). *Management teams: Why they succeed and fail*. Oxford: Butterworth Heineman.

Berwick, D. (1992). Continuous quality improvement in medicine: From theory to practice: Heal thyself or heal thy system: Can doctors help to improve medical care? *Quality in Health Care*, 1, Supplement S2–S8.

Berwick, D. (2013). "The importance and challenge of clinical leadership": Interview. King's Fund: London (video). www.kingsfund.org.uk/audi-video/don-berwick-importance-and-challenge-clinical-leadership.

Bevan, H. P. J., and Layton, A. (2000). Management issues in health care a "breakthrough" approach to reducing delays and patient waiting times. *Clinical Management*, 9, 27–31.

BMA. (2008). *The role of the consultant contract*. www.bma.org.uk.

Broad, M. (2010 9 December). Cutting consultant SPAs is a false economy. *Hospital Doctor News*.

Careau, E., Biba, G., Brander, R., Van Dijk, J. P., Verona, S., Paterson, M., and Tassone, M. (2014). Health leadership education programmes, best practices and impact on learners' knowledge, skills, attitudes and behaviours and system change: A literature review. *Journal of Healthcare Leadership*, 6, 39–550.

Chapman, A., and Giri, P. (2017). Learning to lead: Tools for self assessment of leadership skills and styles. In: Godbole, Prasad, Burke, Derek, and Aylott, Jill (eds). *Why hospitals fail* (eds). Basel, Switzerland: Springer International Publishing AG 2017.

Crisp, H. (2017). *Delivering a national approach to patient flow in Wales: Learning from the 1000 lives improvement programme*. London: The Health Foundation.

Daly, J., Jackson, D., Manix, J., Davidson, P. M., and Hutchinson, M. (2014). The importance of clinical leadership in the hospital setting. *Journal of Healthcare Leadership*, 6, 75–83.

Deci, E. L., and Ryan, R. M. (2000). The what and why of goal pursuits: Human needs and the self determination of behaviour. *Psychological Inquiry*, 11(4), 227–268.

Deci, E. L., and Ryan, R. M. (1985). *Intrinsic motivation and self determination in human behaviour*. Newcastle: Plenum Press.

Deming, W. E. (1986). *Out of the crisis*. Cambridge, MA: MIT Press.

Deming, W. E. (2000). *Out of the crisis*. Cambridge, MA: MIT Press.

Edmonstone, J. (2014). Wither the Elephant: The continuing development of clinical leadership in the UK national health services. *The International Journal of Heath Planning and Management*, 29(3), 280–291.

Ferlie, E. B., and Shortell, S. M. (2001). Improving the quality of health care in the United Kingdom and the United States: A framework for change. *Millbank Quarterly*, 79, 281–315.

Fillingham, P., and Goodson, S. (2013 23 May). *Developing system wide leadership*. London: The Kings Fund.

Fleckner, M. (2015 10 July). Organ brokers. House Nepal, *Mailonline*.

Forsyth, D. R. (2010). *Group dynamics*, 5th edition. Belmont, CA: Wadsworth, Cenage Learning.

Francis, R. (2012). The mid Staffordshire hospitals public enquiry "The Francis Report". www.midstaffspublicenquiry.com.

Frich, J. C., Brewster, A. L., Cherlin, E. J., and Bradley, E. H. (2015). Leadership development programs for physicians: A systematic review. *Journal of General Internal Medicine*, 30(5), 656–674.

Gaba, D. M. (2004). "The future vision of simulation in health care". *Quality & Safety Health Care*, 13(suppl 1), i2.

Giordano, R. (2010). *Leadership needs of medical and clinical directors*. London: The Kings Fund.

Giri, P., Aylott, J., and Kilner, K. (2017). Self determining medical leadership needs occupational health physicians *Leadership in Health Services*, 30(4), 394–410.

Goleman, D. (2000). Leadership that gets results *Harvard Business Review* March-April issue.

Government of Nepal 2067 PROGRAMME STRATEGY www.advancingpartners.org/sites/default/files/nepal_national_female_chv_program_strategy.pdf.

Hartley, J., and Hinksman, B. (2003) Leadership Development: A systematic Review of the Literature: A Report for the NHS Leadership Centre.

Health Foundation. (2011). *Evidence scan: Improvement science*. London: The Health Foundation.

Hogan, H., Healey, F., Neale, G., Thomson, R., Vincent, C., and Black, N. (2012, 7 July). Preventable deaths due to problems in care in English acute hospitals: A retrospective case record review study. *BMJ Quality Safety*, published online.

Horak, B. J., Cloonan, P., Wolk, A., Montero, A., Moore, E., and Giunta, B. (2014, Summer). Interdisciplinary learning and projects in quality improvement and patient safety at Georgetown university. *The Journal of Health Administration Education*, Summer 2014.

IHI. (2003). The model for improvement. In: Langley, G. L., Moen, R., Nolan, K. M., Nolan, T. W., Norman, C. L., and Provost, L. P. (eds). *The improvement guide: A practical approach to enhancing organisational performance*, 2nd edition. San Francisco: Jossey Bass Publishers.

Jones, P., Shepherd, M., Wells, S., Le Feure, J., and Ameratunga, S. (2014). Review article: What makes a good healthcare quality indicator? A systematic review and validation study. *Emergency Medicine Australasia*, 26, 113–124.

Kotter, J. P. (1996). *Leading change*. Boston: Harvard Business School.

Langley, G. L., Moen, R., Nolan, K. M., Nolan, T. W., Norman, C. L., and Provost, L. P. (2009). *The improvement guide: A practical approach to enhancing organisational performance*, 2nd edition. San Francisco: Jossey Bass Publishers.

Laprise, C., Sridhar, U. S., West, L., Foster, B., and Pilate, L. (2017). Sex and gender considerations in transpopulation research: Protocol for a scoping review. *Systematic Reviews*, 6, 186.

Lewin, K., Lippit, R., and White, R. K. (1939). Patterns of aggressive behaviour in experimentally created social climates. *Journal of Social Psychology*, 10, 271–301.

Marshall, S. P. (2006). *The power to transform, leadership that brings learning and schooling to life*, 1st edition. San Francisco: Jossey Bass.

Moscrop, A. (2012). Clinical leadership: Individual advancement, political authority and a lack of direction? *British Journal of General Practice*, 62(598), 384–386.

Nassef, A., Ramsden, L., Newnham, A., Archer, G., Jackson, R., Davies, J., and Stewart, K. (2017). Factors affecting failure. In: Godbole, Prasad, Burke, Derek, and Aylott, Jill (eds). *Why hospitals fail*. Basel, Switzerland: Springer International Publishing AG 2017.

Nadeem, E., Olin, S., Campbell Hill, L., Eaton Hoagwood, K., and McCue Horwitz, S. (2013). Understanding the components of quality improvement collaboratives: A systematic literature review. *The Millbank Quarterly*, 2, 354–394.

Narine, L., and Persaud, D. D. (2003). Gaining and maintaining commitment to large-scale change in healthcare organisations. *Health Services Management Research*, 16, 179–187.

Narine, L., and Persaud, D. D. (2014). Gaining and maintaining commitment to large-scale change in healthcare organisation. *Health Service Management Research*, 16(3), 179–187.

National Patient Safety Agency (NPSA). (2004). *Seven steps to patient safety*. London. http://www.who.int/patientsafety/events/04/7_Williams.pdf

National Transportation Safety Board. (2010). Loss of thrust in both engines after encountering a flock of Birds and subsequent ditching on the Hudson river US Airways Flight 1549 Airbus A320-214, N106US Weehawken, New Jersey January 15, 2009. Accident Report NTSB/AAR-10/03 PB2010-910403. 49–50. www.ntsb.gov/investigations/Accident Reports/Reports/AAR1003.pdf.

Nelson, E., Batelden, P. B., Huber, T. P., Mohr, J. J., Godfrey, M. M., Headrick, L. A., and Wasson, J. H. (2002). Microsystems in health care: Part 1. Learning from high-performing front-line clinical units. *Journal on Quality Improvement*, 28, 472–493.

Nembhard, I. M. (2009). Learning and improving in quality improvement collaboratives: Which collaborative features do participants value most? *Health Services Research*, 44, 2, part1.

NHS Leadership Academy. (2013). Towards a new model of leadership for the NHS. *NHS Leadership Academy*. www.leadershipacademy.nhs.uk.

Northouse, P. G. (1997). *Leadership theory and practice*. Thousand Oaks, CA: Sage Publications.

Organ Procurement and Transplant Network (OPTN/UNOS). (2010). *Organ transplantation report on equity in access*.

Ottestad, E., Boulet, J. R., and Lighthall, G. K. (2007). Evaluating the management of septic shock using patient simulation. *Critical Care Medicine*, 35, 769–775.

Ovretveit, J. (2002). How to run an effective improvement collaborative. *International Journal of Quality Health Care Quality Assurance*, 15, 192–196.

Ovretveit, J., Bate, P., Clearly, P., Cretin, S., Gustafson, D., McInnes, K., MacLoud, H., Molfenter, T., Plesk, P., Robert, G., Shortell, S., and Wilson, T. (2002). Quality collaboratives: Lessons from research. *Quality & Safety Health Care*, 11, 345–351.

Ovretveit, J., and Gustafson, D. (2003). Using research to inform quality programmes. *BMJ*, 326, 759–761.

Peerally, M. F., Carr, S., Waring, J., and Dixon-Woods, M. (2017). The problem with root cause analysis. *BMJ Quality & Safety*, 26, 417–422.

Peden, C. J., and Rooney, K. D. (2009). The science of improvement as it relates to quality and safety in the ICU. *JICS*, 10(4), 260–265.

Parand, A., Burnett, S., Benn, J., Iskander, S., Pinto, A., and Vincent, C. (2010, October). Medical engagement in organisation wide safety and quality improvement programmes: Experience in the UK safer patients initiative. *Quality & Safety Health Care*, 19(5).

Pfeffer, N. (2011, November). Eggs-ploiting women: A critical feminist analysis of the different principles in transplant and fertility tourism. *Reprod Biomed Online*, 23(5), 634–641.

Puoti, F., Ricci, A., Nanni-Costa, A., Ricciardi, W., Malorni, W., and Ortona, E. (2016). Organ transplantation and gender differences: A paradigmatic example of intertwining between biological and sociocultural determinants. *Biology of Sex Differences*, 7(35).

Qurashi, S. A., Kimatian, S. J., Murray, W. B., and Sinz, E. H. (2011). High fidelity simulation as an experiential model for teaching root cause analysis. *Journal of Graduate Medical Education*, 3(4), 529–534.

Richardson, D., Laurie, N., Poudel, M., and Townsend, J. (2016). Women and citizenship post-trafficking: The case of Nepal. *The Sociological Review*, 64(2), 329–348.

Reed, J. E., and Card, A. J. (2015). The problem with plan do study act cycles. *BMJ Quality & Safety*, 0–6.

Rasmussen, S., Paneru, P., Shrestha, K., and Shrestha, P. (2016). Gender bias and organ transplantation in Nepal. *Himalaya, the Journal of the Association for Nepal and Himalayan Studies*, 36(2).

Ryan, R. M., and Deci, E. L. (2000). Self determination theory and the facilitation of intrinsic motivation, social development and well being. *The American Psychologist*, 55(1), 68–78.

Senge, P. (2006). *The fifth discipline: The art and practice of the learning organisation*, 2nd edition. London: Random House Business.

Shortell, S., O'Brien, J. M., Carman, R. W., Foster, R. W., Hughes, E. F., Boerstler, H., and O'Connor, E. J. (1995). Assessing the impact of continuous quality improvement/total quality management: Concept versus implementation. *Health Service Research*, 30(2), 377.

Tenner, E. (1997). *Why things bite back: Technology and the revenge effect*. London: Fourth Estate.

Skard Brandrud, A., Schreiner, A., Hjortdahl, P., Saevil Helljeson, G., Nyen, B., and Nelson, E. C. (2011). Three success factors for continual improvement in healthcare: An analysis of the reports of improvement team members. *BMJ Quality & Safety*, 20, 251–259.

Simms, E. R., Slakey, D. P., Garstka, M. E., et al. (2012). Can simulation improve the traditional method of root cause analysis: A preliminary investigation. *Surgery*, 152, 489–497.

Thorpe, R., Gold, J., and Lawler, J. (2011). Locating distributed leadership. *International Journal of Management Reviews*, 13, 239–250.

Verguet, S. (2016). Defining pathways and trade-offs toward universal health coverage comment on "Ethical Perspective: Five Unacceptable trade-offs on the path to Universal Health Coverage". *Journal of Health Policy Management*, 11:5(7), 445–447.

VonKorff, M., Gruman, J., Schaefer, J., Curry, S., and Wagner, E. H. (1997). Collaborative management of chronic illness. *Annals of Internal Medicine*, 127, 1097–1102.

Wrazen, R., and Soliman, S. (2017). Effective hospital leadership: Quality performance evaluation. In: Godbole, Prasad, Burke, Derek, and Aylott, Jill (eds). *Why hospitals fail*. Basel, Switzerland: Springer International Publishing AG 2017.

Woods, P. (2004). Democratic leadership: Drawing distinctions with distributed leadership *Integrated Journal of Leadership in Education*, 7, 3–26.

Woods, P. A., and Gronn, P. (2009). Nurturing democracy: The contribution of distributed leadership to a democratic organisational landscape. *Educational Management Administration and Leadership*, 37, 430–451.

Wallace, L. M., Boxall, M., Spurgeon, P., and Barwell, F. (2007). Organizational interventions to promote risk management in primary care: The experience in Warwickshire, England. *Health Services Management Research*, 2, 84–93.

Wright, M., and Butterworth, T. (2014). The impact of a large-scale quality improvement programme on work engagement: Preliminary results from a national cross-sectional-survey of the "'Productive Ward'". *International Journal of Nursing Studies*, 51(12), 1634–1643.

PART 4

Service development

20

AN INTRODUCTION

Jeff Perring

In this section, we will be looking at service development and in particular four examples of service development projects undertaken by clinicians at a local level. However, before we look at these projects, we need to consider how their intended improvements are measured. Some outcomes, such as mortality rates, are easily measured and can show real improvements in service. However, these hard measures are not always useful, either because the rate of that measure is low or because the condition itself is chronic and service improvements may not change the outcome of that condition but will change the quality of life of those living with it.

In this section Fiona Kew considers broader measurements of outcome and in particular those relating to the perspective of patients. To do this, she considers in detail patient-reported outcome measures (PROMs). These measures, which are designed to measure health-related quality of life, are being used increasingly within certain healthcare systems, and Fiona Kew considers whether there is the evidence base to support this.

Following on from this we look at three specific projects: Victoria Hemming undertook work to design and introduce an electronic observation system into a paediatric ward; Samantha Wong looked at person-centred service redesign for young carers in a school setting; and Halla Zaitoun looked at service improvement in paediatric dentistry.

For those new to service improvement, these examples provide an important introduction not just to the processes involved but also to the challenges. Excellent work was achieved within these projects, but not all succeeded in reaching their planned goals; not all service improvement projects succeed as originally intended, but improvements can still made along the way.

The authors have reflected upon their projects and these reflections, collected together at the end of this section and provide vital lessons to those setting out on their own service improvement projects.

21

'PATIENT REPORTED OUTCOME MEASURES': WE HAVE BARELY STARTED TO WALK LET ALONE RUN

Fiona Kew

The vision of the World Health Organization (WHO) is for Universal Health Coverage (UHC) and for all global citizens to have equality of access to skilled and motivated healthcare workers within a performing healthcare system by 2030 (WHO, 2013, 2016). The WHO's focus on improving the competence of healthcare workers and improving the healthcare system is fundamental to improving the quality of care. However, when exploring the funding of healthcare from an individual country's perspective, the understanding of what quality is and how to measure the 'quality' of healthcare becomes much more challenging particularly at a time of global austerity. This chapter critically explores the use of Patient-Related Outcome Measures (PROMs) as a tool that has evolved over time to measure the quality of care.

The complexity of understanding improvements in healthcare is confounded by the way social conditions and health inequalities impact on healthcare. Social improvements such as better housing and smoking cessation alongside public health measures such as the provision of clean water have a positive impact on a society's health. Teasing out the effect of healthcare provision within this is challenging, especially for remitting and relapsing chronic conditions.

In the United Kingdom, Lord Ara Darzi (2008) sought to clarify quality in healthcare by seeking to "systematically measure and publish information about the quality of care from the frontline up". These measurements or 'Quality Accounts' were to include the views of patients on "the success of their treatment and the quality of their experiences". A direct link was made between the quality of care provided and funding for the hospital providing that care.

Similar challenges in the measurement of healthcare quality have been found in the United States healthcare system, where indicators of quality of care have been noted to vary with organisational factors, practitioner skills, data completeness and accuracy as well as external factors such as random variation and severity of illness

(Gross et al., 2000). Furthermore, indicator-specific factors, such as differing data sources, data selection and population inclusion/exclusion, have been shown to cause substantial differences in reported outcomes for the same standard of care. Gross et al. (2000) demonstrated that use of different numerators, denominators and risk adjustments can alter a hospital's position in a league table from a low to a high outlier despite using the same data, where the outcome is something as apparently clear-cut as perioperative mortality. Such statistical pitfalls are widely recognised (Appleby, 2011).

Historically, performance data have tended to focus on easily measurable outcomes, which are not necessarily the outcomes that matter most to patients (Yudkin et al., 2011). Almost inevitably it is easier to measure structure (e.g. how many hospitals are there?) and process (e.g. how many operations have been done? how many people have been prescribed a drug?) than outcome (e.g. did the operation make the patient better? did the drug improve quality of life?) (Donabedian, 1966). However, process and outcome should be considered as complementary, rather than as competing, measures of quality, and a robust system for assessing quality should consider both aspects (Georgiou and Pearson, 2002).

This concentration on process rather than outcome was highlighted by the National Health Service (NHS) Plan in the UK (Department of Health, 2000), which aimed to modernise the NHS. Public consultation showed that the public wanted more and better paid staff using new ways of working, reduced waiting times and high-quality care centred on patients and improvements in local hospitals and surgeries. This was reflected in the structural recommendations of the plan which included over 100 new hospitals, 2,000 more GPs and 20,000 extra nurses whilst patients surveys and forums advocated to 'help services become more patient-centred'. (Department of Health, 2000)

It is striking, however, that mention was made of neither clinically meaningful improvements in care, nor any assessment of outcomes that matter most to patients anywhere in the plan (Department of Health, 2000). The executive summary failed to include even the most basic outcome measure (survival/mortality rates) let alone more subtle outcomes such as improved functioning or improvements in health-related quality of life. This may be why later assessments of the impact of the associated financial investment failed to identify the expected benefits in health outcomes. NHS productivity was found to have decreased by an average of 0.2% per year between 2000 and 2010 whilst productivity in hospitals fell by around 1.4% per year, despite the financial investment (National Audit Office, 2011). This increased funding paid for more, better paid staff, alongside extra goods and services but hospital activity – adjusted to reflect improvements in the quality of care – did not rise at the same rate as these additional resources. However, the adjustments made for quality were challenging and remain at an early stage of development due largely to the lack of data on health gains (National Audit Office, 2010).

Maxwell (1992) theorised that there are six areas to consider when looking at quality: effectiveness, efficiency, access, equity, relevance and social acceptability. He also explored the tension that exists between these different areas such that delivering very highly in one area (e.g. efficiency) could impact on another area (e.g. access). Recent efforts to improve healthcare in the United States have focused on improving access to high-quality care as a means to improve population health, being just as important as looking at process and outcome (US Department of Health and Human Services, 2014). However, Berwick argues that the ultimate measure by which to judge the quality of a medical effort is whether it helps patients (and their families) as they see it. Anything else is, by definition, waste (Berwick, 1997).

Over recent years, greater interest has been taken to determine outcomes that patients value. Patients offer a complementary perspective to that of providers and policymakers and should ideally be involved in the process of assessing care. This means that rather than asking, 'how long did I wait for my operation, and how long was I in hospital?' the emphasis is shifting towards 'did my operation make me better, did it improve my quality of life?' (Browne, 2007; Greenhalgh, 2009) and 'was I satisfied with my care?' (Rademakers et al., 2011). To this end, there has been increasing interest in the use of patient-reported outcome measures (PROMs), which are designed to measure health-related quality of life (HRQoL) in addition to patient-reported experience measures (PREMs). However, it has been shown that satisfaction with care as recorded by PREMs correlates poorly with health-related quality of life (Avery, 2006) but better with experiences of process and, to a lesser extent, structure (Rademakers et al., 2011). This may be because satisfaction is closely related to expectation. Whereas PREMs are useful in gaining an understanding of the patient experience, interest in terms of assessing quality of care has, therefore, focused more on PROMs, rather than on PREMs (Avery, 2006; Rademakers et al., 2011).

Patient-reported outcome measures (PROMs)

PROMs are usually in the form of questionnaires, either paper or electronic, which contain a series of questions from which a score can be developed (Snyder et al., 2012) to determine a patient's health-related quality of life (HRQoL). Many different tools are in use (Patient Reported Outcomes Measurement Group, 2005), and these tools vary from the general such as the SF36 (Ware et al., 1992), the General Health Questionnaire (Goldberg et al., 1997) and theEQ5D (Carr-Hill, 1992) to the more specific such as the EORTOC-QLQ EN 24 (Greimel et al., 2011) for endometrial cancer and the Oxford Hip Score (Dawson et al., 1996).

Speight and Barendse (2010) recognised that "any initiative that puts patients at the centre of treatment decisions is welcome providing these measures are selected and interpreted appropriately and related precisely to a prior hypotheses regarding treatment outcome". Remarking on the US Food and Drug Administration's guidelines on using PROMs to support claims in product literature for medications (US Food and Drug Administration, 2013), it was remarked that "the basic principles are undoubtedly relevant for a range of stakeholders" providing the tool measured the intended outcome.

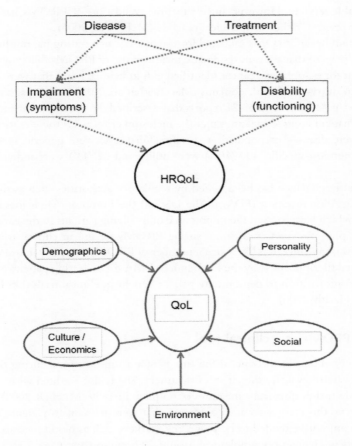

FIGURE 21.1   The inter-relationship between Quality of Life (QoL), Health-Related Quality of Life (HRQoL), health and the environment

Over recent years, there have been moves within the NHS in England to use PROMs that have been validated for use in research trials and clinical settings at the individual patient level as a means of measuring and comparing quality of clinical care across organisations (Department of Health, 2009) in a meaningful way (Darzi, 2008).

Does the use of patient-reported outcome measures (PROMs) measure quality?

The origins of PROMs can be traced back to the early 1970s when they were developed as a health indicator to quantify health beyond simple absolute measures such as mortality and morbidity (Kind and Rosser, 1988) in order to evaluate and plan health services. However, since this time, validation of PROMs has mainly been for research rather than clinical practice (McDowell, 2006).

The number of PROMs validated for use in a research setting has mushroomed over the years so that a recent systematic review of use of PROMs following radical treatment for oesophageal cancer identified 606 individual items that were categorised into thirty-two health domains (Macefield et al., 2014). As long ago as 2002, Garratt et al. (2002) found 3,921 reports that described the development and evaluation of patient assessed measures met the inclusion criteria. Of these reports, 1819 (46%) were disease- or population-specific, 865 (22%) were generic, 690 (18%) were dimension-specific, 409 (10%) were utility and 62 (1%) were individualised measures.

Recently, guidance has been issued by regulatory authorities such as the Food and Drug Administration (FDA) in the US and the European Medicines Agency (EMA), which have stressed the importance of involving patients in the early stages of developing new and evaluating existing PROMs for use in clinical trials. As a result of this guidance, it is likely that a number of PROMs currently in use will not be deemed fit for purpose by the FDA and/or EMA for collecting patient-reported outcome information to demonstrate patient benefit in clinical trials (US Department of Health, 2006).

Use of PROMs as a clinical tool

Florence Nightingale was one of the first people to insist on measuring the outcome of care to evaluate the effect of treatment. She is also credited with creating the world's first performance measures of hospitals in 1859 (Mitchell, 2008). However, despite this early foray into outcomes that were relevant to patients, healthcare outcomes have tended to be judged by markers such as blood pressure, blood test results or changes on radiological imaging (Higginson and Carr, 2001). Whilst these outcomes may be beneficial to patients, their illness cannot be taken in isolation from their experience, expectations and social context. This recognition led to interest in using and validating existing PROMs for use in a clinical context.

Higginson and Carr (2001) identified seven potential uses for quality of life measures in routine clinical practice:

1   To prioritise problems
2   To facilitate communication
3   To screen for potential problems
4   To identify preferences
5   To monitor changes
6   To assess response to treatment
7   To train new staff.

Garratt et al. (1993) recognised that the development of an internal market in the NHS would mean that purchaser needed information about the effectiveness of the care they were delivering, otherwise care would be purchased on the basis of cost alone, with potentially serious consequences for quality. They, therefore, assessed the Short Form Health Survey Questionnaire (SF36), a general outcome measure that had previously been validated in an American population (McHorney et al., 1994), for validity, reliability and acceptability in four common conditions: low back pain, menorrhagia, suspected peptic ulcer and varicose veins. They found that there were clear differences in self-reported health between the general population and patients with these four conditions alongside differences between referred and non-referred patients with these conditions. Further, there was a high level of agreement between SF36 scores and general practitioners' perceptions of symptom severity. Their findings confirmed that the psychometric validity and reliability of the SF36 questionnaire remained intact when transferred from a research to a clinical setting.

The SF36 has also been shown to be responsive to changes in people's health in the United States, following total hip replacement (Katz et al., 1992) and cardiac valve surgery (Phillips and Lansky, 1992). This responsiveness to treatment has further been demonstrated in a UK population, using transition questions to demonstrate self-reported changes in health (Garratt et al., 1994). The SF36 has also been shown to be sufficiently reliable to monitor health in groups of patients and, in four of its subscales, suitable for individual patient management (Ruta et al., 1994).

Attempts to validate other PROMs in clinical practice have had varying degrees of success. The EORTC QLQ-C30 is a questionnaire developed to assess the quality of life of cancer patients in international clinical trials (Affleck et al., 1993). However, when validated for clinical use, its use was found to be limited (Determann et al., 2004). Results showed insufficient discriminative and insufficient construct validity. Therefore, it cannot be assumed that PROMs developed for use in clinical trials will be useful at the level of patient care and/or monitoring.

Even when measures have been validated in a clinical context, evidence of benefit from their use in clinical practice has been lacking in systematic reviews (Espallargues et al., 2000; Gilbody et al., 2001; Greenhalgh et al., 2005). This is partly due to the heterogeneity of methodology that limits the ability to generalise any findings to a broader population (Valderas et al., 2008). In many cases, papers assessed the impact of PROMs on the process of care, rather than changes in patient outcome (Valderas et al., 2008). For example, the use of feedback scores in depression rating scales has been shown to have no impact on the process of patient care or subsequent patient outcomes (Hoeper et al., 1984; German et al., 1987; Gilbody et al., 2001). Further, the choice of instrument may have been based on convenience or available resources rather than the specific outcomes required (Bayliss, 2012).

In order to produce a benefit, patients' problems must be identified and dealt with and treatment decisions based on the patient's priorities and preferences (Higginson and Carr, 2001). Several randomised trials have assessed the use of PROMs in clinical settings. Velikova et al. (2004) found no benefit in HRQoL and emotional functioning in a group of oncology patients commencing treatment. A subsequent qualitative study in this population found that explicit mention of PROMs data in the consultation may strengthen opportunities for patients to elaborate on their problems (Greenhalgh et al., 2013). However, whilst a positive longitudinal impact of the intervention on symptom discussion has been observed, the same impact was not seen in function discussion (Takeuchi et al., 2011), suggesting that potentially serious problems may remain unaddressed. Further training of clinicians in responding to patient-reported functional concerns may increase the impact of this intervention (Takeuchi et al., 2011; Greenhalgh et al., 2013).

Greenhalgh developed a theory-driven approach to the use of HRQoL measures in clinical practice (Greenhalgh et al., 2005), which requires the following:

1   The provision of HRQoL information to clinicians in order to prompt them to discuss HRQoL with their patients;
2   HRQoL information is used to enable clinicians to detect unrecognised problems and/or monitor the impact of treatment;
3   On detecting a problem or a decrease in HRQoL in response to treatment, the clinician will intervene to address this – either by changing or stopping treatment or by addressing side effects with effective management;
4   The act of monitoring responses to treatment, or actual treatment changes, may result in changes to patient behaviours such as treatment adherence;
5   This may then lead to improvements in the patient's health or satisfaction with his or her care.

These complex requirements for use of PROMs in a clinical setting may explain why many studies have failed to show any change in HRQoL when their routine use is introduced and why training of clinicians in their use may change this.

Use of PROMs to assess quality

The majority of PROM-related literature (Bayliss, 2012; Greenhalgh et al., 2005; Espallargues et al., 2000) has considered the impact of their use on individual clinical care rather than considering the use of widespread PROMs to compare quality of care between services and institutions or to compare different interventions in a cost-limited service. As the use of PROMs in clinical practice has become more widespread, there has been an increasing interest in their use to assess quality. It has been postulated that they may provide an effective and efficient way of both improving and evaluating the processes and outcomes of care that contribute to healthcare quality (Marshall et al., 2006).

Use of PROMs to assess quality of providers in the United Kingdom

In 1998, British United Provident Association (BUPA), an independent healthcare provider in the United Kingdom, set out to collect outcomes data for elective surgery in their hospitals. The SF36 was completed pre-operatively and post-operatively and feedback of results, by way of change in scores, sent to the relevant providers, including to the consultant surgeons (Vallance-Owen et al., 2004). The primary aim was to facilitate continuous quality improvement, partly by using out-lier data to direct further audit of outcome measures such as readmissions, com-plaints and variance from standard care pathways.

Experience in the independent sector and increasing political interest in assess-ing meaningful outcomes from the NHS led to several major pieces of work being undertaken. The 2005 review of government outputs and expenditure (Atkinson, 2005) recommended that a number of dimensions of quality should be measured with results weighted by marginal social valuation. The review also recommended longitudinal data collection on health outcomes to demonstrate changes over time. The political imperative was reinforced in *High Quality Care for All: NHS Next Stage Review Final Report* (Darzi, 2008), where the focus of NHS improvement moved from 'quantity of care to one that focuses on improving the quality of care'. As a result, data are being collected in orthopaedic surgery (knee and hip replace-ment) and general surgery (varicose vein surgery and hernia repair) (Department of Health, 2009).

The NHS PROMs initiative has been collecting around 8,000 new records per month (Appleby, 2011), although it remains unclear as to whether the differences seen in health gain between procedures are of any significance.

International use of PROMs

In Sweden, a programme of nationwide prospective observational follow-up has been in place since 1979 (Rolfson et al., 2011). The use of PROMs began in 2002 and gradually expanded to include all units performing total hip replace-ment in Sweden. The tools used are the EQ-5D, the Charnley Classification and visual analogue scales for pain and satisfaction. Questionnaires were completed pre-operatively and 1 year post-operatively. This is a small register, with 960 cases reported between 2002 and 2011.

In the United States, the only national programme for collecting patient-reported outcomes is within Medicare (Safran, 2001), where a validated PROM (VR-12) and Medicare's own HOS questionnaires were used.

In Australia, a nationwide programme was introduced to systematically collect outcomes data in Mental Health services in 2003 (Burgess et al., 2012). Although the use of this data was limited (Meehan et al., 2006 and Callaly et al., 2006), it was used in a series of benchmarking forums to try to compare services and improve quality. Participants in these forums found the examination of intra-organisational variability to be useful in informing service improvements. However, they needed considerable support to generate the required information and to interpret it meaningfully (Burgess et al., 2012).

Data presentation

Although PROMs have been subjected to extensive testing of their measure-ment properties, less attention has been paid to the range of metrics that can be derived from before and after PROMs data (Hildon et al., 2012). BUPA found they encountered multiple problems with the form in which data were presented (Vallance-Owen et al., 2004). The use of histograms and league tables failed to identify appropriate areas for audit and did not take account of normal variation, leading to a proportion of hospitals being incorrectly labelled. This led to data being presented as control charts and the use of league tables being abandoned.

Hildon et al. (2012) undertook a review of the PROMs used in the NHS PROMs programme and identified four suitable metrics for use:

1   Mean follow-up score
2   Mean change in score
3   Proportion reaching a specified 'good' threshold at follow-up
4   Proportion reaching a minimally important difference usually based on the clinician or the patient reporting an improvement and correlating it to the score.

These were derived from six studies that included PROMs (Round et al., 2004; Campbell, 2005; Siggeirsdottir et al., 2005; Ryan et al., 2006; Browne, 2007) although none of them were designed to evaluate the PROMs themselves. Studies also varied in their use, their patient populations and the questionnaires used. Browne recognised that most PROMs have been evaluated for use only in the monitoring of individual patient care, and not for comparative audit (e.g. comparing performance across institutions). Whilst favoured by some other authors, Browne (2007) also rejected 'minimally important difference' as a usable outcome due to methodological uncertainties with the measure.

Biases

Carr et al. (2001) hypothesised that people have different expectations and that this may result in differences in outcome measures. People may be at different points in their illness when their quality of life is measured and their expectations may change with time. This occurs because expectations are learnt from experiences, vary between individuals and are subject to differences in social, psychological, socioeconomic, demographic and other cultural factors (Figure 21.1). For example, older people have described the need to adapt to their changing circumstances as a means of successfully coping with ageing.

Existing measures of quality of life do not account for expectations of health; they do not incorporate the boundaries within which levels of expectation and experience are measured. The result is that someone with an experience of poor health who has low expectations might not evaluate the experience as having an impact on their quality of life because their expectations are correspondingly low. Further, patients from more deprived areas tend to rate their pre-operative health-related quality of life as worse than those from less deprived areas (Appleby, 2010). In general, higher utilisation of outpatient and inpatient services has been shown to be more strongly associated with higher morbidity as calculated by diagnosis code than with patient-reported disease burden, anxiety or depressive symptoms.

In contrast, patient-reported outcomes are strongly and more frequently associated with subjective predictors of patient-reported disease burden and emotional symptoms (Bayliss, 2012).

The impact of comorbidity on PROMs is also recognised (Devlin and Appleby, 2010). In patients with end stage renal failure, comorbidity was one of the factors associated with alterations in SF36 score (Wight et al., 1998). Mild symptoms of anxiety and depression have been shown to be associated with selected outcomes, independent of both clinical and self-report of morbidity, indicating the importance of assessing symptoms of mental well-being as part of completely quantifying morbidity (Bayliss, 2012). Both self-reported morbidity and mood symptoms are, therefore, important in understanding the contribution of morbidity burden for investigations using patient-reported outcomes (Bayliss, 2012). Without this, even cross-referencing PROMs with hospital episode and statistics data will under represent the levels of comorbidity.

The level of recruitment may bias the outcome from PROMs collection, although little research has been undertaken in this area (Browne, 2007). The NHS PROMs programme recommends a recruitment level of 80%, which was found in the BUPA study to be difficult to achieve, with only 62% completing the baseline questionnaire, rising to 75% when reminders were sent out. This level still caused concerns about the validity of the data other than to attempt to detect special cause variation (Vallance-Owen et al., 2004).

Sample size is also important. Hutchings et al. (2012) observed that providers with fewer than fifty patients completing the PROMs could not be assessed due to difficulty with data accuracy in these units. Yet hospital volume and surgeon speciality have been shown to affect outcome in the treatment of lung cancer (von Meyenfeldt et al., 2012), total hip arthroplasty (Ravi et al., 2014), colorectal cancer (Liu et al., 2015), radical cystectomy (Leow et al., 2014) and gynaecological oncology (Junor et al., 1999), to name but a few although this is not universally agreed on the basis that disease outcome needs to be interpreted in light of disease severity and comorbidity in the patient population (LaPar et al., 2012). This makes it difficult to assess low volume providers reliably despite their possibly being at greater risk of providing poorer quality of care.

If PROMs are to be used to compare centres, it has been estimated that an adequate sample size to make meaningful comparisons would be 150 patients, as this would detect a difference of 1 standard error of the measure, with 95% power and statistical significance of $p < 0.002$ for hernia repair and varicose vein surgery, although the power is slightly less for the disease specific measures for hip and knee surgery (Browne, 2007).

Late or non-responders need to be considered. In the NHS PROMs programme, there were higher levels of non-response in men, younger patients, non-white patients, patients in the most deprived areas, those who lived alone and those who had more comorbidities. These late responses were associated with worse outcomes (Hutchings et al., 2012). Other studies have shown that non-responders have poorer outcomes (Emberton and Black, 1995; Sales et al., 2004 and Kim et al.,

2004). The NHS PROMs scheme also excluded patients judged to be incapable of completing a written questionnaire in English because of cognitive impairment, poor sight, literacy or language comprehension problems (Browne, 2007). Participants from minority ethnic groups may be multiply disadvantaged; they may be poor, socially excluded, have multiple comorbidities or be illiterate in any language. Ignoring these groups contributes significant bias to any data collection (Boynton et al., 2004).

There are potential ways to improve the participation rates in some of these groups by physically altering the questionnaires and providing privacy and support when completing them (Jahagirdar et al., 2012). Communicating an understanding of the purpose of them may also encourage people to engage with the process (Jahagirdar et al., 2012). Even if this is not possible, the potential biases described need to be considered when interpreting PROMs data particularly in the context of service provision.

There has been little research assessing recruitment bias in research studies and audits (Browne, 2007). An increase of 20% of those eligible participating is associated with a decrease in pre-operative mean EQ-5D scores, and this is unlikely to be due to chance.

BUPA found problems with the proportion of patients completing the questionnaires. Information on the number of patients completing the post-operative questionnaire was not reported. As such, there is likely to be huge biases and errors in the data being collected (Vallance-Owen et al., 2004).

Collection of self-reported morbidity data may be under utilised because it is resource intensive. This may result in incomplete morbidity adjustment, for example, by using administrative data such as coding, which underestimates the number and severity of comorbidities (Bayliss, 2012). A widespread pilot in the NHS found significant drop-out rates, mostly due to time constraints limiting their ability to collect data (Browne, 2007).

Other uses of PROMs

Much elective surgery is aimed at primarily improving patient perceived health-related quality of life. It has, therefore, been hypothesised that pre-operative HRQoL should be below a certain threshold, otherwise they will have little to gain by undergoing surgery. Browne (2007) showed that many patients undergoing surgery have high self-reported HRQoL using disease-specific measures and may, therefore, have little capacity to benefit from surgery according to such measures. It may, therefore, be possible to set thresholds in pre-operative PROMs data at which surgery is indicated, a suggestion also put forward by Devlin and Appleby (2010).

The UK Health and Social Care Information Centre (2014), who host the reports for the NHS PROMs programme, additionally proposes the use of PROMS for comparing the quality of care between providers, describing effectiveness and cost-effectiveness of different techniques and 'supporting the reduction of health inequalities'.

However, this comes at a cost. The current NHS PROMs programme costs in the order of £40 million per year to administer (Devlin and Appleby, 2010), against an expected expenditure of £800 million on the four procedures assessed (Devlin and Appleby, 2010). Evidence is starting to emerge of some potential benefits from the programme (Basser, 2015), but this has taken 6 years at a cost to the service of approximately £240 million. The value of the scheme is, therefore, questionable, especially in the context of the plan to extend PROMs progressively across other conditions within 3 years (Maynard and Bloor, 2010), including mental health, cancer care, asthma, chronic obstructive pulmonary disease, diabetes, epilepsy, heart failure and stroke. However, this has yet to happen on a systematic basis. This may be because the measurement of elective surgical work using PROMs, however difficult, is relatively easy compared with the measurement of chronic, relapsing and remitting diseases such as those proposed.

Conclusion

Widespread use of PROMs in healthcare systems is still uncommon and limited to the UK, Sweden, Australian mental health services and parts of the US, but only in England has this been done to compare providers' performance as opposed to improving clinical care (Black, 2013). However, there are moves to extend the use of PROMs in the US to reimbursement mechanisms for health maintenance organisations in the hope that the level of reimbursement will be linked to the value that patients' ascribe to the outcome of their treatment.

However, before comparing provider performance a number of factors need to be considered:

1   The measures used need to be validated in order to demonstrate they measure the desired outcome. Whilst the PROMs in use in the NHS programme were extensively reviewed before implementation (Browne, 2007), triangulation with other measures of quality does not appear to have been undertaken.
2   The data must be suitable for comparison. This requires that an adequate assessment of comorbidities is made, including subjective and objective measures of morbidity alongside assessments of mood (Bayliss, 2012).
3   Any data generated have to be appropriately corrected for non-response to take into account that non-responders are over-represented in groups such as non-English speakers and people with disabilities. There is a risk that those with disabilities and low literacy may be systematically excluded (Jahagirdar et al., 2012; Kroll et al., 2014) from PROMs measurements, thereby further disadvantaging them.
4   A reasonable sample size needs to be achieved. A sample size of 150 has been shown to be reasonable to compare services. Low volume providers are a particular risk because they may not achieve the level of activity to provide a meaningful comparison whilst being as risk of providing poor quality of care.
5   Data need to be presented in a way that is meaningful to managers, commissioners, clinicians and patients.

Concerns remain about the ability of the NHS programme to detect meaning-ful differences between healthcare providers, other than in the shape of negative or positive outliers, that is, those more than 3 standard deviations from the mean. Their use in establishing league tables, or informing commissioners on decisions as to which organisations they purchase care from, has to be questioned.

Whilst many laud the NHS for being the first health service in the world to attempt to collect this type of data on health outcome, rather than just health out-put (Devlin and Appleby, 2010), the system has been allowed to run without having learnt to crawl let alone walk. No data have been produced validating this data as a measure of quality of a service, let alone an individual clinician. Furthermore, the list of potential uses of the PROMs data, based on the unproven assumption that it reflects quality of care, continues to grow (Devlin and Appleby, 2010; Black, 2013). This includes a suggestion that they could be used to decide who requires surgery based on their baseline HRQoL (Browne, 2007), arguing that those with a high HRQoL have little to gain from surgery. It seems unlikely that patients would choose to have surgery without any potential gain. Would the PROMs result be better used to inform expectations?

As Maynard observed in 2010:

> the creation of a system of PROMs, in conjunction with patient level costs and improved use of activity date, could transform patient care. . . (but) there has been inadequate consideration of the management of the ambitious sys-tem. . . . In this exciting, innovative and potentially world-leading endeavor we must not forget to learn to walk before we run.
>
> *(Maynard and Bloor, 2010)*

22

SERVICE IMPROVEMENT TO REDUCE EARLY DEATHS OF CHILDREN IN HOSPITAL

The design of an electronic observation system

Victoria Hemming

With increasing paediatric admissions to hospital, there is a need to develop a hospital IT system to record patient observations and calculate an early warning score (EWS) to aid the early identification of unwell patients. A number of systems have been put in place for adults admitted to hospital, but paediatric systems have been slower to implement due to complexities in the development and implementation of a paediatric early warning score (PEWS).

It is recognised that many children in hospital who have a cardio-respiratory arrest and need resuscitation showed signs of deterioration in the 24 hours prior to their arrest. Early recognition, escalation and intervention in deteriorating patients should improve outcomes through reducing morbidity and mortality (Tume et al., 2013). The Confidential Enquiry into Maternal and Child Deaths recommended the use of early warning scores in paediatric departments (Chapman et al., 2010; Pearson, 2008). Following this report, the use of paediatric EWS has increased and the majority of departments use some form of EWS (Roland et al., 2014). The Royal College of Paediatrics and Child Health (RCPCH) Situational Awareness for Everyone (SAFE) project aims to improve paediatric outcomes and patient safety. One strand is improving early identification of deterioration. The use of a paediatric EWS is the main tool for this alongside increasing awareness of the potential for deterioration (RCPCH, 2016).

However, the identification of sick children who are likely to deteriorate is difficult, and there is limited evidence for individual paediatric EWS with most validated only on the data set that created them and few prospectively validated (Morgan et al., 2015). Many scores are sensitive but not specific for those who go on to be transferred to PICU or have cardio-respiratory arrests (Parshuram et al., 2011). There is, therefore, no nationally recognised paediatric EWS. One regional paediatric EWS is the Yorkshire Paediatric Advanced Warning Score, or PAWS (Whiteley, 2009). Although it is recognised that EWSs are used extensively internationally, further research is required to investigate EWS as a complex health-care intervention, assessing its complex multifaceted sociotechnical system embedded in the wider safety culture of the organisation (Lambert et al., 2017).

The NHS has been challenged to go paperless by the Health Secretary to save administration time, thereby allowing for more time for patient care (Pricewater-houseCoopers and Department of Health, 2013). Computer systems are being introduced to record observations electronically, calculating and automatically alerting medical staff to improve clinical attendance in unstable patients (Jones et al., 2011). Electronic calculation of EWS is more accurate and result in more correct clinical interventions whilst inputting into electronic systems can be faster than recording with pen and paper (Prytherch et al., 2006).

In response to this need, a service improvement project was initiated within a single general hospital with a paediatric department to develop and implement an electronic system for recording observations and calculation of the Yorkshire PAWS to improve morbidity and mortality of children admitted to the ward. Objectives for the project were to collect baseline data, develop an electronic system with the local IT department and nursing staff, train system users, implement the system and collect post-implementation data.

Process

On the paediatric ward, patient observations are taken by nursing staff and health-care assistants (HCAs). The observations are then recorded on an age-appropriate PAWS chart. There are five different charts depending on the age of the patient. The PAWS is calculated and, dependent on the score, escalation takes place to a doctor. The PAWS also determines the frequency of observations. Process mapping (Figure 22.1), fishbone analysis (Figure 22.2) and stakeholder analysis (Figure 22.3) were undertaken to review the process. The process map and fishbone analysis showed that recognition and escalation of the deteriorating child is complex, supporting Lambert et al.'s (2017) findings from a systematic review of the literature. Therefore, this project was further focused on the measurement of observations and the method of their recording.

Process measures were used to show the current practice in recording observations (Figures 22.4 and 22.5) comparing those from general ward patients to those requiring transfer to a paediatric intensive care unit (PICU). This was used as a reflection of morbidity and mortality because there is a low mortality rate within paediatrics.

Learning from current practice was also undertaken both internally by speaking to staff and externally through visits to other Children's Hospitals. These visits emphasised staff involvement, staff training and planning for the 'go live' stage of the project, including a clear communication strategy. Stakeholder analysis was also undertaken.

The first part of the process was writing a new monitoring and escalation policy for paediatrics which previously had not fully met the escalation requirements of

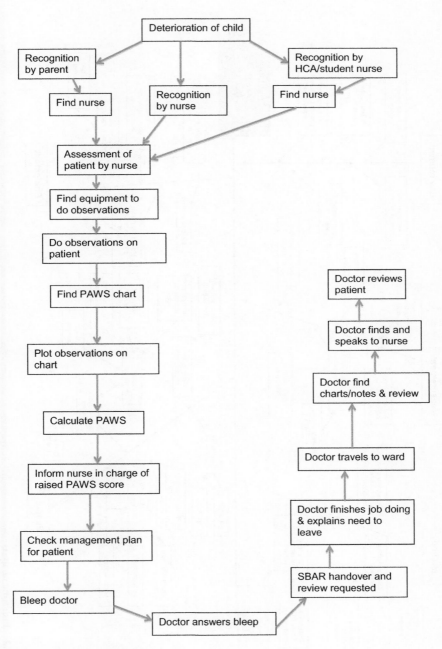

FIGURE 22.1 Process mapping

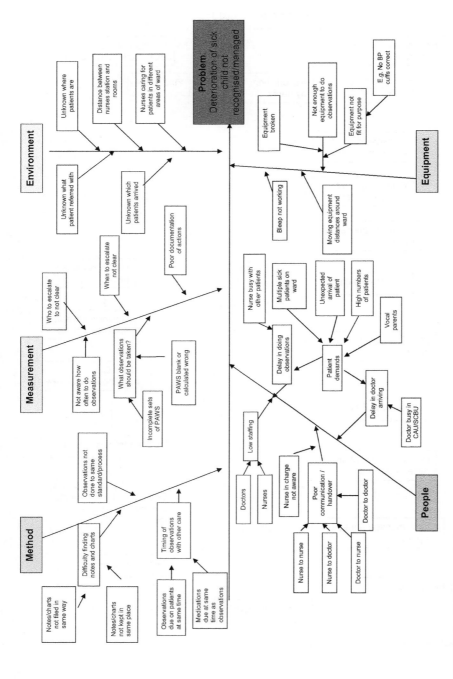

FIGURE 22.2 Fishbone analysis

	Satisfy	*Manage*
HIGH POWER	SCBU Sister	Paediatric Ward Sister
	CCG	Paediatric Deputy Sisters
	Trust CEO	Lead Sister for CAU
	Trust board	Nurses
	Deanery leadership programme team	Healthcare Assistants
		Consultants
	School of paediatrics	Registrars
	Patient Safety team	Junior doctors
	Learning and resource centre	Directorate Manager
	Corporate efficiency team	IT manager
	Workforce team	IT programmer
		Corporate improvement team
		Finance for hardware and systems
		IT hardware support
		Patient Safety Team
LOW POWER	SCBU Staff	Patients
	Simulation team	Parents
	Other hospitals with electronic PAWS	Student nurses
		Effectiveness team
	Monitor	*Inform*
	LOW IMPACT/ STAKEHOLDING	**HIGH IMPACT/STAKEHOLDING**

FIGURE 22.3   Stakeholder analysis

	Baseline		*Seven Weeks Post-Implementation*	
Process Measure	*General ward patients*	*Patients transferred to PICU*	*General ward patients*	*Patients transferred to PICU*
Correct age chart	96%	44%	100%	100%
PAWS score correct	80%	31%	95%	98%
Frequency of observations recorded	16%	22%	99%	89%
Medical review documented when triggered (PAWS ≥ 3)	56%	100% (89% ≤ 1 hr)	80%	Yes 46% Aware 27%

FIGURE 22.4   Process measures

PAWS. The policy was written using evidence-based guidelines (National Institute for Health and Care Excellence, 2007; National Institute for Health and Care Excellence, 2014) and escalation policies from within the department and other paediatric departments within the region. The policy was agreed by the paediatric consultants' team and ratified by the Trust's Patient Safety committee.

	Baseline		Seven Weeks Post-Implementation	
Total Number of Observations Reviewed	375		102	
Saturations	362	96%	101	99%
Heart rate	360	96%	101	99%
Respiratory rate	359	96%	101	99%
Oxygen requirement	355	95%	101	99%
Level of consciousness	331	88%	101	99%
Temperature	308	82%	102	100%
Capillary refill time	146*	75%	97	95%
Blood pressure	40	10%	18	18%

*193 possible measurements

FIGURE 22.5 Individual observations recorded

Many NHS improvement projects are initiated in a top-down manner, with frontline staff having little influence on them (Bate et al., 2004). However, success and sustainability of projects are improved when frontline staff drive them (Bate et al., 2004; Doyle et al., 2013). Although electronic observations were being introduced at the behest of managers, frontline staff needed to feel part of the project for it to be a success, in particular ward nursing staff who were identified from the initial stakeholder analysis as having high power and high influence for the successful implementation of the project. Therefore, appreciative inquiry was used with nurses and HCAs to seek their views on electronic PAWS.

A strategy of engagement enabled nursing staff and clinical managers to express that they felt there had been a lack of training opportunities for paediatric staff caring for acutely ill children. A training programme for paediatric staff in assessment and recognition of sick children was developed, incorporating the Royal College of Nursing standards for performing observations (2013). The training was delivered in small groups to encourage discussion and draw upon staff experiences. Patient stories, baseline audit data and the new formal escalation policy were shared. The patient stories allowed people to engage more fully with the reasons for the introduction of electronic PAWS and drive improvement (Wilcock et al., 2003).

Empathic authoritative leadership was used to drive change (Swanwick and McKimm, 2011). It was made clear why electronic observations would be implemented and the evidence for it, and the concerns of users would be addressed in real time as the issues surfaced. It was a planned rather than an emergent change, but the culture on the ward at the time did not support emergent change (West et al., 2014). Schein's change theory steps were used with unfreezing of current practice using disconfirming baseline information about how the system worked prior to implementing the change. Time was also spent creating psychological safety to overcome learning anxiety with the new system. Change took place with role modelling behaviour with early adopters alongside supportive training workshops (Schein, 1995, 2010).

The electronic PAWS system was developed as a collaboration programme with IT staff with clinical experience, paediatric nursing sisters and paediatric doctors. Once the system had been developed, training was offered to paediatric nursing staff and HCAs with a minimum of two one-to-one sessions each with a trainer alongside the production of written information. Additional sessions were offered to those who had difficulty with the system, and I made myself personally available for staff to have support to practice in their own time and to flag any concerns. Training took place during rostered shifts, 'on the job training' allowing staff to acquire skills through direct experience and observing others demonstrating social learning (Bandura, 1971). Staff reported that the system was easier to use than they had expected. Junior doctors and consultants had the system demonstrated to them during timetabled teaching sessions and written instructions were also e-mailed. It was acknowledged that the system would change with time and feedback from staff was encouraged and shared with the IT team.

Once the system was tested, a 'go live' implementation date was set. Following learning from other departments, it was decided that for the first two weeks both the electronic and paper charts would be used and a decision made by the nursing team when to stop using the paper charts. Trainers were available for support during the first few days after 'go live'. In the longer term, the paediatric nurse educator, who had been involved in developing the system, led the nursing team, and the paediatric clinical director led the medical team and provided continued executive level support for the system.

Following implementation, it was quickly realised that adult rather than paediatric data limits had been used for some observations, a situation that needed to be corrected rapidly. Dual running of the paper and electronic system allowed for the early recognition of this issue.

Evaluation

Staff engagement was the first priority of the project. It allowed communication of evidence for the intervention and patient stories were used to improve and sustain clinical engagement. Feedback to staff emphasised how the use of the system can: (1) aid clinical decision making and (2) how the system supports and improves the development of clinical skills. This appeared to encourage staff and had a positive effect on motivating clinical involvement and engagement. In addition feedback was given to staff on what the system would be capable of, whilst being realistic and acknowledging that it would not be a perfect system. Being open about what was and what might not be possible ensured staff were realistic prior to the implementation.

Nursing staff commented during the training period that they felt the system was easier to learn and use than they expected. Social learning, modelling behaviours and giving direct experience with feedback was critical to the success of learning to change (Bandura, 1971). The medical staff, particularly consultants, found the system difficult following implementation. They had not received the same engagement and training as nursing staff and raised questions that needed to be addressed following implementation. It was acknowledged that systems cannot be taken in isolation and changes may have unexpected consequences on other areas of working practice (Kirchner et al., 2010).

Following implementation, post-implementation quantitative data were collected for seven weeks, giving information on process measures from the electronic system. Improvements were shown in most areas (Figures 22.4 and 22.5). Further data needs to be collected, including outcome measures such as morbidity, mortality and PICU transfers alongside patient experience. Return on investment needs to be assessed not just in cost but also in the value of improvements in patient safety and patient outcomes (Phillips and Phillips, 2004). The returns for this project will take time to become apparent, as significant reductions in mortality and reductions in admissions to PICU will not be calculable for a number of years.

23

INNOVATIONS IN PERSON-CENTRED SERVICE REDESIGN FOR YOUNG CARERS

Samantha Wong

The numbers of children who care for a sick parent or a parent with a disability is increasing, and in the UK, there has been recognition of the role services need to play in the support of young carers. Young carers are defined as children and young people under 18 years of age who provide regular and ongoing care and emotional support to a family member who has a physical or mental illness, has a disability or misuses substances (ADASS, ADCS and The Children's Society, 2012). According to the latest census (Office for National Statistics, 2013), there are 177,918 young unpaid carers (5–17 years old) in England and Wales. This is likely to be only the tip of the iceberg (The Children's Society, 2013).

It is widely appreciated that being a young carer can have significant and long-lasting effects on a young person's health and well-being (Carers Trust, 2014). On average, young carers have lower educational attainment at GCSE level (national examinations taken in year 11) equating to nine grades lower overall than their peers (The Children's Society, 2013). There is also a clear association between being a young carer and having lower future job prospects, fewer further educational opportunities and greater likelihood of working in lower skilled occupations (The Children's Society, 2013).

Further, children who care for others are reported to have poorer general health (Office for National Statistics, 2013). However, they rarely make themselves known to their general practitioner and often avoid seeking help (RCGP, 2013). Despite their additional needs, there is no strong evidence that young carers are any more likely than their peers to come into contact with support agencies (The Children's Society, 2013).

These young people have first-hand experience in healthcare through their additional roles. Heyman and Heyman (2013) identified potential learning and career opportunities arising from skills built up in this role including maturity beyond their years and vocationally valuable practical skills. The young carers also reported greater opportunities for developing a career related to their experience of caring. Nevertheless, minimal research has been done to support this. One study by Brannen (2009) discussed the possible childhood life experiences that encourage people into a caring career. Reports of significant difficult life events led individuals to consider assisting others with similar problems. One case specifically mentions the impact of caring for her father, describing how it fuelled an interest in medicine and illnesses.

One reason for the lack of literature is that encouraging children into caring roles may be considered controversial. A key principle of practice for young carers and their families is to safeguard children by preventing them from undertaking inappropriate care of any family member (Frank and McLarnon, 2007). There is, however, a need to build on the strength and experience of young people and to acknowledge and reward those who may have sacrificed their personal development in order to look after someone else. Recognising their caring skills and supporting their development of a formal caring role can encourage them to use their experience to their advantage in becoming a healthcare professional.

This service improvement project set out to increase the identification, support and aspirations of young carers in a city in the north of England. The proposal was initiated and set up by a local school pastoral support officer who recognised that young carers are often educationally disadvantaged by their role; however, they will also have developed valuable skills to give them a good lead into a career in healthcare. The project set out to identify these young people and raise their ambitions whilst introducing them to a range of healthcare careers.

Two schools were involved in this project: W Academy (WA), a high achieving secondary school in the south of the city and LW Academy (LWA), secondary school in a more deprived area of the city. WA is the workplace of the pastoral support officer leading this study. Both WA and LWA were aware of young carers attending their schools but had neither formal register, nor any regular review system. Only informal and ad-hoc support was given. This is likely to be true of many schools across England despite the specific mention of meeting the needs of young carers in the Common Inspection Framework (OFSTED, 2015).

In advance of the project, both stakeholder and force field analyses were undertaken to inform the project. These analyses (Figures 23.1 and 23.2) were not exhaustive but focus on the key groups whom this project may influence or be influenced by. The populations placed in the 'high interest, high power' area of the stakeholder analysis (Figure 23.1) were found to be similar to the groups placed in the 'forces AGAINST change' area of the force field analysis (Figure 23.2). Although these groups are assumed to have high interest, they have other priorities which may take precedence. Schools have clear and important investment in the health and well-being of vulnerable students, however they also have a strict and inflexible educational agenda.

The young carers and parents/guardians also have conflicting priorities. The young people may see the benefit of additional support but this potentially comes with further isolation from their student body and fears around identification (The

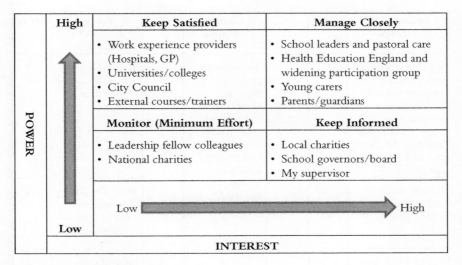

<table>
<tr><td rowspan="4" style="writing-mode: vertical-lr">POWER</td><td>High</td><td>Keep Satisfied</td><td>Manage Closely</td></tr>
</table>

		Keep Satisfied	Manage Closely
	High	• Work experience providers (Hospitals, GP) • Universities/colleges • City Council • External courses/trainers	• School leaders and pastoral care • Health Education England and widening participation group • Young carers • Parents/guardians
POWER		Monitor (Minimum Effort)	Keep Informed
		• Leadership fellow colleagues • National charities	• Local charities • School governors/board • My supervisor
	Low	Low ⟶ High	
		INTEREST	

FIGURE 23.1   Stakeholder analysis

Source: Template adapted from Stakeholder Analysis video and article found at mindtools.com (2016a).

Children's Society, 2013). Involving and informing guardians was an essential part of the process; however, it also ran the risk of creating barriers with a defensive dialogue and fear of repercussions from identification (Department for Education, 2016).

Phase 1 – school engagement

A level of support in WA was assumed because of the working environment of the project lead. At LWA, an initial, informal introduction by the project lead was followed by a meeting with the student well-being and careers team. This relationship was developed further by delivering an NHS careers taster day for thirty of the school's students. Included in this taster day was a first-aid training session, delivered by the local ambulance service. This was a significant event in building a mutually beneficial relationship with the senior team in the school (Toledano et al., 2010). In addition, a local charity agreed to deliver a series of awareness-raising assemblies around young carers to LWA. Significantly, these sessions included all students and form coaches in the school.

Phase 2 – identify young carers and design programme

A screening form to identify young carers was developed from a previous in-house screening questionnaire previously used in WA. WA rolled out the screening questionnaire to all students with a limited return on the completed questionnaires. Those that were returned required significant administrative input which was not

Forces FOR change	Score		Change proposal		Forces AGAINST change	Score
Improve suboptimal educational, employment and health outcomes for young carers (supported by both leadership fellow and school pastoral care)	5		Young carers project: increase identification and support for young carers in schools Offer taster healthcare training and work experience		Limited time for school leaders to engage	5
Improve health and well-being of young carers	5				Difficulty taking young carers out of normal educational activity	4
Leadership Fellow Project	5				Difficulty engaging young carers	3
HEE widening participation and workforce strategies	3				Difficulty engaging parents/guardians	4
Improve OFSTED inspection	2				Limited funding available from HEE	2
Contribute to very limited literature on subject	4				Time limited project for leadership fellow	4
Increase engagement with local young carers charity	3				Safeguarding (work experience etc.)	4
Total score:	27				**Total score:**	26
Score 1 (low significance) → Score 5 (high significance)						

FIGURE 23.2   Force field analysis – the pressures for and against change

Source: Template adapted from mindtools.com (2016b).

supported by the school's senior team and the project was put on hold. LWA was wary of the potential workload and, therefore, opted out of the screening questionnaire, favouring awareness-raising and encouraging self-identification. This was done through school-wide assemblies and signposting handouts to all students and staff.

Phase 3 – engage with young carers and adjust programme

Identified young carers from years 8 to 10 at LWA were invited to a focus group. In order to comply with the projects, ethical approval, letters, information sheets and consent forms for both the students and parent/guardians were sent home prior to the session. Of the six young carers invited, four attended.

These young carers were asked to complete a written questionnaire which gathered qualitative data on the nature of their caring activities and how they felt about their role. They were invited to share their ideas of future employment and what they hoped to gain from this programme. This information was used to shape the activities provided. An emotional well-being score was recorded based on the 'Positive and Negative Outcomes of Caring' (PANOC-YC20) questionnaire by Joseph et al. (2012), the scoring to be repeated at the end of the programme to assess impact.

Phase 4 – implement programme (training, work experience)

A morning of first-aid training was delivered to twenty year 9 students who then received a certificate of attendance. The young carers were given priority for the training which was also offered to health and social care students.

A second event planned was a local hospital visit that could not be facilitated, and therefore students attended a 'trauma care' workshop, arranged by the city's medical school, followed by a series of short talks from the schools of nursing, midwifery and social care.

Phase 5 – sustainability and handover

The project is unlikely to be sustainable because of a lack of dedicated resources. However, LWA has plans to host the awareness-raising assemblies annually with the local charity. The ambulance service also intended to hold more training at the school alongside and further visits to the medical school. WA is planning to continue their identification process.

Measuring the impact and cost-effectiveness of this project has been challenging. The intention to gather repeated emotional well-being scoring 'pre' and 'post' the intervention had limited success because only a single student was able to attend all three interventions.

Feedback was gathered for the events, with all but one student describing a 'good' or 'very good' experience, the remainder rating it 'ok'. Overall, 74% expressed an interest in a future healthcare career following the events, with nine students changing from being 'unsure' about a career in healthcare to 'very interested' or 'somewhat interested'. However, these data are not sufficient to demonstrate a long-term change in behaviour or life choices.

Conclusions

The project set out fairly ambitious aims to collaborate across the public sector joining the NHS with state education. Although it was a very small-scale project with multiple barriers, it has achieved raised awareness and identification of young carers in the area. As a result of the programme, these young carers and other young people have gained experience in healthcare increasing their consideration of a future healthcare career. Although this project is unlikely to continue, both schools plan to continue offering additional support to their young carers. LWA has also made plans to further collaborate with the local charity, ambulance service and the university faculty medical school on an annual basis.

24

SERVICE IMPROVEMENT IN PAEDIATRIC DENTISTRY

Halla Zaitoun

Hospital dentistry is provided for children with extreme dental requirements that are unable to be provided by the child's community dentist. However, there has been a dramatic increase in referrals to hospital dentistry, suggesting a rise in poor dental hygiene and a lack of prevention work (e.g. through lifestyle choices such as sugary drinks). This service improvement project had the following aims:

1   To improve patient throughput and experience in paediatric dentistry by improving the booking, cancellation and refilling of clinic with appointments in a timely manner;
2   To examine the reliability and validity of data regarding patients outside the 18-week referral to treatment target;
3   Over the longer term, to become a 'learning organisation' (Senge, 2006), applying improvement methods as a tool to enable development of more effective and efficient systems to deliver the service.

The project was undertaken within the paediatric dentistry unit of a university dental hospital (DH), providing both a secondary and tertiary referral centre within the north of England. Approximately 4,500 referrals are received per annum and 1,500 of these patients are subsequently referred to nearby children's hospital (CH) for dental treatment under general anaesthesia on a joint care pathway. Their management is completed by the same dentists in the DH. The new patient activity is delivered on an outpatient basis at the DH from a list of consultant graded referral letters. Despite concerted effort from the team and numerous boosts to activity from waiting list initiatives, the team have repeatedly struggled to meet capacity. This is further complicated by a sustained increase in referral growth in new patient referrals, due to external factors such as changes to dental contracts for primary care practitioners and increasing immigration into the region. This has resulted in an overall increase of 18% since 2010–2011 (Figure 24.1).

This growth alongside fluctuations in referrals requires a highly responsive administrative process to meet the demands placed upon it. However, this has not been provided to an administrative team who are under constant pressure, undertaking complex and often repeated fixed processes, in a system that is inflexible and unresponsive resulting in extended waiting lists.

In December 2015, there were 760 patients on the paediatric dentistry new patient waiting list (DH) with an average wait between 17 and 22 weeks. As a large proportion of the dental treatment provided for children is undertaken at the CH, there is a shared pathway. This means that any delay at the DH can result in the CH breaching the national 18 weeks for referral to treatment. These breaches result in a series of fines that may cause the service to become financially and economically challenged (Figure 24.2). Avoiding these fines puts additional strains on the team to see additional patients or work additional hours.

In December 2015, the length of the waiting list triggered action from CH with stipulation that if the DH patients were referred to CH with over 11–12 weeks' wait, DH would pick up the breaches and associated fines. This new proviso spurred

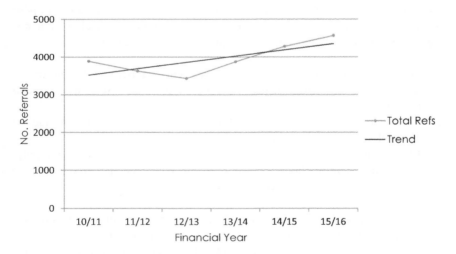

FIGURE 24.1 Referrals to paediatric dentistry

Trust Targets	Cost of Breach
>52-week wait	£5,000 per individual
< 92% patients with 18-week wait	£100 per individual

FIGURE 24.2 Cost of potential breaches 2015–2016 (Department of Health, October 2015)

DH into action to reduce the waiting list and a requirement was set that the paediatric dentistry department would have to see an additional 300 patients by the end of March 2016. In addition to this, DH management identified a need to nurture sustainable improvements to further reduce and manage the ever-increasing waiting list.

One further difficulty in addressing the waiting list issue was the reliability and validity of the data, as there are anomalies on the system in relation to key factors including migration of data to the new electronic patient administration system, and the existence of multiple waiting lists and multiple access plans for individual patients.

Part 1 – review of referral criteria

Referral criteria to the DH was reviewed as a consultant group to ensure that only referrals which met our acceptance criteria were accepted, a standard letter being sent out for inappropriate referrals. This was approved by the Dental Commissioner before being used.

In addition, referral and waiting list concerns were presented to the regional Oral Health Advisory group. Support was agreed from the Local Dental Council Chair and Consultant in Dental Public Health to raise the bar for referrals to DH with immediate effect. In particular, dentists would be required to write the date they had last applied a protective fluoride vanish rather than, as previously, just ticking a box. This would encourage dentists to apply the varnish, as they cannot mistakenly apply a tick without a date. Further, only referrals written on a standard proforma would be accepted, with all others returned with a copy of the proforma.

Part 2 – reducing the 18-week wait

The 18-week waits for the paediatric dentistry department required improvement. Three strategies were employed to do this: improving the completion of outcome forms to show that treatment had been completed or was not required, using waiting list initiatives to reduce the number of patients on the waiting lists to a more manageable level and streamlining the overall patient pathway.

Initial reluctance to complete outcome forms accurately was partially overcome by recruiting nurses' help to check the outcome codes on behalf of the dentist. Positive feedback from this intervention has encouraged greater numbers of outcome forms to be completed. Going forward, this process may be enhanced by the use of electronic outcome forms, which would reduce administrative time and incorporate safeguards so that clinicians have to complete the whole form in order for the patient to be given a further appointment.

To provide a short-term solution, waiting list initiatives were set up to reduce the backlog of patients by 300, thereby achieving a waiting time of 11–12 weeks. It was recognised that this improvement would not be maintained, and therefore strategies to provide a sustainable improvement in activity were considered. This required a longer-term effort between clinical lead and managers to process map the new patient booking pathway to identify where improvements could be made considering areas such as capacity, maximising bookings, improved timetabling and improved methods for dealing with non-attenders and cancellations.

A more formal, whole-team process map of the patient's journey would further support this process – work undertaken with the local service improvement team. This work identified a number of areas for intervention including booking systems, transfer of waiting list, capacity and non-attenders, which are discussed in more detail ahead.

Part 3 – system change

1 Improve efficiency of new patient bookings systems

Major inefficiencies were found to exist in the new patient appointment system. For example, the referral letter from primary care was received by the secretaries on the ground floor, taken up to the third floor to be entered onto the electronic system and then brought back down to be placed in the consultant pigeon holes for grading. Once graded, the referral letters were placed in the reception pigeon hole to go back to central appointments for a booking letter to be sent to the patient.

Process mapping showed that there were major inefficiencies in the system for processing referral letters, improvements in which would ensure earlier bookings, thereby improving patient care and contribute to reducing the 18-week wait.

2 Improve efficiency of transfer of patient to the children's hospital waiting list

Following concern raised regarding delay in receipt of waiting list cards from the dental to the children's hospital and previous confidentiality issues, a collaborative process mapping team came together to find solutions to the referral process. The aim was to explore ways of increasing efficiency without compromising confidentiality and to always maintain a paper trail for auditing purposes. The session had a positive outcome. and now the dental hospital team scans the waiting list cards and sends them across to the children's hospital by secure e-mail. This reduces the need for re-entering information, saving time at the dental hospital and reducing the likelihood of error. Further review of this process is not currently required, as both parties were satisfied with the outcome.

3 Reviewing capacity

The sustained increase in referrals has led to an increase in new and follow-up activity (Figure 24.3). Although more staff have been recruited, maximising activity from existing staff has also been undertaken, including a review of the clinical time-table. This was a comprehensive exercise which involved securing staff agreement

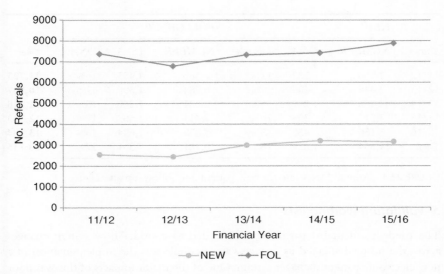

FIGURE 24.3   Outpatient bookings for paediatric dentistry – new patients and follow-up

to increase the number of patients seen on clinics. Revision of the timetable provided additional new patient activity resulting in an additional 16.75 new patient appointments per week (92.25–109), equivalent to nearly three additional new patient clinics per week.

4 Patient Did Not Attend (DNA) appointments

One important area for system change was in attempting to reduce non-attenders to clinics (DNA rate), which historically has run between 8% and 13% for new patients and 15–18% for follow-ups (Figure 24.4).

The dental hospital has historically offered new appointments through a partial booking system, whereby a letter is sent to the parent or carer inviting them to make contact to book an appointment, increasing their choice as to when to attend. However, this meant that the administrative team was able to send out letters only in measured batches (3 weeks' worth of letters) because they could deal with only a certain number of parents or carers calling to make appointments at any one time.

The decision was made to change the process so that appointments were sent out directly to parents or carers who could either accept them or ask for them to be changed. This meant that clinics could be booked out to 6 weeks. The effect of this was to instantly reduce the number of patients waiting without an appointment, although it did not reduce the overall waiting times. On reviewing the change, it was found that it had resulted in a sharp increase in the number of DNAs. The change had made for a more efficient booking system but had resulted in an increase in the number of DNAs rather than a reduction.

	NEW			FOLLOW-UP			
Year	NUMBER	DNA	DNA%	NUMBER	DNA	DNA%	Total
11/12	2,550	332	12%	7,386	1,455	16%	**11,723**
12/13	2,448	235	9%	6,784	1,390	17%	**10,857**
13/14	2,998	269	8%	7,321	1,260	15%	**11,848**
14/15	3,212	338	10%	7,411	1,562	17%	**12,523**
15/16	3,156	455	13%	7,879	1,694	18%	**13,184**
Total	14,364	1,629	10%	36,781	7,361	17%	**60,135**

FIGURE 24.4   Annual DNA rate for new patient and follow-up attendances

5 Validating waiting lists

The paediatric dental department also needed to consider how system changes across the hospital affected its service. One example was the implementation of a new electronic patient manager system. One of the major impacts of this was poor migration of data including access plans across to the new system. This meant that waiting list data were inaccurate, and several tiers of validation work had to be undertaken to correct this.

Having completed this work it resulted in improved information on waiting lists which is now available to the team, including the number of patients referred, how many have been seen and the length of their waits. These objective data are enablers to objectively assess any new intervention designed to reduce the waiting list or improve DNA rates.

Part 4 – Reduce pressure on clinic registration

The paediatric dentistry department was acutely aware that by increasing the footfall of patients through the department, this had increased pressure on reception staff and this in turn was delaying the patient journey. This has been exacerbated by the introduction of an electronic patient record system, which was found to be slower than its predecessor.

A quality improvement programme was targeted at this area to reduce pressure on the reception staff at to improve the patient experience. This was undertaken using a multifaceted approach including data gathering, team work and identification of specific patient- and staff-related goals.

Available information was used to understand clinical capacity and activity within the department enabling timetables to be modified to support the required increase in activity. One further stage was to set the 'capacity/demand' plan as a team approach, thereby giving broader ownership of both the problem and the solution to the team.

In order to do this, the departmental culture needed to be considered, in particular understanding team engagement; what would make people 'go the extra mile' to help support the changes that needed to be made? Regular engagement with the outpatient and clerical team opened up a channel of communication which was established with the specific aim to encourage proactive and meaningful discussion about process improvement, meaning that problems were communicated and acted upon at an earlier stage.

Inherent within the service improvement project to reduce pressure on clinic registration was the need to improve the patient experience. In order to do this, patient feedback was required, and this was achieved through two sources: first, the 'friends and family test', and second, a patient engagement event held to support commissioning guidance. The main themes from these were that patients found the reception area too small, reception staff were not always friendly and that waits were too long both to receive an appointment and on the actual day of their appointment. On the positive side, patients gave positive feedback to the dentists and nurses, and many reported how they enjoyed coming to dental hospital.

These findings were reported to the team and to departmental and hospital managers, encouraging positive engagement and resulting in an understanding from both the department and the children's hospital about efforts undertaken in quality improvement. This also resulted in an increased understanding of what the issues are the level of process improvement being applied by staff. Patient experience was found to be a strong driver for change for the department and a sound rationale for the allocation of resources including raising awareness of the need to refurbish the clinic's waiting room.

25

REFLECTIONS ON SERVICE IMPROVEMENT BY MEDICAL LEADERS

Jeff Perring, Fiona Kew, Victoria Hemming, Samantha Wong and Halla Zaitoun

The clinicians who undertook these service improvement projects reflected upon the lessons they had learnt from them. These lessons have been collated to provide key themes for consideration by those setting out on their own service improvement journey. They are not exhaustive but come out of personal experience from those undertaking a service improvement project for the first time.

1 Stakeholder analysis and engagement for planning and intervention

Undertaking a stakeholder analysis, at the start of a project, was important to identify those groups and individuals with high power and high impact on the project. This knowledge was used to inform both project plans and leadership strategy. It highlighted those groups who required targeted engagement and enabled the development of a plan to engage and communicate with them.

These stakeholders may be not only clinical staff and managers but also service users who have a very personal understanding of the system as was found in the paediatric dentistry projects. Involving these stakeholders from an early stage can help in both the identification of problems and the creation of meaningful aims for the project. Working with service users can be challenging, but even though hard to reach, these stakeholders are significant and should be engaged.

In the PAWS project, nursing staff were identified as a high-impact group who had high power to decide if the electronic PAWS project would be successful. However, they had not been consulted before the decision was made to implement the project. This lack of engagement could have seriously impacted on the project (Juciute, 2009; West and Dawson, 2011), and therefore the project leader made certain that she started by engaging with this staff group early and frequently through informal discussions and training opportunities. Quantitative data and qualitative patient stories were used to show the impact of current practice, thereby highlighting the need for improvement.

In the young carers project, stakeholders were engaged through a collaborative approach designed to drive improvement and innovation, thereby building relationships and finding mutual goals that could be used to improve the service offered even in the context of multiple priorities and limited resources.

Where engagement was limited with a key stakeholder this did not happen; either momentum was not established or key groups failed to support the changes being made. In the young carers project, the leader did not engage with the senior team in one of the schools, resulting in differing priorities being set by the senior team, thereby limiting the benefits of the programme. It cannot be assumed that having one motivated individual in the organisation is enough; one person alone cannot lead significant change (DeChurch et al., 2010).

In the PAWS project, senior medical staff were identified as high power and high impact in the analysis but the focus was not on engagement with them. This meant that at the end of the project, some consultants were disengaged with the implementation and raised concerns about it. These consultants had not received the focused training that other staff had received, and therefore had difficulty engaging with the system. The lead consultant (clinical director) was engaged with the project, but it was an incorrect assumption that the rest of the consultant team would follow. Regular communication with senior medical staff throughout the project would have ensured that they were aware of developments and would have created in them more realistic expectations of the system being implemented. Traditional behaviours and social hierarchy in medicine impact on improvement projects and makes changes difficult to implement (Swanwick and McKimm, 2011; Berwick et al., 1992; Friedman et al., 2015; West et al., 2014). In particular, status asymmetry and authority gradients are a key dynamic in healthcare and can contribute to communication failures (Friedman et al., 2015). In this service development project, there was a clear hierarchical difference between the project leader undertaking the system implementation and the senior medical staff who were amongst its intended recipients. Medical hierarchy, therefore, influenced this project and may still impact on how the system is used in the future.

2 Good and sustained communications

The importance of good and sustained communications was noted in all of the projects. Networking with those involved with or affected by a project built connections and kept these stakeholders informed (Association for Project Management, 2016). This ensured that two-way communication was maintained. As we have already described, where this communication was limited (e.g. by hierarchy), the success of the project was put at risk.

Successful communication means that the received meaning is the same as the meaning intended to be transmitted (Association for Project Management, 2016). However, people respond differently to that information; for some, data are important, whereas others respond to patient stories to engage interest and demonstrate why change is needed. Communication, therefore, has to be directed to the needs of the recipients to maximise the potential for engagement with improvement projects.

Understanding this dynamic allowed one of the project leaders to review how she engaged with staff by being aware that her own preference may not be shared by others, and therefore may not motivate others in the same way (Wilcock et al., 2003; Huitt, 1992). She understood that she needed to adapt her style to meet the needs of those with whom she was communicating.

3 Developing a clear plan with measurable goals

Framing ideas to create a clear plan was found to be vital in project development. There can be many influences on a plan, but stakeholder engagement can help to frame that plan, teasing out issues to provide the clarity required. For example, what is the plan's desired outcome, and how can that outcome can be measured? Both are required to show a successful outcome but maybe difficult to achieve. In the first part of this section, it was shown how difficult it can be to provide a measurable outcome that reflects both the changes put in place and an improvement in the quality of care provided.

Even when the plan is clear and measurable, the project leader may still have to show flexibility and adaptation to changing internal and external environments (Senge, 2006), something that may be new but ultimately fruitful and rewarding.

4 Consider smaller projects to start with

Starting with a smaller project can provide useful information for the project leader. In the PAWS project, the leader implemented a smaller improvement project for recording nursing handover information electronically. Completing this project allowed her to learn valuable lessons about how to present the information to nursing staff, the importance of senior nurses in understanding and acknowledging the need for change and how best to frame the change as part of a patient safety narrative. It also made her realise that she would need to actively seek out and train staff rather than expect them to learn independently from worksheets. Finally, it enabled the project leader to identify staff who were early adopters and could champion change. These staff members were then actively engaged in the larger project, to encourage colleagues taking into account that people are most likely to be influenced by colleagues in a similar position (Kirchner et al., 2010).

These smaller projects may also allow relationships to be built with key stakeholders and for these key stakeholders to see that engagement in the larger project may be mutually beneficial. This was found to be particularly the case in the young carers project.

Larger projects can also be broken down into smaller, more manageable elements. These elements should also have a clear implementation plan and measurable outcomes. As with other, smaller projects, they allow relationships to be built and show that positive improvements can be made.

The service improvement project itself may ultimately be a development of the small projects, which can build into a much larger 'system transformation' project with more strategic and transformational changes required to facilitate service improvement. This was found with the paediatric dentistry project.

5 Effective leadership is visible

These service improvement projects highlighted the need for effective leadership to be visible and available (Bohmer, 2012). Conscious action was required to create opportunities to network and develop relationships, even when time was pressing.

Emotional intelligence may be common to all good leaders (Goleman, 2004) but so is the skill of good communication, which includes active inquiry, reframing situations, sharing the vision, motivating and admitting fallibility to build up a team (Swanwick and McKimm, 2011; Bohmer, 2012; Goleman, 2004). Leadership styles were variable and found to change depending upon the situation, but it was important to remain approachable and consciously aim for a low authority gradient. In doing so, the project leaders could build an effective team with a clear vision, support and trust (Swanwick and McKimm, 2011; Bohmer, 2012).

6 The project leader is a resource

These case studies show that the project leaders provided a resource in terms of both time and specialist knowledge. Fiona Kew facilitated the development of new 'evidence-based knowledge' to support a greater understanding of the theory and evidence base that underpins quality improvement. Victoria Hemming and Samantha Wong were leadership fellows who had time to develop good communication, networking and to build relationships. Fiona Kew and Halla Zaitoun, however, had to make time within their existing roles, which presented a substantial challenge to them and often required investment of their own personal time.

It is easy for a project leader to undervalue her time as a resource either directly or indirectly, for example, through failure to delegate efficiently and effectively, which requires trust that others can complete the task. This is an area which first-time leaders often find difficult.

We have also seen examples of the development of specialist knowledge. In the PAWS study, the project leader informed herself about different electronic systems, thereby becoming an authority on the subject within the department and enabling her to provide information to others as well as guide expectations. In the young carers project, knowledge was also used to evidence the case for change and motivate others.

In paediatric dentistry, the project leader developed an understanding of administrative data and processes, which enabled her to further develop and define her improvement projects, whereas in the young carers project, it was important to understand the relevant legislation in order to underpin the project plan and provide flexibility to overcome barriers. For example, the moving and handling training initially proposed was seen as 'teaching' the young people to care, whereas first-aid training was acceptable as a new skill.

Conclusion

The service development projects discussed in this section provide good examples of work that is taking place across health services to improve quality of care. That a successful outcome was limited in some of the projects reflects an everyday reality in service improvement. However, even when success was limited, important lessons can be learnt, project leaders can reflect upon these lessons to gain a greater understanding of their work and use these real world lessons to increase their chances of future success. The way forward is to explore practical ways to embed continuous quality improvement and service development into everyday clinical practice.

References for Part 4

Affleck, G., Aaronson, N. K., Ahmedzai, S., Bergman, B., Bullinger, M., Cull, A., Duez, N. J., Filiberti, A., Flechtner, H., Fleishman, S. B., De Haes, J. C. J. M., Kaasa, S., Klee, M., Osoba, D., Razavi, D., Rofe, P. B., Schraub, S., Sneeuw, K., Sullivan, M., and Takeda, F. (1993). The European organization for research and treatment of cancer QLQ-C30: A quality-of-life instrument for use in international clinical trials. *Journal of Personality and Social Psychology*, 51, 1173–1182.

Appleby, J. (2010). PROMs: Not an election issue. *British Journal of Healthcare Management*, 16(5), 217.

Appleby, J. (2011). Patient reported outcome measures: How are we feeling today? (online). *BMJ*, 343, 8191.

Association for Project Management. (2016). *Golden rules of project management*. (online). www.apm.org.uk/golden-rules. (Last Accessed on 14 August 2016).

Association of Directors of Adult Social Services (ADASS), Association of Directors for Children's Services (ADCS) and the Children's Society. (2012). *Working together to support young carers and their families*. (online). ADASS, ADCS and The Children's Society. www.youngcarer.com/sites/default/files/imce_user_files/PTP/mou_young_carers_2012.pdf.

Atkinson, A. B. (2005). *The Atkinson review: Final report. measurement of government output and productivity for the national accounts*. Basingstoke, England: Palgrave Macmillan.

Avery, K. N., Metcalfe, C., Nicklin, J., Barham, C. P., Alderson, D., Donovan, J. L., and Blazeby, J. M. (2006). Satisfaction with care: An independent outcome measure in surgical oncology. *Annals of Surgical Oncology*, 13(6), 817–822.

Bandura, A. (1971). *Social learning theory*. (online)New York: General Learning Press, pp. 1–46.

Basser, M. R. (2015). *"Patient reported outcome measures (PROMs)"outputs*. Health and Social Care Information Centre 13/3/2015.

Bate, P., Robert, G., and Bevan, H. (2004). The next phase of healthcare improvement: Learn from social movements? *Quality and Safety in Health Care*, 13, 62–66.

Bayliss, E. A., Ellis, J. L., Shoup, J. A., Zeng, C., McQuillan, D. B., and Steiner, J. F. (2012). Association of patient-centered outcomes with patient-reported and ICD-9-based morbidity measures. (online). *Annals of Family Medicine*, 10(2), 126–133.

Berwick, D., Enthoven, A., and Bunker, J. (1992). Quality management in the NHS: The doctor's role II. *British Medical Journal*, 304, 304–308.

Berwick, D. M. (1997). Medical associations: Guilds or leaders? *BMJ: British Medical Journal*, 314(7094), 1564.

Black, N. (2013). Patient reported outcome measures could help transform healthcare. *BMJ: British Medical Journal*, 346.

Bohmer, R. (2012). *The instrumental value of medical leadership: Engaging doctors in improving services*. London: The King's Fund.

Boynton, P. M., Wood, G. W., and Greenhalgh, T. (2004). Reaching beyond the white middle classes. *BMJ* (clinical research ed.), 328(7453), 1433–1436.

Brannen, J., Mooney, A., and Statham, J. (2009). Childhood experiences: A commitment to caring and care work with vulnerable children. *Childhood*, 16(3), 377–393.

Browne, J., et al. (2007). *Patient reported outcome measures (PROMs) in elective surgery*. Report to the department of health, 12.

Burgess, P., Coombs, T., Clarke, A., Dickson, R., and Pirkis, J. (2012). Achievements in mental health outcome measurement in Australia: Reflections on progress made by the Australian mental health outcomes and classification network (AMHOCN). *International Journal Mental Health Systems*, 6(1), 4.

Callaly, T., Hyland, M., Coombs, T., and Trauer, T. (2006). Routine outcome measurement in public mental health: Results of a clinician survey. *Australian Health Review*, 30(2), 164–173.

Campbell, A. (2005). The evaluation of a model of primary mental health care in rural Tasmania. *Australian Journal of Rural Health*, 13(3), 142–148.

Carers Trust. (2014). *Protecting the health and wellbeing of young carers*. (online). Carers Trust. https://professionals.carers.org/protecting-health-and-wellbeing-young-carers.

Carr, A. J., Gibson, B., and Robinson, P. G. (2001). Measuring quality of life: Is quality of life determined by expectations or experience? *BMJ* (clinical research ed.), 322(7296), 1240–1243.

Carr-Hill, R. A. (1992). Health related quality of life measurement – Euro style. *Health Policy*, 20(3), 321–328.

Chapman, S., Grocott, M., and Franck, L. (2010). Systematic review of paediatric alert criteria for identifying hospitalised children at risk of critical deterioration. *Intensive Care Medicine*, 36, 600–611.

The Children's Society. (2013, May). *Hidden from view: The experiences of young carers in England*. (online). The Children's Society. www.childrenssociety.org.uk/what-we-do/resources-and-publications/publications-library/hidden-view.

Darzi, A. (2008). *High quality care for all: NHS next stage review final report*. London: Department of Health.

Dawson, J., Fitzpatrick, R., Carr, A., and Murray, D. (1996). Questionnaire on the perceptions of patients about total hip replacement. *Journal of Bone & Joint Surgery*, British volume, 78(2), 185–190.

DeChurch, L. A., Hiller, N. J., Murase, T., Doty, D., and Salas, E. (2010). Leadership across levels: Levels of leaders and their levels of impact. *The Leadership Quarterly*, 21, 1069–1085.

Department for Education. (2016 February). *The lives of young carers in England: Qualitative report to DfE*. (online). Department for Education. www.gov.uk/government/publications/the-lives-of-young-carers-in-england.

Department of Health. (2000). *The NHS plan: A plan for investment, a plan for reform*. London: Department of Health.

Department of Health. (2009). *Guidance on the routine collection of patient reported outcome measures (PROMs)*. London: Department of Health.

Department of Health. (2015 October). *Referral to treatment consultant-led waiting times rules suite*. (online). www.gov.uk/government/uploads/system/uploads/attachment_data/file/464956/RTT_Rules_Suite_October_2015.pdf.

Determann, M. M., Kollenbaum, V. E., and Henne-Bruns, D. (2004). Utility of the questionnaire for quality of life EORTC-QLQ-C30 in psycho-oncological outcome research. *Zentralblatt fur chirurgie*, 129(1), 14–17.

Devlin, N. J., and Appleby, J. (2010). *Getting the most out of PROMS*. London: The Kings Fund, Office of Health Economics.

Donabedian, A. (1966). Evaluating the quality of medical care. *The Milbank Quarterly*, 44(3), 166–233.

Doyle, C., Howe, C., Woodcock, T., Myron, R., Phekoo, K., McNicholas, C., Saffer, J., and Bell, D. (2013). Making change last: Applying the NHS institute for innovation and improvement sustainability model to healthcare improvement. *Implementation Science*, 8, 127.

Emberton, M., and Black, N. (1995). Impact of non-response and of late-response by patients in a multi-centre surgical outcome audit. *International Journal for Quality in Health Care: Journal of the International Society for Quality in Health Care/ISQua*, 7(1), 47–55.

Espallargues, M., Valderas, J. M., and Alonso, J. (2000). Provision of feedback on perceived health status to health care professionals: A systematic review of its impact. *Medical Care*, 38(2), 175–186.

Frank, J., and McLarnon, J. (2007). *Key principles of practice for young carers and their families*. Young Carers Initiative, The Children's Society. https://www.childrenssociety.org.uk/sites/default/files/supporting-young-carers-and-their-families.pdf

Friedman, Z., et al. (2015). Power and conflict: The effect of a superior's interpersonal behaviour on trainees' ability to challenge authority during a simulated airway emergency. *Anesthesia*, 70, 1119–1129.

Garratt, A. M., Ruta, D. A., Abdalla, M. I., Buckingham, J. K., and Russell, I. T. (1993). The SF36 health survey questionnaire: An outcome measure suitable for routine use within the NHS? *British Medical Journal*, 306(6890), 1440–1444.

Garratt, A. M., Ruta, D. A., Abdalla, M. I., and Russell, I. T. (1994). SF 36 health survey questionnaire: II. Responsiveness to changes in health status in four common clinical conditions. *Quality in Health Care*, 3(4), 186–192.

Garratt, A., Schmidt, L., Mackintosh, A., and Fitzpatrick, R. (2002). Quality of life measurement: Bibliographic study of patient assessed health outcome measures. *BMJ* (clinical research ed.), 324(7351), 1417.

Georgiou, A., and Pearson, M. (2002). Measuring outcomes with tools of proven feasibility and utility: The example of a patient-focused asthma measure. *Journal of Evaluation in Clinical Practice*, 8(2), 199–204.

German, P. S., Shapir, S., Skinner, E. A., Von Korff, M., Klein, L. E., Turner, R. W., Teitelbaum, M. L., Burke, J., and Burns, B. J. (1987). Detection and management of mental health problems of older patients by primary care providers. *JAMA*, 257(4), 489–493.

Gilbody, S. M., House, A. O., and Sheldon, T. A. (2001). Routinely administered questionnaires for depression and anxiety: Systematic review. *BMJ* (clinical research ed.), 322(7283), 406–409.

Goldberg, D. P., Gater, R., Sartorius, N., Ustun, T. B., Piccinelli, M., Gureje, O., and Rutter, C. (1997). The validity of two versions of the GHQ in the WHO study of mental illness in general health care. *Psychological Medicine*, 27(1), 191–197.

Greenhalgh, J., Long, A. F., and Flynn, R. (2005). The use of patient reported outcome measures in routine clinical practice: Lack of impact or lack of theory? *Social Science & Medicine*, 60(4), 833–843.

Greenhalgh, J. (2009). The applications of PROs in clinical practice: What are they, do they work, and why? *Quality of Life Research*, 18(1), 115–123.

Greenhalgh, J., Abhyankar, P., McCluskey, S., Takeuchi, E., and Velikova, G. (2013). How do doctors refer to patient-reported outcome measures (PROMS) in oncology consultations? *Quality of Life Research*, 22(5), 939–950.

Goleman, D. (2004, January). What makes a leader? *Harvard Business Review*, 1–11.

Greimel, E., Nordin, A., Lanceley, A., Creutzberg, C. L., van de Poll-Franse, L. V., Radisic, V. B., Galalae, R., Schmalz, C., Barlow, E., Jensen, P. T., Waldenström, A. C., Bergmark, K., Chie, W. C., Kuljanic, K., Costantini, A., Singes, S., Koensgen, D., Menon, U., and Daghofer, F. (2011). Psychometric validation of the European organisation for research and treatment of cancer quality of life questionnaire-endometrial cancer module (EORTC QLQ-EN24). *European Journal of Cancer*, 47(2), 183–190.

Gross, P. A., Braun, B. I., Kritchevsky, S. B., and Simmons, B. P. (2000). Comparison of clinical indicators for performance measurement of health care quality: A cautionary note. *British Journal of Clinical Governance*, 5(4), 202–211.

Heyman, A., and Heyman, B. (2013). "The sooner you can change their life course the better": The time-framing of risks in relationship to being a young carer. *Health, Risk & Society*, 15(6–7), 561–579.

Higginson, I. J., and Carr, A. J. (2001). Measuring quality of life: Using quality of life measures in the clinical setting. *BMJ* (clinical research ed.), 322(7297), 1297–1300.

Hildon, Z., Neuburger, J., Allwood, D., Van Der Meulen, J., and Black, N. (2012). Clinicians' and patients' views of metrics of change derived from patient reported outcome measures (PROMs) for comparing providers' performance of surgery. *BMC Health Services Research*, 12(1), 171.

Hutchings, A., Neuburger, J., Grosse Frie, K., Black, N., and Van Der Meulen, J. (2012). Factors associated with non-response in routine use of patient reported outcome measures after elective surgery in England. (online). *Health & Quality of Life Outcomes*, 10, 34.

Huitt, W. (1992). Problem solving and decision making: Consideration of individual differences using the Myers-Briggs type indicator. *Journal of Psychological Type*, 24, 33–44.

Hoeper, E. W., Nycz, G. R., Kessler, L. G., Burke, J. D., and Pierce, W. E. (1984). The usefulness of screening for mental illness. *The Lancet*, 323(8367), 33–35.

Jahagirdar, D., Kroll, T., Ritchie, K., and Wyke, S. (2012). Using patient reported outcome measures in health services: A qualitative study on including people with low literacy skills and learning disabilities. *BMC Health Services Research*, 12, 431.

Jones, S., Mullally, M., Ingleby, S., Buist, M., Bailey, M., and Eddleston, J. M. (2011). Bedside electronic capture of clinical observations and automated clinical alerts to improve compliance with an early warning score protocol. *Critical Care and Resuscitation*, 13(2), 83–88.

Junor, E. J., Hole, D. J., McNulty, L., Mason, M., and Young, J. (1999). Specialist gynaecologists and survival outcome in ovarian cancer: A Scottish national study of 1866 patients. *BJOG: An International Journal of Obstetrics & Gynaecology*, 106(11), 1130–1136.

Juciute, R. (2009). ICT implementation in the health-care sector: Effective stakeholders' engagement as the main precondition of change sustainability. *AI & Society*, 23, 131.

Joseph, S., Becker, F., and Becker, S. (2012). *Manual for measures of caring activities and outcomes for children and young people*, 2nd edition. London: Carers Trust.

Katz, J. N., Larson, M. G., Phillips, C. B., Fossel, A. H., and Liang, M. H. (1992). Comparative measurement sensitivity of short and longer health status instruments. *Medical Care*, 10, 917–925.

Kim, J., Lonner, J. H., Nelson, C. L., and Lotke, P. A. (2004). Response bias: Effect on outcomes evaluation by mail surveys after total knee arthroplasty. *The Journal of Bone and Joint Surgery*, American Volume, 86-A(1), 15–21.

Kind, P., and Rosser, R. (1988). The quantification of health. *European Journal of Social Psychology*, 18(1), 63–77.

Kirchner, J., Parker, L. E., Bonner, L. M., Fickel, J. J., Yano, E. M., and Ritchie, M. J. (2010). Roles of managers, frontline staff and local champions, in implementing quality improvement: Stakeholders' perspectives. *Journal of Evaluation in Clinical Practice*, 18(1), 63–69.

Kroll, T., Wyke, S., Jahagirdar, D., and Ritchie, K. (2014). If patient-reported outcome measures are considered key health-care quality indicators, who is excluded from participation? *Health Expectations*, 17(5), 605–607.

Lambert, V., Matthews, A., Macdonnell, R., and Fitzsimons, J. (2017). Paediatric early warning systems for detecting and responding to clinical deterioration in children: A systematic review. *BMJ Open*, 7.

Lapar, D. J., Kron, I. L., Jones, D. R., Stukenborg, G. J., and Kozower, B. D. (2012). Hospital procedure volume should not be used as a measure of surgical quality. *Annals of Surgery*, 256(4), 606–615.

Leow, J. J., Reese, S. W., Jiang, W., Lipsitz, S. R., Bellmunt, J., Trinh, Q. D., Chung, B. I., Kibel, A. S., and Chang, S. L. (2014, September). The impact of surgeon volume on the morbidity and costs of radical cystectomy in the United States: A contemporary population-based analysis. *European Urology*, 66(3), 569–576.

Liu, C., Chou, Y. J., Teng, C. J., Lin, C. C., Lee, Y. T., Hu, Y. W., Yeh, C. M., Chen, T. J., and Huang, N. (2015). Association of surgeon volume and hospital volume with the outcome of patients receiving definitive surgery for colorectal cancer: A nationwide population-based study. *Cancer*, 15, 121(16), 2782–2790.

Macefield, R. C., Jacobs, M., Korfage, I. J., Nicklin, J., Whistance, R. N., Brookes, S. T., Sprangers, M. A., and Blazeby, J. M. (2014). Developing core outcomes sets: Methods for identifying and including patient-reported outcomes (PROs). *Trials*, 15, 49-6215-15-49.

Marshall, S., Haywood, K., and Fitzpatrick, R. (2006). Impact of patient-reported outcome measures on routine practice: A structured review. *Journal of Evaluation in Clinical Practice*, 12(5), 559–568.

Maxwell, R. J. (1992). Dimensions of quality revisited: From thought to action. *Quality in Health Care*, 1(3), 171.

Meehan, T., McCombes, S., Hatzipetrou, L., and Catchpoole, R. (2006). Introduction of routine outcome measures: Staff reactions and issues for consideration. *Journal of Psychiatric and Mental Health Nursing*, 13(5), 581–587.

McDowell, I. (2006). *Measuring health: A guide to rating scales and questionnaires.* Oxford: Oxford University Press.

McHorney, C. A., Ware, J. E., Lu, J. F., and Sherbourne, C. D. (1994). The MOS 36-item short-form health survey (SF-36): III. Tests of data quality, scaling assumptions, and reliability across diverse patient groups. *Medical Care*, 32(1), 40–66.

Maynard, A., and Bloor, K. (2010). Patient reported outcome measurement: Learning to walk before we run. *Journal of the Royal Society of Medicine*, 103(4), 129–132.

Mindtools.com. (2016a). *Stakeholder analysis: Winning support for your projects.* (online). www.mindtools.com/pages/article/newPPM_07.htm.

Mindtools.com. (2016b). *Force field analysis: Analyzing the pressures for and against change.* (online). www.mindtools.com/pages/article/newTED_06.htm.

Mitchell, P. H. (2008 April). Defining patient safety and quality care. In: Hughes, R. G.(ed). *Patient safety and quality: An evidence-based handbook for nurses.* Rockville: Agency for Healthcare Research and Quality (US); Chapter 1. www.ncbi.nlm.nih.gov/books/NBK2681/.

Morgan, J., Day, E., and Phillips, R. (2015 April). PAWS for thought. *Archives of Disease in Childhood*, 100(4), 417.

National Audit Office. (2010–11). *Management of NHS hospital productivity*. London (HC491).

National Institute for Health and Care Excellence. (2007). *Acutely ill adults in hospital: Recognising and responding to deterioration*. London: NICE. NICE guidelines (CG50).

Office for Standards in Education, Children's Services and Skills (OFSTED) (2015). *The Common inspection framework: Education, skills and early years*. (online). OFSTED, England. www.gov.uk/government/publications/common-inspection-framework-education-skills-and-early-years-from-september-2015.

Office for National Statistics. (2013). *2011 Census, detailed characteristics for local authorities in England Wales release: Providing unpaid care may have an adverse affect on young carers' general health*. (online). Office for National Statistics. http://webarchive.nationalarchives.gov.uk/20160105160709/www.ons.gov.uk/ons/rel/census/2011-census-analysis/provision-of-unpaid-care-in-england-and-wales – 2011/sty-unpaid-care.html. (Released on 4 June 2013).

National Institute for Health and Care Excellence. (2014). *Head injury: Assessment and early management*. London: NICE. NICE guidelines (CG176).

Parshuram, C., Duncan, H. P., Joffe, A. R., Farrell, C. A., Lacroix, J. R., Middaugh, K. L., Hutchison, J. S., Wensley, D., Blanchard, N., Beyene, J., and Parkin, P. C. (2011). Multicentre validation of the bedside paediatric early warning system score: A severity of illness score to detect evolving critical illness in hospitalised children. *Critical Care*, 15, R184.

Patient Reported Outcomes Measurement Group. (2005). *Instrument selection*. (online). http://phi.uhce.ox.ac.uk/instruments.php.

Phillips, R. C., and Lansky, D. J. (1992). Outcomes management in heart valve replacement surgery: Early experience. *The Journal of Heart Valve Disease*, 1(1), 42–50.

Phillips, P., and Phillips, J. (2004). ROI in the public sector: Myths and realities. *Public Personnel Management*, 33(2), 139–149.

Pearson, G. (2008). *Why children die: A pilot study 2006; England (South West, North East and West Midlands), Wales and Northern Ireland*. London: CEMACH.

Pricewaterhousecoopers and Department of Health. (2013). *A review of the potential benefits from the better use of information and technology in health and social care*. London: PWC.

Prytherch, D. R., Smith, G. B., Schmidt, P., Featherstone, P. I., Stewart, K., Knight, D., and Higgins, B. (2006). Calculating early warning scores – A classroom comparison of pen and paper and hand-held computer methods. *Resuscitation*, 70(2), 173–178.

Rademakers, J., Delnoij, D., and De Boer, D. (2011). Structure, process or outcome: Which contributes most to patients' overall assessment of healthcare quality? *BMJ Quality & Safety*, 20(4), 326–331.

Ravi, B., Jenkinsonm, R., Austin, P. C., Croxford, R., Wasserstein, D., Escott, B., Paterson, J. M., Kreder, H., and Hawker, G. A. (2014). Relation between surgeon volume and risk of complications after total hip arthroplasty: Propensity score matched cohort study. *BMJ* (clinical research ed), 348, g3284.

Roland, D., Oliver, A., Edwards, E. D., Mason, B. W., and Powell, C. V. (2014). Use of paediatric early warning systems in Great Britain: Has there been a change of practice in the last 7 years? *Archives of Disease in Childhood*, 99, 26–29.

Rolfson, O., Kärrholm, J., Dahlberg, L. E., and Garellick, G. (2011). Patient-reported outcomes in the Swedish hip arthroplasty register: Results of a nationwide prospective observational study. *Journal of Bone and Joint Surgery*, 93(7), 867–875.

Round, A., Crabb, T., Buckingham, K., Mejzner, R., Pearce, V., Ayres, R., Weeks, C., and Hamilton, W. (2004). Six month outcomes after emergency admission of elderly patients to a community or a district general hospital. *Family Practice*, 21(2), 173–179.

Royal College of General Practitioners (RCGP). (2013). *Supporting carers in general practice: Summary report on GP practice journeys towards improved carer identification and support*. London: Royal College of General Practitioners.

Royal College of Nursing. (2013). *Standards for assessing, measuring and monitoring vital signs in infants, children and young people. RCN guidance for nurses working with children and young people.* https://my.rcn.org.uk/__data/assets/pdf_file/0004/114484/003196.pdf.

Royal College Paediatrics and Child Health. (2016). *S.A.F.E 4: Recognising deterioration.* (online). www.rcpch.ac.uk/safe-resource/introduction-resource-pack/4-recognising-deterioration/safe-4-recognising-deterioratio (Last Updated 5 July 2016).

Ruta, D. A., Abdalla, M. I., Garratt, A. M., Coutts, A., and Russell, I. T. (1994). SF 36 health survey questionnaire: I. Reliability in two patient based studies. *Quality in Health Care,* 3(4), 180–185.

Ryan, T., Enderby, P., and Rigby, A. S. (2006). A randomized controlled trial to evaluate intensity of community-based rehabilitation provision following stroke or hip fracture in old age. *Clinical Rehabilitation,* 20(2), 123–131.

Safran, D. G. (2001). Measuring, monitoring and reporting functional health outcomes: Opportunities and challenges in a bold national initiative. *International Journal for Quality in Health Care: Journal of the International Society for Quality in Health Care/ISQua,* 13(1), 7–8.

Sales, A. E., Plomondon, M. E., Magid, D. J., Spertus, J. A., and Rumsfeld, J. S. (2004). Assessing response bias from missing quality of life data: The Heckman method. *Health Qual Life Outcomes,* 2, 49.

Schein, E. (1995). Kurt Lewin's change theory in the field and in the classroom: Notes toward a model of managed learning. *Systems Practice,* 9(1), 27–47.

Schein, E. (2010). *Organizational culture and leadership.* (online), 4th edition. New Jersey, US: Jossey Bass Ltd.

Senge, P. (2006). *The fifth discipline: The art and practice of the learning organisation,* 2nd edition. London: Random House Business.

Siggeirsdottir, K., Olafsson, O., Jonsson, H., Iwarsson, S., Gudnason, V., and Jonsson, B. Y. (2005). Short hospital stay augmented with education and home-based rehabilitation improves function and quality of life after hip replacement: Randomized study of 50 patients with 6 months of follow-up. *Acta Orthopaedica,* 76(4), 555–562.

Snyder, C. F., Jensen, R. E., Segal, J. B., and Wu, A. W. (2012). Patient reported outcomes: Putting the patient perspective in patient centred outcomes research. *Medical Care,* 51(803), 73–79.

Speight, J., and Barendse, S. M. (2010). FDA guidance on patient reported outcomes. *BMJ,* 340.

Swanwick, T., and McKimm, J. (eds.) (2011). *ABC of clinical leadership.* ABC series. London: BMJ Books.

Takeuchi, E. E., Keding, A., Awad, N., Hofmann, U., Campbell, L. J., Selby, P. J., Brown, J. M., and Velikova, G. (2011). Impact of patient-reported outcomes in oncology: A longitudinal analysis of patient-physician communication. *Journal of Clinical Oncology,* 29(21), 2910–2917.

Toledano, N., Urbano, D., and Bernadich, M. (2010). Networks and corporate entrepreneurship: A comparative case study on family business in Catalonia. *Journal of Organizational Change Management,* 23(4), 396–412. Emerald Group Publishing Limited.

Tume, L., Sefton, G., and Arrowsmith, P. (2013). Teaching paediatric ward teams to recognise and manage the deteriorating child. *Nursing in Critical Care,* 19(4), 196–203.

US Food and Drug Administration. (2013). *Guidance for industry patient-reported outcome measures: Use in medical product development to support labeling claims.* Washington, DC: US Department of Health and Human Services Food and Drug Administration.

US Department of Health and Human Services. (2014). *Annual report to congress.* www.acf.hhs.gov

UK Health and Social Care Information Centre. (2014 14 July). *A guide to PROMs methodology.* (online). www.hscic.gov.uk/media/1537/A-Guide-to-PROMs-Methodology/pdf/PROMs_Guide_V8.pdf. (Last Accessed on 17 July 2014).

U.S. Department of Health and Human Services FDA Center for Devices and Radiological Health. (2006). Guidance for industry: Patient-reported outcome measures: Use in medical product development to support labeling claims: Draft guidance. *Health and Quality of Life Outcomes*, 4, 79.

Valderas, J. M., Kotzeva, A., Espallargues, M., Guyatt, G., Ferrans, C. E., Halyard, M.Y., Revicki, D.A., Symonds, T., Parada, A., and Alonso, J. (2008). The impact of measuring patient-reported outcomes in clinical practice: A systematic review of the literature. *Quality of Life Research*, 17(2), 179–193.

Vallance-Owen, A., Cubbin, S., Warren, V., and Matthews, B. (2004). Outcome monitoring to facilitate clinical governance: Experience from a national programme in the independent sector. *Journal of Public Health (Oxf)*, 26(2), 187–192.

Velikova, G., Booth, L., Smith, A. B., Brown, P. M., Lynch, P., Brown, J. M., and Selby, P. J. (2004). Measuring quality of life in routine oncology practice improves communication and patient well-being: A randomized controlled trial. *Journal of Clinical Oncology*, 22(4), 714–724.

Von Meyenfeldt, E. M., Gooiker, G. A., Van Gijn, W., Post, P. N., Van De Velde, C. J., Tollenaar, R. A., Klomp, H. M., and Wouters, M. W. (2012). The relationship between volume or surgeon specialty and outcome in the surgical treatment of lung cancer: A systematic review and meta-analysis. *Journal of Thoracic Oncology*, 7(7), 1170–1178.

Ware, J. R., John, E., and Sherbourne, C. D. (1992). The MOS 36-item short-form health survey (SF-36): I. Conceptual framework and item selection. *Medical Care*, 30(6), 473–483.

West, M., and Dawson, J. (2011). *Employee engagement and NHS performance.* London: King's Fund.

Wilcock, P., Brown, G., and Carver, J. (2003). Using patient stories to inspire quality improvement within the NHS modernization agency collaborative programmes. *Journal of Clinical Nursing*, 12(3), 422–430.

Wight, J. P., Edwards, L., Brazier, J., Walters, S., Payne, J. N., and Brown, C. B. (1998). The SF36 as an outcome measure of services for end stage renal failure. *Quality Health Care*, 7(4), 209–221.

Whiteley, S. (2009). *Development of a Paediatric Advanced Warning Score (PAWS).* http://rapidresponsesystems.org/downloads2009/Whiteley_PAWS.pdf.

World Health Organization. (2016). *Universal health coverage, fact sheet.* http://www.who.int/news-room/fact-sheets/detail/universal-health-coverage-(uhc)

West, M., Lyubovnikova, J., Eckert, R., and Denis, J-L. (2014). Collective leadership for cultures of high quality health care. *Journal of Organizational Effectiveness*, 1(3), 240–260.

World Health Organization. (2013). *Research for universal health coverage: World health report.* http://apps.who.int/iris/bitstream/handle/10665/85761/9789240690837_eng.pdf;jsessionid=0BB5871A938FB6BEE28BE1A0700E44CC?sequence=2

World Health Organization. (2014). *A universal truth: No health without a workforce.* http://www.who.int/workforcealliance/knowledge/resources/GHWA-a_universal_truth_report.pdf

Yudkin, J. S., Lipska, K. J., and Montori, V. M. (2011). The idolatry of the surrogate. *BMJ* (Clinical Research, ed.), 343, d7995.

PART 5
System transformation

26

INTRODUCTION TO CRITICAL ISSUES IN HEALTH SYSTEM TRANSFORMATION

Jill Aylott and Ahmed Nassef

Future healthcare services need a 'system wide focus on improvement and leadership' which requires a different set of leadership skills and knowledge to those used in 'service' or 'quality' improvement (Smith Review, 2015). Quality Improvement projects require clinical leaders to develop skills in leadership and quality improvement methods (as illustrated in case studies in Part 4 of this book). Quality Improvement is usually located within one's own area of clinical specialism, and strategies are utilised to engage teams to sustain improvement initiatives over time. However, transforming healthcare services will need a different type of leader with skills in understanding strategic data in relation to forecasting patient demand; understanding trends in technology in relation to telehealth and social media, strategic marketing, strategic finance, large-scale change management; developing working partnerships with patients to comply with the legal requirement to consult and engage with patients and developing effective, motivated and innovative teams. Leaders will also need to apply a wide range of strategic leadership skills to work across professional boundaries and enter new types of working relationships across organisations and professional groups. These core skills are taught on Health or Medical Leadership MBAs and recognised as a key requirement for senior clinicians who are developing their career in healthcare. In the UK, senior clinicians have been encouraged to consider a Health MBA (Hunt, 2016; Aylott and Montisci, 2017).

In an ideal world, system transformation programmes would scale-up quality improvement projects, where data sources indicate that specific changes are required. However, the UK English NHS alongside all other global healthcare systems are under considerable pressure to transform services through system transformation while at the same time develop and achieve continuous quality improvement. This is particularly apparent in England, with the forty-four Sustainability and Transformation Partnerships (STP) (NHS England, 2016a), with some planning for a 30%

reduction in some areas of hospital activity including outpatients, A&E and emergency inpatient services (Imison et al., 2017). Not only is this a major challenge but also clinicians and managers continue to deliver frontline services with minimal time available to review, advance, improve and transform those same services. However, successful transformation depends on medical engagement and skilled medical leaders engaging with patients and their families and clinical and non-clinical teams.

A major study on transformational systems change identified evidence on what works to transform services and the authors (Lukas et al., 2007) concluded that five elements need to be in place (Table 26.1):

TABLE 26.1 What works to transform services

1   Impetus to transform
2   Leadership commitment to quality
3   Improvement initiatives that actively engage staff in meaningful problem solving
4   Alignment to achieve consistency of organisation-wide goals with resource allocation and actions at all levels of the organisation
5   Integration to bridge traditional intra-organisational boundaries between individual components

Source: Lukas et al. (2007).

An additional and critical element for the transformation of healthcare services is the importance of engaging with patients and the public. In England, UK, the Health and Social Care Act 2012 provides a legal requirement to consult with the public regarding any changes in services, yet patient and public engagement are often 'one-off' events. The involvement of patients and the public is intended to keep services focused on quality as defined by patients and act as the driver for transformation. This approach is more likely to create 'fit for purpose' services and to get them right first time. The values of new 'patient-centred' partnerships with medical leaders and the wider multidisciplinary team will form a collective focus for steering transformation and change. Working within a model of 'coproduction' establishes more meaningful and constructive relationships with patients and the public for all proposed transformation of healthcare.

Reflecting on our own experience in the facilitation of transformation programmes with clinical and medical leaders in NHS hospital Trusts, we have found that much of our discussion focused on the barriers within 'systems' and 'infrastructure'. Examples of barriers to transformation that we have heard reported include:

1   *Tension between delivering clinical activity and transforming services*

In a time of austerity, there are critical pressures that create tension between balancing the delivering of a volume of clinical activity with patients within agreed waiting times and time available to improve and transform services. Much of this pressure moves the focus of system transformation away from patients and to the board room, where senior clinicians work with managers to decide the mapping of future services.

2   *A focus on elective or emergency services*

With a national and global shortage of medical and nursing staff, there has to be decisions as to how to deliver a balanced service to patients. This requires a team-based approach across all services, as decisions made in one area will have a significant impact in another. Clinical decision-making teams need support to access quality data across the local population to identify where resources need to be focused. This requires substantial skills in types of data used for system transformation, forecasting, statistical process control measures, managing people, leadership styles, skills and approaches, managing change and managing finance. There also needs to be an understanding of the key elements required to change a hospital's organisational culture which may currently deliver many smaller services across a large organisation and instead will need to centralise some core services.

3   *Adapting and changing work and practice for people to work differently*

A need for a HR infrastructure particularly in relation to equity and fairness of medical staff travelling to work across the Trust. Changes in working practice to be developed with the medical staff and agreed as a new way of working to support the transformation of services.

4   *Nursing staff development programmes*

Nursing staff to develop skills across traditional intra-organisational boundaries (e.g. the development of a training programme and protocol to deliver hospital services such as intravenous antibiotics in a community setting)

5   *New integrated training and development models to include administration and clerical staff*

Administration and clerical support staff are often working within historical lines of accountability, which delays medical leadership decision making to advance change. 'System Transformation' training programmes need to include administrative and clerical staff along with patients and families in partnership with clinicians.

6   *Insufficient time* to generate reliable and valid data to support strategic medical leadership decision making. Clinicians frustrated with minimal time available to devote to strategic thinking and system transformation. Planned time required to facilitate the transformation and integration of services.

This section explores Healthcare System Transformation in practice, by identifying case studies that demonstrate the application of elements of the Lukas et al. (2007) framework in a range of areas of clinical practice.

Branko Perunovic sets the scene for horizon scanning the future model of integrated services in England. He reviews models and approaches to integrated services and outlines some of the challenges to transformation. Rachael Baines and Prasad Godbole explore the development of a strategy to engage staff teams in healthcare transformation. They examine what factors are likely to stall the transformation of healthcare and how best to support staff through the process.

Surgeons and Anaesthetists worked with managers and administrators to provide a reflective account of the group learning acquired while steering a project to transform theatre services in an English NHS Foundation Trust. The complexity and challenge of transformation is evident as clinicians and non-clinicians engaged in a planned way with the collection of primary and secondary data and met monthly to undertake real time data analysis and propose process improvements.

Prakash Subedi and colleagues present a case study from an English NHS Foundation Trust where he and others have been developing a new and alternative medical workforce model in the provision of a Hybrid (Quality Improvement and Medical Leadership) medical speciality training in Emergency Medicine. This work follows recommendations from the General Medical Council (2017) to create more flexible pathways for specialty training that are competency based as opposed to 'programmed over time'. Keeping with Emergency Medicine, Elizabeth Hutchinson explores the multiple challenges faced with transforming services in Accident and Emergency departments and concludes how a quality improvement project demonstrated a need for a stable workforce in A&E to facilitate its future transformation.

Finally as we consider the need for the system transformation of health and social care, Jonathan Sahu examines the urgent need for mainstream health and social care services to change and adapt in line with equalities legislation and the Health and Social Act 2012 to challenge health inequalities for people with a learning disability and/or autism. This chapter calls for hospitals to adopt an advocacy charter and for Learning Disability Liaison nurses to be appointed to oversee the compliance of the hospital in relation to 'reasonable adjustment' under equalities legislation. Across the globe, as people are living longer there is a higher prevalence of complex and multiple disabilities. With increased demand for services, there is a need to consider the quality of these services. Pradeep Thumbikat reviews the national Spinal Injuries Care pathway and identifies further work required to standardise the quality of care for patients on this national pathway.

27

SYSTEM TRANSFORMATION FOR HEALTH AND SOCIAL CARE

Branko Perunovic

In the UK, several factors synergistically challenge the sustainability of the NHS as a healthcare service of the type and funding model that has been established since its inception in 1948. Apart from economic factors which are largely a consequence of a debt-fuelled national economy and a budget deficit (Statistics, 2016), there is a progressive demographic shift comprising an expanding and ageing population at the same time as an increase in the numbers of people with chronic illness. It is estimated that 20–25% of the world population will be over 65 years old by 2030 (United Nations, 2015) and data available for the UK mirror this demographic trend (Society, 2015; UK Parliament, 2016). Currently, 58% of population over 60 years old have long-term or multiple conditions, and the number of people with three or more chronic conditions will have reached 2.9 million in 2018. The long-term conditions are significantly more prevalent and severe in deprived socioeconomic groups (Barnett et al., 2012; Kings Fund, 2016). These population changes, coupled with scientifically and technologically more advanced disease management options, create a gradual shift from life-threatening to chronic diseases which inevitably fuel an increase in volume and complexity of healthcare demand, cost per patient and total cost of healthcare. The management of patients with long-term conditions is estimated to require an additional £5 billion by 2018 (Barnett et al., 2012; Kings Fund, 2016).

The existing health and social care models are not adequately equipped to deal with these challenges. So far, the care has been provided by the number of organisationally and functionally loosely connected entities (hospitals, general practice surgeries, nursing homes, care agencies, families, etc.), each incentivised to deal with their own constraints and manage own clinical, operational and financial performance, rather than to optimise the whole system. The net effect is a 'twin care and cash crisis' (Warner and O'Sullivan, 2015), comprising a service model that is neither fit for purpose nor affordable.

The concept of *integrated care* is not a new one; various aspects of integration between NHS organisations and local authorities have been aspiration of policy-makers and health reforms since the 1960s (Shortell et al., 2014; Department of Health, 2008). The idea and experimentation with a range of models of integration of care has been on the agenda in other countries as well (Shortell et al., 2014; Mac-Adam, 2008; World Health Organization, 2008; Watson, 2012). The basic postulate around the concept of integrated care is that *improving coordination of care around the needs of individual patients, service users and carers will positively affect quality of care and its cost-effectiveness* (Lewis et al., 2010; Goodwin et al., 2012). However, bringing care closer to the patient has been identified as not always being cost effective and. in some cases, may cost more (Imison et al., 2017).

There is neither a single model for integration of care, nor a definite evidence for a 'best model'. The emerging evidence highlights that planners and providers need to have a service user-centric perspective as the organising principle (Shaw et al., 2011, Lloyd and Wait, 2005). Essentially, clinical and service-level integration needs to focus around the needs of individuals, especially when its delivery spans across professional and organisational boundaries (Curry and Ham, 2010). Also, the concept does not imply conventional mergers of NHS providers, aiming to address acute operational or financial crises or achieve the 'critical masses' without changing traditional models of care (Collins, 2015, Gaynor et al., 2012, Ham and Curry, 2011). In fact, there is no evidence that organisational integration is required or is sufficient to deliver desired outcomes (Goodwin et al., 2012, Ham and Curry, 2011).

Due to the changing pattern of demand, meeting the needs of the population will require a shift of emphasis from acute care towards prevention, public health and self-care as well as more consistency in primary care (Goodwin et al., 2012). Because the potential for most tangible and long-lasting benefits could be expected from the interventions in these domains, many programmes of integration have been and will be focusing at the interfaces between primary and social care and primary and secondary care (Naylor et al., 2016, Addicott and Ham, 2014, Ham and Alderwick, 2015, Naylor et al., 2015). However, this is not the only perspective. Plausible effects of integration are also expected to come from 'horizontal' integration of acute hospitals (Naylor et al., 2015, Department of Health, 2014) and integration of mental and physical care (Naylor et al., 2016).

The UK 'Five-Year Forward View (5YFV)' puts forward seven broad areas for transformation (NHS England, 2014). The document and subsequent reviews and options appraisals put a clear emphasis on the need for the whole system transformation, effective leadership and coordination of efforts between the stakeholders around personalised, proactive and effective programmes of care (Addicott and Ham, 2014; Ham and Murray, 2015; Imison, 2014; Naylor et al., 2015; Timmins, 2015; Department of Health, 2014).

The UK Cities and Local Government Devolution Act (The Parliament, 2016) created another powerful impetus for transformation through transfer of significant body of healthcare functions to local or regional authorities. It is too early to understand the implications of the Act, especially the potential vulnerabilities of local financial constructs in view of competing priorities (Nuffield Trust, 2015; Hudson, 2015; Gregory, 2016), but a number of areas have already developed ambitious devolution agendas (BBC News, 2016; Greater Manchester Combined Authority, 2016; Gloucestershire County Council, 2016).

In order to give momentum to the system-wide changes and incentivise integration processes, NHS England, in conjunction with NHS Improvement, the Care Quality Commission, Public Health England, Health Education England and NICE has issued new 'NHS Shared Planning Guidance 16/17–20/21' (NHS England, 2016a). Although individual organisations will be required to produce plans for 2016–2017, the new *place-based system of care* framework will aim to ensure that the decisions for common pools of resources are taken collectively by local systems, comprising providers, commissioners and local authorities.

Key legislative and policy changes brought about by the Care Act (2014) and the Children and Families Act (2014) introduce a number of reforms to the way that care and support for adults with care needs are met. Under the Care Act 2014, "local authorities must carry out an assessment of anyone who appears to require care and support, regardless of their likely eligibility for state funded care". (The Care Act: Assessment and Eligibility – social care institute for Excelllence) www. scie.org.uk/care-act-2014. Within the Care Act 2014, the needs of young carers are clearly required to be identified (which provided a rationale for Samantha Wong's project in Chapter 23), with the legislation extending the right to an assessment of the support needs of all young carers under the age of 18.

The Care Act 2014 outlines a significant role for carers in the new model of health and social care transformation in the UK. System transformation proposes a vision of alternative models of integrated services (NHS England, 2014; 2016c) across the acute and primary care interface that integrates the patient/service user and carers' perspective. These services will require providers to adapt and design integrated services around patients (Imison et al., 2014). Successful methods to facilitate this have been documented elsewhere, with the use of communication profiles for vulnerable children and adults who use non-verbal communication and alternative and augmentative communication methods (Aylott, 2010, 2015) in conjunction with the use of patient personas, for example, the 'Esther project' in Sweden (Gray et al., 2016), which provide the impetus for person-centred system transformation.

There should be no 'one-size-fits-all' and 'organisational forms' should deliver the models of care which best suit local circumstances – they must not be centrally dictated (Dalton Review, 2014). The health and social care legislation in the UK requires local authorities to adopt a whole system, whole council, 'whole family approach', coordinating services and support around the person and their family, including children.

28

A STRATEGY FOR ENGAGING TEAMS AND MOTIVATING STAFF THROUGH SYSTEM TRANSFORMATION

Rachael Baines and Prasad Godbole

Although drivers are in place to provide the legislative framework for the future transformation of health and social care services, staff teams will need to be engaged at a time when there is 'change fatigue' across the NHS workforce (Rose Report, 2014). Evidence of what works well with large-scale change in healthcare is sparse and what evidence is available is quite complex and nuanced (Best et al., 2012).

'Large-scale improvement' and 'scale-up' are terms that refer to efforts that seek to stimulate positive and sustainable change within the organisation and beyond on a regional and national basis, through the mobilisation of hundreds or thousands of healthcare workers (Perla et al., 2011a). In particular, large-scale system transformations are described as interventions aimed at coordinating system-wide change affecting multiple organisations and care providers, with the goal of significant improvements in the efficiency of healthcare delivery, the quality of patient care and population-level patient outcomes (Best et al, 2012).

The existing evidence suggests that there are several large-scale change programme drivers (Perla et al., 2011a; Benn et al., 2009), and these drivers are not dissimilar to what Brandrud et al. (2011) described in the factors for successful continuous Quality Improvement programmes. However, the combination of continuous Quality Improvement with major healthcare transformation in the English NHS is unprecedented. The large-scale change drivers have been combined with the characteristics of a successful microsystem project (Nelson et al., 1998, 2002, 2011) and presented in Table 28.1.

All large-scale planned improvement initiatives involve supporting humans to operate and change in complex social settings, and one example that enables the facilitation of this process is the Microsystems Coaching Academy (MCA) (Nelson et al., 2002; Narine and Persaud, 2003, 2014; Mohr and Batalden, 2002). The MCA has undertaken extensive research to understand the cognitive dimension of spread and how people and groups think about, interact with and are affected by

TABLE 28.1 Drivers for large-scale change programme utilising clinical microsystems as the 'process of change'.

Primary Drivers	Secondary Drivers
1. Planning and Infrastructure	Leadership
	Clear Vision and Aim
	Information Technology
	Resources
2. Individual, Group,	Culture
Organisation and Systems	Previous QI Knowledge
Factors	Capability and Capacity Development
	Staff and Patient Focus
	Learning Networks and Support
3. The Process of Change	Change Theory Used 'Clinical Microsystems coaching'
4. Outcomes	Performance Patterns
	Outcomes – Measurement and Feedback

innovation (Nelson et al., 2002; Narine and Persaud, 2003, 2014; Mohr and Batalden, 2002; Perla et al., 2011a). Such research is critical to developing knowledge about what works and how to support people with large-scale change initiatives.

Engaging people in the process of change

Leadership is the key to change with "strong and capable leadership being the key to driving transformational change and the taking of bold decisions" (Rose Report, 2014). Strong leadership is required to develop a new culture of collaboration and co-operation for the good of the patient and their family and for good practice to be actively shared.

Healthcare administrators have sought to improve the quality of healthcare services by using organisational change as a lever. Unfortunately, evaluations of organisational change efforts in areas such as total quality management (TQM), continuous quality improvement (CQI) and organisational restructuring have indicated that these change programmes have not always fulfilled their promise in improving service delivery (Narine and Persaud, 2003). Research on a large scale shows that if cost and quality outcomes are to improve dramatically, it will be through the engaged improvement efforts of frontline clinical teams that do the work, effectively supported by their leaders (Bevan et al., 2008; Bibby et al., 2009; King and Peterson, 2007). Bevan et al., 2011 proposes ten key principles when considering large-scale change programmes (see Table 28.2).

In producing a strategic approach, change needs to be considered in terms of how it spreads in complex adaptive systems, how skills relate to daily work and how far systems, organisations, teams and individuals have already come in their own development journey (Bevan, 2010). Large-scale training programmes that train literally hundreds of thousands of people in change skills with a 'sheep dip'

TABLE 28.2 Bevan's ten key principles of large-scale change

No.	Principle
1	Movement towards a new vision is better and fundamentally different from the status quo
2	Identification and communication of key themes that people can relate to and that will make a big difference
3	Multiples of things
4	Framing the issues in ways that engage and mobilise the imagination, energy and will of a large number of diverse stakeholders in create a shift in the balance of power and distribute the leadership
5	Mutually reinforcing change across multiple processes subsystems
6	Continually refreshing the story and attracting new active supporters
7	Emergent planning and design, based on monitoring progress and adapting as you go
8	Many people contribute to the leadership of change beyond organisational boundaries
9	Transforming mindsets, leading to inherently sustainable change
10	Maintaining and refreshing the leader's energy over the long haul (Bevan et al., 2011)

approach will fail (Bevan, 2010). The traditional static strategies of 'command and control' approach, in which the top of the organisation does the thinking and the rest is supposed to comply (Senge et al., 1999), will not work.

How an individual reacts to change can vary (Blacker and Shimmin, 1984). For example, change may raise issues with fear of job security, and therefore threaten the security of family and/or property and may be overtly demonstrated as extreme resistance (Wittig, 2012). Literature indicates that a high proportion of change initiatives are unsuccessful (Beer and Nohria, 2000; Waldersee and Griffiths, 1996). Employee resistance is suggested to be the foremost cause of change failure (Bovey and Hede, 2001). Every individual has needs ranging from basic to higher order (see Maslow's Hierarchy of Needs (1943) in Figure 28.1); if the lower order needs are threatened, the higher order needs are compromised.

Similarly, Herzberg (1966) proposed the motivational theory for people at work, which can also affect how people react to change. This is depicted in Figure 28.2. What works well and what can be improved within a given change initiative will highlight the motivators and dissatisfiers and allow the facilitator of change to focus on specific areas to target improvement.

There are many factors that may contribute to the well-being of an individual. As most individuals spend a significant amount of time in the workplace, pressures, stresses and strains within the workplace have been identified as a potentially important health factor. It is postulated that there is a direct link between organisational/workplace stress and well-being (Cooper, 1999). Kenny et al. (2000) and Cooper (1999) have shown a growing evidence that changing work practices and trends in employment conditions may be eroding levels of job satisfaction.

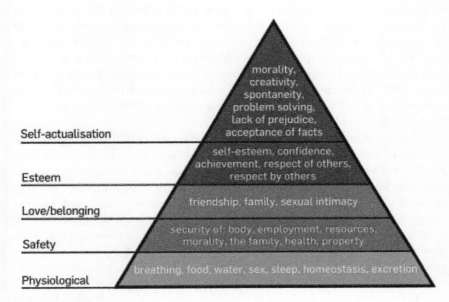

FIGURE 28.1 Maslow's Hierarchy of Needs

FIGURE 28.2 Herzberg's Hygiene and Motivational Factors

Job satisfaction has been defined in different ways. One view is that job satisfaction reflects the positive emotional and attitudes an individual has towards their job (Oshagbemi, 2003). Other views are of a bi-dimensional construct consisting of intrinsic/extrinsic dimensions of satisfaction (Warr et al., 1979) or dissatisfaction/lack of dissatisfaction dimensions (Winefield et al., 1988). This is in keeping with the Herzberg Hygiene and Motivational Factors described and illustrated in Figure 28.2. Studies on job satisfaction in medical teams have been carried out extensively, with most studies focusing on nurses (Blegen, 1993; Adams and Bond, 2001; Mueller and McCloskey, 1990).

Correct evaluation of job satisfaction became fundamental for any organisation as shown by Faragher et al. (2005) in their meta-analysis, for improving employees' physical and mental well-being. Job satisfaction was much more strongly associated with mental/psychosocial problems than with physical complaints like cardiovascular disease and musculoskeletal disorders. The authors discussed whether organisations should develop stress management policies, including counselling services, helping to identify job dissatisfaction and getting employees to find solutions. According to McNeese-Smith (1999), nurse satisfaction derives mainly from patient care, balanced workload, relationships with co-workers, salary, professionalism and nurses' cultural background and job security.

The Finnish study by Makinen et al. (2003) examines the relationship between methods of organising nursing and employee satisfaction and shows that the strongest contributor to nurses' satisfaction with supervision was mainly the opportunity to write patients' nursing notes, patient-focused work allocation and accountability for patient care. The outcomes of a quality improvement project showed that when Clinical Nurse Specialists are trained, supported and trusted to lead a Nurse led clinic for patients post-operatively, their job satisfaction increased alongside higher patient satisfaction rates and a return on investment of 1.71. This means that for every £1 spent on this quality improvement project, the income generated was £1.71 (Patel and Aylott, 2017:45). Zangaro-Soeken's (2007) meta-analysis of thirty-one studies examined the strengths of the relationship between job satisfaction and autonomy, job stress and nurse-physician collaboration amongst registered nurses working in staff positions. Job satisfaction was most strongly correlated with job stress, followed by nurse-physician collaboration and autonomy.

A literature review by Lu et al. (2012) also contributed to define the relative importance of the many identified factors to nurse job satisfaction. The factors with very strong relationship are job stress, organisational commitment, depression and cohesion of the ward nursing team. Authors underlined that more research was required to produce a strong causal model incorporating organisational, professional and personal variables for the development of interventions to improve nurse retention. It is important to distinguish between intrinsic satisfaction (with autonomy) and extrinsic satisfaction (hours of work) as this is key to the study (Warr et al., 1979 and Winefield et al., 1988).

Transforming services can result in the production of a stressful working environment which can impact on job satisfaction, employee retention and group cohesion Kapur et al. (1998). As health and social care services undergo substantial transformation, there is an important role for senior leaders to create a positive work environment with reduced stress and increased job satisfaction. There is evidence to show that when staff are supported through the change process, there is a positive relationship between employees and employer, with high job satisfaction and positive business outcomes Harter et al. (2002). When clinical staff are supported in the workplace, job satisfaction can increase (Giallonardo, 2010).

29

TRANSFORMING OPERATING THEATRE SERVICES WITH MEDICAL LEADERSHIP

Ahmed Othman, Jayarama Mohan, Prabhakar Motkur, Salma Noor, Milind Rao, Adam Wolverson, Amit Shukla, Gurdip Singh Samra, Mohit Gupta, Chloe Scruton, Jill Aylott, Karen Kilner and Prasad Godbole

The aim of transforming theatre services is to provide a better patient experience, increase the quality of services and improve patient flow but perhaps most significantly to prevent cancellations of operations on the day. The secondary aim in the transforming of theatre services is to improve efficiencies by increasing the way theatres are utilised and thereby provide the Trust with returns on investment. However, theatre services are concerned with multiple layers of complexity across elective and emergency procedures as they deal with emergency and elective procedures across multiple clinical specialties, within times of austerity, amidst a backdrop of shrinking resources and gaps in the medical and nursing workforce.

Each clinical and technical group (e.g. Nursing, Operating Department Practitioners (ODP), Medical staff, and Physicians Assistants/Associates) has their own culture of practice, shift patterns and different codes of professional practice, which will all serve to support the development of their own different professional identities. Transforming theatre services requires clinicians from a range of different clinical disciplines to stand back from their own clinical speciality and to explore the wider 'system' from a more strategic perspective. Medical leaders already have mechanisms to communicate across medical specialties as they share a culture of medical practice over the years from their early beginnings in medical school. Medical leaders are best placed to lead the transformation of theatre services with a multidisciplinary and multi-agency group through action learning and facilitation. This case study is the shared work of surgeons (AO, PM, JM, AO, SN, MR, MG, AS, PG), anaesthetists (AW, GS), and an operational manager (CS) with two academic Medical Leadership facilitators (JA, KK). Following a business case 'A Tale of Three Case Studies' outlining the Return on Investment to the NHS Foundation Hospital Trust led by JM, PM and AO, a cross-speciality transformation group of doctors and surgeons received support from their NHS Hospital Trust Executive, and the programme was sponsored by the medical director. The group became the 'Theatre Utilisation Transformation Action Learning (TUTAL) group', led by senior doctors across the NHS Foundation Trust.

TABLE 29.1 Extraction of 2016 NHS England data on 'Cancelled operations on the day' across England, UK

Organisation	Number of last-minute elective operations cancelled for non-clinical reasons	Number of patients not treated within 28 days of last-minute elective cancellation
England (Excluding Independent Sector)	19,399	1,229
England (Including Independent Sector)	19,515	1,233

Surgeons and anaesthetists drove the transformation programme from the bottom up, as they were concerned about several issues that were affecting the quality of service provided to patients. Their main concern was the increased number of cancelled operations on the day, which for England totalled 19,515 patients in 2016 (Table 29.1). This figure was up significantly from 2015, where the total cancellation of operations on the day was 16,414 in the same quarter (NHS England, 2016b). The Patients Association produced a report, *Feeling the Wait: Annual Report on Elective Surgery Waiting Times* (2016), reporting on a Freedom of Information request to NHS Trusts on the number of cancelled operations. Cancelled operations can have a devastating effect on patients emotionally, psychologically and financially.

There is a clear rationale to drive up improvements in the system to prevent even more cancellation of operations on the day. A general principle is that when cancelled operations go up, theatre utilisation goes down and the income to the Trust is reduced. Cancelled operations and theatre utilisation are interrelated. A Norwegian Hospital improvement programme showed that when cancelled operations were reduced from 8.5% to 4.9%, the volume of operations increased by 17% (Hovlid et al., 2012). System improvement resulted through the involvement of frontline clinicians, use of information technology and the engagement of middle managers (Hovlid et al., 2012).

The TUTAL programme had five distinct phases: (1) Securing medical engagement from across the Trust to lead the transformation programme, (2) generating system-wide data on theatre performance and patient satisfaction, (3) facilitating new skills in statistical analysis and medical leadership through a process of action learning, (4) testing out and evaluating new processes (with the use of PDSA cycles) and, finally, (5) proposing new NHS Trust wide process change with an implementation strategy.

1 Securing medical engagement from across the Trust to lead the transformation programme

The nature of medical leadership (as discussed in Part 1 of this book) is of a 'hybrid leader role' with limited time for doctors to devote to leadership, management, service improvement and system transformation. Doctors are busy 'doing the doing' and with very little time to devote to service improvement and system transformation. Engaging the right medical leaders, and working together to create a programme in co-production, as well as securing the support from various stakeholders across the Trust took approximately 11 months with this project. An external academic facilitator (JA) kept the individuals and the group engaged through e-mail communication and telephone contact to develop a programme that would fit the needs of 'hybrid leaders', allow for their attendance on the medical leadership programme and foster their commitment to change. Securing medical engagement is a complex process and needs 'early adopters' (suggested to be about 14% of people who are the first to try new ideas and processes in the 'diffusion of innovation theory', Rogers, 1962) early in the process. It is worth mentioning that surgeons JM and AO were the innovators and who as early adopters led from the inside across different geographical areas of the organisation. They co-opted clinical and non-clinical individuals on to the group and sustained their unwavering commitment to transforming systems in theatres. In addition, there needed to be top-down support and buy-in for this transformation programme which was maintained by the medical director and the Executive Board. Although certain elements of the programme were supported by the senior medical leaders (statistical analysis of data and systems/process review with academic improvement facilitators, JA/KK), it was not until a senior surgeon/medical leader, external to the hospital Trust (PG) and a senior operational manager (CS) began to work closely with the group on delivery did the group start to develop some momentum with system and process change. PG was able to ask difficult and challenging questions and action was supported by CS. We secured support from a lead anaesthetist from the Trust (AW) who had significant skills in quality improvement methods and the programme started to move into a more 'operational and delivery' stage. Our approach supports the evidence in Figure 29.1 that large-scale change needs to spend more time upfront on building readiness for change, as this will result in better use of time and resources overall. This approach suggests that more sustainable change and greater return on investment will be achieved in the longer term.

The key message here is to be completely open to methods and processes to secure medical engagement and to continue to seek to get the right team together, as there are too many variables that constitute constraints and barriers to system transformation that could make the project flounder and fail.

2 Generating system-wide data on theatre performance and patient satisfaction

Learning sessions were facilitated with a skills-based approach to support senior clinicians to take a more Trust wide 'systems approach' to understanding data and analysis. The sessions were facilitated in an external venue to the Trust, but close enough to reduce travel time for busy clinicians. The focus of the learning sessions was to collect and analyse primary and secondary data on start and finish times in theatre and to agree a consensus on the core definitions of the terms used. Surgeons

*The **'Top-Down'** classic approach to large-scale change minimises the time spent preparing for change in the initial stages. It gives the appearance of saving time and being efficient, but the enormity, scope and impact of the change stays with a small minority at the top of the structure.*

The **'Bottom-up'** approach works with the people who will be the recipients of the change and by spending more time upfront building a readiness for change, we can work with people's fears, anxieties and their lack of confidence in the change process. We can also use a PDSA method to 'test out' small-scale change to build experience, confidence and skills in the change process. This approach to large-scale change will be built on a stable foundation and will result in more sustainable change in the long term, bringing returns on investment.

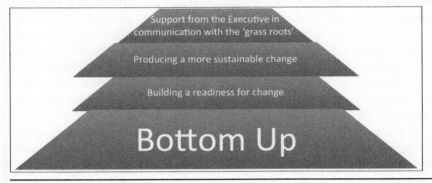

FIGURE 29.1 'Top-down' vs 'bottom-up' approach to large-scale change

Source: Adapted from Patel and Aylott (2017:37–47).

define the start time from 'knife to skin', but good practice guidance suggests looking at the start from the beginning of a 16-week patient journey. Having a debate on the concepts and agreeing a consensus was time worth spent to ensure the robustness of the design of the tools that were used for collecting primary data.

We undertook an audit for one day across all theatres (for elective and day case) to determine start, finish times, waiting between patients on the list, reasons for cancellation on the day and devised an audit template using national benchmarking criteria.

We set out to establish the cost of the variation in theatre utilisation so that we could have an effective baseline by which to measure the costs and levels of improvement as an outcome of our system transformation project.

3 Facilitating new skills in statistical analysis and medical leadership through a process of action learning

We booked laptop computers for our learning sessions and worked with senior medical leaders to develop new skills in management science. (We were able to work with 'real' NHS Trust data in 'real time' learning.) We generated learning and action from this process to inform a reflective group action plan to be undertaken before the next learning session. The academic facilitator (JA) took on the role as 'project manager' to ensure the action plan was pushed along and managed in between sessions, to keep everyone on board with the programme, maintain motivation and medical engagement and keep the project team on task.

4 Testing out and evaluating new processes

Bringing all the staff on board with this project requires the engagement and development of the workforce in theatres which is in line with the recommendations of the consensus paper by Greenwell et al. (2003) on theatre efficiency and maintaining a safe and sustainable workforce. CS actively engaged a wide group of non-clinical staff who were invited to a presentation by the clinicians to listen to ideas for process improvement. It was interesting to observe how some of the administrative and clerical staff had been testing out similar ideas for improvements in the administrative processes. We also engaged the lead for patient engagement and complaints about the development a strategy to engage patients in this transformation project.

Fitzsimmons (2012) describes the challenge facing frontline workers in providing a high-quality service to patients. She describes the feeling of being powerless as frontline staff seek to challenge out-dated practices. She describes the factors enabling workers to provide high-quality care to patients as good leadership, support, good team working and a high level of control about how the work is undertaken. Realigning shift patterns of different professional and technical staff may address this issue within the theatre department. Poorly aligned shift patterns and on-call arrangements for nursing and ODP staff can cause a delay in providing an on-call service in a timely fashion. In another hospital trust, (PG) shared his own experiences of system transformation in barriers in the nursing and anaesthetic staff rotas, which prevented staff being available at a weekend at 8am as part of their shift. Such barriers had to be dealt with efficiently so that the overall improvement momentum would continue to be maintained across a vast group of stakeholders.

5 Proposing new NHS Trust wide process change with an implementation strategy

The TUTAL group were clear that their job as systems leaders was to keep the Executive NHS Trust Board in the loop with regular communications. One of the TUTAL group members was also a Deputy Medical Director (GS) who took on the role of regularly briefing the Medical Director's office of the project group's activities and actions. The TUTAL group's work is still continuing, as the transformation of theatres remains high on the NHS Trust's agenda.

30

TRANSFORMING THE EMERGENCY MEDICINE MEDICAL WORKFORCE

A new 'hybrid' doctor with integrated specialty training and a competency-based Fellowship in Quality Improvement (FQim)

Prakash Subedi, Jill Aylott, Naushad Khan, Prosenjit Giri and Lesley Hammond

Hospitals in the UK are led by the 'triumvirate of disciplines' (Nurse Director, Clinical Lead and General Manager), and this relationship is an important relationship to drive through transformational change (Rose Report, 2014). However, the complexity of emergency medicine raises some questions as to the best fit of this model with the complex and multiple systems of emergency medicine and the challenging short supply of a medical workforce in Emergency Medicine.

A major contributory factor to the current problems in emergency medicine is the flawed assumption that emergency care demand can be 'managed downwards' (Hughes, 2013, Mason, 2011). Instead, there is evidence that the problems of Emergency Medicine are 'systems related'. A large study in 2004 undertaken with 137 Emergency Departments (ED) found patients were likely to wait longer if the ED had high visit numbers and more serious cases (accounting for 14% variation in mean waiting time) (Mason, 2011). In addition to high-volume and complex/more serious cases, waiting times worsened where EDs failed to be proactive in the development of working relationships with other agencies on the boundary (such as radiology, laboratories, community care and the acute ward setting). In addition to these systems factors, this study found that there was larger variation in relation to human factors. Thirty-three percent (33%) of the variation was due to a less democratic clinical leader which resulted in higher staff sickness (Mason, 2011). Further research findings recommend a 'whole system' approach to tackle the problems in urgent and emergency care (Turner et al., 2014), which has seen increases in demand double over forty years and a five-fold increase in the emergency care departments' inability to meet the 4 hour wait target (Turner et al., 2014). A summary of the key problems from a 'whole system' perspective are: too many access points and hand-offs between services, too much duplication of services, too few community options, too little focus on type of demand and fragmented leadership and coordination (Turner et al., 2014).

In a devolved 'medical leadership' culture within Emergency Medicine Departments, there is evidence to show that where clinicians are supported to self-determine solutions to the 'system' (a bottom up rather than top-down approach), consultants will gravitate to these working environments. For example, in Wrexham, UK, consultants work full night shifts, and there is also a full complement of EM consultants working in the department with fewer costs incurred to pay locum staff (Sen et al., 2012). It is the poor working environment in Emergency Medicine Departments that is a significant factor contributing to the low take up of doctors specialising in this field of medical practice. Reasons stated for not choosing EM are poor working conditions, a harsh work-life balance, target-driven culture and a lack of 24-hour support in ED (Turner et al., 2014). This suggests that a more supportive, 'medical leadership', self-determined culture, with a focus on quality improvement as opposed to a traditional 'triumvirate model', may offer an alternative solution to creating an environment where doctors want to work.

Despite the evidence that improvements in ED can be made by systems changes and by creating a supportive and 'values-based' culture, emergency medicine departments in the UK are predominantly performance managed from the top of the organisation down. The Department of Health declared that '*by 2005, 98% of all patients must be in and out of the emergency department within 4 hours*'. The 98% 4-hour cut-off was not based on any good research evidence, and this target was not demanded anywhere else in the world (Mason, 2011). The 98% target was later relaxed by the Department of Health in the UK in 2010.

To achieve the 4-hour target, hospitals undertook a range of measures (from a 4-hour monitor role, improved access to beds, additional nursing hours and triage by senior staff). The biggest influence on the improved performance was the number of measures rather than any specific measure (Mason, 2011). The 4-hour target did encourage change, but this was not cost neutral and the lessons learnt from the implementation of the target was that it emphasised the role and responsibility of the whole organisation. Disproportionate effort was focused on achieving the 4-hour target rather than on developing a quality service for patients.

To date, there is no evidence that the 4-hour target has benefitted patient care, and findings suggest that it has encouraged target-led care rather than needs-led care. An analysis of the research literature shows that there is a rising proportion of patients who have dispositions in the last 20 minutes of the 4-hour interval, which strongly suggests that a stringent absolute cut-off may not be the best way to manage ED crowding (Mason, 2011). A target-driven culture can have a demotivating effect on the medical workforce, and it has been suggested that as soon as the target is breached, the incentive is lost. This can be demoralising to work in this environment, where consultants are told they are failing the target but their values and their intrinsic motivation and rewards are in meeting their patient's clinical needs.

An over-stretched and limited medical workforce in Emergency Medicine, where the English NHS currently has a shortage of 2,200 Emergency Medicine Consultants (Royal College of Emergency Medicine, 2017), has created significant barriers to transforming the system of emergency departments and enabling a quality improvement culture. The low levels of emergency medicine registrars with a vacancy rate of 50% (Turner et al., 2014) and the high dependency on locum doctors serve as a significant barrier to achieving the 4-hour target. However, more devolvement of leadership to senior consultants in the Emergency Department will enable more freedom to decide on how the emergency department should be run in collaboration with the emergency team and patients. Such an approach requires the development of a Quality Improvement governance structure as outlined in Chapter 18 (e.g. Continuous Quality Improvement Collaborative). This approach has more potential to create a more positive and dynamic culture in Emergency Medicine and for creative and innovative solutions to achieve higher levels of job satisfaction, retain staff and achieve higher levels of patient satisfaction.

An alternative emergency medicine workforce model: a combined Certificate of Eligibility of Specialist Registration (CESR) and integrated Fellowship in Quality Improvement (FQim)

The Certificate of Eligibility of Specialist Registration (CESR) is an alternative model of enabling the registration of speciality doctors after years of equivalence of training, experience and practice in one of the sixty-six clinical specialties. CESR doctors usually follow a 'self-directed' and 'self-managed' period of training for 6 years or more and then apply for assessment and registration of their e-portfolio (currently, the GMC accepts only paper applications) by the Royal College of Emergency Medicine. However, many doctors find this a challenging route through speciality training, as there are often gaps in their experience that are difficult to negotiate within a hospital. The biggest challenge for individual doctors will be clinical supervision and mentoring (as Consultants are not usually job planned to do this). Another challenge is to secure rotation into other specialties, for example, acute medicine, ITU and anaesthesia, as the hospital will lose money and the consultants in other specialties have usually been unprepared to supervise CESR doctors from other specialties. With no money in the system to train the CESR doctors, Consultants are sometimes unsure what to do with the CESR doctors, as they may be unfamiliar with the CESR training route and the curriculum model. With such substantial challenges for doctors with self-managing their own training programme and learning experiences, that when they finally do submit their e-portfolio, the evidence is that the pass rate is just 50% (Table 30.1). This can be demoralising and serve as yet another barrier to train doctors in this speciality. Although there has been a slight increase in the numbers of doctors undertaking the CESR registration route since 2012, the pass rate has maintained at around 50% (Table 30.1).

TABLE 30.1 Numbers of CESR applications granted and rejected (2012–2016)

2012		2013		2014		2015		2016	
Total	*501*	*Total*	*523*	*Total*	*551*	*Total*	*537*	*Total*	*593*
Granted	Rejected	Granted	Rejected	Granted	Rejected	Granted	Rejected	Granted	Rejected
254	247	252	271	246	305	264	273	314	279
Pass rate 50%		Pass rate 48%		Pass rate 44%		Pass rate 49%		Pass rate 52%	

Source: GMC annual reports on speciality training application registrations.

Case Study: Doncaster and Bassetlaw NHS Trust

In 2015, a business case proposal was prepared for the NHS Trust to set up an structured integrated clinical and leadership programme for doctors on the CESR programme. Accident and Emergency Medicine requires a substantial amount of core competencies in areas defined as non-clinical, in leadership, quality improvement, audit, critical appraisal, coaching and mentoring and team work. PS and JA worked together to explore the mapping of the core non-clinical components of the A&E speciality curriculum against the core subject benchmarks of an MBA. This mapping process produced a 6-year integrated programme for doctors (Table 30.2). The leadership and quality improvement curriculum was integrated with the weekly clinical teaching and all doctors on the CESR programme. In addition, we offered a personalised learning pathway for each doctor, with a planned end date for submission of their portfolio to the GMC for registration. The programme has proved popular with doctors, and it has now recruited twenty-four doctors. Our first doctor (NK) has now successfully registered with the General Medical Council specialist register as an Emergency Medicine Consultant.

The General Medical Council argued that postgraduate medical training has to change as the training is "out of date and urgently needs reform" (GMC, 2017). More flexible training is required to respond to the needs of doctors who want a more balanced programme to fit around family and other commitments. Table 30.3 outlines the specific features of our programme to ensure maximum motivation and support to trainees.

We have now developed the programme set out in Tables 30.2 and 30.3 as a Hybrid International Emergency Medicine programme (HIEM) (Table 30.4). The programme works within the Medical Training Initiative (MTI), which is a mutually beneficial scheme that provides doctors from all over the world with the

TABLE 30.2 The Doncaster CESR-FQim

Year 1 Fellowship in Quality Improvement (leading to an MBA)

Year 1 Fellowship in Quality Improvement (60 credits)	Teams and Effective Teamwork (15 credits) (EM CC1, CC2, CC12, CC13, CC7, CC8)	Transformation and Change (15 credits) (EM, CC10, CC14, CC24)
	Leadership for Improvement (15 credits) (EM CC8, CC15, CC24)	Operations Management and Quality Improvement (15 Credits) (EM, CC4, CC5, CC6, CC11, CC14, CC22, CC9, CC25)
Year 2		
	Strategic Management and Strategic Marketing – (EM CC14, CC16, CC19) (15 credits)	Research Methodology, Patient Co-design and Critical Appraisal (15 credits) (EM CC20, CC21)
	Finance and Patient Safety (15 credits) (EM CC9, CC17, CC25)	Train the trainer – teaching quality improvement to scale up change (15 credits) (EM CC18, CC23)

Year 3, Year 4 Final Stage MBA Dissertation that focuses on a strategic project across a hospital/community/Primary Care Services

TABLE 30.3 Core features of the Doncaster structured CESR – Fellowship in Quality Improvement (FQim)

Recruitment and pre-enrolment
- Doctors can join at any level of experience – we assess their competence and place them at different stages of the programme between pre-CESR to CESR 1–6 years
- We identify doctor's area of sub-specialist interest using Self Determination Theory (motivation theory) to agree the terms of their contract for the programme

Enrolment and CESR contract
- Each doctor has a personalised rota to support them to work the hours that they want to fit around family commitments
- A timeline for completion is based on an assessment of competencies and the expectations of the doctor
- A flexible personal learning plan, learning objectives and tailored mentorship
- Agreed progress review twice a year

Personalised programme plan
- A route map with specific training experience scheduled over time
- An integrated Fellowship in Quality Improvement that teaches leadership development from the start of their programme
- Doctors follow an internal rotation pattern within the NHS Hospital Trust instead of travelling to different hospitals across a region and are supervised by doctors who are trained to support CESR doctors
- Weekly teaching sessions
- 1 in 9 week Fellowship in Quality Improvement sessions and once a year Quality Improvement summer school
- 1 in 9 week librarian-led session to support the development of search strategies for evidence-based search and review
- Trained mentors for feedback, signing off clinical competencies and signposting to further learning resources.

TABLE 30.4 The CESR-Fellowship in Quality Improvement (FQim) and Hybrid International Emergency Medicine Programme (HIEM)

Year	CESR-FQim programme	HIEM programme	
1	UK Acute Care Common Stem (ACCS) – Emergency Medicine (6 months); ACCS – Acute Medicine (6 months)	Home country	F2 competencies (6 months) Introduction to the NHS Acute Care Common Stem (ACCS) – Emergency Medicine (6 months) 3 months of ITU 3 months of Anaesthesia Module 1 – FQim
2	UK ACCS Anaesthetics (6 months); ACCS Intensive Care (6 months)	UK	Acute Care Common Stem (ACCS) – Emergency Medicine (6 months) Specialty Training (ST3) Adult Emergency (6 months) Module 2 – FQim
3	UK Specialty Training (ST3) Adult Emergency Medicine (6 months); Paediatric Emergency Medicine (6 months)	UK	Higher Specialty Training (ST4) Module 3 – FQim
4	UK Higher Specialty Training (ST4)	Home country	Paediatric Emergency Medicine (3 months) ACCS – Acute Medicine (3 months) Home country local emergency medicine management (6 months) Module 4 – FQim
5	UK Higher Specialty Training (ST5)		
6	UK Higher Specialty Training (ST6)		

opportunity to work and train in the UK NHS, while giving NHS Hospital Foundation Trusts a high-quality, longer-term alternative medical workforce solution to using locums to fill rota gaps (The Royal College of Physicians, 2017). Through the MTI initiative, a 4-year programme is offered to doctors, with the first year in the country of origin, second and third years international rotation (in the UK NHS) and the final year back in the country of origin.

The programme developed in Table 30.4 outlines how both the CESR-FQim and the Hybrid International Emergency Medicine (HIEM) programme relate to each other. Although the UK CESR-FQim is planned over 6 years, the programmes are both competency-based programmes and can be delivered in a bespoke way and personalised to each individual doctors timeline. The HIEM programme will meet requirements for postgraduate emergency medicine training in the home country and will also support the completion of each module of the Fellowship in Quality Improvement over the four years of the programme (Table 30.4). If the HIEM doctors wish to continue with the programme they can study for a further three years to complete the Certificate of Eligibility for Specialist Registration (CESR).

31

QUALITY IMPROVEMENT AND SYSTEM TRANSFORMATION IN EMERGENCY MEDICINE

Elizabeth Hutchinson

It is now generally agreed that a dashboard of additional quality and safety measures will be required in EM to ensure an optimum balance of safety, quality and timeliness in emergency care (Heyworth, 2011; Mason, 2011). In the UK, a set of quality indicators was developed between the Royal College of Emergency Medicine, The Royal College of Nursing and Department of Health (Heyworth, 2011). The quality indicators were developed to reflect timeliness, quality and safety and are presented in Table 31.1.

The quality indicators in Table 31.1 should function as indicators and not as targets for organisations to measure current performance. Although the former are encouraged to be seen as part of a quality dashboard, it is difficult to see how they relate to other elements of the quality definition set out by the Institute of Medicine. It is also difficult to see how they are a balanced set of measures against Donabedian's (1966) structure, process and outcome model of quality. An evaluation study found that when measuring the performance of 'Unscheduled Return Visits' or Unplanned re-attendance (Indicator 3), there were major inconsistencies in the way URVs or Unplanned re-attendance are defined and measured across EDs in the UK and that there are four different reasons why this occurs: patient related, illness related, system related and clinician related (Trivedy and Cooke, 2015). The single largest cause is related to the patient's illness, particularly abdominal pain where the symptoms are vague. While 73% of ED agreed to calculate URV within a 72-hour period, this would not pick up all the chronic conditions. The authors reported variation for URV of between 0.4% and 49.3% (Trivedy and Cooke, 2015).

Two recent studies outside of the UK (Denmark and Australia) have defined quality in EM by using Donabedian's 'Structure, Process Outcome' Model (Donabedian, 1966; Madsen et al., 2016; Jones et al., 2014) and the Institute of Medicine's definition of quality as patient centredness, access, timeliness, equity, effectiveness, efficiency and safety (Madsen et al., 2016; Jones et al., 2014). Using a definition

TABLE 31.1 Quality indicators in emergency departments in the UK

1. Service user experience – quarterly feedback from patients, carers and staff
2. Those who leave ED without being seen should be below 5%.
3. Unplanned re: attendance within 7 days – to be seen by a different and more senior clinician. Rates above 5% indicate poor quality, and rates below 1% may reflect excessive risk aversion.
4. Time to initial assessment – to include a pain score and to occur within 15 minutes of patients' arrival
5. Time to treatment to a clinical decision maker within 60 minutes of arrival, with more prompt assessment, for example, for sepsis, stroke myocardial infarction (a median above 60 minutes from arrival to see a decision-making clinician, may trigger intervention)
6. Total time in ED – excessive total time in the ED is linked to poor outcomes. A 95th percentile wait above 4 hours for admitted patients and non-admitted patients is not good practice. The single longest wait should not be more than 6 hours.
7. Consultant sign-off – to increase the number of patients who are reviewed in person by the ED consultant, to improve quality of care for high-risk conditions and to derive the agenda for increasing emergency medicine consultant numbers
8. Ambulatory care – Cellulitis and DVT better managed as an outpatient following assessment and diagnosis from ED

of quality helps to develop a balanced set of indicators. The Danish Health and Medicine's Authority worked with a panel of fifty-four experts (the majority were clinicians) to develop a set of nine quality indicators (Table 31.2). This was undertaken after completing a global literature review where the authors "found limited evidence for most emergency department performance indicators, with the majority presenting a low level of evidence" (Madsen et al., 2015). The authors reviewed 6,440 articles to conclude that no indicators can be currently recommended on the basis of the review of the literature (Madsen et al., 2015). Further work with the Medicine's authority agreed a final set of quality indicators (Table 31.2).

In the UK, against a backdrop of Quality Indicators set out in Table 31.1, a quality improvement project undertaken in an emergency medicine department in a hospital in the UK resulted in unexpected learning in relation to wider systems failing. What started out as a focused quality improvement project to identify the quality of clinical practice with community acquired pneumonia (CAP) resulted in an identification of a systems failure to fail to provide compliance to the protocol for CAP. This case study illustrates the complexity of the interrelationship between quality improvement and health system transformation.

Approximately 175,000 people were admitted to hospital with community acquired pneumonia (CAP) in 2013–2014 (online), costing the NHS £441 million/year (Barlow, 2007). Untimely recognition and treatment of CAP leads to poorer patient outcomes and longer stays in hospital, costing the NHS millions of pounds (British Thoracic Society, 2009, 2014). The saving for each bed day avoided would be £192 (NICE, 2014). Not only would this benefit the patient by reducing the risk of hospital acquired infections and further complications, but also it would

TABLE 31.2 Quality indicators in emergency medicine: The Danish example

1. Short-term mortality after arrival in ED
2. Measure rate of return within 72 hours
3. Time to treatment for stroke
4. Time from first hospital contact to coronary arteriography in patients with STEMI
5. Time to surgery for suspected gastrointestinal perforation
6. Time to X-ray the wrist
7. Time of hemodynamic stabilisation of acute gastrointestinal bleed
8. Time to triage
9. Time to be seen by a medical doctor for all patients

Source: Madsen et al. (2015).

lead to improved efficiency in bed allocations for providers along with a long-term saving for commissioners in conjunction with reduced length of bed stay below the national tariff point (NICE, 2014).

The COST care bundle was launched within the ED as a registrar-led improvement project. All patients who were admitted via the ED with a query diagnosis of pneumonia were included in the data source. Any patient who was found not to have pneumonia post validation was excluded from the cohort. Validation of results was done on a quarterly basis, with the number of eligible patients compared with the number of patients that who every component of the bundle. Performance was broken down monthly to assess variation.

Results of quantitative data analysis

The data were collected over a 21-month time period from September 2012 (baseline recordings) until June 2014, with a 2-month period between April and June 2013 with no data collection (see Figure 31.1).

A run chart (Figure 31.1) clearly demonstrates a substantial improvement (nearing nearly 100% compliance) in the percentage of patients receiving the full care bundle in comparison with the baseline data. This improvement was consistent over a 6-month period. The chart then goes on to indefinitely demonstrate a mass reduction in the number of patients receiving the full bundle from July 2013 to March 2014, reflecting in the re-adjustment of the median value demonstrated on the graph. The percentage compliance then seems to plateau along the median during this time without variation. From April 2014 until the end of data collection in June 2014, there was a significant new trend of improvement as signified on the chart. Unfortunately, there was no further data collection to assess whether this was a true shift (six or more points are needed to be able to state this) (Perla et al., 2011b) or to whether the improvement was sustainable.

The raw data demonstrate seasonal variation in patients admitted via the ED, with more presentations of pneumonia in the winter months. Between November 2012 and February 2013, compliance was at an all-time high despite higher

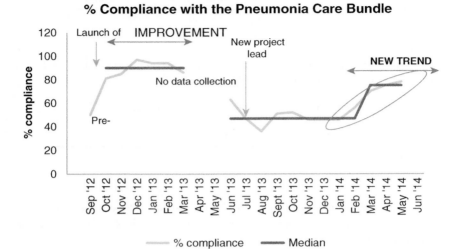

FIGURE 31.1   Chart 1: A run chart to demonstrate the percentage compliance with the pneumonia care bundle

numbers of patients with pneumonia. Although initial costs would have been high, secondary costs would be expected to be much reduced, namely due to reduced hospital stay and reduced mortality in accordance with the BTS evidence for the pneumonia care bundle.

However, the opposite may be said for the following winter period with a much lower compliance of bundle completion. Poorer implementation of the bundle will likely to have led to increased lengths in hospital stay, increased readmission rates and higher mortality rates.

Data were collected over a total of 21 months, giving a generous time frame for data to be analysed at certain points in time and for implementation or improvement strategies to be adopted.

The collection of data was laborious and time consuming. It involved reviewing all of the patient notes that were flagged as pneumonia or chest infection. First, a diagnosis of pneumonia needed to be confirmed as per X-ray appearance or from formal reports that had been written since the patient admission. Second, the elements and evidence of use of the bundle often required searching throughout the handwritten notes or on the observation charts. The easiest notes to collect the data from were where the clinician had clearly written 'COST' with a tick to confirm bundle completion on the front of the notes.

Data tended to be analysed on a 3-monthly basis, which then formed the quarterly report for the CQUIN. There were many times that the analysis of the data would be taking place a couple of days before the deadline. On reflection of this, quarterly analysis was not effective at all. It formed the risk of identifying pitfalls in the compliance rate potentially 2 or 3 months after it had occurred, and therefore not enabling the opportunity to intervene sooner. Data should have ideally been collected on a fortnightly or, at the very least, a monthly basis in order to identify any patterns, whether positive or negative.

The data have been displayed using a run chart, which is a relatively simple analytical tool used in quality improvement (see Figure 31.1). It is a method of plotting data in graphical form in time order (Perla et al., 2011b). This is the first time that this set of data has been displayed in this way and has been adapted from a tabular form. The main advantage of the run chart is that it displays the data in such a form to make performance visible as well as showing clearly whether strategic changes resulted in improvement (Perla et al., 2011b). The main drawback of run charts is that they cannot determine whether a process is stable. For this, a control chart would be needed (Provost and Murray, 2011; Speroff and O'Connor, 2004; Shewhart, 1931). Although the data were analysed quarterly, I have presented the data monthly in order to aid meaningful analysis.

The dark line represents the median, which is the point at which half of the values are expected to be either side of the line. By inputting the median onto the chart, it is easy to visualise negative or positive trends in the data and overall aids in the understanding of the impact of changes and interventions over the time period (Perla et al., 2011b).

Looking at the data in more detail, it is obvious to see that there was vast improvement in compliance of the care bundle after the formal launch. This was highly sustained over a 5-month period through staff education, advertisement and motivation. The period represented as having no data collection was when the registrar left the department, clearly demonstrating that a lack of leadership resulted in poorer performance. As the new project lead in August 2013, I was already faced with analysing retrospective data from an Emergency Department that had lost their original project lead, their inspiration and enthusiasm. This was clearly evident from the compliance rate dropping to half within 4 months. Although this is evident from the tabular data, the run chart makes this failing visually obvious. Had the data been collected on a more regular basis, we may not have seen the plateauing effect from October 2013 to February 2014, as actions may have been agreed on to improve performance sooner.

Judging by the low compliance rate of bundle completion, action was needed. It was decided to validate data on a monthly basis to ensure any issues could be identified sooner. I also 'reinvented' the project, as the Emergency Department has a high turnover of clinical staff, and it became obvious that maybe the current clinicians had not been exposed to the same educational activity as their previous counterparts. Posters were redesigned, as the previous ones had become 'part of the furniture'. From the data analysis, it was identified that the non-recording of the CURB severity score was mainly the reason of poor compliance, as most clinicians tended to do the other three elements spontaneously. I, therefore, focused on this during educational sessions in order to try and raise compliance. The inclusion and exclusion criteria were also modified, as certain evidence shows that the CURB severity score is not as sensitive in the over-75 age group (Lim et al., 2003; Conte et al., 1999; Ewig et al., 1999).

From March 2014, following action, there was seen to be a new increasing trend peaking to 78% compliance in June 2014. Strictly speaking, a trend is a collection of five or more consecutive points either going up or down (Olmstead, 1945). Although there are only four points showing a potential positive trend, forecasting should predict that compliance should stay around the 75% mark with the further aim to increase this even more.

Run charts require more regular monitoring of data to be effective (Perla et al., 2011b). Had the data been plotted every 3 months as per data collection, the chart would have looked very different and would have posed difficulties in detecting the correct points to action improvement. It is obvious that once data were collected on a monthly basis, there was a far better understanding of the processes occurring, improvement was actioned upon and the outcome was satisfyingly seen as a steep and rising trend in compliance of bundle completion.

Although the production of data is shown to have stopped by June 2014, the pneumonia care bundle pathway is a continuous project in the department. However, unfortunately, again there is no defined project lead and due to clinical capacity and departmental pressures, the data have been unable to be validated. Learning from and using the run chart as a predictor as well as taking these factors into account, I suspect that the compliance rate will have dropped back to the levels seen in July 2013 to March 2014. Without further intervention and improvement action, this will likely remain the same.

32

TRANSFORMING THE QUALITY OF HOSPITAL CARE THROUGH ADVOCACY FOR PEOPLE WITH A LEARNING DISABILITY AND/OR AUTISM

Jonathan Sahu

People with a learning disability (LD) and/or autism remain one of the most vulnerable and socially excluded groups (Valuing People, DH, 2001; Valuing People Now, DH, 2009; Mencap, 2007; Flynn, 2012). In 2007, Mencap reported on the deaths of six people with a learning disability ('Death by Indifference', Mencap, 2007) and concluded that a label of a 'learning disability' was a risk factor in terms of mortality in hospital. Whilst individuals with LD are valued by families, friends and circles of support and recognised as having a wide range of abilities, capabilities, health and social care needs; society generally negatively appraises disability and devalues difference. There is evidence that such negative value impacts on the decision-making processes of healthcare professionals and can lead to health inequalities and even death ('Death by Indifference', Mencap, 2007). Glover and Ayub (2010) concluded that

> people with learning disability are 58 times more likely to die before the age of 50 than the general population from associated congenital conditions, but also from preventable secondary health conditions. They are significantly more likely to suffer additional health problems with a life expectancy 10 years shorter than the rest of the population.

The most common reasons for the premature deaths include delayed problems with diagnosis and treatment, problems identifying needs, lack of coordination of care between service providers and sporadic care provision. There is also evidence that GPs are not undertaking annual health checks with at least 50% of the population of people with a learning disability (Hatton et al., 2016) despite various government incentives to enable this to happen (Atkinson et al., 2013).

Following the highly critical reports from MENCAP, 'Death by Indifference' (2007) and 'Death by Indifference, 74 Deaths and Counting' (2012), identifying key contributory factors, the Department of Health, in association with the British Institute for Learning Disability (BILD) and MENCAP, commissioned a survey in 2013 to assess the care, treatment and experience of people with LD and their families, within the NHS. A total of seventy-five people with LD and 191 family members responded to the survey. Table 32.1 summarises the main findings from the survey.

TABLE 32.1 Survey of people with a learning disability, family and carers

Themes from the Survey	Response from Individuals with LD, Family and Carers
Communication	54% of LD and 64% of carers stated that staff did not ask how they would like to be communicated with.
Accessible information	70% LD and 84% carers said that healthcare staff did not ask the individual with LD in what form the information should be presented to them. 46% LD could not fully understand the information provided.
Being listened to	46% of LD and 66% carers indicated that staff listened to them sometimes. 38% of LD and 20% of carers stated that they were always listened to. 7% of LD and 9% of carers said that they were never listened to.
Taking pain seriously	40% of individuals with LD and 39% of carers said that staff sometimes responded to them when they or the individual with LD had pain. 4% of individuals with LD and 11% of carers stated that staff never responded to pain.
Respect	62% of individuals with LD felt that they were shown respect by healthcare staff. However, only 40–50% of carers felt that their family member with LD was shown respect some or all of the time. 34–48% of carers felt that they were shown respect all or some of the time, respectively.
Level of care	46% of individuals with LD felt that the staff were caring, whereas only 38% of carers felt that this was the case.
Receiving a diagnosis	43% of carers were unhappy with the length of time taken before a diagnosis was reached.
Staff knowledge	63% of carers said that staff had poor knowledge of how to support individuals with LD.
Inclusion in decision making	40% of individuals with LD and 44% of carers said they were not included (either all or some of the time) in decision making about their care.
Compliance with Mental Capacity Act 2005	20% of carers had been asked to sign on behalf of the individual with LD despite the LD individual being able to do so.
Being offered a LD nurse	73% of individuals and carers stated they had not been offered an LD nurse.
Personal care	61% of carers had attended to the personal care of the individual with LD.
Complaint procedure	77% of the carers who complained found the complaints process difficult or very difficult.

Source: Adapted from BILD and MENCAP (2013).

People with a learning disability often have significant communication difficulties (Gaag, 1998; Jones, 2000) and difficulties with social interaction, and therefore may well require a level of personalisation in communication methods between service providers and the person and their family (ASLHA, 1993; Bradley, 2013). Advocacy is a concept that has been developed to support the enablement of communication methods and is particularly important when people with a learning disability/autism encounter new situations and new environments. Gray and Jackson (2002) define advocacy as a 'right to a voice', whereas the Citizen's Information Centre (2008) is more emphatic, deliberate and challenging by defining this as 'a process of empowerment'. The concept and foundations of advocacy are well established; its potential role for individuals who lack capacity, independence, self-determination and self-realisation (Wullink et al., 2009) is undisputed, but its uptake, legal foundation and acceptance by wider society is less clear.

The Care Act 2014 introduced a new type of advocacy called 'independent advocacy'. This form of advocacy, for the first time, accepted that the person with a learning disability and their family needed support by an independent person to enable the facilitation of communication and to advocate for the right services to meet the person's needs. In addition, legislation, in the form of the Equality Act (2010), Autism Act (2009) and the Human Rights Act (1998), clearly state that all

TABLE 32.2 Equality Act, 2010: reasonable adjustments for people with a learning disability and/or autism

Premises	Taking into account hypersensitivities experienced by people with autism, quiet areas, low lighting
Processes	Scheduling appointments either as first or last patients, extra time, flexible with communication methods
Policy	All public service providers have an Equality Act Duty to make reasonable adjustments and consider changes to policy and how they will impact on the lives of people with a disability.
Communication	Avoiding ambiguous questions, not pressurising people in conversation, sensitive not to use touch or use touch in a way that is preferred by a person with autism, all forms of communication to be accessible and in easy read.
Planning and Preparation	People with autism to be supported to visit to see the setting, the waiting room and the clinical room to help prepare to process the environment in relation to their planned appointment.
The Individual Practitioner	Some people with autism will be hypersensitive to smell and may find some environments difficult; this can also inhibit the processing of information; not expecting the person with autism to look while you are speaking if the person is unable to process through more than one of the senses at a time; taking responsibility that creating accessible health and social care environments will mean making personal changes in one's own communication style if this helps the person with autism to process information and reduce the strain of processing information.

Source: Sahu and Aylott (2017).

individuals, irrespective of age, sex, ethnicity, religion or disability must be treated equally with equal rights. The Acts refer to all aspects of life, including health and social care. The Equality Act (2010) introduced the concept of '*reasonable adjustments*' to be applied to individuals with disability as well as others with protected characteristics under the act to enable better access to health and social care (Hatton et al., 2011). Reasonable adjustments can be developed in a range of ways and summarised in Table 32.2

TABLE 32.3 Summary of the increased incidence and prevalence of conditions affecting individuals with a learning disability and/or autism

Morbidity	LD Population
General health status	2.5–4.5 times poorer for LD children
Cancer	Generally lower incidence 12–18% vs 26% general population
	Proportionately higher rates of gastrointestinal cancer – 48–59% vs 25% general population
Coronary heart disease	A major cause of death in 14–20% LD individuals
Respiratory disease	Main cause of death – 44–52% vs 15–17% general population. High rates of asthma in LD
Endocrine disorders	Hypothyroidism in Down syndrome
	Higher rates of type 1 and type 2 diabetes
Osteoporosis	Possible increase prevalence in LD
Injuries, accidents and falls	Higher rates
Sensory impairments	Higher rates of visual impairments (8–200 times)
	40% hearing impairment
Pain	Higher rates of acute and chronic pain
Dementia	Higher rates in older LD – (22% vs 6% 65+ years)
Epilepsy	Up to 20 times higher than general population and leading cause of premature death
Sleep disorders	Prevalence 9–34%. 9% LD individuals have significant sleep problems
Mental health and challenging behaviour	High prevalence – 36% vs 8% children in general population. Anxiety, aggression, self-injurious behaviour
Oral health	1 in 3 adults have unhealthy teeth and gums; 80% in Down syndrome
Dysphagia	Difficulty in eating and drinking may affect up to 8%
Gastroesophageal reflux	Up to 50% in international studies
Constipation	17–51% of LD individuals in supported living
Weight	Significantly higher rates of obesity and individuals who were underweight
Women's health	Higher rates of menorrhagia, premenstrual syndrome

Source: (Leeder and Dominello, 2005; Carlisle, 2000; Lennox et al., 2004; Fisher, 2004; Glover and Ayub, 2010; Tyrer et al., 2007; Krahn et al., 2006; Michael and Richardson, 2008; Emerson, 2005; Emerson et al., 2014; Emerson and Baines, 2011; Beange et al., 1995; Hove, 2004; Kennedy et al., 1997; Mencap, 1991; McIntosh, 2002; McConkey, 2004).

Advocates can enable a 'a reasonable adjustment plan' that allows an independent advocate to speak up on the person's behalf or for paid support workers to communicate the plan to the healthcare provider. The transformation of primary and secondary services for people with a learning disability and/or autism aims to reduce the healthcare inequalities and premature death. A summary of the main healthcare issues are presented in Table 32.3.

Transforming services for people with LD/autism through advocacy

All hospitals need to undertake an Equality Impact Assessment under the Equality Act (2010). It is proposed that hospital services need to transform through compliance with the legislation and to demonstrate their accountability to all members of the public including the most vulnerable by making reasonable adjustments (Turner and Robinson, 2011). The following action is suggested:

1   *Embed an advocacy charter in all provider and commissioning services*

Action for Advocacy, a voluntary organisation, published an Advocacy Charter in 2002. The principles were adopted and incorporated into the Quality Standards for Advocacy Schemes (2006): Clarity of purpose; Independence; Putting people first; Empowerment; Equal opportunity; Accessibility; Accountability; Supporting advocates; Confidentiality; Complaints

The Charter requires written and supported evidence to monitor and ensure adequate standards.

2   *Establish a communication plan for all people with a learning disability and/or autism* (Figure 32.1)

A clear written strategy for people with a learning disability and/or autism must be in place to accompany the person for assessment and treatment. The support person accompanying the person should follow the advocacy charter.

Communication plan

3   *Mandate training on autism awareness for all staff (compliance with Autism Act 2009)*
4   *Appoint an autism/learning disability specialist to oversee compliance, quality standards and mortality review* (Sahu, 2016)

There is growing evidence of the key role of learning disability liaison nurses/ acute liaison teams (Stewart and Todd, 2001; Foster, 2005) in bridging this gap and providing effective, efficient care and support for individuals with learning disability and/or autism together to work with and support staff.

1. How is verbal communication used with the person? How effective is verbal communication?
2. What non-verbal methods of communication are used?
3. Does communication change when the person's anxiety levels increase?
4. If the person has autism, has a sensory profile been completed? If yes, what are the reasonable adjustments needed to enable effective communication?
5. What needs to be in place to prevent anxiety and distress in the communication process?
6. What is the person's special interest?
7. Does the person use a communication aid or any assistive communication device? If yes, how will this be used in communication with the person?

Summary and recommended method of communication for the consultation?

Reasonable Adjustments?

Source: Aylott (2015).

FIGURE 32.1 Communication plan

33

TRANSFORMING SERVICES FOR PATIENTS WITH SPINAL CORD INJURY – A NATIONAL REVIEW OF STANDARDS AND PRACTICE

Pradeep Thumbikat

Spinal cord injury (SCI) is a relatively rare and complex impairment which will result in some degree of loss or reduction in voluntary muscle activity, sensory deprivation and disruption of autonomic function related to the level and severity of the spinal cord damage. Specialist SCI care incorporates the core components of acute care, restorative rehabilitation, reintegration into the community and long-term follow-up into a seamless clinical service (Kent Local Specialist Commissioning Group, 2003). There is evidence that a specialist programme of care for SCI patients improves mortality and morbidity (DeVivo et al., 1990; Smith, 2002). Patients with spinal cord injury are cared for in specialist spinal injury centres, eleven of which are now operational within the United Kingdom (Barr, 2009).

A review carried out between 2007 and 2009 on behalf of the Spinal Injuries Association (SIA) identified that the number of beds and facilities available across the spinal centres were not standardised (Barr, 2009). Although common principles of care underpinned the services provided by the spinal cord injury centres, no universal model of care had been adopted across the service, which in turn reflected the lack of high-quality evidence to support a preferred model of care as identified by Cochrane reviews (Jones, 2004). There was variation in the quality of admission criteria, absence of clear service specifications, absence of clinically valid outcome measures, difficulty in accessing spinal injury centres, difficulty in retrieval of basic patient information and problems with SCI centre host trust utilisation of specialised commissioning funding (Barr, 2009).

The NSCISB (National Spinal Cord Injury Strategy Board) was established in 2010 under the aegis of the National Specialised Commissioning Group, with representation from all ten Specialised Commissioning Groups and all eight Spinal Cord Injury Centres in England. The purpose was to agree on a coordinated and common approach across England to the delivery and commissioning of services for people with a spinal cord injury (SCI) and to ensure improved health outcomes for people with spinal cord injury in England by effective commissioning of appropriate high-quality and cost-effective services (UK Parliament/Crown copyright, 2011). The NHS clinical advisory groups report on management of people with SCI laid down the key clinical considerations and service requirements.

Pilot pathways of care and clear linkages between the major trauma centres and spinal cord injury centres were introduced. A national database and registry system was introduced along with a requirement for SCI patients to be referred to an SCI centre within 4 hours of identification of the spinal cord injury/impairment. Liaison and outreach working from SCI centres was also to be strengthened. In 2012, the pathways of care were officially published. The six pathways covered acute management and acute rehabilitation of ventilated and non-ventilated patients, review and outpatient pathways for ventilated and non-ventilated patients, acute secondary admission pathway, planned secondary admission pathway and community support outreach pathway (Barr, 2013).

The development of the National Spinal Cord Injury service has been the biggest attempt at creating a national programme for spinal cord services, which included creating a uniform set of standards, introducing clear service specifications and creating common (single) commissioning arrangements while addressing many of the long-standing issues raised by service user groups. The pathways component of the programme can be looked upon as the development of an integrated care pathways spanning multiple services. The SCI initiative is of international interest, as it is the first time that an attempt has been made to transform spinal cord injury treatment pathways at a national level with an aim to standardise the quality of the SCI service.

Undertaking the review

In 2015, an evaluation was undertaken (Thumbikat, 2015) to review existing data from available sources including NHS England, publications, formal and informal reviews, data from the spinal cord injury database, dashboard data submitted to NHS England by the SCIC, data collected in preparation for national service reviews and data submitted to the All Party Parliamentary Group on Spinal Cord Injury. A publication from the All Party Parliamentary Group proved particularly valuable (All Party Parliamentary Group on Spinal Cord Injury, 2015).

Key stakeholders were identified through brainstorming with senior medical and nursing colleagues and members of the clinical reference group. The review engaged key stakeholders including the clinical reference group, project lead, spinal injury centres, spinal injury association (user group) and professional groups such as the British Association of Spinal Cord Injury Specialists (BASCIS) and MASCIP (Multidisciplinary Association of Spinal Cord Injury Professionals). Stakeholders as used in this context are individuals, groups or organisations who can affect or who are affected by a review process or its findings. 'Key' stakeholders are a subset of this group, but who is identified as a 'key stakeholder' will always be a judgement call and a matter for negotiation (Bryson and Patton, 2010). Patton views primary intended users as a subset of key stakeholders (Patton, 2008).

A logic model was created (Taylor-Powell and Henert, 2008) and used to graph-ically represent the relationship between the programme's activities, inputs, out-puts and its intended outcomes (US Department of Health and Human Services Centers for Disease Control and Prevention, 2011; McLaughlin and Jordan, 2010). This helped inform the review by clearly identifying the context, flow, process and expected outcomes. This was based on the pathway developed by the national path-way lead. A pathway review was then carried out using the data obtained through the national spinal cord injury database and other data sources. Appropriate per-missions were sought from the Information Management Subgroup of the Clinical Reference Group in SCI for use of anonymised data. Key indicators of perfor-mance and outcome as outlined in the national pathway were collected and ana-lysed. At this stage of the programme, it was felt that the most appropriate measures to review were those related to process such as time taken to referral, time taken to transfer, time taken to admission, length of stay, length of waiting list, time taken to liaison visit, incidence of complications and so forth. The approach used in this review broadly fits in with the six-stage quality improvement framework recom-mended by the NHS institute for Innovation and Improvement. It is expected that the National Spinal Cord Injury Programme will improve quality and outcomes at least in part through a reduction in service variation across the country, and for this a detailed analysis of the process data is essential (Gage, 2013).

The views of key participants were obtained through two focus group meetings. The review of the Spinal Cord Injury Program aimed to understand how peo-ple involved in the intervention (frontline staff, clinical reference group members) shaped their experiences from their own perspectives (Marks and Yardley, 2004). As this was a national review, logistically telephonic focus groups were chosen as the participants were widely distributed geographically and it would have been difficult to arrange a face-to-face focus group.

Findings of the review

1 Poor quality data

Although the programme had been running in all areas for at least the last 2 years, the quality and availability of data was poor. The data were not publicly available, and when it was obtained, there was inconsistency in data obtained from different sources (dashboard data and NHS England specialised services data), although the raw data used were the same for both sources. The information contained within the database, although very useful for commissioning purposes, was not granular enough to address many of the questions raised in this review.

Even where data are reliably available, interpretation of data has to be done cau-tiously. Powell and colleagues observed that one of the ways in which quality of care is currently assessed is by taking routinely collected data and analysing them quantitatively (Powell et al., 2003). The use of routine data has many advantages, but there are also some important pitfalls. The natural inclination when there is variation is to assume that such variations imply rankings: that the measures reflect quality and that variations in the measures reflect variations in quality. Particularly in chronic problems (such as SCI), a range of interventions may be provided by different health professionals, both in hospital and in the community, and thus may not be amenable to a single quality measure. Poor quality data can compound the inherent problems of interpretation of routine data and can undermine even the most sophisticated quality assessment tool. Yet, even in well-resourced, well-organised research studies, it is difficult to ensure that data are complete and of a consistently high quality (Davies and Crombie, 1995).

2 Variation in the process for patients falling outside the major trauma pathway

There was widespread awareness and adoption of some aspects of the programme but not others. The referral system and the database were being used widely. Some centres had made arrangements to include information about the pathway as a part of the induction programme for doctors and nurses. This was in part because referrals could not be made to a spinal injury centre other than through this system. There was poor compliance with the pathway specifications such as contact with the spinal injuries centres within 4 hours and referral within 24 hours. Referral of patients falling outside the major trauma pathway was seen as a problem, as there was no single pathway that operated for these patients and many such patients were treated outside of major trauma centres. There was limited awareness of the care pathways outside the MTCs and SCICs. Participants unanimously expressed a desire to see the pathway work effectively, as they felt it could help to improve patient outcomes and patient flow.

Care pathways were cited in the Lord Ara Darzi health policy report as a form of quality improvement to be implemented in the NHS (Darzi, 2008). Clinical guidelines are usually developed in a top-down fashion, whereas care pathways are more often derived from the bottom up, so that the pathway precisely fits the configuration of the local health service (Evans-Lacko et al., 2010). Such pathways may adapt to nuances between institutional cultures by including teams of clinical service providers and managers in their local creation and implementation. Moreover, the process of creating a pathway calls for individuals from all sectors to be involved in defining their own roles, in terms of responsibilities and relationship to others in the local 'healthcare economy'. Consequently, there is likely to be a sense of participation in pathway design but also accountability in terms of implementation.

The findings from this review suggest that as the pathway development in SCI followed such a process and as there was involvement of clinicians and local managers across the trauma pathway, there has been a sense of ownership across the trauma pathway. The difficulties with the non-trauma referrals may reflect that lack of early engagement, consequent lack of ownership and also the considerably larger number of referral centres that may have only the occasional patient, and therefore does not engage with the pathway frequently. Interest in care pathways has rapidly increased within the NHS, and it is important to appreciate that the evidence base on pathway creation greatly exceeds what is known on how to engage providers and how to modify their practice (Grimshaw et al., 2001). Several studies suggest that simply providing information alone does not impact evidence-based practice (Dennehy et al., 2007; Feldman et al., 1998).

3 Barriers to implementation

Barriers to implementation that were identified in this study included change weariness, other organisational changes, lack of morale, understaffing and inadequate focus on the non-acute pathways resulting in patients with a delayed discharge creating a block in the system. Interestingly, the participants in both focus groups were welcoming of change. Whether this is truly representative of all staff working across the pathway is unclear. Barriers which impede clinical engagement and uptake of care pathways may occur at the staff (clinician or management) or healthcare organisation (management, resources and financial or institutional structures) level or be influenced by external factors (broader health and social policies or patient characteristics).

4 Quality standards across the system

The available data were very limited, and it was not possible to determine whether there has been any detectable change as a result of the pathways and associated initiatives. There was a trend towards fewer pressure ulcers and a shorter length of stay. As only 2 years of poor quality data were available and there is no prior data to compare this with, it is difficult to know whether this is a normal variation or whether it indeed reflects the impact of the pathway. The national referral system is being consistently used and the catchment areas, identified as a result of the MTC-SCIC linkage project, are being adhered to. However, on other measures such as timely contact with SCI centres, timely referrals and timely admissions, there seems to be considerable delays. Centres reported greater number of referrals, suggesting that patients previously missing out on spinal rehabilitation are now being referred. Focus group participants confirmed this trend but reported a mismatch between resources (beds and staff) and the number of referrals. Top-level outcomes such as long-term quality of life changes, reintegration into society measures and return to work outcomes were not available.

Participants highlighted that although the pathway addressed the needs of many people with spinal cord injury who were willing to travel to the specialist units for rehabilitation, there was a significant subgroup who were either unwilling to travel or were not in a position to travel because of comorbidities. This group is mainly composed of the elderly, who generally have poorer rehabilitation potential and who are likely to be more affected by being away from family and friends in a rehabilitation centre geographically removed. A need for more local support was articulated.

The perception of many participants was that although outreach support was effective, this needed to be on a continuous basis, which can realistically be done only with the development of local expertise in referring hospitals. This is to address the care of not only the acutely spinal cord injured patients, but also those who are not transferred to spinal injury centres and to facilitate the care of long-term spinal cord injury patients who are admitted with medical complications. Although the outreach service was considered valuable, it was felt further refinement and support was required.

Conclusions

Attempts to transform SCI services within a nationally defined patient framework have worked in some areas. One aspect of the programme that has been effective was the introduction of the national registry, which was easy to implement and did not require major change in behaviour from staff. In other areas, the results have been mixed. The referral system and pathways work have resulted in a larger number of referrals, due to uncovering of patients previously not referred into the system. Although the pathways are mostly working well for trauma patients, the non-trauma patients are not accessing the pathway uniformly. There are no drivers currently to change behaviour in agencies external to SCI centres, which has resulted in delayed referrals and discharges. Many of the pathway specifications such as 4-hour contact and 24-hour referrals are not being met. There are delays in patients being admitted to SCI centres. Clinicians in referring hospitals recognised that there are always going to be capacity issues and would like the development of local skills and knowledge, which would be supported by an SCIC centre outreach service. There was a clear perception that the outreach support from SCIC requires enhancement, that it has to be more frequent and continuous and requires a wider clinical mix (including senior doctors). There is absence of reliable data and feedback on how the different elements of the programme are working. Clinicians working at SCIC and MTC felt that more open data and outcome measures access are required to embed change. There was a perception that there has been lack of resources to facilitate change. Future reviews need to include the patient voice and explore appropriate means and methods to engage those patients with complex needs.

References for Part 5

Adams, A., and Bond, S. (2001). Hospital nurses' job satisfaction, individual and organizational characteristics. *Journal of Advanced Nursing*, 32(3), 536–543.

Addicott, R., and Ham, C. (2014). *Commissioning and funding general practice: Making the case for family care networks*. London: The Kings Fund.

All Party Parliamentary Group on Spinal Cord Injury. (2015), *A paralysed system – report*. APPG – SCI/ Spinal Injuries Association. https://www.spinal.co.uk/wp-content/uploads/2015/11/SIA-APP-Paralysed-System-Report-FINAL-lo-res.pdf

American Speech-Language Hearing Association. (1993). *About communication disorders.* www.ksha.org.

Atkinson, D., et al. (2013). *The health equalities framework (HEF) an outcomes framework based on the determinants of health inequalities.* Bristol: Improving Health and Lives, Learning Disabilities Observatory.

Aylott, J. (2010). Improving access to health and social care for people with autism. *Nursing Standard*, 24(27), 47–56.

Aylott, J. (2015). *Developing specialist skills in autism practice.* Middlesex: RCNi, Department of Health. https://rcni.com/sites/rcn_nspace/files/RCNi-Autism-Booklet-2015.pdf

Aylott, J., and Montisci, L. (2017 4 August). Nurses are ready for the MBA – so lets bring it on. *Learning Disability Practice On-Line*, 20(4), 13.

Barlow, G., et al. (2007). Reducing door-to-antibiotic time in community acquired pneumonia: Controlled before-and-after evaluation and cost-effectiveness analysis. *Thorax*, 62, 67–74.

Barnett, K., Mercer, S. W., Norbury, M., Watt, G., Wyke, S., and Guthrie, B. (2012). Epidemiology of multimorbidity and implications for health care, research, and medical education: A cross-sectional study. *The Lancet*, 380(9836), 37–43.

Barr, F. (2009). *Preserving and developing the national spinal cord injury service phase 2 – seeking the evidence.* Milton Keynes: UK: Spinal Injuries Association. https://www.spinal.co.uk/wp-content/uploads/2015/07/234-590487.pdf

Barr, F. (2013). *New national SCI pathways.* www.spinal.co.uk/userfiles/pdf/Portal/May%20 2013%20-%20National%20SCI%20Pathways.pdf [2014, 11/1].

BBC News. (2016 1 April). NHS spending devolved in Greater Manchester. *BBC News.*

Beange, H., McElduff, A., and Baker, W. (1995). Medical disorders of adults with mental retardation: A population study. *American Journal on Mental Retardation*, 99(6), 595–604.

Beer, M., and Nohria, N. (2000, May–June). Cracking the code of change. *Harvard Business Review*, 133–141.

Benn, J., Burnett, S., Parand, A., et al. (2009). Studying large-scale programmes to improve patient safety in whole care systems: Challenges for research. *Social Science & Medicine*, 69(12), 1767–1776.

Best, A., Greenhalgh, T., Lewis, S., et al. (2012). Large-system transformation in health care: A realist review. *The Milbank Quarterly*, 90(3), 421–456.

Bevan, H. (2010). How can we build skills to transform the healthcare systems? *Journal of Research in Nursing*, 15(2), 139–148.

Bevan, H., Ham, C., and Plesk, P. E. (2008). *The next leg of the journey: How do we make high quality care for all a reality?* Coventry: NHS Institute for Innovation and Improvement.

Bevan, H., Winstanley, L., and Plesk, P. (2011). *Leading large-scale change.* NHS Institute for Innovation and Improvement. https://www.england.nhs.uk/wp-content/uploads/2017/09/practical-guide-large-scale-change-april-2018-smll.pdf

Bibby, J., Bevan, H., Carter, E., Bate, P., and Rovert, G. (2009). *The power of one, the power of many – Bringing Social movement thinking to healthcare and healthcare management.* Coventry: NHS Institute for Innovation and Improvement.

Bild and Mencap. (2013). *Consultation questionnaire results: Is healthcare "Getting Better" for people with a learning disability?* London: Department of Health.

Blacker, F., and Shimmin, S. (1984). *Applying psychology in organisations.* London: Metheun.

Blegan, M. A. (1993). Nurses' job satisfaction: A meta-analysis of related variables. *Nursing Research*, 42(1), 36–41.12(4), 419–450.

Bovey, W. H., and Hede, A. (2001). Resistance to organizational change: The role of cognitive and affective processes. *Leadership and Organization Development Journal*, 22(8), 372–382.

Bradley, H. (2013). Assessing and developing successful communication. In: *People with profound & multiple learning disabilities: A collaborative approach to meeting*. Routledge, p. 50.

Brandrud, A. S., Schreiner, A., Hjortdahl, P., et al. (2011). Three success factors for continual improvement in healthcare: An analysis of the reports of improvement team members. *BMJ Quality Safety*, 20(3), 251–259.

British Thoracic Society. (2009). BTS guideline for the management of CAP. *Thorax*, 64, 1–55.

British Thoracic Society. (2014). The British thoracic society pilot care bundle project: A care bundles-based approach to improving standards of care in chronic obstructive pulmonary disease and community acquired pneumonia. *British Thoracic Society Reports*, 6(4).

Bryson, M. J., and Patton, M. Q. (2010). Analysing and engaging stakeholders. In: Wholey, J. S., Hatry, H. P. and Newcomer, K. E. (eds). *Handbook of practical program evaluation*, 3rd edition. San Francisco: Jossey-Bass.

Carlisle, S. (2000). Health promotion, advocacy and health inequalities: A conceptual framework. *Health Promotion International*, 15(4), 369–376.

Citizens Information Centre. (2008). *Advocacy project resource pack*. www.citizensinformation board.ie.

Collins, B. (2015). *Foundation trust and NHS trust mergers 2010–2015*. London: The Kings Fund.

Conte, H., Chen, Y., Mehal, W., Scinto, J., and Quagiiarello, V. (1999). A prognostic rule for elderly patients admitted with community-acquired pneumonia. *American Journal of Medicine*, 106, 20–28.

Cooper, C. L. (1999). Can we live with the changing nature of work? *Journal of Managerial Psychology*, 14, 569–572.

Curry, N., and Ham, C. (2010). *Clinical and service integration: The route to improved outcomes*. London: The Kings Fund.

Dalton, D. (2014). *Examining new options and opportunities for providers of NHS Care: The Dalton review*. London: The Kings Fund.

Darzi, A. (2008). *High quality care for all NHS next stage review final report*. (online). Great Britain: Department of Health.

Davies, H. T., and Crombie, I. K. (1995). Assessing the quality of care. *BMJ* (Clinical research ed.), 311(7008), 766.

Dennehy, E. B., Bauer, M. S., Perlis, R. H., Kogan, J. N, and Sachs, G. S. (2007). Concordance with treatment guidelines for bipolar disorder: Data from the systematic treatment enhancement program for bipolar disorder. *Psychopharmacology Bulletin*, 40.

Department of Health. (2008). *High quality care for all*. Department of Health. www.gov.uk

Department of Health. (2008). *High quality care for all*. (online). www.gov.uk/government/uploads/system/uploads/attachment_data/file/228836/7432.pdf.

Department of Health. (2014). *Examining new options and opportunities for providers of NHS care*. The Dalton Review. Department of Health.

Devivo, M. J., Kartus, P. L., Stover, S. L., and Fine, P. R. (1990). Benefits of early admission to an organised spinal cord injury care system. *Paraplegia*, 28(9), 545–555.

Donabedian, A. (1966). Evaluating the quality of medical care. *Milbank Quarterly*, 83(4), 691–729.

Emerson, E. (2005). Underweight, obesity and exercise among adults with intellectual disabilities in supported accommodation in Northern England. *Journal of Intellectual Disability Research*, 49(2), 134–143.

Emerson, E., and Baines, S. (2011). Health inequalities and people with learning disabilities in the UK. *Tizard Learning Disability Review*, 16(1), 42–48.

Emerson, E., et al. (2014). Trends in age-standardised mortality rates and life expectancy of people with learning disabilities in Sheffield over a 33-year period. *Tizard Learning Disability Review*, 19(2), 90–95.

Equality Act. (2010). www.legislation.gov.uk/ukpga/2010/15/contents.

Evans-Lacko, S., Jarrett, M., McCrone, P., and Thornicroft, G. (2010). Facilitators and barriers to implementing clinical care pathways. *BMC Health Services Research*, 10(1), 1–6.

Ewig, S., Kleinfield, T., Bauer, T, Seifert, K., Schafer, H., and Goke, N. (1999). Comparative validation of prognostic rules for community acquired pneumonia in an elderly population. *European Respiratory Journal*, 14, 370–375.

Faragher, E. B., Cass, M., and Cooper, C. L. (2005). The relationship between job satisfaction and health: A meta-analysis. *Occupational and Environmental Medicine*, 62, 105–112.

Feldman, E. L., Jaffe, A., Galambos, N., Robins, A., Kelly, R. B, and Froom, J. (1998). Clinical practice guidelines on depression: Awareness, attitudes, and content knowledge among family physicians in New York. *Archives of Family Medicine*, 7.

Fisher, Kathleen. (2004). Health disparities and mental retardation. *Journal of Nursing Scholarship*, 36(1), 48–53.

Fitzsimmons, B. (2012). *What can hospital staff do to improve the quality of care for patients?* London: The Kings Fund.

Flynn, M. (2012). *South Gloucestershire safeguarding adults board: Winterbourne view hospital*. A Serious Case Review. CPEA Ltd. http://www.southglos.gov.uk/news/serious-case-review-winterbourne-view/

Foster, J. (2005). Learning disability liaison nurses in acute hospitals: Is there evidence to support the development of this role? Julie Foster examines the current literature to discover the effectiveness of the liaison nurse role and to look for evidence to inform the development of learning disability liaison nurse roles in acute healthcare settings. *Learning Disability Practice*, 8(4), 33–38.

Foster, S. T. (2007). Does Six Sigma Improve Performance? *Quality Management Journal*, 14(4), 7–20.

Gaag, A. (1998). Communication skills and adults with learning disabilities: Eliminating professional myopia. *British Journal of Learning Disabilities*, 26(3), 88–93.

Gage, W. (2013). Using service improvement methodology to change practice. *Nursing Standard*, 27(23), 51.

Gaynor, M., Laudicella, M., and Propper, C. (2012). Can governments do it better? Merger mania and hospital outcomes in the English NHS. *Journal of Health Economics*, 31, 528–543, 16p.

General Medical Council. (2017). *Adapting for the future: A plan for improving the flexibility of UK postgraduate medical training*. London: General Medical Council.

Giallonardo, L. M., Wong, C. A., and Iwasiw, C. L. (2010). Authentic leadership of preceptors: Predictor of new graduate nurses' work engagement and job satisfaction. *Journal of Nursing Management*, 18(8), 993–1003.

Gloucestershire County Council. (2016). *Gloucestershire's bid for more power forges ahead* (online). www.gloucestershire.gov.uk/article/119686/Gloucestershires-bid-for-more-power-forges-ahead. (Accessed on 05 May 2016).

Glover, G., and Ayub, M. (2010). *How people with a learning disability die*. Durham: Improving Healthy Lives, Learning Disability Observatory.

Goodwin, N., Smith, J., Davies, A., Perry, C., Rosen, R., Dixon, A., Dixon, J., and Ham, C. (2012). *Integrated care for patients and populations: Improving outcomes by working together*. London: The Kings Fund and Nuffield Trust.

Gray, B., and Jackson, R. (2002). *Advocacy and learning disability*. London: Jessica Kingsley Publishers.

Gray, B., Winblad, U., and Sarnak, D. O. (2016). *Sweden's Esther model: Improving care for elderly patients with complex needs*. www.commonwealthfund.org/publications/case-studies/2016/sep/sweden-esther-case-study.

Greater Manchester Combined Authority. (2016). *Taking charge of health and social care* (online). www.gmhsc.org.uk/. (Accessed on 4 May 2016).

Greenwell, S.W., et al. (2003). *Theatre efficiency, safety, quality of care and optimal use of resources*. Association of Anaesthetists of Great Britain and Ireland, 21 Portland Place, London: W1B1PX.

Gregory, S. (2016). *How do the health care systems in the United Kingdom compare with others internationally?* www.kingsfund.org.uk/blog/2016/04/how-uk-health-systems-compare-internationally 2016.

Grimshaw, J. M., Shirran, L., Thomas, R., Mowatt, G., Fraser, C., Bero, L., Grilli, R., Harvey, E., Oxman, A., and O'Brien, M. A. (2001). Changing provider behavior: An overview of systematic reviews of interventions. *Medical Care*, 39.

Ham, C., and Alderwick, H. (2015). *Aligning public services: Strategies for local integration. PF perspectives: CIPFA and public finances.* http://www.cipfa.org/cipfa-thinks/perspectives/aligning-public-services

Ham, C., Berwick, D., and Dixon, J. (2016). *Improving quality in the English NHS*. London: The Kings Fund.

Ham, C., and Curry, N. (2011). *Integrated care: What is it? Does it work? What does it mean for the NHS?* London: The Kings Fund.

Ham, C., and Murray, R. (2015). *Implementing the NHS five year forward view: Aligning policies with plans*. London: The Kings Fund.

Harter, J. K., Schmidt, F. L., and Keyes, C. L. M. (2002). Well being in the workplace and its relationship to business outcomes: A review of the Gallup studies. In Keyes, C. L., and Haidt, J. (eds). *Flourishing: The positive person and the good life*. Washington, DC: American Psychological Association, pp. 205–224.

Hatton, C., Glover, G., Emerson, E., and Brown, I. (2016). People with learning disabilities in England 2015: Main report. *Learning Disabilities Observatory: Public Health England.* https://assets.publishing.service.gov.uk/government/uploads/system/uploads/attachment_data/file/613182/PWLDIE_2015_main_report_NB090517.pdf

Hatton, C., Roberts, H., and Baines, S. (2011). *Reasonable adjustments for people with learning disabilities in England 2010: A national survey of NHS trusts*. Durham: Improving Health & Lives, Learning Disabilities Observatory.

Herzberg, F. (1966). *Work and the nature of man*. Cleveland, OH: World Publishing Company.

Heyworth, J. (2011). A&E quality indicators *Academic Emergency Medicine*, 18, 1239–1241.

Hove, Oddbjørn. (2004). Weight survey on adult persons with mental retardation living in the community. *Research in Developmental Disabilities*, 25(1), 9–17.

Hovlid, E., Oddbjorn, B., Haug, K., Aslakson, A. B., and von Plessen, C. (2012). A new pathway for elective surgery to reduce cancellation rates. *BMC Health Services Research*, 12, 154.

Hudson, B. (2015 24 November). Devolution bill poses a serious threat to the NHS. *The Guardian*.

Hughes, G. (2013). The emergency medicine taskforce: An interim report. *Emergency Medicine*, 30, 348.

Hunt, J. (2016). *NHS providers conference.* Keynote Speech. www.gov.uk/government/speeches/nhs-providers-annual-conference-keynote-speech.

Imison, C. (2014). *Future organisational models for the NHS: Perspectives for the Dalton review*. London: The King's Fund.

Imison, C., Sonola, L., Honeyman, M., and Ross, S. (2014). *The reconfiguration of clinical services; What is the evidence?* London: King's Fund.

Imison, I., Curry, N., Holder, H., Castle-Clarke, S., Nimmons, D., Appleby, J., Thornly, R., Lombardo, S. (2017). *Shifting the balance of care: Great Expectations*. Nuffield Institute. https://www.nuffieldtrust.org.uk/research/shifting-the-balance-of-care-great-expectations

Jones, J. (2000). A total communication approach towards meeting the communication needs of people with learning disabilities. *Tizard Learning Disability Review*, 5(1), 20–26.

Jones, L., and Bagnall, A. M. (2004). Spinal injuries centres (SICs) for acute traumatic spinal cord injury. *Cochrane Database of Systematic Reviews*, 4.

Jones, P., Sheperd, M., Wells, S., Le Feure, J., and Ameratunga, S. (2014). Review article: What makes a good healthcare quality indicator? A systematic review and validation study *Emergency Medicine Australasia*, 26, 113–124.

Kapur, N., Borrill, C., and Stride, C. (1998). Psychological morbidity and job satisfaction in hospital consultants and junior house officers: Multicentre, cross sectional survey. *British Medical Journal*, 317(7157), 511–512.

Kennedy, M., et al. (1997). Nutritional support for patients with intellectual disability and nutrition/dysphagia disorders in community care. *Journal of Intellectual Disability Research*, 41(5), 430–436.

Kenny, D.T., Carlson, J. G., McGuigan, F. J., and Sheppard, J. L. (eds) (2000). *Stress and health: Research and clinical application.* Amsterdam: Harwood Academic Publisher.

Kent, Surrey, and Sussex Local Specialist Commissioning Group. (2003). *Standards for Patients Requiring Spinal Cord Injury Care.* Kent, Surrey and Sussex: Local Specialist Commissioning Group.

King, S., and Peterson, L. (2007). How effective leaders achieve success in critical change initiatives. *Healthcare Quarterly*, 10(3), 58–62.

Kings Fund. (2016). *Long-term conditions and multi-morbidity.* (Online). @TheKingsFund. www.kingsfund.org.uk/time-to-think-differently/trends/disease-and-disability/long-term-conditions-multi-morbidity. (Accessed on 15 May 2016).

Krahn, G. L., Hammond, L., and Turner, A. (2006). A cascade of disparities: Health and health care access for people with intellectual disabilities. *Mental Retardation and Developmental Disabilities Research Reviews*, 12(1), 70–82.

Leeder, S. R., and Dominello, A. (2005). Health, equity and intellectual disability. *Journal of Applied Research in Intellectual Disabilities*, 18(2), 97–100.

Lennox, N., et al. (2004). Are a health advocacy diary and health assessment welcomed by those who use them? *Journal of Intellectual Disability Research*, Blackwell Scientific, 354.

Lewis, R., Rosen, R., Goodwin, N., and Dixon, A. (2010). *Where next for integrated care organisations in the English NHS?* Nuffield Trust. https://www.nuffieldtrust.org.uk/research/where-next-for-integrated-care-organisations-in-the-english-nhs

Lim, W., Van Der Earden, M., Laing, R., Boersma, W., Karalus, N., and Town, G., et al. (2003). Defining community acquired pneumonia severity on presentation to hospital: An international derivation and validation study. *Thorax*, 58, 377–382.

Lloyd, J., and Wait, S. (2005). *Integrated care a guide for policymakers: The international longevity centre UK and alliance for health and the future.* https://www.google.com/url?sa=t&rct=j&q=&esrc=s&source=web&cd=2&ved=2ahUKEwir8OCRz73cAhWTV8AKHWK_AoMQFjAB egQIBBAC&url=http%3A%2F%2Fwww.ilcuk.org.uk%2Fimages%2Fuploads%2Fpublicat ion-pdfs%2Fpdf_pdf_7.pdf&usg=AOvVaw3bGP-eKbQAuQwg-rSLlB77

Lu, H., Barriball, K. L., Zhang, X., and While, A. E. (2012). Job satisfaction among hospital nurses revisited: A systematic review. *International Journal of Nursing Studies*, 49(8), 1017–1038.

Lukas, C., Holmes, S. K., Cohen, A. B., Rostuccia, J., Cramer, I. E., Shwartz, M., and Charns, M. P. (2007). Transformational change in healthcare systems: An organisational model *Healthcare Management Review*, 32(4), 309–320.

Macadam, M. (2008). *Frameworks of integrated care for the elderly: A systematic review.* CPRN. http://brainxchange.ca/Public/Files/Primary-Care/HQPC/Care-of-the-Eldery-inte grate-care.aspx

Madsen, M., Halgreen Eiset, A., Mackenhauer, J., Odby, A., Christiansen, C., Kurland, L., and Kirnegaard, H. (2016). Selection of quality indicators for hospital based emergency care in Denmark, informed by a modified-Delphi process. *Scandinavian Journal of Trauma, Resuscitation and Emergency Medicine*, 24, 11.

Madsen, M., Kiuru, S., and Castren, M. (2015, October). The level of evidence for emergency department performance indicators: Systematic review. *European Journal of Emergency Medicine*, 22(5), 298–305.

Makinen, A., Kivimaki, M., Elovainio, M., Virtanen, M., and Bond, S. (2003). Organization of nursing care as a determinant of job satisfaction among hospital nurses. *Journal of Nursing Management*, 11(5), 299–306.

Marks, D. F., and Yardley, L. (2004). *Research Methods for clinical and health psychology*. Thousand Oaks, CA: Sage Publications, p. 68.

Maslow, A. H. (1943). A theory of human motivation. *Psychological Review*, 50(4), 370–396.

Mason, S. (2011). Keynote address: United Kingdom experiences of evaluating performance and quality in emergency medicine. *Journal of Emergency Medicine*, 18, 1234–1238.

McConkey, R. (2004). *Pressures, possibilities and proposals: Northern Ireland review of day services for people with learning disabilities*. Belfast: Eastern Health and Social Services Board.

McIntosh, B. (2002). *The strategies for change project: Modernising day services – lessons learnt in the changing days programme*. London: Community Care Development Centre, Kings College.

McLaughlin, J. A., and Jordan, J. B. (2010). Using logic models. In Wholey, J. S., Hatry, H. P., and Newcomer, K. E. (eds). *Handbook of practical program evaluation*, 3rd edition. San Francisco: Jossey-Bass.

McNeese-Smith, D. K. (1999). A content analysis of staff nurse descriptions of job satisfaction and dissatisfaction. *Journal of Advanced Nursing*, 29(6), 1332–1341.

Mencap. (1991). *Empty days . . . empty lives: Mencap report on day services*. London: MENCAP.

Mencap. (2007). *Death by indifference*. London: MENCAP.

Mencap. (2012). *Death by indifference: 74 deaths and counting*. London: MENCAP.

Michael, J., and Richardson, A. (2008). Healthcare for all: The independent inquiry into access to healthcare for people with learning disabilities. *Tizard Learning Disability Review*, 13(4), 28–34.

Mohr, J. J., and Batalden, P. B. (2002). Improving safety on the front lines: The role of clinical microsystems. *Quality & Safety in Health Care*, 11(1), 45–50.

Mueller, C. W., and McCloskey, J. C. (1990). Nurses' job satisfaction: A proposed measure. *Nursing Research*, 39(2), 113–117.

Narine, L., and Persaud, D. D. (2003). Gaining and maintaining commitment to large-scale change in healthcare organisations. *Health Services Management Research*, 16, 179–187.

Narine, L., and Persaud, D. D. (2014). Gaining and maintaining commitment to large-scale change in healthcare organisation. *Health Service Management Research*, 16(3), 179–187.

Naylor, C., Alderwick, H., and Honeyman, M. (2015). *Acute hospitals and integrated care From hospitals to health systems*. London: The Kings Fund.

Naylor, C., Das, P., Ross, S., Honeyman, M., Thompson, J., and Gilburt, H. (2016). *Bringing together physical and mental health: A new frontier for integrated care*. London: The Kings Fund.

Nelson, E., Batelden, P. B., and Godfrey, M. M. (2011). *Quality by design: A clinical microsystems approach*. San Francisco, CA: Jossey-Bass Publication.

Nelson, E., Batelden, P. B., Huber, T. P., Mohr, J. J., Godfrey, M. M., Headrick, L. A., and Wasson, J. H. (2002). Microsystems in health care: Part 1. Learning from high-performing front-line clinical units. *Journal on Quality Improvement*, 28, 472–493.

Nelson, E. C., Batelden, P. B., Mohr, J. J., and Plume, S. K. (1998). Building a quality future. *Frontiers of Health Services Management*, 15(1), 3–32.

NHS England. (2014). *Five year forward view*. NHS England.

NHS England. (2015). *Five year forward view*. Time to Deliver.

NHS England. (2016a). *Delivering the forward view: NHS planning guidance 2016/17–2020/21*. NHS England.

NHS England. (2016b). *Cancelled operations*.

NHS England. (2016c). *Sustainability and transformation partnerships*.

NICE. (2014). *Costing statement: Pneumonia – diagnosis and management of community and hospital acquired pneumonia in adults. Implementing the NICE guideline on pneumonia (CG191)*.

Nuffield Trust. (2015). *Cities & local government devolution bill: Report stage*. Nuffield Trust. https://www.nuffieldtrust.org.uk/resource/parliamentary-briefing-cities-and-local-government-devolution-bill-2nd-reading

Olmstead, P. I. (1945). Distribution of sample arrangements for runs up and down. *Annals of Mathematical Statistics*, 17, 24–33.

Oshagbemi, T. (2003). Personal correlates of job satisfaction: Empirical evidence from UK universities. *International Journal of Social Economics*, 30(12), 1210–1231.

The Parliament. (2016). *Cities and local government devolution act 2016*.

Patel, K. and Aylott, J. (2017). Assessing the return on investment (ROI) through appreciative inquiry (AI) of Hospital Improvement Programmes. In: Godbole, P., Burke, D., and Aylott, J. (eds.). *Why hospitals fail*. Springer.

Patients Association. (2016). *Feeling the wait: Annual Report on elective surgery waiting times*.

Patton, M. Q. (2008). *Utilization focused evaluation*, 4th edition. Thousand Oaks, CA: Sage Publications.

Perla, R. J., Bradbury, E., and Gunther-Murphy, C. (2011a). Large-scale improvement initiatives in healthcare: A scan of the literature. *Journal for Healthcare Quality*, 1, 1–11.

Perla, R. J., Provost, L. P., and Murray, S. K. (2011b). The run chart: A simple analytical tool for learning from variation in healthcare processes. *BMJ Quality Safety*, 20, 46–51.

Powell, A. E., Davies, H. T., and Thomson, R. G. (2003). Using routine comparative data to assess the quality of health care: Understanding and avoiding common pitfalls. *Quality & Safety in Health Care*, 12(2), 122–128.

Provost, L., and Murray, S. (2011). *The healthcare data guide: Learning from Data for Improvement*. San Francisco: Jossey-Bass.

Quality Standards for Advocacy. (2006). *Quality standards for advocacy schemes: Based on the advocacy charter. Action for advocacy*. www.aqvx59.dsl.pipex.com/Quality%20Standards%20Doc.pdf.

Rogers, E. M. (1962). *Diffusion of innovations*. London: Collier MacMillan Publishers, The Free Press.

The Rose Report. (2015, June). *Better leadership for tomorrow: NHS leadership review*. London: Department of Health.

Royal College of Emergency Medicine. (2017). *Royal college emergency medicine vision 2020*. www.rcem.ac.uk/RCEM/Quality_Policy/Policy/RCEM_Vision_2020/RCEM/Quality-Policy/Policy/Vision_2020.aspx?hkey=44955e65-f65e-4846-be91-b31ea7eba89d.

Sahu, J. (2016). MBA Dissertation Thesis, *An evaluation of the pathway though mainstream hospital for people with a learning disability and or autism: A case study*. Submitted to Sheffield Hallam University.

Sahu, L., and Aylott, J. (2017). *ACESSIA, sensory simulation issues in autism training workshop*, Sheffield, 2017.

Sen, A., Hill, D., Meson, D., Rae, F., Hughes, H., and Roop, R. (2012). The impact of consultant delivered service in emergency medicine: The Wrexham model. *Emergency Medicine Journal*, 29, 366–371.

Senge, P., Kleiner, A., Roberts, C., Ross, R., Roth, G., and Smith, B. (1999). *The dance of change: The challenge of sustaining momentum in learning organizations*. New York: Doubleday.

Shaw, S., Rosen, R., and Rumbold, B. (2011). *What is integrated care?* Nuffield Trust. https://www.nuffieldtrust.org.uk/research/what-is-integrated-care

Shewhart, W. A. (1931). *The economic control of quality of manufactured product*. New York: D Van Nostrand.

Shortell, S., Addicott, R., Walsh, N., and Ham, C. (2014). *Accountable care organisations in the United States and England: Testing, evaluating and learning what works*. https://www.king

sfund.org.uk/sites/default/files/field/field_publication_file/accountable-care-organisa tions-united-states-england-shortell-mar14.pdf

Smith, E. (2015). *Review of improvement and leadership development*. London: NHS Leadership Academy.

Smith, M. (2002). Efficacy of specialist versus non-specialist management of spinal cord injury within the UK. *Spinal Cord*, 40(1), 10–16.

Society, R. G. (2015). *21st century challenges: Britain's greying population*. (online). @wordpress-dotcom. https://21stcenturychallenges.org/britains-greying-population/. (Accessed on 15 May 2016).

Speroff, T., and O'Connor, G. (2004). Study designs for PDSA quality improvement research. *Quality Management Health Care*, 13, 17–32.

Statistics, O. F. N. (2016). *Home – Office for national statistics*. (online). www.ons.gov.uk/ (Accessed on 15 May 2016).

Stewart, D., and Todd, M. (2001). Role and contribution of nurses for learning disabilities: A local study in a county of the Oxford – Anglia region. *British Journal of Learning Disabilities*, 29(4), 145–150.

Taylor-Powell, E., and Henert, E. (2008). Developing a logic model: Teaching and training guide. *Benefits*, 3, 22.

Thumbikat, P. (2015). MBA Dissertation Thesis, *An evaluation of the national spinal cord injury pathway*. Submitted to Sheffield Hallam University, Sheffield, UK.

Timmins, N. (2015). *The practice of system leadership: Being comfortable with chaos*. London: The Kings Fund.

Trivedy, C., and Cooke, M. (2015). Unscheduled return visits (URV) in adults to the emergency department (ED): A rapid evidence assessment policy review. *Journal of Emergency Medicine*, 32, 324–329.

Turner, J., Nicholl, J., Mason, S., O'Keefe, C., and Anderson, J. (2014). *Whole system solutions for emergency and urgent care*. Sheffield, UK: ScHARR, University of Sheffield.

Turner, S., and Robinson, C. (2011). Reasonable adjustments for people with learning disabilities: Implications and actions for commissioners and providers of health care. In: *Improving Health and Lives: Learning Disabilities Observatory*. Durham: Evidence into Practice Report, p. 3.

Tyrer, F., Smith, L. K., and McGrother, C. W. (2007). Mortality in adults with moderate to profound intellectual disability: A population-based study. *Journal of Intellectual Disability Research*, 51(7), 520–527.

U.S. Department of Health and Human Services Centers for Disease Control and Prevention. Office of the Director, Office of Strategy and Innovation. (2011). *Introduction to program evaluation for public health programs: A self-study guide*. Atlanta, GA: Centers for Disease Control and Prevention.

UK Parliament/Crown copyright. (2011). October 2011-last update. *Written evidence from the National Spinal Cord Injury Board (COM 82)*. www.publications.parliament.uk/pa/ cm201011/cmselect/cmhealth/513/513vw77.htm.

UK Parliament. (2016). *Political challenges relating to an aging population: Key issues for the 2015 Parliament*. (Online). @UKParliament. www.parliament.uk/business/publications/ research/key-issues-parliament-2015/social-change/ageing-population/. (Accessed on 15 May 2016).

United Nations. (2015). *World population prospects The 2015 revision: Key findings and advance tables*. New York: United Nations.

Valuing People. (2001). *Valuing people a new strategy for learning disability for the 21st century*. London: Department of Health.

Valuing People Now. (2009). *Valuing people now: A new three year strategy for people with learning disabilities "Making it happen for everyone"*. London: Department of Health.

Waldersee, R., and Griffiths, A. (1996). *The changing face of organisational change*. CCC Paper no 065. Sydney: Centre for Corporate Change, Australian Graduate School of Management. The University of New South Wales.

Warner, N., and O'Sullivan, J. (2015). *Letting go: How English devolution can help solve the NHS care and cash crisis*. http://www.reform.uk/wp-content/uploads/2015/03/Letting-Go.pdf

Warr, P., Cook, J., and Wall, T. (1979). Scales for the measurement of some work attitudes and aspects of psychological wellbeing. *Journal of Occupational Psychology*, 52, 129–148.

Watson, J. (2012). *Integrating health and social care from an international perspective*. London: The International Longevity Centre.

Winefield, A., Tiggerman, M., and Goldney, R. (1988). Psychological concomitants of satisfactory employment and unemployment in young people. *Social Psychiatry and Epidemiology*, 23, 144–157.

Wittig, C. (2012). Employees reactions to organizational change. *OD Practitioner*, 44(2), 23–28.

World Health Organization. (2008). *The world health report 2008 – primary health care (Now More Than Ever)*. http://www.who.int/whr/2008/whr08_en.pdf

Wullink, M., Widdershoven, G., van Schrojenstein Lantman-De Valk, H., Metsemakers, J., and Dinant, G. J. (2009). Autonomy in relation to health among people with intellectual disability: A literature review. *Journal of Intellectual Disability Research*, 53(9), 816–826.

Zangaro, G. A., and Soeken, K. L. (2007). A meta-analysis of studies of nurses' job satisfaction. *Research in Nursing and Health*, 30(4), 445–458.

INDEX

AAROGYA Foundation 166
absenteeism 97–98
active listening 27
advocacy 259–262; independent 259
advocacy charter 261
adult learning 6, 38, 40
affiliative leadership style 10
analytical support 132
appraisal 101
Arora, Sanjeev Dr. 4
assistant workforce 4
audit 134–135
authoritative leader 5, 10, 145, 194
autism 257–262; act 2009 259
autocratic vs. authoritative leader 146

barriers for CESR 246
barriers to change 267
barriers to system transformation 240
behavioural leadership theories 11
behaviourism 11, 39
bespoke medical Leadership 38
BMA 135
born to lead 10
burnout 87, 96

cancelled operations on the day 238–239
Care Act 2014, The 231, 259
Care Quality Commission 28, 88, 90, 97
case for change 9, 135
change, planned 194
clinical audit 132
clinical errors 3

clinical leadership ix
clinical microsystems 16–21, 44–45
coaching 114; behaviour 21; style 10, 14
codesign leadership programmes 38
coerciveness 10
cognitive resource theory 11
cognitivism 40
collaboration 4, 10
collaborative leadership 131, 146
collective leadership 15, 34
common cause variation 139
communication care plan 261–262
communities of practice 6, 39, 42–43
community acquired pneumonia
    252–256
competency frameworks 3
completer-finisher 148
conceptually different workforce 4
conceptual model, medical leadership 6
conflict 111, 116; resolution 10
connectedness 110
contingency theories 11
continuous quality improvement
    130, 214, 233
continuous quality improvement
    collaborative 130, 153
contributory factors framework 139
control charts 254–256
coproduction 5, 6, 16
core values 112
cost of healthcare 6
CQUIN payments 254–256
critical reflection 40

cultural issues 12
culture of improvement 3

Darzi 9, 10, 176, 266
Darzi, Lord ix, x
data 132; analysis 132; analysts 132–136
deaths by indifference 257
decision process theory 11
dehumanising 25
Deming 17
democratic leadership 10, 145
democratisation of professional
    knowledge 4
deprivation 61
Did Not Attend appointments 207
diffusion of innovation theory 240
dignitiy of patients 29
discharge planning 31
disputed professional boundaries 4
distributed leadership 5
diverse workforce 12
duty of candour 25

ecological framework 82–83
economic health inequalities 131
effective communication 10
eighteen week pathway 203–209
electronic observation system 189–196
emergency medicine 251–256
emotional intelligence 4, 9, 108
emotional literacy 9
empathy 111
empowered leaders ix
engaged front line teams 233
engaged medical workforce 6
engagement 86–94, 95–105, 109, 115
Equality Act 2010 259
equality and diversity 10
ergonomics 140
ethical leadership 163
evidence based guidelines 193
experience based design 5
experiential learning 38
extrinsic motivation 134

Faculty of Medical Leadership and
    Management (FMLM) 3, 114
failures in healthcare 3
fear 27
fear of falling 31
feedback 135, 138, 196
Fellowship in Quality Improvement
    246–250
Fielder's contingency theory 11
fishbone analysis 192
Five Year Forward View 230

focus groups 201, 264–265, 267
force field analysis 200
Francis, Sir Robert 3, 24, 25, 26, 138
Francis report 100
Full Range Leadership Model 12, 13, 14

gender inequalities 12, 167
General Practice Forward View 33
geopolitical influence 12
global shortage of health workers 4

happiness 8, 10
Health and Social Care Act, 2012 33
health assistant workforce 4
Healthcare Alliance Model 3
Healthcare Leadership Model 141–144
hegemonic ambiguity 12
hermeneutic inquiry 5, 22–32
Hersey and Blanchards Life Cycle
    theory 11
Herzberg 234–235
high quality care for all ix, 176, 266
hip fracture patients 22–32
Hippocratic oath 6
hospital standardised mortality ratio
    (HSMR) 99
human factors 139–140
Human Rights Act 2010 259
human transplantation health system 131, 164
hybrid international emergency medicine
    247–250

identity theory 41
improvement science 129–130, 140
independent advocacy 259
inequality 61
inspirational leaders 14
institute for healthcare improvement 90
integrated leadership and management 5
integrated services 35, 230
integrated systems of service delivery 6
International Hospital Federation 3
international model of medical leadership 3
interpretative phenomenological approach 30
intrinsic motivation 135

job satisfaction 236, evaluation 236

Kirkup Report 3

Laissez-Faire Leadership 145
large scale change 225–226, 232, 234
Leader Member Exchange Theory
    (LMX) 151
leadership and management standards 3
leadership as influence 8

leadership competencies 3
leadership definition 8, 9
leadership development tools 130
leadership diagnostic tools 130,
  140–152
leadership framework 3
leadership qualities framework 3
leadership qualities social care 3
leadership skills 149
leadership styles: authentic 109; distributed
  108–109, 111; situational 107, 112, 115;
  transformational 107–109, 111, 116;
  transactional 107–108
leaders with patients ix
lean 20
learning disability 257–262
least preferred co-worker (LPC)
  110–111, 115
lived experience 24
logic model 265
long term conditions, cost 229

macro system 131
management by exception 14
management definition 8
management science 129
Managerial Grid Model 12
Managerial v affective leadership 145
managing change 10
Mafraq obstetric emergency programme
  (MOEP) 79–85
Marmot review 61
Maslow's Hierarchy of Needs 30, 235
MBA Medical/Healthcare 225
McGregor's Theory 12
Measurement Feedback 135–136
medical engagement 5, 35, 36, 239; scale 36,
  88–90
medical leadership competency
  framework 3
medical leadership general practice 6
mentorship 114
Microsystems Coaching Academy
  (MCA) 163
Mid Staffordshire NHS Foundation Trust
  24, 28, 138
model for improvement 129, 163
moral leadership 14, 163
morbidity 196, 257–262
mortality, increased vulnerability 196,
  257–262
motivated workforce ix
motivation 100, 111; theory 41
Multifactor Emotional Intelligence Scale
  (MEIS) 9
multi-source feedback 114

National Institute for Health and Care
  Excellence (NICE) 78
National Institute of Clinical Excellence
  (NICE) 24
national leadership schemes ix
National Skills academy for social care 3
National Spinal Cord Injury Strategy
  Board 263
networking 114
NHS Constitution 96
NHS Healthcare Leadership Model
  141–144
NHS Leadership Academy 3
NHS Leadership framework 3
NHS Medical leadership competency
  framework 3

organisational change 34
organisational culture 3, 134
organisational decision making 34
organisational effectiveness 29
organisational learning 130, 137, 138
organisational performance 34, 88–91, 109

pace setting 10
Paediatric Advanced warning Score
  (PAWS) 189–196
Paediatric Early warning score (PEWS)
  189–196
pain 28, 30
participative leadership behaviours 34
participatory methods 266
path-goal theory 11
person centred improvement 165
person centred macro health system 165
path dependency 73–74
patient centred outcome measures
  176–188
patient centred service improvement 32
patient centred values 27
patient-centric care ix, 29
patient engagement 16
patient experience 22–32; framework 25
patient fear 27
patient focused care 25
patient information 30
patient injury 28
patient involvement 6, 16
patient recovery 28
patient rehabilitation 31
patient reported experience measures
  (PREMs) 88
patient reported outcome measures
  (PROMs) 88
patient safety 29; network 79
patients association 239

patient surveys 24
PDSA 129, 132, 137
performance evaluation 129
personal development 130
personal identity theory 41
phenomenological approach 23, 28, 30
plan of care 27
population demographics 229
population health 61
power 12
practical obstetric multi-professional
    training 79
primary care 61–64
process mapping 190–191
professionalised health workforce
    planning 4
profound knowledge 130

quality and safety agenda ix
quality improvement 5, 16
Quality Improvement Collaborative 131
quality improvement projects 132
quality improvement strategy 16
quality indicators 252–253
quality international healthcare 4
quality outcomes framework 73, 75

reasonable adjustments 259
reflection 110; on practice 210–214
reflective practice 38
rehabilitation for patients 28
respect for patients 28
returns on investment 196, 241
revalidation 130
risk awareness 30
risk management 138
role theory 92–93
Root Cause Analysis (RCA) 137–140
run charts 254–256

safety measures 251
scope of professional practice 4
Self Determination Theory (SDT) 6, 38, 41,
    42, 133–134, 146, 245
self motivation 9
self regulation 9
sense of identity 25
service development 175, 189–214
shared decision making 78
shared leadership 5, 34, 131, 145
shortage of health workers 4
simulation 138–140
Sir Robert Francis 3, 24
Social Identify Theory (SIT) 6, 38, 40, 41

Social Learning Theory (SLT) 40
special cause variation 139
spinal cord injury 263–268
staff engagement toolkit 97, 102
stakeholder analysis 193, 199, 210–211, 264
stakeholders 131
Statistical Process Control (SPC) 254–258
strategic change 35
structural power imbalance 12
succession planning 34
suffering 27
Sustainability and Transformation Plans 33
systems of care 35
systems thinking 139

task orientated *vs.* relationship
    orientated 147
team building 10
team effectiveness 80, 82–83
teams ix
team working 79–85, 101
technical improvement 165
'top down' *vs.* 'bottom up' change 241, 266
total quality management 233
Toyota Production System (TPS) 20
training in data collection 135
trait theory 10
transactional leadership 12, 14, 15
transformational leaders 14, 15
transformational leadership 12, 14, 34
transformative learning 38, 40
transforming services 226, 236
Transplant Act in Nepal 166

UK Cities and Devolution Act 2016
    230–231
United Nations 229
Universal Health Care 3

values in leadership development 5
values of leadership 5
Vanguard projects 33
variation 65–78; common cause 139; in
    data quality 265–266; of healthcare
    265–266; seasonal 253
visionary leadership 10

waiting list 204
WHO, Safer-surgery checklists 12
work based learning 38
workforce planning 4
World Health Organisation 3, 176, 230

young carers 197